Metalanguage

W
DE
G

Language, Power and Social Process 11

Editors

Monica Heller
Richard J. Watts

Mouton de Gruyter
Berlin · New York

Metalanguage

Social and Ideological Perspectives

Edited by

Adam Jaworski
Nikolas Coupland
Dariusz Galasiński

Mouton de Gruyter
Berlin · New York

Mouton de Gruyter (formerly Mouton, The Hague)
is a Division of Walter de Gruyter GmbH & Co. KG, Berlin.

Library of Congress Cataloging-in-Publication Data

Cardiff Roundtable in Sociolinguistics (3rd : 1998 : Newtown, Powys, Wales)
    Metalanguage : social and ideological perspectives / edited by Adam Jaworski, Nikolas Coupland, Dariusz Galasinski
      p. cm. − (Language, power, and social process 11)
    Includes bibliographical references and index.
    ISBN 3-11-017877-X (cloth : alk. paper) − ISBN 3-11-017878-8 (pbk. : alk. paper)
    1. Metalanguage − Congresses.   2. Sociolinguistics − Congresses.   3. Ideology − Congresses.   I. Jaworski, Adam, 1957−
II. Coupland, Nikolas, 1950−   III. Galasinski, Dariusz, IV. Title.
V. Series.

P40.5.M48C37   1998
306.44−dc22

                               2004053092

♾ Printed on acid-free paper which falls within the guidelines of the ANSI to ensure permanence and durability.

ISBN 3-11-017877-X hb
ISBN 3-11-017878-8 pb

Bibliographic information published by Die Deutsche Bibliothek

Die Deutsche Bibliothek lists this publication in the Deutsche Nationalbibliografie; detailed bibliographic data is available in the Internet at <http://dnb.ddb.de>.

Cover design: Christopher Schneider.
Printed in Germany.

Preface

The 3rd Cardiff Round Table in Sociolinguistics, organised by the Cardiff University Centre for Language and Communication Research, was held at the University of Wales Conference Centre, Gregynog Hall, Newtown, Hall, Mid Wales between 1–3 June, 1998. The theme of the Round Table was "The Sociolinguistics of Metalanguage". Our broader rationale for the Cardiff Round Table series is to identify, for each meeting, a new cross-disciplinary research theme of international interest, systematically explore its conceptual range, and bring together a unified but diverse set of innovative research papers to demonstrate its importance and carry it forward.

At this Round Table we brought together researchers with various perspectives on metalanguage, sociolinguistic reflexivity and language ideology, intending to establish these areas as a new and more integrated field of sociolinguistics and discourse studies. These perspectives included language awareness, the social psychology of language attitudes, folklinguistics, metapragmatics, political and media discourse analysis, and critical linguistics/CDA. Each of these is a reasonably well-established sub-field in the study of linguistics and human communication. However, our ambition for the Round Table was primarily to explore links and relationship between these approaches as they impinge on some conception of processes, and to reassess their importance to sociolinguistics.

Issues of social actors' knowledge about language and representations of language (e.g., representations of dialects, styles, utterances, stances and goals) have, in our view, been largely absent from or implicit within sociolinguistic theory, sociolinguistic accounts of language variation, and accounts of linguistic usage generally. The conference addressed strategic and ideological aspects of metalanguage in face-to-face, intergroup, institutional and media communication. In this way, its remit extended empirically across a wide range.

The contributions commissioned for this volume (with one exception) began life as papers first presented at the Round Table. Some of the authors bring critical reformulations of well-established and recognised approaches to the study of metalanguage, while others develop new insights into the study of metalanguage on the basis of new empirical research.

The *Sociolinguistics of Metalanguage* Round Table finds its place in a series of such events. The first (1995) and second (1997) Round Tables were jointly funded by Blackwell Publishers and by Longman, respectively. Theoretical and empirical studies linked to the first meeting were published by Blackwell (1998) under the title *Approaches to Media Discourse* (edited by Allan Bell and Peter Garrett). Longman/ Pearson Education published research emanating from the second meeting, titled *Sociolinguistics and Social Theory* (edited by Nikolas Coupland, Srikant Sarangi and Christopher N. Candlin). Two further Round Tables have been held, with related books either published – *Discourse, the Body and Identity* (edited by Justine Coupland and Richard Gwyn, Palgrave, 2003), or forthcoming – *Sociolinguistic Approaches to Narrative* (edited by Joanna Thornborrow and Jen Coates, John Benjamins).

For the present volume, we gratefully acknowledge all Round Table participants' involvement in the presentations and discussions which generated these ideas, whether or not those individuals' contributions appear as chapters here.

The Editors

Contents

Part 3. Metalanguage and social evaluation

Part 4. Metalanguage and stylisation

Commentary

Contributors

Deborah Cameron
University of Oxford
deborah.cameron@worc.ox.ac.uk

Nikolas Coupland
Cardiff University
coupland@cardiff.ac.uk

Dariusz Galasiński
University of Wolverhampton
d.galasinski@wlv.ac.uk

Peter Garrett
Cardiff University
garrettp@cardiff.ac.uk

Adam Jaworski
Cardiff University
jaworski@cardiff.ac.uk

Tore Kristiansen
University of Copenhagen
tore.kristiansen@hum.ku.dk

Ulrike Hanna Meinhof
University of Southampton
u.h.meinhof@soton.ac.uk

Dennis R. Preston
Michigan State University
preston@pilot.msu.edu

Kay Richardson
University of Liverpool
kay100@liv.ac.uk

Itesh Sachdev
Birkbeck College
i.sachdev@bbk.ac.uk

Theo van Leeuwen
Cardiff University
vanleeuwent@cardiff.ac.uk

Jef Verschueren
University of Antwerp
jef.verschueren@ipra.be

Angie Williams
Cardiff University
williamsa@cardiff.ac.uk

John Wilson
University of Ulster
j.wilson@ulst.ac.uk

Introduction

Metalanguage: Why now?

Adam Jaworski, Nikolas Coupland and Dariusz Galasiński

The starting point for all studies of metalanguage is the familiar observation that language is a unique communicative system in that it can be used to describe and represent *itself*. This idea opens up a perspective on a general set of processes that define "the metalinguistic function of language". Communicators may refer in their speech or writing to any aspect of language use, including their own. We can describe the sounds of language, grammatical structures, differences in word meanings, intended meanings of utterances, or people's strategic purposes in talk; we can discuss styles and genres of talk and make comparisons between languages and dialects. Texts can sometimes, curiously, refer to themselves, as in the fictional case of a notice erected in an urban backstreet saying "PLEASE DO NOT THROW STONES AT THIS NOTICE". And so on.

However, the metalinguistic function of language is not merely a self-serving capacity of language and an interesting "design feature". How people represent language and communication processes is, at one level, important data for understanding how social groups value and orient to language and communication (varieties, processes, effects). This approach includes the study of folk beliefs about language, language attitudes and language awareness, and these overlapping perspectives have established histories within sociolinguistics. Metalinguistic representations may enter public consciousness and come to constitute structured understandings, perhaps even 'common sense' understandings – of how language works, what it is usually like, what certain ways of speaking connote and imply, what they *ought* to be like. That is, metalanguage can work at an ideological level, and influence people's actions and priorities in a wide range of ways, some clearly visible and others much less so. When we approach language use as discourse and social practice, we naturally view language as a form of social action. But it is in the interplay between usage and social evaluation that much of the social "work" of language – including pressures towards social integration and division, and the policing of social boundaries generally – is done. This is one of the reasons why metalanguage matters to sociolinguistics.

In another regard, speakers and writers make active and local use of the metalinguistic function of language in goal-directed ways *in* communicative acts and events themselves. Metalanguage, in the sense of direct or indirect quotation of previous utterances, or commentary on language performance, style or rhetorical function, can therefore often be a resource for strategic communication. In doing metalinguistic commentary, for example "What I was trying to say was ...", we can influence and negotiate how an utterance is or should have been heard, or try to modify the values attributed to it. We can mark our personal or group identities, display expertise, claim incompetence, and do many other sorts of "personal identification work" or "social relationship work". This approach addresses the metapragmatics of discourse, including metacommunication through various framing devices, stylisation, verbal art and play, humour, and so on. The implication here is that metalanguage needs to be conceptualised *within* as well as outside of or as an adjunct to language use. How we theorise metalanguage and its cognate concepts (metapragmatics, metacommunication) must reflect this.

The chapters that follow all address these issues in particular ways, some mainly theoretical but most of them in the context of new data-based research. One of our ambitions for the book is that the chapters should enliven sociolinguistic debate about metalanguage and build bridges between this concept (or family of concepts) and a wide range of broadly sociolinguistic research perspectives. These include established traditions of functional analysis in linguistics and communication (originally deriving from Hockett, Halliday, Hymes, Bateson, Mey and others); perspectives on reflexive language and communicative performance in linguistic anthropology and cultural studies (where the work of Bauman, Gumperz, Philips, Lucy, Briggs, Irvine, Hanks, Silverstein and others has been highly influential); overlapping research in language ideology analysis (by Gal, Woolard, Schieffelin, Harris, Cameron and others); sociolinguistic studies of linguistic evaluation (by Labov, Giles, Lambert, Preston and others); sociolinguistic studies of style and identity (developed again by Labov, and more recently by Johnstone, Rampton, Ochs, Eckert, Hill, Bell and others, in many respects influenced by the critical writings of Bakhtin); and critical discourse analysis and metapragmatics (following important work by Verschueren, Blommaert, Fairclough, Van Dijk, Kress, Van Leeuwen and others).

Our contention is that a notion of "metalanguage" lies close to the core of all these approaches – daunting as the list is. But of course it is not a simple or uniform notion of metalanguage. "Language about language" is too literal a formulation for many of these perspectives, and perhaps for all of them. "Language in the context of linguistic respresentations and evaluations" is a better short-hand, pointing to a shared assumption that, for the analysis of language use in social life, we need to engage explicitly with a "meta" component, a set of social and cognitive processes "alongside" or "about" the forms and substances of speech, writing or other symbolic material. The main challenges for the book are to debate what range of "meta" processes need to be recognised and theorised in sociolinguistics, how we should view them in relation to each other, and how we can approach these dimensions methodologically in different social contexts of language use.

Why should the "meta" component of language use be a more pressing concern now, as opposed to earlier expositions of sociolinguistic agendas? One broad answer is that sociolinguistics has gradually powered up its accounts of social meaning, on the one hand, and of social context, on the other. In Labov's seminal accounts of phonological variation (e.g., 1972), sociolinguistic variables appeared to attract social meaning by virtue of their distributional characteristics. To take one very familiar example, the meaning of (ng) (the alternation between velar and alveolar variants of the nasal consonant in English present progressive *-ing* verb morphemes and in some other linguistic environments) seemed to be adequately explained by noting that the alveolar forms marked lower socio-economic status, or less formal speaking contexts, and might therefore be in some general sense called a "stigmatised" variant. In the earliest discussions of sociolinguistic variation, however, Labov pointed out that the study of social evaluation needed to accompany the explicit study of social differentiation (distribution), because it was likely that the evaluated meanings of forms would help explain statistical patterns of social distribution. This is why he instigated "subjective reaction tests" as one sort of empirical procedure to collect evaluative data. It has become clear that the social meanings of variables, styles and ways of speaking need to be studied in all their richness and multiple dimensions, across different speech communities. This requires detailed study of language perceptions and folklinguistics within and across social groups, and also more ethnographic study of how social meanings surface as effects of timing and placement in specific groups' communicative acts and genres. The "meta-lives" of sociolinguistic styles have surfaced as an important sociolinguistic paradigm (see Eckert and Rickford 2001 for an extensive recent treatment of "style" in sociolinguistics). To follow up on the (ng) instance, Eckert suggests that the alveolar variant of (ng) "is not stigmatized in itself, but is associated with formality and informality (which in itself may have different interpretations depending on the more general style in which they emerge)" (2001: 122).

Whereas we could once define social context in terms of the places and times where language is used, there has been a steady shift towards appreciating the contextual*ising* as well as the contextual*ised* dimension of language (e.g., Auer and di Luzio 1992; Gumperz 1982; Goodwin and Duranti 1992). If language is used in ways that actively give shape to social contexts, then we are forced to consider the "meta zone" where contextualisation happens. Many different but overlapping accounts of these processes have been developed (see the review in Coupland and Jaworski's chapter), including frame analysis, metapragmatics, theories of performance, stylisation and language-ideological analysis. Socio-linguistics now theorises social context, rather as Dell Hymes had anticipated it should (Hymes 1972), as a dynamic interaction between language forms and an array of "situational components", which include cultural norms of production and interpretation, generic and stylistic conventions, communicative motiva-tions, inter-speaker relationships, discursive moves and strategies.

If we ask the same "why now?" question from the social rather than the lin-guistic direction, we can find a quite different answer. This is not so much to do with the maturing of an academic perspective; more a matter of, at least argu-ably, rather fundamentally transformed patterns of social life. It may be true that metalinguistic sensitivity is, in a certain sense, a hallmark of contemporary so-cial life, *tout court*. This is the theory of "reflexive modernity" (Beck, Giddens and Lash 1994). Modernity, as theorised by Giddens (1991: 20), is "essentially a post-traditional order". Late-modernity in particular – the present-day social configuration, at least in the "developed" world – is an order characterised by the routines of every-day life having become detached from pre-established social structures, traditions or customs. These no longer provide a sufficient account of the meaning of what social actors do, and social actors are in urgent need of resolving the perpetual dilemma of "how to live". Reflexivity, Giddens goes on to say, refers to the "susceptibility of most aspects of social activity, and material relations with nature, to chronic revision in the light of new informa-tion or knowledge" (ibid.). Our social lives are less determined and less durable than they would have been in earlier times.

The volatile modern self and a social condition of heightened reflexivity im-ply the possibility of taking up different ideological stances and alignments, and questioning dominant ideologies. Chouliaraki and Fairclough (1999) point out that reflexivity is caught up in social struggle. And while reflexivity challenges naturalised discourse – that is, ways of using language as self-evident (p. 95) – at the same time it challenges ideology resulting in fragmentation of consciousness. Late-modernity offers a chance to question ideological discourses permeating society. In fact, Chouliaraki and Fairclough (1999) argue that nowadays people are generally more aware not only of their practices but also of the discourses underpinning them. For example, a growing number of people are aware of what kind of language can be viewed as sexist or racist, and can use that awareness to defend and warrant their own socio-political stances, whatever they are.

An interesting example of by-now institutionalised challenge and attempt to de-naturalise discourse is what has been for some time termed "political correctness" (see Suhr and Johnson 2003 for a recent debate). Designed to counter what was perceived as racist and sexist imagery in media and education discourses, for example, the proponents of the "new language" openly challenged the taken-for-granted ideologies of gender or race. As Cameron (1995: 33) observes, the "movement for the so-called "politically correct" language does not threaten our freedom to speak as we choose" but "threatens only our freedom to imagine that our linguistic choices are inconsequential". The new language, however, has quickly been dubbed "political correctness", a label which at least in British public life stands for a half-mad obsession of scrutinising every word as to its all-encompassing appropriateness. The reflexivity which offered a chance to resist prejudicial ways of speaking has in turn been challenged by "common sense" ideologies resulting, for example, in the publication of dictionaries of politically correct terms in need of translation into "plain English".

The following chapters are structured into four main parts: "Approaches to metalanguage", "Metalanguage and ideological construction", "Metalanguage and social evaluation", "Metalanguage and stylisation". The final chapter stands alone as a coda to the sociolinguistic story of metalanguage which this book aims to recount. Deborah Cameron's *Commentary*, "Out of the bottle: The social life of metalanguage", recaps on, recontextualises and at least to a degree synthesises the arguments of the other papers. Most importantly, not unlike some other authors (e.g., Verschueren, Van Leeuwen), Cameron finds it counterproductive to discuss metalanguage in a wholly traditional fashion, focusing on the identification of its various forms and specific functions. She argues that, at a theoretical level, making a distinction between "language" and "metalanguage" cannot ultimately be sustained. Despite this, Cameron argues, metalanguage remains an important analytic category which needs to be deployed in accounting for various sociolinguistic phenomena, such as those highlighted in this book: metalanguage for ideological construction, the social evaluation of language, and strategic stylisation in discourse.

In our section introductions, we give summary overviews of the individual chapters and make links with other chapters in the book.

References

Auer, Peter and Aldo di Luzio (eds.)
  1992   *The Contextualization of Language*. Amsterdam: John Benjamins.
Beck, Ulrich, Anthony Giddens and Scott Lash
  1994   *Reflexive Modernisation: Politics, Tradition and Aesthetics in the Modern Social Order*. Cambridge: Polity Press.

Cameron, Deborah
   1995   *Verbal Hygiene*. London: Routledge.

Chouliaraki, Lilie and Norman Fairclough
   1999   *Discourse in Late Modernity: Rethinking Critical Discourse Analysis*. Edinburgh: Edinburgh University Press.

Eckert, Penelope
   2001   Style and social meaning. In Eckert, Penelope and John Rickford (eds.), *Style and Sociolinguistic Variation*. Cambridge: Cambridge University Press, 119–126.

Eckert, Penelope and John R. Rickford (eds.)
   2001   *Style and Sociolinguistic Variation*. Cambridge: Cambridge University Press.

Giddens, Anthony
   1991   *Modernity and Self-identity*. Cambridge: Polity Press.

Goodwin, Charles and Alessandro Duranti
   1992   Rethinking context: An introduction. In Duranti, Alessandro and Charles Goodwin (eds.), *Rethinking Context: Language as an Interactive Phenomenon*. Cambridge: Cambridge University Press, 1–42.

Gumperz, John J.
   1982   *Discourse Strategies*. Cambridge: Cambridge University Press.

Hutcheon, Linda
   1985   *A Theory of Parody*. New York: Methuen.
   1994   *Irony's Edge: The Theory and Politics of Irony*. London: Routledge.

Hymes, Dell
   1972   Models of the interaction of language and social life. In Gumperz, John J. and Dell Hymes (eds.), *Directions in Sociolinguistics*. New York: Holt, Rinehart and Winston, 35–71.

Labov, William
   1972   *Sociolinguistic Patterns*. Philadelphia: University of Pennsylvania Press.

Suhr, Stephanie and Sally Johnson (eds.)
   2003   Political correctness. Special issue of *Discourse & Society* 14/1.

Part 1. Approaches to metalanguage

Introduction to Part 1

Adam Jaworski and Nikolas Coupland

The concept of metalanguage is neither new nor lacking in extensive treatment in various traditions of sociolinguistic research. The usefulness and productivity of the concept have ensured that there is a steady stream of work which places metalanguage at the centre of its interest, both as a direct object of study and an explanatory tool for linguistic analysis. By the same token, accelerated interest in the metalanguage debate has been one of the motivations for the publication of this volume, mainly due to the availability of new empirical sociolinguistic research orienting to the "meta" level. Therefore, as editors, we have been faced with the task of manageably overviewing the huge existing literature in this area, while also showcasing new empirical work in the chapters of this book, and suggesting new, integrated theoretical perspectives. This Part of the volume, and Deborah Cameron's "Commentary" are specifically concerned with the first and third of these tasks.

Each chapter in Part 1, in its particular way and according to its own conceptual schema, critically overviews the sociolinguistic territory where metalanguage comes into play. Our own introductory chapter, "Sociolinguistics and metalanguage: Reflexivity, evaluation and ideology" elaborates on the initial comments in the general Introduction to provide a mainly historical review of different approaches to the "meta" theme in sociolinguistics and cognate fields. In this chapter, we begin by challenging early views that language in use can be accounted for in purely distributional terms, as self-contained and "innocent" linguistic "behaviour". Although some versions of sociolinguistics have given the impression that they are content with this view, we point out that the core idea of "social meaning" in sociolinguistics has always implied that the distribution of linguistic forms is underpinned by patterns of social evaluation. Then we trace the earliest accounts of metalanguage in functional linguistics and their legacy, as it appears in several different sociolinguistic traditions (of the sorts, again, indexed in the general Introduction). One of these is the language evaluation paradigm, which itself has different guises. Another is linguistic anthropology, with its emphases on normative rituals and the performative framing of communicative events. Two other broad traditions where "meta" issues are focal are the explicit study of language representations (quotations, reformulations, etc.), and the fast-developing paradigm in language ideology critique.

Taking a much more specific disciplinary line, Jef Verschueren's chapter, "Notes on the role of metapragmatic awareness in language use", deconstructs the notions of *metalanguage, metapragmatics, metapragmatic awareness*, and relates them to a broad-based pragmatic theory encompassing cognitive, social and cultural processes. For Verschueren, *metapragmatic awareness* and *reflexivity* are general terms implying communicators' constant self-monitoring in speaking and interpreting others' talk. This sort of monitoring leaves important linguistic traces, which makes it possible to investigate reflexivity empirically. Such indicators of reflexivity can be more or less explicit (see also Galasiński, this volume) and include modes of categorisation (e.g. of speech events), intertextual links (e.g. to earlier or later parts of talk), explicit metapragmatic descriptions (e.g. of certain linguistic activities), metapragmatic markers (such as quotation marks), and so on. Verschueren argues that all metapragmatic uses of language are interpretive and, consequently, responsible for creating ideologies of language and participants' identities in talk (e.g. through code choice in bilingual communication).

The third chapter in this scene-setting Part of the book combines the social psychological approach to language attitudes with the insights from sociolinguistic studies of language variation. Here Dennis Preston, in his chapter "Folk metalanguage", discusses various types of lay metalanguage. Preston draws a distinction between folk and expert (linguists') metalanguages, and demonstrates how the two types of description may categorise what is apparently the same linguistic form, e.g. "nasality", in significantly different ways, without needing to suggest that lay categorisations are simply "wrong" or "redundant" (Verschueren's chapter raises similar issues). Preston also demonstrates how "naïve" comments on language typically draw on contrasts (real or imaginary) between one's own speech variety and those of others, often based on the belief that one's own way of speaking is somehow more correct than others' are. (These issues are developed in relation to extensive Danish data in Kristiansen's chapter, in Part 3.)

According to Preston, studying explicit folk metalanguage (which is one of Verschueren's indicators of reflexivity, mentioned above) enables us to study a different type of *im*plicit metalanguage, i.e., a body of shared folk knowledge about language. Speakers may refer to others' linguistic varieties, and these references may contain, for example, derogatory descriptive categories (e.g. "lazy talk") and/or derogatory performances intended as imitations of this variety (e.g. "hybyayhubyhuby" in reference to African American Vernacular English). References of this sort are part of the shared metalanguage of the speaker's community and of this group's cultural model of the world. The link between these two dimensions of metalanguage – explicit commentary and implicit belief – is at the centre of the chapters in Part 3.

It is in this part of the book that the strongest links are made to the area of sociolinguistics which has probably been most closely associated with the study of metalanguage – Anthropological Linguistics. In our overview of the notion of metalanguage against the backdrop of the gradually falsified idea of "language as innocent behaviour', we point to the important work of Silverstein, Lucy, Hanks, Urban, Gumperz, Hill, Irvine and others in demonstrating how the continual reflexivity of language users is a necessary and indispensable element of creating meaning, including social meaning and ideology (see also Preston, Cameron, this volume). These issues are further discussed in greater detail by Verschueren, who building on Silverstein's work, specifically sets out to examine the 'link between the study of metalanguage or metapragmatics and pragmatics in general'.

Sociolinguistic perspectives on metalanguage: Reflexivity, evaluation and ideology

Nikolas Coupland and Adam Jaworski

1.   Language as "innocent behaviour"

What would language use be like without it involving a metalinguistic dimension? What would we have to say about it? Speaking (and writing and other forms of symbolic practice) would be seen as self-contained and autonomous, in various senses. Speaking would be treated as "behaviour", a flow of language forms between speakers and listeners equipped with all necessary processing equipment to play their productive and receptive roles. (This is "the conduit model", critiqued among others by Reddy 1993 [1979], see also Jaworski 1997.) Linguistic meanings would be inherent in those linguistic forms, and as a result those meanings would be uncontroversial, uncontested and "innocent". There would be no social investment in particular ways of speaking, or effects to be achieved through deploying them, because meaning conventions and demands would be universally shared and predictable. Speakers would have fully invested in the meanings they are communicating, and would fully "own" those meanings. There would be no social penumbra around meanings. Communicating would be a one-shot affair, with no scope for strategic revision, clarification or retellings. In short, nothing of any significance would be going on at the contextual margins of speaking, and there would be nothing that might deserve to be called "social meaning", "discursive negotiation" or "inferential work".

The descriptive project of linguistics has sometimes appeared to believe in linguistic innocence of this sort, in ways that we do not need to dwell on here. When language is assumed to be a set of structural forms and items, and when it is studied in isolation from its human and social functioning, the myth of autonomous, monologic, asocial linguistic behaviour survives intact. Of course, even for arch descriptivists, there *is always* a metalinguistic domain it is the domain of the linguist himself or herself. In this view, linguists are privileged as *the only* party able to analyse language and with an investment in "reading" it. Engagement with "the meta" starts and ends with them. The further implication of this orientation is that there is a necessary gulf between the academy and the lifeworld. The lifeworld is treated as the domain of innocent, asocial behaviour, whereas the academy is the domain of critique and of commentary. Describing linguistic structure may seem to be one of life's most benign activities, and therefore in its own way "innocent" too, but in this separation of domains we can see at least a potentially political issue, an elitism of critique. Language and its innocent users are treated as "out there", to be sampled and dissected by linguistically aware and strategically active experts.

As we go on to say in the rest of this chapter, these assumptions have for the most part been roundly rejected in sociolinguistics. In fact, it would be reasonable to suggest that sociolinguistics came into existence specifically to articulate the limitations of seeing language as innocent, socially disconnected behaviour. As we suggested in the general Introduction, sociolinguistics has developed rich and varied models of language as a contextualised and contextualising phenomenon, and as a set of strategic, often reflexive, socially imbued practices. Metalinguistic processes are at the heart of these models in one way or another. But it seems most accurate to describe contemporary sociolinguistics as existing in a state of tension between more *and less* metalinguistically-oriented perspectives.

We organise the remainder of this chapter under five main sections, reflecting the sociolinguistic traditions in which metalanguage in different senses has played a significant role. First, we trace the history of the notion of metalanguage, beginning in early functionalist approaches to language, then carried forward mainly in linguistic pragmatics and anthropology, especially in studies of performance events. Second, we sketch the history of social psychological research on "language attitudes" and its interface with dialect-focused, variationist sociolinguistic research. As a third tradition, we review research on language representation, spanning conversational and literary approaches to quotation, linguistic reformulation and similar processes. Fourthly, we examine research into the poetics of speech style and stylisation, heavily influenced by the writings of Mikhail Bakhtin and increasingly influential on sociolinguistic theory. Finally, we overview the burgeoning field of language ideology, where political, ideological and again pragmatic/discursive emphases are dominant.

It becomes clear in the review that these five themes overlap substantially, so that it would be a mistake to use the headings we have just introduced to try to locate any one study as part of a unique sub-field. In fact our aim for the chapter is the contrary one of showing how sociolinguistic fields as apparently diverse as language attitudes, dialect variation studies, performance studies, anthropological linguistics and critical discourse analysis can find common ground in theorising the "meta" dimension of language use.

2. Developments in the formulation of "metalanguage"

Linguistics owes to Ferdinand de Saussure the seminal idea, developed in the early years of the 1900s, that language itself needs to be viewed as a system of signs which, in themselves, are only indirectly associated with worldly phenomena (for a short biographical retrospective on Saussure see Cobley 1996: 2; see Saussure 1974 [1916]). The "arbitrariness" of the linguistic sign opens up the possibility that language can take as its "object" not only material objects but abstractions, and "language" itself as one of these. To put this in Roland Barthes's technical semiotic terms, in metalanguage "the signifieds of the second system are constituted by the signs of the first [system]" (Barthes 1996: 131). What we call "words", as they are written or spoken, are therefore not so much signs and "metasigns" as items which refer to meaningful clusters of experience coded in human languages. Roy Harris (1996) comments extensively on how there is a persistent tendency for people to confuse metasigns with signs themselves, and so to attribute autonomy and permanence to words. An interest in metalanguage in this fundamental semiotic sense, as a recursive quality, or an in-built self-referential potential of linguistic systems, then surfaces in many of the formative movements of early linguistics – the Prague School, American and European Structuralism, Russian Formalism, and others.

"What human language is like", in structural and semiotic terms, is closely related to "what human language can do". It became common for early theorists of language to develop taxonomic accounts of "the functions of language". Roman Jakobson (1960, 1980) identified language as having not only a referential (referring and predicating) function, an emotive (expressive) function and a conative (person-influencing and change-effecting) function, but also metalinguistic (self-commenting) and poetic (creative, non-literal) functions. Charles Hockett's list of the "design features" of human language (Hockett 1958, 1963) similarly included a metalinguistic function. Hockett identified this function as a resource that allows humans, perhaps distinctively from other species, to be creative, to imagine worlds other than their own, and to tell lies. Metalanguage in this conception takes on a quality of cognitive liberation and human transcendence.

Michael Halliday's influential tripartite taxonomy of the functions of language (e.g. Halliday 1978), as the heart of his systemic-functional model of language, includes the ideational function (language used in referring and exchanging information), the interpersonal function (language in self-presentation and in negotiating relationships with other people), and the textual function. This third function or dimension is where Halliday locates the complex of processes through which linguistic utterances are organised sequentially and in relation to their social contexts, including what others have called "framing" or "frame signalling" (see below). It is language ordering itself, or speakers ordering their language, for its/their communicative contexts and purposes, and therefore metalinguistically. Although in any taxonomic system of language functions, each function can be treated as an analytic isolate, it is clear that language use, even at the level of the individual utterance, is thoroughly multifunctional (Tracy and Coupland 1990). The implication is that metalanguage, however we orient to it theoretically, cannot be hived off to the margins of linguistic usage, even if it is useful to treat it as such for certain analytic purposes.

So we can look back at the beginnings of an interest in metalanguage which are rather abstract and, one might say, universalist. The key insights summarised in the term "metalanguage" were relevant to debates about what linguistic systems were universally like in semantic/semiotic/functional terms. Behind them we can see linguists' ambitions to establish linguistics as an autonomous field of scientific inquiry, which required a careful mapping out of the core concept "language" – what it is and what it can do. Behind Hockett's listing of "design features" we can see a debate about the potential uniqueness of human language (vis-à-vis non-human primate and other communication systems) which went on to become an enduring theme in psycholinguistics. In Halliday's three "macro-functions" we can see his ambition to develop a comprehensive theoretical model of language in use which would be more socially attuned than the models of theoretical syntax that dominated in the 1970s and later decades. But these early formulations of metalanguage are sociolinguistic in a general rather than a particular sense, if "sociolinguistic" implicates the practical as well as the abstract, the empirical as well as the theoretical, the local and the variable as well as the universal, and language as socially constitutive as well as socially constituted.

John Lucy's (1993) overview of the study of reflexive language identifies three broad traditions of research, which he calls *philosophical-linguistic, semiotic-functional* and *literary-performance*. The first two of these categories in fact summarise very well the emphases we have just noted. The philosophical-linguistic tradition is primarily concerned with the universal properties of human language as a code and the principles of relations between object language (i.e. language used to describe extra-linguistic reality) and metalanguage (i.e. language used to describe language). The semiotic-functional approach again begins with the general properties of semiotic systems, making observations on the functional affordances of linguistic systems ("what can they do communicatively?") as a special case. Yet it *is* possible to see important sociolinguistic principles in the functional theory of metalanguage. As Lucy points out:

> The semiotic-functional approach moves beyond a concern with the relation of
> linguistic reference to knowledge and considers language use as a form of social

action, most particularly, as communicative action. From this perspective, reflexive activity is essential to language use. Metacommunicative and metalinguistic activity takes place all the time to help structure ongoing linguistic activity.

(Lucy 1993: 18)

If a "meta" dimension of language continually structures social interaction, then all manner of social outcomes and effects can be attributed to it. Sociolinguists' classical concerns with linguistically mediated social relationships, social identities, power imbalances, institutional constraints on communication and processes of social change need to encompass this "meta" dimension. Language is not so socially innocent after all.

This social practice/pragmatic theme was articulated early on by Gregory Bateson in his (1972 [1955]) work on the metalinguistic and metacommunicative "messages" of utterances. "Metalinguistic" here deals once again with language as the topic or object of a discourse, while "metacommunicative" for Bateson relates specifically to relationships between conversational partners (similar, then, to Halliday's "interpersonal" macrofunction). According to Bateson, metacommunicative messages *frame* communication; that is, they "explicitly or implicitly [give] the receiver instructions or aids in his attempt to understand the messages included within the frame" and define "the set of messages about which it communicates" (1972: 188; quoted in Lucy 1993: 15).

The phrase "explicitly or implicitly" in this quotation opens a Pandora's Box of sociolinguistic interpretation, challenging us to find ways to account for framing instructions which may *or may not* be visible at the surface of language texts. It has become conventional in discourse analysis and pragmatics to assume that the meanings (and especially the social meanings) of utterances are radically underspecified in the semantics of utterances themselves (cf. Hanks 1993, 1996a, 1996b). As John Gumperz and Stephen Levinson suggest (1996: 225), meanings are "systematically enriched by contextual parameters and principles of use". They mean that there are social values and expectations that fill out particular social contexts of language use, and that analysing meaning – for communicators as well as for analysts – requires a critical sensitivity to such factors "in the meta zone", and to how they can be made relevant in particular instances. One might even say that the *primary* goal of sociolinguistics is to account for the metalinguistic processes of social contextualisation, in the widest sense, through which linguistic utterances find their meanings.

In his own empirical work (e.g. 1982, 1992), Gumperz has tended to emphasise those context-building features of spoken delivery which *are* isolable at the surface of texts, and which he calls *contextualisation cues*. Gumperz defines a contextualisation cue as "one of a cluster of indexical signs ... produced in the act of speaking that jointly index, that is invoke, a frame of interpretation for the rest of the linguistic content of the utterance" (Gumperz 1996: 379). His examples include prosodic and rhythmical cues, the phonological features associated with "accent" (dialectal pronunciation), and code-switching. Each of these can be used in ways that position a speaker socio-culturally and may influence interpretations of that speaker's stance, purpose, social alignment or even referential meanings, perhaps particularly in social encounters that can be labelled intergroup (e.g. interethnic). Gumperz makes the important point that, in a globalising world where it is increasingly misleading to develop research based on the assumption that people live and move in bounded, stable communities, it is increasingly important not to presuppose group membership or affiliations (cf. Beck, Giddens and Lash 1994; Chouliaraki and Fairclough 1999). In contrast, by studying the more active indexical displays and inferences people make in particular social encounters, we may gain a truer perspective on the sociolinguistics of culture. As Gumperz succinctly puts it, "cultural differences are becoming increasingly functional and less structural" (1996: 401). In relation to our starting point of socially innocent language, Gumperz's position gives us another reason to doubt the adequacy of approaching language as a simple, observable, "out there", socially given, behavioural phenomenon.

Social constructivism predisposes the use of interpretive, ethnographic approaches to sociolinguistic data, because they can create better opportunities for researchers to appreciate the close detail of how meanings are generated in social interaction. It is not surprising, then, that qualitative, ethnographic, discourse analytic approaches are coming to dominate in most research which recognises the "meta" sociolinguistic dimension (cf. Urban 1991; Gumperz 1996). As we shall see later in the chapter, this is true of some recent approaches to stylistic variation, and certainly of approaches to language ideology analysis, which builds much of its theory around the notion of metapragmatics. The link to ideology from the ideas from Bateson and Gumperz that we have been outlining is that the *non*-specified, *non*-isolable metalinguistic "messages" in many communicative events are the received, taken-for-granted, normative and sometimes repressive assumptions and "discourses" that colour social interaction. As we shall see, qualitative methods have *not*, however, been characteristic of language attitudes research, which approaches the topic of social and ideological contexts with very different assumptions and generates different sets of insights.

Returning to Lucy's three-way analysis of dominant trends in linguistic reflexivity research, we have yet to comment on his third category, literary-performance approaches. It is in this domain that we find an overtly *socio*linguistic perspective, to date. It is associated with Richard Bauman and colleagues' theorising of performance (e.g. Bauman 1977, 1992, 1996; Bauman and Briggs 1990; Silverstein and Urban 1996), mainly applied to set-piece, ritualistic events in different ethnic communities. Curiously enough, this meshes well with Erving Goffman's less empirically grounded, sociological observations on western, urban norms and mini-rituals of interactional conduct (Goffman 1974, 1981).

For Bauman (1992: 46), performance events have the qualities of being scheduled, spatio-temporally bounded, programmed, co-ordinated, generally public occasions which articulate a sense of heightened communicative intensity. Performance is inherently reflexive, in different regards:

> Perhaps the principal attraction of cultural performances for the study of society lies in their nature as *reflexive* instruments of cultural expression ... First of all, performance is formally reflexive – signification about signification – insofar as it calls attention to and involves self-conscious manipulation of the formal features of the communicative system ... making one at least conscious of its devices. At its most encompassing, performance may be seen as broadly metacultural, a cultural means of objectifying and laying open to scrutiny culture itself, for culture is a system of systems of signification ... In addition to formal reflexivity, performance is reflexive in a socio-psychological sense. Insofar as the display mode of performance constitutes the performing self as an object for itself as well as for others, performance is an especially potent and heightened means of taking the role of the other and of looking back at oneself from that perspective.
>
> (Bauman 1996: 47–48)

The "metacultural" facet of performance is apparent in those events that occupy acknowledged positions within cultural groups. As an instance, we might think of the Welsh National Eisteddfod with its set-piece choral and poetry competitions, centring on predetermined poetic forms and norms. The Eisteddfod, now held annually in Wales but having spawned hundreds of smaller-scale events in its image in Welsh communities around the world, is intensely metacultural. It is a studied and orchestrated cultural event, ideologically bound to the politics of Welsh language revival and to the maintenance of what are believed to be traditional Welsh cultural forms. Bauman and Briggs (1990) make the interesting observation that, as part of such events' reflexivity, they tend to *decontextualise* their textual content, making it more consumable as an independent and memorable cultural form.

But it is more of a challenge to read the metacultural dimension of less formal, less institutionalised, and more spontaneous cultural practices, where performance is nevertheless a defining characteristic. We discuss some of these below under the heading of the poetics of style and stylisation, although what we can call "everyday performance" should occupy a prominent place on the sociolinguistic agenda. This is particularly true if, as we speculated in the general Introduction and as Gumperz also hints, social life is tending to take on an increasingly reflexive character in the context of more globalised and less given and pre-structured identities. In fact it was Goffman who first alerted the social sciences to the dramaturgical element of everyday encounters. It is through his extensive use of a theatrical metaphor for communication, in which such terms as "actor" and "performance" often replace "speaker" or "listener", and "talk" or "behaviour", respectively. The notions of "poise" (self-control) and "face" suggest stage "masks" that people carefully select and "wear" to conjure up specific images and effects. Thus, for Goffman, interaction is a fine-tuned, collaborative engagement among social actors in a sequence of strategic performances (or rituals) for the construction and management of individuals" identities and group relations. The signalling of a performance is dependent on a series of keying devices and amalgamation of signals, multiple laminations (Goffman 1974), which warrant creativity and the artistic quality of the performance.

As we shall also see in a later section, literary-performance approaches have concentrated on the use of indirect and direct speech in narratives (and their genres) for reporting purposes (presenting speaker's or another person's point of view) and for their aesthetic value. Reflexive language is therefore closely linked to the poetic function of language (Jakobson 1960, see above) in which the message becomes foregrounded for its own sake (Lucy 1993: 20–21).

Verbal art and play, performance and other types of reflexive talk are said to orient more towards the formal and aesthetic qualities of language use (e.g. Briggs 1993, Kirshenblatt-Gimblett and Sherzer 1976; Goffman 1981; Schilling-Estes 1998). But the multifunctionality of talk not only allows but also requires some orientation to the propositional content, even in "nonsense" poetry, or small talk and other forms of phatic communion (Malinowski 1923). Even formulaic small talk involves information exchange, e.g. giving someone your name in a self-introduction (Jaworski 2000). In fact, some participants engaging in small talk and swapping the first-tellings of their stories actually value highly the *newness* and *newsworthiness* of these stories (J. Coupland and Jaworski 2003). Of course, this is not to say that the interpersonal and reflexive value of such story exchanges is undermined. On the contrary, the conventionality of strategies with which participants respond to the newsworthiness of their stories suggests a strong sense of self-monitoring and co-constructedness of talk.

The speaker's ability to mix or even manipulate different communicative goals in a single utterance locates *strategising* in the "meta" level of communication, because it requires speaker's engagement with creating desirable inferences (cf. Wilson, this volume) and adding multiple laminations onto the frame structure of one's talk. In this way, the speaker can, for example, present new information disguised as fabrication (see Coupland, this volume), or challenge old interpretation through irony (Clift 1999).

Although we agree with Lucy that "reflexivity is so pervasive and essential that we can say that language is, by nature, fundamentally reflexive" (Lucy 1993: 11), we make a case for isolating the "meta" level of communication from the totality of communication (linguistic and otherwise), for the sake of theoretical argument when it offers distinctive sociolinguistic insights. Like Lucy, we nevertheless see these processes as ultimately inextricable from the whole communicative picture (see also Cameron, this volume). The cluster of approaches we turn to next finds common ground in explicitly evaluative forms of meta-talk and linguistic meta-representation.

3.   Language attitudes, folklinguistics and language awareness

Outside of metapragmatics and anthropological linguistics (both of which we return to below), by far the most sustained "meta" oriented sociolinguistic re-search has been done under the headings of language attitudes, folklinguistics and language awareness. Language attitudes research is a core field of the social psychology of language (e.g. Giles and Coupland 1990; Robinson and Giles 2001; see also the *Journal of Language and Social Psychology* published by Sage) which has entered into a critical dialogue with variationist sociolinguis-tics since the 1970s. Folklinguistics has existed as a broad field interested in popular everyday understandings about language and traditional uses of lan-guage, subsuming traditional dialectology (Chambers and Trudgill 1990; Wake-lin 1977). More recently, Dennis Preston has refocused folklinguistics, specifi-cally through the new sub-discipline of perceptual dialectology (e.g. Preston 1986, 1999; Garrett, Coupland and Williams 1999). Perceptual dialectology has developed an explicit rationale for the "folk" perspective and built valuable bridges to both social psychological studies and variationist sociolinguistics. Research carried out in the language awareness tradition has been mainly con-cerned with pedagogical issues: the role of explicit knowledge of language in first- and second-language learning and teaching (see Hawkins 1984; James and Garrett 1990, and the journal *Language Awareness* published by Multilingual Matters).

Preston (1999) offers a comprehensive justification for folklinguistics, which also stands as a distinctive argument in favour of a "meta" focus for sociolinguistics as a whole. Folkloric awareness is a reality, he argues, whether or not community views accord with scientific fact. The "language in society" brief subsumes community opinion and discourse about language as well as description of language use. There may be systematic influence between the two domains of experience, and we should not ignore the possibility that folk perceptions and categories actually drive the agenda of scientific research. Then, folk representations may well provide better explanations of social trends (including language change) than do scientifically-derived generalisations. Overall, Preston challenges the fixity of a "folk" vs. "science" opposition, in ways that chime with recent ideological critiques of sociolinguistic research method and relationships between researchers and researched populations (Cameron et al. 1992; see also below).

In relation to dialect variation and change, William Labov has always recognised the importance of social-evaluative data. What Weinreich, Labov and Herzog (1968: 183–187) labelled "the evaluation problem" for a theory of language change has to do with the following questions:

> What subjective factors of speakers and hearers correlate with the observed change in the [speech] variable? What do the forms involved in the change "socially mean" to the speakers, consciously or unconsciously? And how does this relate to the process of change, if it does?
>
> (William Downes's summary – Downes 1998: 236)

Labov developed empirical and rather experimental techniques to study popular evaluations of particular speech variables. For example in New York City, he (1966) asked New Yorkers to judge the job suitability of speakers who had differing degrees of postvocalic /r/ in their speech, with rhoticity (audible /r/) in fact signalling suitability for high-ranking occupations. Evidence of this sort allowed Labov to make the case that the social meaning of postvocalic /r/ – its overtly acknowledged high status in the community – exerted pressure for more people to adopt the form in their own speech, and to use it more frequently in more formal speaking situations. At the same time, it emerged that another component of the social meaning of postvocalic /r/ in New York City was "toughness" (Downes 1998: 265), because informants felt that /r/ *non*-users would be more likely to come out on top in a fight than /r/ users.

From the 1970s onwards, the social psychology of language was developing other, progressively more standardised methods for studying language attitudes of this sort, and applying them to various forms of speech "stimulus", some to do with accent and dialect variables in different speech communities but others relating to all manner of communicative style variables – such as speech rate, lexical density and language choice in multilingual settings. (See Garrett, Coupland and Williams 2003 for a methodologically-oriented review.) Wallace Lambert (see, e.g. Lambert et al. 1960) developed the "matched guise technique", as a way of accessing attitudinal information indirectly – that is, without having to ask direct self-analytic questions about the meanings of speech styles. Vocal "guises" were generated by speakers with excellent imitative repertoires (sometimes they were professional actors), which fooled listeners into thinking they were hearing different speakers saying similar things, or reading the same texts. The central idea was that the "guising" procedure allowed experimenters to control out speech features other than the dependent variables (being targeted by the research), adding a useful degree of experimental control. A good deal of this sort of research was developed by Howard Giles and his associates, for example in relation to Welsh and Canadian speech communities (see Giles and Powesland 1975 for an early introduction to such studies, also Giles and Coupland 1990 and sources we have cited above, for more recent reviews).

Language attitudes research has been based on a far wider range of methods than the matched guise technique (see, e.g. Bourhis and Giles 1976; Kristiansen, this volume; Garrett, Williams and Coupland, this volume) even though "the MGT" still stands as its prototype. Mapping techniques associated with Preston's perceptual dialectology offer a quite different empirical approach, where informants are typically asked to draw boundary lines on maps, for example of the United States (see Preston 1986, 1999), and to describe the characteristics of the speech they associate with the speech communities they have identified. A map drawing stage is often followed by more controlled coding and evaluation tasks, where people might assign numerical values to stereotyped speech styles or speakers on pre-determined judgement scales (such as intelligence, social attractiveness or dynamism). But the epistemological principle behind this sort of research is an empiricist one, and the basic design is the surveying of attitudes and evaluations across relatively large populations, using some form of questionnaire instrument. As such it obviously differs in some fundamental ways from the committedly ethnographic, discourse analytic approaches to metalanguage and metapragmatics we introduced in the previous section. The question arises whether these different approaches are at all compatible with each other, also whether they might even have some useful complementarity of design.

Those questions have already been asked *within* the social psychology of language, and answered with a resounding *no* by the group of researchers who self-identify as *discursive psychologists*. Jonathan Potter and Margaret Wetherell's (1987) book, *Discourse and Social Psychology: Beyond Attitudes and Behaviours*, set out to subvert the experimental "attitudes" paradigm in social psychology, of which language attitudes was and largely still is a part. Their arguments were that attitudes have insufficient permanence – or at least cannot be demonstrated to have this quality – to be researched as durable "psychological states". Rather, they argued for a critical scepticism of psychological research which made (as they saw it) premature appeals to cognition, and for a form of discourse analysis which would expect "attitudes" to be speakers' accounts made in local circumstances of talk, for the moment (see Edwards and Potter 1992; Antaki and Widdicombe 1998 for more recent treatments of these and overlapping themes in discursive psychology).

In our view the discursive critique of "attitudes" is valuable but has tended to be overplayed. It is valuable for the same reasons as metapragmatics is valuable – in that it opens up a sociolinguistic agenda on contextualisation processes in situated interaction. But its overly radical stance against cognitivist interpretations also seems to undermine at least a part of the case for a sociolinguistics of metalanguage. That centres on the point we have already emphasized – that social interaction *is*, as well as contextual*ising*, contextual*ised* by prior expectations and assumptions, which must be carried cognitively, as Gumperz, Hanks, Silverstein and others have argued in their appeals to concepts like conversational "framing", "inferencing" and indeed "social meaning" itself. It follows from this that we need research paradigms that can help to build generalisations about which dimensions of social meaning are active in which social environments, and how they relate to sociolinguistic practices, styles and features. To put this another way, it would seem sensible to come at the issue of social meaning from both available directions – from the ethnographic and conversation-analytic study of situated interaction *and* from the social surveying of social groups and communities. The "meta" dimension of language in use points precisely to an *interaction* between socially structured meanings and values for talk and their activation in local contexts under local contingencies (see, e.g. Silverstein 2001 [1981] on the pragmatic constraints of meta-pragmatic awareness and their implications for the socio-cultural study of language).

As for complementarity, it again seems reasonable to acknowledge the potentially severe limitations of *all* footings for sociolinguistic research. The obvious causes for concern with survey-type attitude elicitation measures are a risk of pre-specifying dimensions of value judgement, and indeed presuming the existence of "emically" significant judgements in everyday circulation, and the possibility that attitudes coded up under experimental conditions – as a special case of a discursive context – will be tailored to match the perceived priorities of attitude researchers. (That is, a version of one of the discursive psychologists' main concerns.) These problems are of course not unknown to survey researchers, and various techniques have been developed in an effort to counter their effects. But in parallel, the causes for concern with ethnographies and analysis of situated discourse are that they may overgeneralise from local (con)textual happenings in small data sets, and may overinterpret (or misinterpret) speakers' and listeners' evaluations and attributions of linguistic sequences and items.

Sociolinguistics seems to be at a stage when it is making good its earlier lack of engagement with social theory (see Coupland, Sarangi and Candlin 2001) and redressing an over-investment in quantitative survey-based dialect research. But this is not a warrant for the exclusive use of ethnography. We return to language awareness perspectives at the end of the chapter.

4. Approaches to language representation

Our basic tenet of the lost "innocence" of language can be traced back to Bakhtin (e.g. 1981, 1984, 1986), whose ideas have already been referred to and will reappear in a later section. For him, language cannot be considered in terms of single, individual utterances. Rather, language is characterised by heteroglossia, i.e. various combinations of linguistic forms, the co-existence of past and present linguistic forms, and competing voices of different socio-ideological groupings and traditions (see Woolard 1999). This makes language dialogic, in that any discourse echoes any number of earlier (or future) discourses, all competing for ideological supremacy. Discourse is also emergent and co-constructed in that every utterance responds not only to the myriad of past linguistic forms or possible, anticipated ones, but also to the ongoing interactive "nowness".

The conceptualisation of language as heteroglossic is another way of encapsulating the metalinguistic nature of communication, in which speakers alternate and accommodate their speaking styles (registers, dialects, languages, etc.) to the speaking styles of others (see below). Each choice of a linguistic form or language variety is strategic, i.e. it is part of the speaker's communicative competence (Hymes 1972a, 1972b, 1996), and his/her sense of how each utterance fits in their linguistic universe and what it can achieve for them. Bakhtin makes a distinction between "heteroglossia alone" (unconscious switching between different language varieties), and "heteroglossia with awareness" (conscious manipulation of language choices) (see Cazden 1988 for discussion). But it would seem that whether linguistic choices are conscious or not, they always rely on the speaker's internalised knowledge of other linguistic forms, and that their choices are always "meta" choices as they copy, approximate or contrast with other language forms. In other words, each instance of language use is an act of linguistic representation indexing the actual or potential other linguistic forms.

To illustrate heteroglossia (with awareness) Courtney Cazden cites Roger Shuy's autobiographical comment:

> There is a natural conflict between acceptability by teacher and acceptability by peers even within the classroom. Personally I remember very clearly my school

conflicts between peer pressure and teacher expectations. One strategy to avoid this conflict is to give the right answer to the teacher but to do so in either non-standard or informal English.

(Shuy 1981: 170–171, quoted by Cazden 1988: 124)

The type of conflict described above may result in the student saying: "La Paz ain't the capital of Peru" (Shuy's example), which illustrates Bakhtin's "hetero-glossic utterance" – one that orients to two types of audiences and allows the speaker to project two types of identities at once: "good student" and "one of the boys". At the same time, this utterance indexes two sociolinguistic styles: "non-standard or informal English" through the use of *ain't* and "standard and formal English" through the conspicuous absence of *isn't*.

The heteroglossic view of language implies that interactants unavoidably subscribe to, offer or challenge representations of the communicative task at hand. That is, there is never unframed "behaviour". This is an inferential model, which asserts that all communicative interaction is undertaken knowingly. But just as in Bakhtin's distinction between heteroglossia alone and heteroglossia with awareness, we can find instances of language use which invoke the "meta" level more overtly than in others. These have been studied extensively in sociolinguistics under such headings as speech representation, reported speech ("direct", "indirect" and other types), linguistic reformulation and repetition.

At one level, the essential characteristic of language to refer to itself can be seen as a stylistic resource for speakers to attend to the contents of their own and others talk. Florian Coulmas (1986) overviews different forms of reported speech: "direct", "indirect" and, following Voloshinov's (1973) terminology, "quasi-direct discourse", which is typical of much literary style, for example, and in which the voices of the narrator and the hero are not explicitly separate but nonetheless discernible. Although reported speech might seem to be adequately accounted for by the phrase "talk about talk", the main emphases in sociolinguistic approaches to reported speech have been on the social contexts and consequences of reported speech rather than its content (insofar as they can be separated). It is commonly accepted that even in direct speech, the quoted part of the utterance is rarely a verbatim representation of the "original" utterance, if there was any in the first place (see Myers's 1999 study of hypothetical reported discourse). As Mike Baynham and Stef Slembrouck (1999a) observe, "it is probably best not to think in terms of 'originals' and 'copies', but rather to restrict oneself to stating chronological relationships of antecedence between 'versions'" (p. 453). Deborah Tannen (1986) suggests that what is referred to as "reported speech" or "direct quotation" in storytelling or conversation should be termed more appropriately "constructed dialogue", used to create multiple voices for more vivid narration and to conjure up distant or imagined worlds (see also Sternberg 1982; Philips 1985; Baynham 1996, 1999). For Tannen, constructed dialogue, alongside repetition (Tannen 1987, 1989; Johnstone 1987a, 1994), is part of the speaker's repertoire to poeticise conversation or narrative, which again echoes the link between Jakobson's metalinguistic and poetic functions.

Speakers have a wide range of stylistic devices at their disposal to introduce constructed dialogue in the form of "dialogue introducers" or "quotatives" (Johnstone 1987b), such as verbs *say, think, go, yell, whisper*, the lexical collocation *be like* and a zero form. Some of these quotatives, e.g. *be like*, have traditionally been associated with the representation of thoughts or attitudes of a character (or internal dialogue) (Tannen 1986) although its rapid spread across different varieties of English demonstrates an increased use of this form to introduce direct speech as well as internal dialogue (Tagliamonte and Hudson 1999). What is important here is that such obvious exploitation of the "meta" level in doing forms of quotation is used by speakers as a conventionalised resource to create different effects. For example, other things being equal, the predominant use of *go* or zero quotative, as opposed to the use of *think* or a lower ratio of quotatives overall, may create a greater sense of animation and immediacy in narratives and/or involvement between interlocutors (Tagliamonte and Hudson 1999).

Repetition stands out as a prime example of a metalinguistic resource available to speakers (and writers) although it is commonly derided and cited as a sign of "bad style", in contrast to creativity, originality and uniqueness (Kelly 1994; Tannen 1987). In 1936 Walter Benjamin (1968 [1936]) considered the rise of mass photographic reproduction as detrimental to the status and significance of art. But art has continued to flourish even though the boundaries between "original" and "reproduction" have been blurred even further. The most celebrated example is, of course, Andy Warhol, whose silk-screened repetitive images of Marilyn, Liz, Elvis, Campbell's Soup cans, Coca-Cola bottles, and so on, elevated repetition to the highest form of art.

Likewise, linguistic repetition is fundamental to verbal art and literature as well as "ordinary" talk, not least in the form of formulaic language (see Coulmas 1981; Wray 2002). Repetition operates at every level of linguistic analysis from phonological (e.g. alliteration) to repetition of larger chunks of discourse such as greetings and other politeness formulae, song choruses, prayers, poems, plays, lectures, or indeed any other linguistic form large and small. As Barbara Johnstone (1994) and her various contributors suggest, the functions of repetition are as varied and numerous as those of language itself. Let us repeat here Johnstone's list of the functions of repetition:

> Repetition functions didactically, playfully, emotionally, expressively, ritualistical-
> ly: repetition can be used for emphasis or iteration, clarification, confirmation; it can
> incorporate foreign words into a language, in couplets, serving as a resource for en-
> riching the language. People repeat to produce trance, as in mantras or the Lamaze
> method for overcoming pain. Actors repeat to learn their lines; academics copy out
> quotes when they read in a new are. Repetition can be bridging device in conversa-
> tion, a way of dealing with an interruption, or a way of validating what another speak-
> er has said. Repetition is a persuasive device. It is one of the primary forms of play.
>
> (Johnstone 1994: 6)

No doubt, the above list could be refined, extended and illustrated with numerous examples. But as Johnstone suggests, regardless of whether repetition is
formal, semantic, cognitive, immediate or displaced, exact or non-exact, self-
or other-repeating, it is always metalinguistic as it focuses our attention on
(earlier) discourse and intertextuality as evidenced by "translation, plagiarism,
allusion, parody, private and shared jokes, instructions, summation, quoting,
anaphora, reporting" (p. 13).

This broad-based view of repetition suggests that all language is at some level repetitive, or at least brings the promise of repetition. This is a radically different emphasis from the early Chomskyan view (e.g. Chomsky 1965), which
gives precedence to the generative nature of grammar to produce potentially
infinitely long and novel sentences, i.e. those that no-one has ever said before.
We certainly do not want to argue against the notion of creativity in language,
but it needs to be seen in a dialectic relationship with repetition, and however
paradoxical this may sound, even the creation of novel sentences or utterances
is metalinguistic on at least two counts. First, "knowing" that an utterance is
original, unique or novel requires a degree of metalinguistic awareness, as it
must be distinguished as "new" or "different" from all other utterances (or at
least be trusted to be so). Second, each time a novel utterance is made, it enters
the universe of potentially repeatable utterances, making it really possible for
an utterance to be "original" only once.

Apart from the broadly stylistic uses of reported speech/constructed dialogue,
quotation, voicing, repetition, and so on, these metalinguistic resources have
another important function, widely recognised in sociolinguistics – representing
other people and their social realities. This, in turn, helps the speaker project
desirable images of self and create interpersonal or intergroup closeness and
distance, and power imbalances. Two areas in which speech representation gains
much ideological significance are those of institutional discourse and the media.

Papers gathered in Baynham and Slembrouck (1999b), for example, demonstrate how social actors in different institutional settings use the resource of
reported speech to pursue individual, localised conversational goals and align

themselves with broader institutional practices. Janet Maybin (1999) demonstrates how pupils in a primary school setting repeat or appropriate teachers' voices of authority in teacher-pupil dialogue in the classroom as part of their induction to school procedures, and as a strategy for evaluating their teachers in pupil-pupil dialogue in the playground. Mike Baynham (1999) examines how nursing students take up writing positions and, more broadly, positions in a disciplinary practice through the mechanisms of quoting and referencing. Elizabeth Holt (1999) discusses a telephone conversation between two employees of a gas supply company, in which they use reported speech to portray a "difficult" client and to ironically represent other customers. Voicing here works in two ways: "othering" of clients and an affiliation-building between the two employees. Hall, Sarangi and Slembrouck (1999) draw on the data from social work to show how the representation of somebody's speech or writing is used by social workers to authenticate their versions of events and their discursive positions in conversation, and how these processes are subordinate to maintaining and legitimating the institutional goals and practices of social work. Greg Myers (1999) discusses how members of a focus group use hypothetical reported speech as a rhetorical device to enact and explore tensions between opposing points of view they may hold.

In those studies, speech representation is shown to act as an integral part of ideological positioning of speaking subjects in discourse conceived of as situated social action. Similar concerns have been attended to in Critical Discourse Analysis (CDA) with regard to media discourse. Norman Fairclough (1992a) distinguishes two types of metalinguistic (or metatextual) processes: "manifest intertextuality" and "interdiscursivity". This latter term, with its strong links to Bakhtin's dialogism, stresses the hybrid nature of texts as ad-mixtures of genres and discourses. This is an important notion with respect to what Fairclough calls the "orders of discourse", i.e. interdependent genres and discourses structuring different types of social practice into particular social orders (Fairclough 1989). These genres and discourses are characterised by shifting flows and boundaries, which leads to the hybridisation of discourse. This is another manifestation of the significance and ubiquity of the metalinguistic level in discourse. Fairclough's examples include the "conversationalization" of public discourse (Fairclough 1994), such as mixing the genre of (celebrity) media interview with political interview (Fairclough 1989; see also Fairclough and Wodak 1997), and the blending of military and religious discourses in a published account of government and religious leaders' comments on nuclear deterrence (Fairclough 1992b). There is a clear link here between intertextuality and multivoicing found in performative and stylized uses of language (see chapters by Coupland, Richardson, Meinhof, this volume).

The notion of "manifest intertextuality" lies close to the problems of speech representation discussed earlier in this section (see also chapters by Van Leeuwen, Galasiński, Wilson, this volume), as it refers to the mixing of elements of real or imagined texts within a text in the form of "reported speech", "indirect speech", "free indirect speech" or "discourse representation" (see Fairclough 1988, 1995). It is CDA's approach to (media) discourse that makes it clear that metalinguistic expressions such as "manifest intertextuality" do not merely refer to language. They can, and do, introduce the speaker's or other parties' voices as a gloss on the ideational layer of meaning of the text. The reporting of someone's words is not just a "neutral" account of what has been said. The act of retelling something involves the speaker's control both of what is being retold as well as how the retelling is structured and organised, depending on the speaker's view of the world, position of power, which will dictate the choice of the quotatives and the more or less interpretative account of the other's words (see, e.g. Caldas-Coulthard 1994; Short 1989; Cook 1992; Fairclough 1995; Roeh and Nir 1990; Zelizer 1989).

Similar intertextual links of metapragmatic representation have been shown to operate across different modalities. Barthes (1977), Hall (1981), Jaworski and Galasiński (2002) demonstrate how the connotative and associative meanings of press photographs are modified, reinforced or "inflected" by their headlines and captions. For example, Stuart Hall (1981) comments on the interpretative work of photo captions, which he illustrates with the newspaper photographs of the Tory politician Reginald Maudling on the day of his resignation over the Poulson affair. The newspapers showed the same or very similar photographs and variously chose to interpret Mr Maudling's expression as "angry" or "tragic". Thus, the photo "is linked with a particular interpretation which exploits its connotative value" (Hall 1981: 238), and the text bridges the theme of the message and the dominant ideology reinforced by an imposed reading of an image. Likewise, Jaworski and Galasiński (2002) discuss how President Clinton's facial expressions and hand gestures in his grand jury testimony video in August 1998 are reported in the British press with different, often conflicting "interpretations" ranging from accusing him of lying and rudeness to praising him for highly dignified behaviour. These studies are especially useful in revealing the power of metapragmatic comments, as non-verbal behaviour seems to be more indeterminate than most linguistic communication.

The above examples of representation of speech (and more broadly, communication) lie at the heart of the conception of metalanguage as a useful analytic category, which may be deployed for the discussion of various sociolinguistic phenomena, such as ideological construction, social control and (strategic) stylisation (see Cameron, this volume). It is part of a broader socio-pragmatic model, which similarly asserts that what is done through language constitutes a higher order of communicative organisation, above the organisation of linguistic forms and realisations. Pragmatic function has its own metalanguage – labelled speech acts such as "disagreeing with", "niggling", "buttering up", "sounding off", and so on. The fact that speakers routinely use these labels to comment on what is being achieved in conversation, for example, "What are you going on about?" or "Why are you slagging him off?", suggests that metapragmatics is a key notion for the understanding of micro- and macro-level discourse processes (but see Verschueren, this volume for criticism of other uses of the term "metapragmatics").

5.   The poetics of style and stylisation

Classical variationist conceptions of speaking "style" can be called "innocent", in the use of the term we offered at the head of this chapter. William Labov (e.g. 1966, 1972) introduced a sociolinguistic perspective on style viewed as the repertoire of spoken varieties that individuals use across different social situations of speaking, as a neutral dimension of language variation. It was neutral in that it was not necessarily associated with any specific design or social motivation for style-shifting. For Labov it was more an observation on a cultural tendency – the tendency to shift one's dialect style in quantitative terms towards the standard model in more formal contexts of talk. Although Labov has recently (2001) restated and confirmed his conception of sociolinguistic style, many different conceptualisations of style have appeared in recent decades. They include Allan Bell's (1984, 1991, 1992, 1999) explication of an audience design model, where speakers' style choices are believed to be made strategically in relation to listeners' speech characteristics, and Howard Giles and his colleagues' similar approach to sociolinguistic accommodation (see Giles, Coupland and Coupland 1991 for a historical review and collection of empirical studies). In accommodation theory the strategies of symbolically converging to and diverging from audience members' speech norms or communicative demands are formalised. Again, Nikolas Coupland (1984, 1985, 1988, 2001a) emphasises the strategic potential of style-shift as a resource for speakers to project relationally significant social personas, and Judith Irvine (2001) theorises style as personal and social "distinctiveness".

Several of these authors and others are contributors to a new volume of research on the sociolinguistics of style (Eckert and Rickford 2001). This book along with a few others (perhaps especially Rampton 1995 and Eckert 2000) amount to a new wave of more open, theoretically engaged research on sociolinguistic variation, style and identity. Its main strengths are its maintenance of the linguistic detail and rigour in the analysis of sociolinguistic variables (typically phonological variables with salient social class, gender, age and personality associations) as pioneered by Labov, while paying much more systematic attention to local contextualisation and social meaning dimensions. Theoretically it has drawn on and illuminated Mikhail Bakhtin's concepts of double voicing and heteroglossia (see references given above), while connecting with non-sociolinguistic approaches to style (e.g. Hebdige 1979), Bauman, Goffman and others' work on communicative performance (as we reviewed it above), and various interdisciplinary perspectives on social identity (including LePage and Tabouret-Keller's 1985 "acts of identity" framework).

Although there are important differences within this set, we would again like to emphasise its members' general recognition of a metalinguistic dimension. Style as innocent variable behaviour is replaced by style as reflexive social action. In the Bell and Giles approaches, communicative strategies are quite explicitly theorised. A "stylistic strategy" requires a speaker to achieve a degree of analytic distance, both from his/her speech and from the communicative event in which it features, designing speech to achieve (consciously or not) an anticipated personal or relational outcome. Cognitively, stylistic strategies also require a modelling of a speaker's own process of selection – of a language style or feature from a repertoire of referentially equivalent but relationally non-equivalent alternative forms ("stylistic variants"). These processes are clearly metalinguistic in character. They are very reminiscent of LePage and Tabouret-Keller's summary of how acts of identity are generated:

> Each individual creates his systems of verbal behaviour so as to resemble those common to the group or groups with which he wishes from time to time to be identified.
> (LePage and Tabouret-Keller 1985: 115)

There are obviously constraints on the range of "resemblances" or distinctively meaningful social images and associations that speakers are able to employ (or, better, *de*ploy) in particular cases. Once again we run up against the risk of overplaying the openness, contingency and negotiation potential of social interaction. But it is interesting to speculate that globalised modernity is widening the "normal repertoires" available for creative selection by many speakers.

The distinction between styled and *stylised* utterance is difficult to draw, but bringing the concept of stylisation into the sociolinguistics of style (as illustrated in three chapters of this volume) further increases the scope to theorise metalinguistic operations. In his theory of sociolinguistic *crossing*, Ben Rampton has in mind situations "in which the conventional persona normatively associated with one situation is transposed to another setting where it initially seems anomalous but subsequently makes sense as some kind of artful effect" (Rampton ms., cf. Rampton 1998: 302–306; 1999). Crossing indicates language styles "out of place", whose interpretation requires complex inferencing work by listeners in an attempt to work out how a speaker came to voice that image at that moment. Doing and interpreting crossings are fundamentally metapragmatic processes. Rampton (ms., note 5) gives a range of heuristic criteria for identifying stylisations in his data. They include exaggerated sociolinguistic features, sequences marked by a high density of marked phonetic features, sometimes by quotative verbs, abrupt prosodic or voice quality shifts, often with formulaic lexis and characterising personas stereotypically.

But in terms of metapragmatics, the key issue is ownership. Partly building on Rampton's data, Coupland (2001b, see also Coupland, this volume) suggests that stylisation systematically complicates speaker modality – the speaker's inferable relationship to the content and function of what is said. Stylised utterance is "as if" utterance, when a speaker gives reason for a listener to doubt whether s/he is the owner (in Goffman's terms the "principal" and "author" as well as the "animator") of his/her utterance. Similar complexities are theorised by Bakhtin in his concepts of *uni-directional* and *vari-directional double-voicing* (Bakhtin 1984), discussed and applied to sociolinguistic data by Rampton (1995: 222–223, 299–300). In the uni-directional case, a speaker voicing a prior style endorses or validates it. In the vari-directional case, the speaker voices the style with the intention of discrediting it (that is, parodies it). So, animators of stylised language recontextualise themselves as well as their talk, to the point of not necessarily self-presenting as themselves: they may be "ventriloquating" (another concept from Bakhtin), but often without offering evidence of the mimicked source they intend, which might or might not be themselves (cf. Hill and Hill 1986). This is the focal quality of stylisation, which links it to verbal play and even, occasionally, broad farce. It patterns with Eastman and Stein's (1993) idea of "language display", and Schilling-Estes's (1998) account of "performance speech" in Ocracoke.

Indeed, with stylisation we are clearly back in the domain of language performance, with all of its metalinguistic and metacultural implications. Goffman's ideas on ritualistic social interaction are also apposite, when he writes that ritualised language is achieved "through such ethologically defined processes as exaggeration, stereotyping, standardization of intensity, loosening of contextual requirements, and so forth" (1981: 84). Stylised performances "loosen" context by embedding another context within the current one – in the manner of Blom and Gumperz's (1972) "metaphorical style-shifting", but potentially more radically, in cancelling the assumption that we are even hearing "the same" speaker. In the same passage, Goffman writes about "self talk" and suggests that there are rather restricted "apparently permissible habitat[s]" for self talk. He is thinking of when we address an absent other or "address ourselves in the name of some standard-bearing voice" (1981: 79). He writes that, in self-talk, "we split ourselves in two" (p. 83). He compares the consequent participation frameworks with representations of cartoon figures' sentiments in balloons above their heads, "providing a text that the other figures in the pictured world can't perceive but we real people can" (p. 84). For Goffman, the lone self-talker is generating "a mimicry of something that has its initial and natural provenance in speech between persons ... one might want to say that a sort of impersonation is occurring" (p. 82). However, he goes on to make it clear that self-talk is *not* the mere citation or recording of what a monitoring voice would say, or what we would say to another if given a chance, but "the stage-acting of a version of the delivery, albeit only vaguely a version of its reception. What is set into the ongoing texts is not merely words, but their animator also – indeed, the whole interactional arrangement in which such words might get spoken" (p. 83). Goffman's self-talk is a reflexive stylisation of conversation.

6.   Language ideology analysis

Beyond agreeing to disagree with Marx's famous definition of ideology as "false consciousness", theorists rarely commit to defining the concept. Jan Blommaert and Jef Verschueren (1998: 25) define ideology "as any constellation of fundamental or commonsensical, and often normative ideas and attitudes related to some aspect(s) of social 'reality'". They bring forward other attributes, such as that ideologies tend to persist over time, are rarely questioned, but can be easily refashioned and transferred in the form of familiar "topoi" from one powerful group to another. Kathryn Woolard's review (1998) of *language* ideologies (ideological beliefs or discourses specifically about language or linguistic varieties – cf. Joseph and Taylor 1990; Schieffelin et al. 1998) debates the question where we should locate them. Do they inhere *in* language use itself, in explicit talk *about* language (that is, in metalanguage), in implicit metapragmatics (indirect signalling within the stream of discourse), or at least partly as "doxa", "naturalized dominant ideologies that rarely rise to discursive consciousness" (p. 9)? The answer is surely all of these, as we have already suggested.

The central point is that language is necessarily used against background sets of assumptions – about what is "correct", "normal", "appropriate", "well-formed", "worth saying", "permissible", and so on, but also about what indexical expression x has as its default meaning (Silverstein 1998) – which vary from one time and place to others, and that these evaluative and prescriptive assumptions are ideological. That is to say they are part of specific socio-cultural frames, with particular histories, tied in to particular power struggles and patterns of dominance (cf. Gal and Irvine 1995; Heller 1995; Lucy 1993; Silverstein 1985a, 1985b; Silverstein and Urban 1996; Urban 1993, 1996). The concept of language ideology is the final rejection of an innocent, behavioural account of language and the focus of the strongest claims that sociolinguistics must engage with metalinguistic processes in the most general sense.

It is again in linguistic anthropology where language-ideological processes have been most comprehensively discussed. This may be because of the implicitly or explicitly contrastive perspective that anthropology adopts, and because of its increasingly urgent wish to avoid essentialist or colonial readings of "exotic" cultural practices (Bendix 1997). Understandably, linguistic anthropology has needed to be wary of its own language ideologies and of those it imputes to its informants. But similar issues exist for general sociolinguistics, which has only recently begun to debate its own critical stances on public debates about language (e.g. McKinney and Swann 2001; Heller 1999; Wolfram 1998) and the political implications of researchers' stances relative to those of informants and of the populations it researches (Cameron et al. 1992).

There is no agreed methodology for studying language ideologies, although Gal and Irvine (1995) have proposed that three semiotic processes need to be addressed. The first and most significant is *iconisation*, taking a linguistic form or style to be a transparent depiction of a social group and its members. Woolard (1998) gives the example of "simple folk" being characterised iconically by "plain speech" and of the English language being taken to be a *sine qua non* of democratic thought (in American language policy discriminating in favour of "English-first" policies). In Judith Irvine's own research on the linguistic ideology of the Wolof people of Senegal (e.g. Irvine 1996, 2001), she identifies that the *griots* (bards) are iconised as an active, articulate but low-status group while the Nobles are an inarticulate, inert and high-status group, and so on. The other two of Gal and Irvine's processes are *recursivity*, whereby a meaningful opposition at one level is transposed onto other sorts of language/social organisation relationship, and *erasure*, where specific sociolinguistic evidence is rendered invisible in the drive to keep stereotyped generalisations intact. It should be evident, once again, that these processes can apply as much to academic theorising as to "folk" or "lay" theorising "in the field" (cf. Blommaert 1999).

7.   "The end of the innocence": Language for society

It is a relatively small step from Gal and Irvine's focus on iconisation as part of a critique of language ideology to the much more traditional concept of "social meaning" in sociolinguistics. The step is, however, a step away from a taken-for-granted, relatively transparent, apolitical sense of social meaning to a perspective that seeks out agencies in meaning making, is sceptical about orthodoxies and naturalness, and is attuned to a wider politics of metalanguage. In short, it is a step from a descriptivist stance to a critical stance.

The short history of sociolinguistics can be characterised very grossly as the articulation of dissatisfaction with the practice and emphases of linguistics, and as the consequences of several different strands of opposition coming together under one, broad banner. Elements of this history have been written rather elegantly, for example in Esther Figueroa's (1994) *Sociolinguistic Metatheory*. Under these circumstances it is not surprising that sociolinguistics retains at least some of the hallmarks of dominant theories in linguistics. Examples include Chambers's (2002) reading of what sociolinguistic theory is and should be, and Trudgill's (1978) comments that sociolinguistics is, in effect, a "proper" way of doing linguistics. But if sociolinguistics could be loosened from its history, perhaps the most fundamental question we would ask about the relationship between language and society would be: what are the distinctive social processes that language has allowed humans to engage in? What are the qualities of social life that would have been absent without language? Lucy (1996) takes up this same issue, and his answer is as follows:

> [W]here biologists operate with units such as individual organism and social group, the human sciences also explore questions of self and culture, the nature of reflective consciousness, and the significance of historically developed systems of meaning. All of the latter depend centrally on language.
>
> (Lucy 1996: 39)

In this quotation, and in Lucy's subsequent argument, we find a striking answer to the questions just asked. Lucy's answer is that it is language that has allowed humans to develop "systems of meaning" in the most general sense, including selves and cultures. In short, language is a prerequisite, not for humans to be individual and social, but for humans to have a sense of individuality and a sense of sociality. Language allows us to develop perspectives on lived and changing circumstances and on our individual relationships to experience – it permits, in Lucy's terms, "socialization or objectification of individual activities" (p. 40). What we call sociolinguistics should therefore be elaborated not so much as the study of language in society, but perhaps as the study of language *for* society.

Language can facilitate social and individual perspective-taking because of what Lucy calls its potential for "metasemiotic commentary". Language allows us to represent and so debate and evaluate all forms of communicative signals, including language itself, and in this chapter we have given a flavour of the respects in which it achieves this. Since language is the basis of the social, and since it is specifically the metasemiotic potential of language that achieves this, sociolinguistics and metalanguage must interconnect, and do so in more local and more global respects. The crux of the matter lies in the notion of "language awareness", which has often been identified as a means of resisting language-related prejudice and hegemony. Being "aware of language" is of course a matter of "metalinguistic competence", although there are good reasons to be wary of that notion too. What studies of metalanguage tell us to date, above all, is that the first level of meta-analysis is rarely the last, so that there is likely to be an institution or a social group that has an investment in prescribing what forms of "competence" are "appropriate", "authorisable", and so on (cf. Fairclough 1992d). The madness of infinite regress looms, but at least sociolinguists should prepare themselves to avoid falling at the first hurdle.

One area of sociolinguistics which addresses these issues is Critical Language Awareness (CLA) (Fairclough 1992c; Clark and Ivanič 1999; Cameron 1995, 2000a, 2000b). CLA has arisen in response to the growing importance of linguistic gatekeeping, i.e. an increasing number of individuals and institutions spelling out desirable or required versions of communication in various contexts (cf. Jaworski and Sachdev, this volume). The growth of the service sector at the expense of the shrinking manufacturing industries (in the post-industrial West) in the previous century meant shifting greater emphasis from work on assembly line to professional communication between service sector workers and clients. This has led to the "technologisation" of language, i.e. various organisations' adoption of a more interventionist orientation to language by formulating guidelines for their workers couched in terms of "communication skills" and "techniques". At the same time, the fragmentation of individual identities in late modernity (Giddens 1991, 1994) has also led to the "crisis" of previously stable roles in people's private lives. To a great many people it is no longer clear how to enact the role of a partner, parent or child, as well as citizen, consumer, co-worker, colleague, etc. This uncertainty is linked with many people's inability (or conviction of their inability) to produce and interpret new discourse genres and ways of speaking and writing required of successful professionals, fulfilled citizens and happy individuals. The growing obsession with "good" communication (Cameron 2000a) is filled by a communication industry happily producing prescriptive orders of *meta*-discourse which are constitutive of new social orders. These meta-discourses are based on various regimes of verbal hygiene

(Cameron 1995) and codifications of communication skills (Cameron 2000a). Building new "competences" is then seen as an essential part of coping with contemporary life. CLA examines the patterns of implicit and explicit language training and dissemination of different "models" of language use in education, professional training, the mass media and social/personal life, and unravels their ideological positions.

CLA, however, is itself not just a matter for the academy, allowing socio-linguists engaged in ideology-based research to make links between different types of discourse and different types of social action, or make transparent opaque patterns of power. As Fairclough points out, knowledge is a form of discourse. If we view language as a mere reflection of "natural" and "inevita-ble" states of knowledge, we shall never "question and look beyond existing discourses, or existing relations of dominance and marginalisation between discourses, and so advance knowledge" (Fairclough 1999: 75). Which again brings us to the significance of the "meta" level, this time not so much as a use-ful analytic category for sociolinguists, but as an essential educational tool for everyone, and a crucial component of struggle for social, political, economic and cultural fairness.

References

Antaki, Charles and Sue Widdicombe (eds.)
     1998   *Identities in Talk.* London: Sage.
Auer, Peter and Aldo di Luzio (eds.)
     1992   *The Contextualisation of Language.* Amsterdam: John Benjamins.
Baker, Colin
     1992   *Attitudes and Language.* Clevedon: Multilingual Matters.
Bakhtin, Mikhail M.
     1981   *The Dialogic Imagination.* Edited by Michael Holquist, translated by Caryl
              Emerson and Michael Holquist. Austin: University of Texas Press.
     1984   *Problems in Dostoyevsky's Poetics.* Minneapolis: University of Minnesota
              Press.
     1986   *Speech Genres and Other Late Essays.* Edited by Caryl Emerson and
              Michael Holquist, translated by Vern W. McGee. Austin: University of
              Texas Press.
Barthes, Roland
     1977   *Image – Music – Text.* London: Fontana.
     1996   Denotation and connotation. In Cobley, Paul (ed.), *The Communication
              Theory Reader.* London: Routledge, 129–133. [First published 1973.]

Bateson, Gregory
  1972   A theory of play and fantasy. In *Steps to an Ecology of Mind*. New York:
          Ballantine, 177–193. [First published 1955.]
Bauman, Richard
  1977   *Verbal Art as Performance*. Prospect Heights, IL: Waveland Press.
  1992   Performance. In Bauman, Richard (ed.), *Folklore, Cultural Performanc-
          es, and Popular Entertainments: A Communications-centered Handbook*.
          New York: Oxford University Press, 41–49.
  1996   Transformations of the word in the production of Mexican festival drama.
          In Silverstein, Michael and Greg Urban (eds.), *Natural Histories of Dis-
          course*. Chicago: University of Chicago Press, 301–327.
Bauman, Richard and Charles Briggs
  1990   Poetics and performance as critical perspectives on language and social
          life. *Annual Review of Anthropology* 19, 59–88.
Baynham, Mike
  1996   Direct speech: What's it doing in non-narrative discourse. *Journal of Prag-
          matics* 25, 61–81.
  1999   Double-voicing and the scholarly "I": On incorporating the words of oth-
          ers in academic discourse. In Baynham, Mike and Stef Slembrouck (eds.),
          Speech representation and institutional discourse. Special issue of *TEXT*
          19, 485–504.
Baynham, Mike and Stef Slembrouck
  1999a   Speech representation and institutional discourse. In Baynham, Mike and
          Stef Slembrouck (eds.), Speech representation and institutional discourse.
          Special issue of *TEXT* 19, 439–457.
Baynham, Mike and Stef Slembrouck (eds.)
  1999b   Speech representation and institutional discourse. Special issue of *TEXT*
          19/4.
Beck, Ulrich, Anthony Giddens and Scott Lash
  1994   *Reflexive Modernisation: Politics, Tradition and Aesthetics in the Modern
          Social Order*. Cambridge: Polity Press.
Bell, Allan
  1984   Language style as audience design. *Language in Society* 13, 145–204.
  1991   Audience accommodation in the mass media. In Giles, Howard, Nikolas
          Coupland and Justine Coupland (eds.), *Contexts of Accommodation: De-
          velopments in Applied Sociolinguistics*. Cambridge: Cambridge University
          Press, 69–102.
  1992   Hit and miss: Referee design in the dialects of New Zealand television
          advertising. *Language and Communication* 12, 327–340.
  1999   Styling the other to define the self: A study in New Zealand identity mak-
          ing. *Journal of Sociolinguistics* 3, 523–541.
Bendix, Regina
  1997   *In Search of Authenticity: The Formation of Folklore Studies*. Madison:
          University of Wisconsin Press.

Benjamin, Walter
    1968   The work of art in the age of mechanical reproduction. In *Illuminations*.
            Edited and introduced by Hanna Arendt. New York: Harcourt, Brace &
            World Inc., 211–244. [First published 1936.]
Blom, Jan Petter and John J. Gumperz
    1972   Social meaning in linguistic structures: Code-switching in Norway. In
            Gumperz, John J. and Dell Hymes (eds.), *Directions in Sociolinguistics*.
            New York: Holt, Reinhart & Winston, 407–434.
Blommaert, Jan (ed.)
    1999   *Language Ideological Debates*. Berlin: Mouton de Gruyter.
Blommaert, Jan and Jef Verschueren
    1998   *Debating Diversity: Analysing the Discourse of Tolerance*. London:
            Routledge.
Bourhis, Richard and Howard Giles
    1976   The language of cooperation in Wales: A field study. *Language Sciences* 42,
            13–16.
Briggs, Charles
    1993   Generic versus metapragmatic dimensions of Warao narratives: Who regi-
            ments performance? In Lucy, John A. (ed.), *Reflexive Language: Reported
            Speech and Metapragmatics*. Cambridge: Cambridge University Press,
            79–212.
Caldas-Coulthard, Carmen R.
    1994   On reporting reporting: The representation of speech in factual and fic-
            tional narratives. In Coulthard, Malcolm (ed.), *Advances in Written Text
            Analysis*. London: Routledge, 295–308.
Cameron, Deborah
    1995   *Verbal Hygiene*. London: Routledge.
    2000a   *Good to Talk? Living and Working in a Communication Culture*. London:
            Sage.
    2000b   Styling the worker: Gender and the commodification of language in the
            globalized service economy. *Journal of Sociolinguistics* 4, 323–347.
Cameron, Deborah, Elizabeth Frazer, Penelope Harvey, M. B. H. Rampton and
Kay Richardson
    1992   *Researching Language: Issues of Power and Method*. London: Routledge.
Cazden, Courtney B.
    1988   Contributions of the Bakhtin Circle to "communicative competence". *Ap-
            plied Linguistics* 10, 116–127.
Chambers, J. K.
    2002   *Sociolinguistic Theory*. 2nd edition. Oxford: Blackwell.
Chambers, J. K. and Peter Trudgill
    1990   *Dialectology*. Cambridge: Cambridge University Press.
Chomsky, Noam
    1965   *Aspects of the Theory of Syntax*. Cambridge, MA: MIT Press.

Chouliaraki, Lilie and Norman Fairclough
   1999   *Discourse in Late Modernity: Rethinking Critical Discourse Analysis.* Edinburgh: Edinburgh University Press.
Clark, Romy and Roz Ivanič (eds.)
   1999   Critical language awareness. Special issue of *Language Awareness* 8/2.
Clift, Rebecca
   1999   Irony in conversation. *Language in Society* 28, 523–553.
Cobley, Paul
   1996   Introduction. In Cobley, Paul (ed.), *The Communication Theory Reader.* London: Routledge, 1–32.
Cook, Guy
   1992   *The Discourse of Advertising.* London: Routledge.
Coulmas, Florian (ed.)
   1981   *Conversational Routine: Explorations in Standardized Communication Situations and Prepatterned Speech.* The Hague: Mouton.
   1986   Reported speech: Some general issues. In Coulmas, Florian (ed.), *Direct and Indirect Speech.* Berlin: Mouton de Gruyter, 1–28.
Coupland, Justine and Adam Jaworski
   2003   Stories as small talk: Mutual accomplishment of verbal play and newsworthiness. In Coupland, Justine (ed.), Small talk. Special issue of *Research on Language and Social Interaction* 36, 85–106.
Coupland, Nikolas
   1984   Accommodation at work: Some phonological data and their implications. *International Journal of the Sociology of Language* 46, 49–70.
   1985   "Hark, hark the lark": Social motivations for phonological style-shifting. *Language and Communication* 5, 153–172.
   1988   *Dialect in Use: Sociolinguistic Variation in Cardiff English.* Cardiff: University of Wales Press.
   2001a   Language, situation and the relational self: Theorizing dialect-style in sociolinguistics. In Eckert, Penelope and John R. Rickford (eds.), *Style and Sociolinguistic Variation.* Cambridge: Cambridge University Press, 185–210.
   2001b   Dialect stylisation in radio talk. *Language in Society* 30, 345–375.
Coupland, Nikolas, Srikant Sarangi and Christopher N. Candlin (eds.)
   2001   *Sociolinguistics and Social Theory.* London: Longman.
Downes, William
   1998   *Language and Society.* 2nd edition. Cambridge: Cambridge University Press.
Eastman, Carol M. and Roberta F. Stein
   1993   Language display: Authenticating claims to social identity. *Journal of Multilingual and Multicultural Development* 14, 187–202.
Eckert, Penelope
   2000   *Linguistic Variation as Social Practice.* Malden, MA: Blackwell Publishers.

Eckert, Penelope and John R. Rickford (eds.)
   2001   *Style and Sociolinguistic Variation*. Cambridge: Cambridge University
           Press.
Edwards, Derek and Jonathan Potter
   1992   *Discursive Psychology*. London: Sage.
Fairclough, Norman
   1988   Discourse representation in media discourse. *Sociolinguistics* 17, 129–
           139.
   1989   *Language and Power*. London: Longman.
   1992a   *Discourse and Social Change*. Cambridge: Polity Press.
   1992b   Discourse and text: Linguistic and intertextual analysis within discourse
           analysis. *Discourse & Society* 3, 193–217.
   1992c   The appropriacy of "appropriateness". In Fairclough, Norman (ed.), *Criti-
           cal Language Awareness*. London: Longman, 33–56.
   1994   Conversationalization of public discourse and the authority of the consum-
           er. In Keat, Russell, Nigel Whiteley and Nicholas Abercrombie (eds.), *The
           Authority of the Consumer*. London: Routledge.
   1995   *Media Discourse*. London: Edward Arnold.
Fairclough, Norman (ed.)
   1992d   *Critical Language Awareness*. London: Longman.
Fairclough, Norman and Ruth Wodak
   1997   Critical discourse analysis. In Van Dijk, Teun A. (ed.), *Discourse Studies:
           A Multidisciplinary Introduction. Volume 2: Discourse as Social Interac-
           tion*. London: Sage, 258–284.
Figueroa, Esther
   1994   *Sociolinguistic Metatheory*. London: Pergamon.
Gal, Susan and Judith Irvine
   1995   The boundaries of languages and disciplines: How ideologies construct
           differences. *Social Research* 62, 967–1001.
Garrett, Peter, Nikolas Coupland and Angie Williams
   1999   Evaluating dialect in discourse: Teachers' and teenagers' responses to
           young English speakers in Wales. *Language in Society* 28, 321–354.
   2003   *Investigating Language Attitudes: Social Meanings of Dialect, Ethnicity
           and Performance*. Cardiff: University of Wales Press.
Giddens, Anthony
   1991   *Modernity and Self-identity*. Cambridge: Polity Press.
   1994   Living in a post-traditional society. In Beck, Ulrich, Anthony Giddens and
           Scott Lash (eds.), *Reflexive Modernization: Politics, Tradition and Aes-
           thetics in the Modern Social Order*. Cambridge: Polity Press, 56–109.
Giles, Howard and Nikolas Coupland
   1990   *Language: Contexts and Consequences*. London: Open University Press.
Giles, Howard, Nikolas Coupland and Justine Coupland (eds.)
   1991   *Contexts of Accommodation: Developments in Applied Sociolinguistics*.
           Cambridge: Cambridge University Press.

Giles, Howard and Peter Powesland
1975 *Speech Style and Social Evaluation*. London: Academic Press.
Goffman, Erving
1974 *Frame Analysis: An Essay on the Organization of Experience*. New York: Harper & Row.
1981 *Forms of Talk*. Oxford: Blackwell.
Gumperz, John J.
1982 *Discourse Strategies*. Cambridge: Cambridge University Press.
1992 Contextualization and understanding. In Duranti, Alessandro and Charles Goodwin (eds.), *Rethinking Context: Language as an Interactive Phenomenon*. Cambridge: Cambridge University Press, 229–252.
1996 The linguistic and cultural relativity of inference. In Gumperz, John J. and Stephen C. Levinson (eds.), *Rethinking Linguistic Relativity*. Cambridge: Cambridge University Press, 374–406.
Gumperz, John J. and Stephen C. Levinson
1996 Introduction to Part III. In Gumperz, John J. and Stephen C. Levinson (eds.), *Rethinking Linguistic Relativity*. Cambridge: Cambridge University Press, 225–231.
Hall, Stuart
1981 The determination of news photographs. In Cohen, Stanley and Jack Young (eds.), *The Manufacture of News*. London: Constable, 226–243.
Hall, Christopher, Srikant Sarangi and Stef Slembrouck
1999 Speech representation and the categorization of the client in social work discourse. In Mike Baynham and Stef Slembrouck (eds.), Speech representation and institutional discourse. Special issue of *TEXT* 19, 539–570.
Halliday, M. A. K.
1978 *Language as Social Semiotic: The Social Interpretation of Language and Meaning*. London: Edward Arnold.
Hanks, William F.
1993 Metalanguage and pragmatics of deixis. In Lucy, John A. (ed.), *Reflexive Language: Reported Speech and Metapragmatics*. Cambridge: Cambridge University Press, 127–157.
1996a Language form and communicative practices. In Gumperz, John J. and Stephen C. Levinson (eds.), *Rethinking Linguistic Relativity*. Cambridge: Cambridge University Press, 231–270.
1996b Exorcism and the description of participant roles. In Silverstein, Michael and Greg Urban (eds.), *Natural Histories of Discourse*. Chicago: University of Chicago Press, 160–200.
Harris, Roy
1996 *Signs, Language and Communication*. London: Routledge.
Hawkins, Eric
1984 *Awareness of Language: An Introduction*. Cambridge: Cambridge University Press.

Hebdige, Dick
    1979   *Subculture: The Meaning of Style*. New York: Methuen.
Heller, Monica
    1995   Language, choice, social institutions, and symbolic domination. *Language in Society* 24, 373–405.
Heller, Monica (ed.)
    1999   Sociolinguistics and public debate [Thematic collection of dialogue contributions]. *Journal of Sociolinguistics* 3, 260–288.
Hill, Jane H. and Kenneth C. Hill
    1986   *Speaking Mexicano: Dynamics of a Syncretic Language in Central Mexico*. Tucson: University of Arizona Press.
Hockett, Charles F.
    1958   *A Course in Modern Linguistics*. New York: Macmillan.
    1963   The problem of universals in language. In Greenberg, Joseph H. (ed.), *Universals in Language*. Cambridge, MA: MIT Press, 1–29.
Holt, Elizabeth
    1999   Just gassing: An analysis of direct reported speech in a conversation between employees of a gas supply company. In Mike Baynham and Stef Slembrouck (eds.), Speech representation and institutional discourse. Special issue of *TEXT* 19, 505–537.
Hutcheon, Linda
    1985   *A Theory of Parody*. New York: Methuen.
    1994   *Irony's Edge: The Theory and Politics of Irony*. London: Routledge.
Hymes, Dell
    1972a   On communicative competence. In Pride, J. B. and Janet Holmes (eds.), *Sociolinguistics*. Harmondsworth, Middlesex: Penguin, 267–293.
    1972b   Models of the interaction of language and social life. In Gumperz, John J. and Dell Hymes (eds.), *Directions in Sociolinguistics*. New York: Holt, Rinehart & Winston, 35–71.
    1975   Breakthrough into performance. In Ben-Amos, Dan and Kenneth S. Goldstein (eds.), *Folklore: Performance and Communication*. The Hague: Mouton, 11–74.
    1996   *Ethnography, Linguistics, Narrative Inequality: Toward an Understanding of Voice*. London: Taylor & Francis.
Irvine, Judith
    1996   Shadow conversations: The indeterminacy of participant roles. In Silverstein, Michael and Greg Urban (eds.), *Natural Histories of Discourse*. Chicago: University of Chicago Press,131–159.
    2001   "Style" as distinctiveness: The culture and ideology of linguistic differentiation. In Eckert, Penelope and John Rickford (eds.), *Style and Sociolinguistic Variation*. Cambridge: Cambridge University Press, 21–43.
Jakobson, Roman
    1960   Closing statement: Linguistics and poetics. In Sebeok, Thomas A. (ed.), *Style in Language*. Cambridge, MA: MIT Press, 350–377.

1980   Metalanguage as a linguistic problem. In *The Framework of Language.* Michigan Studies in the Humanities. Ann Arbor: Horace H. Rackham School of Graduate Studies, 81–92.

James, Carl and Peter Garrett (eds.)
1990   *Language Awareness in the Classroom.* London: Longman.

Jaworski, Adam
1997   "White and white": Metacommunicative and metaphorical silences. In Jaworski, Adam (ed.), *Silence: Interdisciplinary Perspectives.* Berlin: Mouton de Gruyter, 381–401.
2000   Silence and small talk. In Coupland, Justine (ed.), *Small Talk.* London: Pearson Education, 110–132.

Jaworski Adam and Dariusz Galasiński
2002   The verbal construction of non-verbal behaviour: British press reports of President Clinton's grand jury testimony video. *Discourse & Society* 13, 629–649.

Johnstone, Barbara (ed.)
1987a   Perspectives on repetition. Special issue of *TEXT* 7/3.

Johnstone, Barbara
1987b   "He says … so I said": Verb tense alternation and narrative depictions of authority in American English. *Linguistics* 25, 33–52.
1994   *Repetition in Discourse: Interdisciplinary Perspectives,* vol. 1 and 2. Norwood, NJ: Ablex Publishing Corporation.

Joseph, John E. and Talbot J. Taylor (eds.)
1990   *Ideologies of Language.* London: Routledge.

Kelly, Katherine E.
1994   Staging repetition: Parody in postmodern British and American theatre. In Johnstone, Barbara (ed.), *Repetition in Discourse: Interdisciplinary Perspectives,* vol. 1. Norwood, NJ: Ablex Publishing Corporation, 55–67.

Kirshenblatt-Gimblett, Barbara and Joel Sherzer
1976   Introduction. In Kirshenblatt-Gimblett, Barbara (ed.), *Speech Play: Research and Resources for Studying Linguistic Creativity.* Philadelphia: University of Pennsylvania Press, 1–16.

Labov, William
1966   *The Social Stratification of English in New York City.* Washington, DC: Center for Applied Linguistics.
1972   *Sociolinguistic Patterns.* Philadelphia: University of Pennsylvania Press.

2001   The anatomy of style-shifting. In Eckert, Penelope and John R. Rickford (eds.), *Style and Sociolinguistic Variation.* Cambridge: Cambridge University Press, 85–108.

Lambert, Wallace E., R. Hodgson, R. C. Gardner and S. Fillenbaum 1960 Evaluational reactions to spoken languages. *Journal of Abnormal and Social Psychology* 60: 44–51.

LePage, Robert and Andrée Tabouret-Keller
    1985   *Acts of Identity*. Cambridge: Cambridge University Press.
Lucy, John A.
    1993   Reflexive language and the human disciplines. In Lucy, John A. (ed.),
            Reflexive Language: Reported Speech and Metapragmatics. Cambridge:
            Cambridge University Press, 9–32.
    1996   The scope of linguistic relativity: An analysis and review of empirical re-
            search. In Gumperz, John J. and Stephen C. Levinson (eds.), *Rethinking
            Linguistic Relativity*. Cambridge: Cambridge University Press, 37–69.
McKinney, Carolyn and Joan Swann
    2001   Developing a sociolinguistic voice: Students and linguistic descriptivism.
            Journal of Sociolinguistics 5, 576–590.
Malinowski, Bronislaw
    1923   The problem of meaning in primitive languages. Supplement to C. K.
            Ogden and I. R. Richards *The Meaning of Meaning*. London: Routledge
            and Kegan Paul, 146–152.
Maybin, Janet
    1999   Framing and evaluation in ten- to twelve-year-old school children's use
            of repeated, appropriated, and reported speech in relation to their induc-
            tion into educational procedures and practices. In Baynham, Mike and Stef
            Slembrouck (eds.), Speech representation and institutional discourse. Spe-
            cial issue of *TEXT* 19, 459–484.
Myers, Greg
    1999   Unspoken speech: Hypothetical reported discourse and the rhetoric of eve-
            ryday talk. In Baynham, Mike and Stef Slembrouck (eds.), Speech repre-
            sentation and institutional discourse. Special issue of *TEXT* 19, 571–590.
Philips, Susan U.
    1986   Reported speech as evidence in an American trial. In Tannen, Deborah and
            James E. Alatis (eds.), *Language and Linguistics: The Interdependence of
            Theory, Data, and Application. Georgetown University Round Table on
            Language and Linguistics 1985*. Washington, DC: Georgetown University
            Press, 154–170.
Potter, Jonathan and Margaret Wetherell
    1987   *Discourse and Social Psychology: Beyond Attitudes and Behaviour*. Lon-
            don: Sage.
Preston, Dennis
    1986   Five visions of America. *Language in Society* 15, 221–240.
Preston, Dennis (ed.)
    1999   *Handbook of Perceptual Dialectology*, vol. 1. Amsterdam: John Ben-
            jamins.
Rampton, Ben
    1995   *Crossing: Language and Ethnicity among Adolescents*. London: Long-
            man.

1998   Language crossing and the redefinition of reality. In Auer, Peter (ed.), *Codeswitching in Conversation*. London: Routledge, 290–317.

ms.   Styling social class: "Acts of identity" or "structures of feeling"? Paper presented at the Colloquium on Acts of Identity, University of Freiburg, February 2002.

Rampton, Ben (ed.)

1999   Styling the other. Special issue of *Journal of Sociolinguistics* 3/4.

Reddy, Michael

1993   The conduit metaphor: A case of frame conflict in our language about language. In Ortony, Andrew (ed.), *Metaphor and Thought*, 2nd edition. Cambridge: Cambridge University Press, 164–201. [First published 1979.]

Robinson, W. Peter and Howard Giles (eds.)

2001   *The New Handbook of Language and Social Psychology*. London: John Wiley.

Roeh, Itzhak and Nir, Raphael

1990   Speech presentation in the Israel radio new: Ideological constraints and rhetorical strategies. *TEXT* 10, 225–244.

Saussure, Ferdinand de

1974   *Course in General Linguistics*. Translated by W. Baskin. Glasgow: Fontana. [First published 1916.]

Schieffelin, Bambi B., Kathryn A. Woolard and Paul V. Kroskrity (eds.)

1998   *Language Ideologies: Practice and Theory*. New York: Oxford University Press.

Schilling-Estes, Natalie

1998   Investigating "self-conscious" speech: The performance register in Ocracoke English. *Language in Society* 27, 53–83.

Short, Mike

1989   Speech presentation, the novel and the press. In Van Peer, Willie (ed.) *The Taming of the Text*. London: Routledge, 61–81.

Shuy, Roger

1981   Learning to talk like teachers. *Language Arts* 58, 168–174.

Silverstein, Michael

1985a   Language and the culture of gender: At the intersection of structure, usage and ideology. In Mertz, Elizabeth and Richard J. Parmentier (eds.), *Semiotic Mediation*. Orlando: Academic Press, 219–259.

1985b   The culture of language in Chinookan narrative texts; or, On saying that… in Chinookan. In Nichols, Johanna and Anthony Woodbury (eds.), *Grammar Inside and Outside the Clause: Some Approaches to Theory from the Field*. Cambridge: Cambridge University Press, 132–171.

1996   The uses and utility of ideology. In Schieffelin, Bambi B., Kathryn A. Woolard and Paul V. Kroskrity (eds.), *Language Ideologies: Practice and Theory*. New York: Oxford University Press, 123–145.

2001   The limits of awareness. In Duranti, Alessandro (ed.), *Linguistic Anthropology: A Reader*. Malden, MA: Blackwell Publishers, 382–402. [First published 1981.]

Silverstein, Michael and Greg Urban (eds.)
1996   *Natural Histories of Discourse*. Chicago: University of Chicago Press.

Sternberg, Meir
1982   Point of view and the indirection of direct speech. *Language and Style* 15, 67–177.

Tagliamonte, Sali and Rachel Hudson
1999   *Be like* et al. Beyond America: The quotative system in British and Canadian youth. *Journal of Sociolinguistics* 3, 147–172.

Tannen, Deborah
1986   Introducing constructed dialogue in Greek and American conversational and literary narrative. In Coulmas, Florian (ed.), *Direct and Indirect Speech*. Berlin: Mouton de Gruyter, 311–332.
1987   Repetition in conversation: Toward a poetics of talk. *Language* 63, 574–605.
1989   *Talking Voices: Repetition, Dialogue, and Imagery in Conversational Discourse*. Cambridge: Cambridge University Press.

Tracy, Karen and Nikolas Coupland
1990   Multiple goals in discourse: An overview of issues. In Tracy, Karen and Nikolas Coupland (eds.), *Multiple Goals in Discourse*. Clevendon: Multilingual Matters, 1–13.

Trudgill, Peter
1978   Introduction: Sociolinguistics and sociolinguistics. In Trudgill, Peter (ed.), *Sociolinguistic Patterns in British English*. London: Edward Arnold, 1–18.

Urban, Greg
1991   *A Discourse-Centred Approach to Culture: Native South American Myths and Rituals*. Austin: University of Texas Press.
1993   The represented functions of speech in Shokleng myths. In Lucy. John, A. (ed.), *Reflexive Language: Reported Speech and Metapragmatics*. Cambridge: Cambridge University Press, 241–259.
1996   Entextualization, replication and power. In Silverstein, Michael and Greg Urban (eds.), *Natural Histories of Discourse*. Chicago: University of Chicago Press, 21–44.

Voloshinov, Valentin Nikolaevic
1973   *Marxism and the Philosophy of Language*. Translated by Ladislav Matejka, and I. R. Titunik. New York: Seminar Press. [First published 1929 and 1930.]

Wakelin Martyn
1977   *English Dialects: An Introduction*. London: Athlone Press.

Weinreich, Ulrich, William Labov and Marvin I. Herzog
  1968   Empirical foundations for a theory of language change. In Lehman, W. P.
          and Y. Malkiel (eds.), *Directions for Historical Linguistics*. Austin: Uni-
          versity of Texas Press, 95–189.
Wolfram, Walt
  1998   Scrutinizing linguistic gratuity: Issues from the field. *Journal of Sociolin-
          guistics* 2, 271–280.
Woolard, Kathryn A.
  1995   Changing forms of codeswitching in Catalan comedy. *Catalan Review* 9,
          223–252.
  1998   Introduction: Language ideology as a field of inquiry. In Schieffelin, Bambi
          B., Kathryn A. Woolard and Paul V. Kroskrity (eds.), *Language Ideologies:
          Practice and Theory*. New York: Oxford University Press, 3–47.
  1999   Simultaneity and bivalency as strategies in bilingualism. *Journal of Lin-
          guistic Anthropology* 8, 3–29.
Wray, Alison
  2002   *Formulaic Language and the Lexicon*. Cambridge: Cambridge University
          Press.
Zelizer, Barbie
  1989   "Saying" as collective practice: Quoting and differential address in the
          news. *TEXT* 9, 369–388.

Notes on the role of metapragmatic awareness in language use

Jef Verschueren

1. Introduction

This chapter argues that metalanguage is an important topic for linguistic research because it reflects metapragmatic awareness, a crucial force behind the meaning-generating capacity of language in use. The reflexive awareness in question is no less than the single most important prerequisite for communication as we know it. It is part of what Tomasello (1999) describes as people's ability to identify with others and thus to work collaboratively towards common goals.[1]

In the second section, the notions of metalanguage and metapragmatics will be briefly introduced and clarified. Section 3 goes into the relevance of metalinguistic or metapragmatic phenomena as reflections of metapragmatic awareness, a notion that will be situated in relation to an overall theory of pragmatics. A fourth section elaborates on some aspects of the functioning of metapragmatic awareness in actual language use. Finally, some of the social implications of this functioning will be reviewed, in particular in relation to language ideologies and identity construction.

2. Metalanguage and metapragmatics

Let's start out by establishing an intertextual link – and thereby engaging in the conscious use of metalanguage. During a meeting of which this chapter is a side product,[2] the issue was raised repeatedly of how useful the notion of META-LANGUAGE was, more often than not with the implication that its usefulness was very limited. Yet, depending on the perspective one takes, the significance of the notion may range from useful and interesting to absolutely necessary. First one may regard "metalanguage" as an identifiable *object*, separable from other manifestations of "language". Applied to the text you have just started to read, the term would cover the use of lexical items such as "intertextual", phrases such as "the text you have just started to read" and "thereby engaging in the conscious use of metalanguage", or utterances such as "... the issue was raised repeatedly of how useful the notion of 'metalanguage' was" or "what Toma-sello (1999) describes as ...". It would cover conversational interventions such as "What do you mean by that?" or "That's not what I said." Such occurrences are pervasive in most types of discourse. Hence, because of its obvious corre-spondence with a range of empirical facts, the notion is necessarily a useful and interesting one. Yet its usefulness, from this perspective, remains limited. One might object, for instance, that what we are concerned with is simply language about language, i.e., manifestations of language in general which happen to have language within their referential scope. We would still have to demon-strate what is so special about it – if anything. We would have to demonstrate that the reflexivity involved is neither fortuitous nor trivial.

A second way of approaching "metalanguage" is to look at it as a *dimen-sion* of language – to be found in *all* language use – rather than a collection of instances of metalinguistic language use. While a discussion of this dimension would have to refer to all metalinguistic phenomena covered by the object notion of "metalanguage", it moves beyond such phenomena into the realm of basic properties of any stretch of discourse, thus significantly expanding the relevance of the notion. This approach has a reasonably long history in linguistics, where the influences of pragmatist semiotics (in particular Peirce's theory of indexical-ity) combined with Prague School structuralism in the person of Roman Jakob-son, who may have provided the single most forceful and influential introduction of "metalanguage" as a linguistic topic. In his "Shifters, verbal categories, and the Russian verb" (1971), Jakobson points out that the two basic ingredients of linguistic communication, the message (M) and the code (C), may both be "utilized" (used) and "referred to" (pointed at, mentioned). "Referring to" is a metalinguistic activity as soon as it has ingredients of linguistic communication within its scope. This activity may take place either within or across message and code, thus yielding four types of metalinguistic usage: messages referring to messages (M/M) are to be found in various forms of quoted and reported speech (for an authoritative treatment of which, in terms of speech about speech, Ja-kobson refers to Vološinov 1930); an instance of code referring to code (C/C) is the proper name, which cannot be defined without circular reference to the code itself (i.e., a name means anyone or anything to whom or to which the name is assigned); messages referring to the code (M/C) are found whenever a word is "mentioned" rather than "used", as in "'Pup' means a young dog" or "'Pup' is a monosyllable" (a topic which has been commonly debated in philosophy at least since Carnap 1937); finally, a case where code and message overlap or where an element of the code makes "compulsory reference to the given message" (C/M) is provided by the category of "shifters" (a term borrowed from Jespersen 1922), i.e., indexical symbols such as personal pronouns, aspect, tense, mood and evidentials, which necessarily "shift" in relation to changes in the context of use and hence in relation to the content of the message. In more general terms, Jakobson (1960, 1985) presented the "metalingual function" as one of his six basic functions of language.[3] Clearly, only Jakobson's M/M and M/C categories of metalinguistic functioning fit into the object notion of "metalanguage", while C/C and C/M can only be conceived in terms of a metalinguistic dimension. This observation gives rise to a rough classification of metalinguistic phenomena into two categories, as visualized in Table 1, one included in the dimension view of metalanguage only (say "implicit metalanguage"), the other included in both the dimension and the object view ("explicit metalanguage").

Table 1. Metalinguistic phenomena

Metalanguage as a **dimension** of language use	
Metalanguage as an **object**	[Jakobson's C/C + C/M] *implicit metalanguage*
[Jakobson's M/M + M/C] *explicit metalanguage*	

Because of its necessary relation to usage phenomena (the proper domain of linguistic pragmatics), *the study of the metalinguistic dimension of language* could be called *metapragmatics*. In fact, the term has been used in this way, e.g., by Michael Silverstein (1976, 1979, 1993). In Silverstein's view, strongly inspired by Jakobson but taking an interdisciplinary (primarily Anthropological Linguistic) point of view, pragmatics encompasses "the totality of indexical relationships between occurrent signal forms and their contexts of occurrence, regardless of whether such contexts are other occurrent signal forms ... or not specifically such ..." (1993: 36). Whatever pragmatic functioning there may be, there is always the possibility of metapragmatic functioning, conceived in terms of *reflexivity*. He goes on to emphasize the importance of reflexivity more strongly still, taking away all suspicion that the phenomenon we are confronted with would be fortuitous or trivial:

> Without a metapragmatic function simultaneously in play with whatever pragmatic function(s) there may be in discursive interaction, there is no possibility of interactional coherence, since there is no framework of structure – here, interactional text structure – in which indexical origins or centerings are relatable one to another as aggregated contributions to some segmentable, accomplishable event(s).
>
> (Silverstein 1993: 36–37)

And, "metapragmatic function serves to regiment indexicals into interpretable event(s) of such-and-such type that the use of language in interaction constitutes (consists of)" (Silverstein 1993: 37). In other words, there is a constant interaction between pragmatic and metapragmatic functioning. This observation definitely lifts metapragmatics or metalanguage (seen as a dimension rather than an object) from the merely interesting and useful to the absolutely necessary if we want to understand language use.

In order to make the vast field of inquiry opened up by this view more manageable, Silverstein identifies three dimensions of contrast along which metapragmatic phenomena can be usefully situated. First, he distinguishes metafunctions according to their *object of meta-semiosis*. Along this dimension, metapragmatics – bearing on a reflexive relation to the pragmatic or indexical dimension of language – is opposed to (while at the same time incorporating) metasemantics, which deals with the reflexivity related to the semiotic realm of sense, i.e., an "abstractable constancy in denotational capacity of grammatically constructed expressions" (1993: 41). A second dimension is formed by degrees and kinds of *denotational explicitness*. Most natural languages have (partially) explicit metapragmatic forms of expression, e.g., in the form of metapragmatic lexical items (such as performative verbs). There are also inherently (hence relatively explicitly) metapragmatic semantico-referential forms such as deictic expressions. At the implicit end of the scale we find metapragmatic indexicality, i.e., indexical signaling of something about indexical signaling. It is here that one may, for example, situate the theoretical contribution of Gumperz's (1982) "contextualization cues", the linguistic means (often prosodic) that speakers use (usually with a very low degree of awareness) to signal how (forms occurring in) utterances are to be appropriately interpreted. Third, types of metapragmatic functioning differ in terms of the *mutual calibration* of the metapragmatic signaling event and the signaled pragmatic event-structure. Put simply, there is a difference, for instance, between cases in which the relationship between the two events is a "reporting on" rather than a "coincidence". It is with reference to this dimension that the double communicative layering inherent in the pragmatic-metapragmatic relationship can be fully accounted for.

It is important to keep such possible distinctions in mind, while it is not necessary to adhere strictly to the associated terminology. For one thing, this author has trouble distinguishing between metapragmatics and metasemantics; even though a theoretical distinction can be made between those aspects of the meaningfulness of signs that are constant across different specific contexts and those that are connected with ongoing usage, they are hard to identify in practice. Aspects of denotational explicitness and mutual calibration between the pragmatic and the metapragmatic, on the other hand, will help to structure the following exposition. At the same time, they should function as a frame of interpretation for what follows; for instance, when we use the contrast explicit–implicit, it should be clear that this is a scale rather than a dichotomy, though because of the difficulty in giving all phenomena a specific place on the scale, the presentation will still look dichotomous.

As already mentioned, a dimension approach to metalanguage, exemplified in the Silversteinian formulation, implies a necessary or crucial link between the study of metalanguage or metapragmatics and pragmatics in general. The following section will be an attempt to define that link. Before doing so, however, let me specify two ways of using the term "metapragmatics" which I want to distance myself from in what follows. Neither of them bears on the "reflexivity" of language itself. The first is "metapragmatics" in the sense of critical discussions of pragmatics; this belongs to the order of endeavors which any self-respecting scientific discipline has to engage in. According to the second, "Metapragmatics studies the conditions under which pragmatic, i.e., users', rules are supposed to hold" (Mey 1993: 277) – a topic which would generally be regarded as the province of pragmatics itself.[4] There is a reason why such confusion could arise, but we can only explain that later. First we have to go deeper into the fundamental relationship between pragmatics and metapragmatics. In the following section we will introduce the notion of "metapragmatic awareness" in relation to a general theory of pragmatics, arguing for the central role it plays in any type of language use, thus strengthening the view of metalanguage as a dimension rather than an object in its own right and demonstrating the relevance – indeed, necessity – of taking metalinguistic or metapragmatic functioning into account when approaching instances of language use.

3.   Pragmatics and the central role of metapragmatic awareness

This section is formulated against the background of a theory of linguistic pragmatics which defines language use as the adaptable and negotiable making of linguistic choices, both in production and in interpretation, from a variable (and constantly varying) range of options in an interactive effort at generating meaning (see Verschueren 1999).[5] The highly dynamic processes that are involved take place in a medium of adaptability which, rejecting any strict dichotomy between society and cognition, could be labeled "mind in society" (following Vygotsky 1978). The mental phenomena characterizing this medium of adaptability that are most visibly at work in the meaningful functioning of language are perception and representation, planning, and memory. In addition to their being determined by the workings of such mechanisms, all meaning-generating processes occupy a specific *status* in relation to the medium of adaptabililty. In other words, not everything that happens in linguistic behavior occupies the same place in consciousness. Various *manners of processing* or *degrees of salience* (a term originally inspired by Errington 1988) may be involved. Just consider the opening sentences of this section:

(1)   This section is formulated against the background of a theory of linguistic pragmatics which defines language use as the adaptable and negotiable making of linguistic choices, both in production and in interpretation, from a variable (and constantly varying) range of options in an interactive effort at generating meaning (see Verschueren 1999). The highly dynamic processes that are involved take place in a medium of adaptability which, rejecting any strict dichotomy between society and cognition, could be labeled "mind in society" (following Vygotsky 1978).

Though writing is a verbal activity involving a generally high degree of consciousness in the making of linguistic choices (in comparison to more spontaneous oral interaction), much in (1) is the product of quite automatic processing. Thus for someone with a reasonable command of English the verb *to be* quite naturally transforms into *is* when a correspondence with *this section* is required in the present, and into *are* when the subject is the plural *processes*. Similarly, following the basic English word order subject-verb-object is hardly a matter of conscious decision-making. Even a conventionalized violation of the "standard" rule requiring implicit subjects of non-finite clauses to be coreferential with the explicit subject of the main clause, resulting in the dangling participle *rejecting*, is not really the product of intentional design. On the other hand, as in most academic writing, word choice and the development of an argumentational structure are (expected to be) highly salient activities, the product of conscious effort. What happens on the interpreter side is roughly analogous.

Being a crucial aspect of what goes on when language is used (whether in uttering or in interpreting), pragmatic analyses have to come to terms with the role of consciousness, awareness, or salience – whatever the preferred term may be – in order to understand linguistic behavior. As is graphically suggested in Figure 1, salience has within its scope all the processes operating on structural choices anchored in context that contribute to the meaningful functioning of language. In other words, language users know more or less what they are doing when using language. Self-monitoring, at whatever level of salience, is always going on.

It is this general aspect of language use in relation to the medium of adaptability that I call *reflexive* or *metapragmatic awareness* (a usage that is in line with the terminology anthropologists use, as reflected in Lucy 1993). Studying

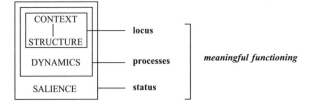

Figure 1. The structure of a pragmatic theory

this type of awareness is crucial to an understanding of verbal *behavior* because, like any other form of social action, language use is always *interpreted*, in the sense that the actors involved attach meaning to it, so that the actors' interpretations become part and parcel of what needs to be described and explained. We will return to this point in Section 3.

On the basis of these observations we may be able to understand Mey's confusion (referred to at the end of Section 2) about metapragmatics in relation to pragmatics: "the conditions under which pragmatic rules are supposed to hold" suggests a distance between conditions and rules; the conditions, however, necessarily belong to the rules (disregarding for the moment the question whether we want to talk about rules rather than principles at all); they form a normative package as it were; but of course there is no normativity without awareness, and the norms involved are constantly negotiated and manipulated; it is at this meta-level of awareness, which is necessarily at work whenever language is used, that the proper domain of metapragmatics is situated, inseparable from but still beyond the "rules-cum-conditions" (which cannot really be broken up into "rules" and "conditions").

Awareness is not measurable, and the notion lends itself to easy speculation. Hence the centrality of metapragmatic awareness could easily mean the end of pragmatics as an empirical enterprise. Fortunately, the self-monitoring in question, at various levels of consciousness or salience, leaves identifiable linguistic traces. Returning to (1), just consider the following features:

– the **self-referential use** of *this section*, which not only refers to the overall activity of which the chosen phrase is itself a constitutive part, but which also **categorizes** that overall activity as a specific genre of language use, thus providing it with a specific frame of interpretation;
– the explicit **intertextual links** that are introduced by *see ..., following ...,* and *formulated against the background of*, where the first two are mainly informative while the last one also instructs the addressees how to interpret what is about to follow;

- the **metapragmatic description** of a verbal activity carried out elsewhere, as with the linguistic action verb *defines*;
- the introduction of a **modality** in *could be*, which draws explict attention to the status of the choice in the author's conceptualization of the ideational state of affairs referred to;
- other **metapragmatic markers** such as the quotation marks in *"mind in society"*, which draw attention to the lexical choice-making itself, as a kind of warning against unreflective interpretation;
- finally, the entire stretch of discourse (and whatever follows it in this text) is about properties of language use, formulated at the meta-level of linguistic theory and analysis, and hence it is one long marker of metapragmatic awareness, abounding with categorizations, suggestions, claims, etc.

Thus, while all linguistic choice-making implies some degree of consciousness (which is not always equally observable), some choices openly reflect upon themselves or upon other choices. Reflexive awareness is so central that all verbal communication is self-referential to a certain degree, or that there is no language use without a constant calibration (to use Silverstein's term) between pragmatic and metapragmatic functioning. This phenomenon forms the proper domain of *metapragmatics*.

The range of indicators of metapragmatic awareness is not restricted to those exemplified with reference to (1) above. It includes all of Jakobson's "shifters", Gumperz's "contextualization cues" (such as instances of code switching), anything ever discussed under the labels "discourse markers/particles" or "pragmatic markers/particles" (such as *anyway, actually, undoubtedly, I guess, you know*, etc.), "sentence adverbs" (such as *frankly, regrettably*), hedges (such as *sort of, in a sense*), instances of "mention" vs. "use" (again as already suggested by Jakobson), as well as direct quotations, reported speech, and more implicitly embedded "voices".[6] Independently of the Silversteinian tradition, though fully compatible with it, the label "metapragmatics" has been used to describe specifically the linguistic study of one category of indicators of metapragmatic awareness, namely "metapragmatic terms" or – more specifically still – "linguistic action verbs" (Verschueren 1985a, 1989b, 1987; Kiefer and Verschueren 1988). This more restricted form of metapragmatics was motivated as an empirical-conceptual approach to linguistic action, i.e., an attempt to come to grips with the varying ways in which linguistic behavior is conceptualized by those engaged in it, by way of scrutinizing empirically observable linguistic reflections of those conceptualizations (such as the verbs and verb-like expressions used, in natural language, to talk about the conceptualized behavior in question). This approach to language on language could be regarded, in a Silversteinian perspective, as a form of "folk-metapragmatics", to be approached with due caution.[7] As Silverstein (2001 [1981]) pointed out, speakers' awareness of pragmatic phenomena (an interesting cross-linguistic study of which is provided in Lucy 1993) does not have to match the linguist's metapragmatic descriptions. Naïvely confusing these two may contribute to the furthering of a specific kind of folk metapragmatics inherent in Western linguistics itself. Assuming that such naïve confusion can be avoided, at least some of my further comments will be based on results obtained in this line of research.

Using the dichotomy introduced in Table 1 (which was declared to be scalar rather than dichotomous), let us assign, for the sake of easy reference in what follows, a "place" to the different indicators of metapragmatic awareness, as reviewed briefly above, in Table 2.

Table 2. Indicators of metapragmatic awareness

Explicit metalanguage	Implicit metalanguage

– metapragmatic descriptions (e.g., by means of metapragmatic lexical items such as speech act verbs or performative verbs)
– self-referential expressions
– discourse markers/particles or pragmatic markers/particles
– sentence adverbs
– hedges
– explicit intertextual links
– quoted and reported speech
– "mention" (vs. "use")
– some "shifters" (e.g., some evidentials)
– some "contextualization cues" (many of the above can be included in this category)
	– most "shifters":
	  – deictic expressions (pronouns, tense, etc.)
	  – aspect
	  – mood and modality
	  – (some) evidentials
	– many "contextualization cues" (e.g., prosodic patterns, code switching, etc.)
	– implicit "voices"
	– [proper names, i.e., Jakobson's C/C, which may not be fully treatable on a par with the other metalinguistic phenomena]

Returning briefly to the scalarity of the distinction, it may be useful to point at a property of (1). The fact that deictic expressions, and in particular personal pronouns, are absent from the example does not mean that there is no person deixis. Clearly, the deictic center is the author and his own work. The degree of implicitness is higher than if there had been personal pronouns. This is a function of the genre of academic writing to which the example belongs. But genre is only one parameter that corresponds to degrees of explicitness. Developmental research (e.g., Hickmann 1993) suggests that there are also age differences in the relative use of more explicit vs. more implicit forms of metalanguage.

4.   The functioning of metapragmatic awareness

Metapragmatic awareness (of which we should remember that it may be present at any level of salience) functions in at least two crucial ways, related to – though not coinciding with – the categories of explicit and implicit metalanguage (see Table 2).

4.1. Anchoring

First of all, forms of more implicit metalanguage such as deictic expressions[8] reflect an awareness of the ways in which utterances or sets of structural choices are situated or anchored in a temporal, spatial, social or discourse context. (This metapragmatic functioning bears on degrees of salience of the line that connects STRUCTURE and CONTEXT in Figure 1.) Without such anchoring, any cognitive processing or interpretation is impossible or, as Silverstein puts it, "there is no possibility of interactional coherence" (1993: 36). This kind of function is also performed by some types of explicit metalanguage, in particular those that establish discourse deixis. In this domain, a special place is occupied by instances of self-reference, and in particular the full self-reference manifested in the performative use of speech act verbs (such as *promise* in *I promise that I will come tomorrow*), requiring the kind of calibration between the metapragmatic signaling event and the signaled pragmatic event-structure that Silverstein would call "coincidence" (a label which corresponds directly with a term used by early 20th-century German specialists in Slavic linguistics for exactly this type of construction: *Koinzidenzfall*). The relation to problems of cognitive processibility is clear from a close study of the constraints on performativity of this kind: only speech act verbs which do not require separate reference to properties of the describing act involved in the use of an explicitly metapragmatic verb (i.e., properties of the metapragmatic signaling event) for an adequate description of their meanings, and can be fully accounted for in terms of properties of the described act (i.e., of the signaled pragmatic event-structure) lend themselves to performative use; if this condition is not satisfied, a conceptual distance is involved which blocks complete self-referentiality (see Verschueren 1995c).

4.2. Reflexive conceptualization

A second type of functioning relates primarily to forms of explicit metalanguage, though its effects are often far from salient or only with difficulty accessible to consciousness. As already suggested, linguistic behavior – as a form of social behavior – cannot be understood without an understanding of the notions in terms of which the behavior is conceptualized by those engaged in it, whether as utterer or interpreter, i.e., without an understanding of the reflexive conceptualization that accompanies production and interpretation choices. (In terms of Figure 1, the metapragmatic functioning in question bears on degrees of salience of the very processes that form the DYNAMICS of meaning generation in language use.) Let us illustrate this with reference to (2), distributed by the United States Information Service on 11 February 1999 (numbers in square brackets added for easy reference; boldface, italics, and underlining added).

(2) [1] **TEXT**: ALBRIGHT *THANKS* MONTENEGRIN LEADER FOR *SUPPORT* ON KOSOVO

[2] (SecState *calls* President Djukanovic Feb. 9)

[3] <u>Washington</u> – Secretary of State Madeleine Albright *expressed U.S. thanks* to the president of Montenegro for *supporting* international *efforts to resolve* the crisis in Kosovo.

[4] In *a call* to President Miklo Djukanovic February 9, Albright *assured* him that "Montenegro's concerns would be kept in mind at the Kosovo *settlement talks* in Rambouillet, France," <u>according to State Department spokesman James Rubin</u>.

[5] **Following is the text** of the *statement*:

[6] (**Begin text**)

[7] <u>U.S. Department of State</u>

[8] <u>Office of the Spokesman</u>

[9] **Press statement** <u>by James P. Rubin, Spokesman</u>

[10] February 9, 1999

[11] Secretary's *Call* to Montenegrin President Djukanovic

[12] On February 9 Secretary Albright *called* Montenegrin President Djukanovic to *thank* him for his government's *continued support* for international *efforts to resolve* the Kosovo crisis. [13] The Secretary *noted* the constructive role Montenegro had played throughout the crisis and *praised* Montenegro for leading the way on democratization and economic reform in the Federal Republic of Yugoslavia (FRY).

[14] The Secretary *took this opportunity to assure* President Djukanovic that Montenegro's concerns would be kept in mind at the Kosovo *settlement talks* in Rambouillet, France. [15] In his February 5 *letter* to the secretary, President Djukanovic had *stressed his government's support* for any *political settlement* reached by the two parties that did not affect Montenegro's constitutional position in the FRY.

[16] Finally, the Secretary *assured* President Djukanovic that *world attention on* the Kosovo situation **does not mean** FRY President Milosevic has a free hand to cause problems elsewhere in the FRY or the region.

[17] (**End text**)

[18] NNNN

Looking at the stretches of explicit metalanguage, we find illustrations for the above claim on two levels, the level of reporting on verbal behavior as well as the self-referential level. First, with the exception of "calls" in [2], "a call" in [4], "Call" in [11], "called" in [12], and "letter" in [15] – which focus on a channel of communication – all *italicized* portions of text show that reporting on verbal behavior is inevitably interpretive. Within the context of this chapter it is not even possible to begin spelling out all implications of social and institutional meaning carried along by "expressed thanks" in [3], "assured" in [4] or even "statement" in [5]. All of these descriptive metapragmatic choices reflect assessments of the communicative status and meaning of the described speech events. The quality of the descriptions, then, depends crucially on the degree to which the reflected assessments match frames of meaning that inform the described events. In contexts of communicative controversy, therefore, the incidence of opposing interpretations, emerging from the descriptive choices, is extremely high. And as with all linguistic choice-making, even without the surfacing of oppositions any choice that is made carries along its contrast sets implicitly.

Second, on the self-referential level, **boldface** portions of text demonstrate clearly the importance that is generally attached to the interpretive status accorded to any speech event and the efforts that are often made to protect such status against contaminating reframings. It is the function of "TEXT" in [1], "Following is the text ..." in [5], "Begin text" in [6], and "End text" in [17] to define the status of the communication as precisely as possible in order to avoid the imposition of unintended frames of meaning. The same can be said of "Press statement" in [9], even though the speech event covered by this term is technically one layer removed from the superordinate structure of (2); I say "technically" because the source of the two layers is the same. Communicative status protection is further accomplished by means of explicit source indications (<u>underlined</u> in [3], [4], [7], [8], and [9]).

Furthermore, there is a cyclic presence of these two levels (indicated here in *bold italic*). Thus "does not mean" in [16] is an attempt to freeze the interpretability of a communicative complex descriptively captured as "world attention". In this case, the form of autoreferentiality that is involved hinges on the fact that the U.S. is one of the main engineers of this "world attention" in spite of the descriptive distancing. (For an interesting study of how all the above metapragmatically shapes the communicative status of specific genres such as press releases, see Jacobs 1999.)

5.   Social implications of the functioning of metapragmatic awareness

5.1. Metapragmatic awareness and language ideologies

Language use, just like other forms of social behavior, is interpreted by the actors involved. In the realm of social life in general, more or less coherent patterns of meaning which are felt to be so commonsensical that they are no longer questioned, thus feeding into taken-for-granted interpretations of activities and events, are usually called ideologies.[9] Similarly, when elements of metapragmatic awareness can be seen to form persistent frames of interpretation related to the nature and social functioning of language which are no longer subject to doubt or questioning, it becomes possible to talk about ideologies of language.[10] The latter become relevant topics of investigation in a variety of ways.

First of all, indeed, there is the inseparability of (local) linguistic practice and (systemic) metalinguistic conceptualization whenever language is used. As could already be concluded from example (2), much of the meaning negotiation that forms the dynamics of linguistic interaction is a struggle over the communicative status of utterances, involving norms (generally accepted or hege-monically imposed even if not generally adhered to) against which the ongoing (or past, or future) behavior can be evaluated. Though this is most clearly the case in institutional settings (witness the acceptability rating of different types of questions and answers during a trial), it is an integral part of what goes on in everyday conversations as well (at any level of choice-making, even at the level of language choice in a multilingual context – see, e.g., Meeuwis 1997), so that understanding these processes is necessary for any adequate pragmatic analysis.

Second, under certain circumstances the "struggle" may be suspended in favor of facile judgment. This is most typically the case when interpretations informed by habitual conceptualizations are not subject to further negotiation. This may be a purely personal or occasion-specific occurrence. But it may also result from the incompatibility of aspects of communicative style (a notion which would not make sense without the metapragmatic level) as documented in the literature on intercultural communication (e.g., Gumperz 1982) or on in-ternational news reporting (e.g., Verschueren 1985b, 1989a). What happens in such cases is that the experience of the naturalness of the invoked normativity, resulting directly from interpretation and conceptualization habits rooted in or related to ideologies of language, interferes with further meaning negotiation (a process which may be greatly enhanced by the absence of any direct interac-tion). Insight into the ingredients of language ideologies may therefore help us to understand what goes on in such specific settings.

By way of illustration, in order to show that none of this is innocent, take example (3) (borrowed from Blommaert 1999), which is an extract from an of-ficial report following interviews with an asylum seeker as part of the procedure to determine eligibility for refugee status in Belgium.

(3)   It has to be noted that the concerned *remains very vague* at certain points. Thus he is *unable to provide details* about the precise content of his job as "political informant". Furthermore, the account of his escape *lacks cred-ibility*. Thus *it is unlikely* that the concerned could steal military clothes and weapons without being noticed and that he could consequently climb over the prison wall.

It is also unlikely that the concerned and his wife could pass the passport control at Zaventem bearing a passport lacking their names and their pic-tures.

Furthermore, the itinerary of the concerned *is impossible to verify* due to a lack of travel documents.

> The statements of the concerned *contain contradictions* when compared to his wife's account. Thus he declares that the passports which they received from the priest were already completely in order at the time they left Angola. His wife claims that they still had to apply for visa in Zaïre.

The phrases in italics are clearly not value-free descriptions. They focus on (i) commonsense plausibility and hence the trustworthiness of the applicants, (ii) the need for documentary evidence, and (iii) the nature of the communicative activities that make up the summarized narrative. The interpretations are characterized by automatic applications of specific types of normativity, the validity of which is not questioned. As to (i), the inability to produce a convincing story is seen as a sign of lying – a judgment that is probably extended beyond the "doubtful" stretches to the very grounds for seeking asylum. As to (ii), the norms of administrative records are imposed on the telling of part of a life story. As to (iii), a notion such as *contradiction* is applied across different narratives as if such an application did not require the careful comparison of entire discourse contexts.

Third, the workings of language ideologies can not only be observed in forms of everyday interaction, institutional discourse, education, political rhetoric, mass communication, and the like, but also linguistic theories and analyses themselves do not escape from their influence. Silverstein (1979) may have been the first to point this out convincingly. Others, mostly linguistic anthropologists, followed suit in their criticisms of the Gricean and Searlean paradigms in pragmatics, confronting what linguists took for granted with observable, situated linguistic practice. That the history of linguistics itself (or pragmatics in particular) is not free from "ideological" fluctuations is easy to observe; just think of the notion of linguistic relativity, proposed as a principle by Whorf, elevated to the level of dogma by his followers, turned into a dirty word among linguists in the sixties and seventies, and resurrected during the last ten to fifteen years (witness Gumperz and Levinson 1996). From such observations we should learn that a constant monitoring of linguistic rhetoric in view of the ideological underpinnings of theories and analyses is not a luxury but a prerequisite for the advancement of linguistic pragmatics. (For an excellent example of such a critical approach to some of the linguistic literature, see Eelen's 1999 study of politeness research.)

5.2. Metapragmatic awareness and identity construction

Example (2) illustrates (in the underlined segments) how explicit attempts may be made to define the identity of the utterer or of the source of a message. The functioning of aspects of "identity" would be hard to understand without reference to metapragmatic awareness. Most of the time it does not take the explicit form exemplified in (2), but it hinges on the subtle signaling involved in category-specific linguistic choices. Typical examples are forms of code switching (Gumperz 1982; Auer 1998) which become symbolic for specific social groups or formations of which membership is typically required for an utterer to be able to use a certain code; similarly, switching to a code one assumes the interpreter to be more familiar with accomplishes a process of other-categorization (see, e.g., Hinnenkamp 1991). In conversation analysis, the entire literature on participation frameworks and membership categorization devices (see, e.g., Antaki and Widdicombe 1998) is fundamentally concerned with the metapragmatics of identity construction. That identities are not "given" but dynamically constructed in discourse – which further strengthens the assumption that metapragmatic awareness must be fundamentally involved – should be clear from a small example such as (4). This example (borrowed from D'hondt 2000) is a fragment from an ordinary conversation in the streets of Dar es Salaam (from which I have eliminated the original Kiswahili and the transcription conventions).

(4)   [N and G talking about a soccer game they want to watch]

    N: If it is granted to us.

    G: Inshallah, inshallah, inshallah.

    N: Eh? But in the mosque I do not see you?

    G: That's where I am going right now.

As D'hondt points out, reference to a future course of events (the watching of a soccer game) – which should not simply be taken for granted by humans who cannot themselves control the future – is followed by the formulaic "If it is granted to us", which is then acknowledged and upgraded by G's series of "Inshallah's" ('If God wishes'). Though there is a categorial relationship between G's utterance and being a muslim, the value of G's linguistic choices as identity markers is variable. The signaling of identity could have been left entirely implicit, and its contextual relevance might have been nil. But then N taps into his metapragmatic awareness of the identity-signaling value or potential of the linguistic choices made by G to topicalize it explicitly in "But in the mosque I do not see you?", a topicalization which is accepted by G in his next response.

6. Conclusion

There is a reason why the title of this chapter is simply "Notes on ..." The task of completing the picture is far beyond its scope. By way of conclusion, I would simply like to draw the attention once more to the fact that metapragmatic awareness – and hence all of its linguistic manifestations – contributes crucially to the generation and negotiation of meaning which, in a pragmatic theory, is the core process of what language use is all about. This is not only the case at the obvious levels of conscious self-monitoring and audience design, but also at much lower levels of salience where it underlies and contributes to the meaning of most aspects of linguistic choice-making. Singling the metalinguistic dimension of language out for separate scientific attention is therefore a valuable heuristic strategy in order not to forget its fundamental contribution to all pragmatic functioning.

Notes

1.   According to Tomasello, this ability to identify with others is the source of cultural learning, the cognitive switch that separates homo sapiens from primates and that explains the complex development of industries and institutions within historical (rather than evolutionary) time.

2.   Observations leading to the writing of this chapter were first presented in a very different lecture on "Metapragmatic awareness and ideologies of language in socially relevant linguistic research" during the 3rd Cardiff Round Table in Sociolinguistics, Gregynog, Wales, 1–3 June 1998. The basic ideas were lifted out of that presentation and further developed in lectures given in Madrid (28 March 2000), A Corunha (29 March 2000), Poitiers (6 September 2000; École thématique "Pragmatique: Langage, Communication et Cognition") and Mar del Plata (21 September 2000; VIII Congreso de la Sociedad Argentina de Lingüística).

3.   For a brief account of the interdisciplinary ancestry or links of these ideas, see Verschueren (1995b).

4.   Both of these senses, as well as the definition used in this chapter, occur in a special issue of the *Journal of Pragmatics* (Caffi 1984) devoted to "Metapragmatics"; see also Caffi (1998).

5.   The theory in question views pragmatics as a general functional perspective on (any aspect of) language, i.e., as an approach to language which takes into account the full complexity of its cognitive, social, and cultural (i.e., "meaningful") functioning in the lives of human beings.

6.   For a more detailed overview of indicators of metapragmatic awareness, see Verschueren (1999: 189–195).

7.   A recent plea for the study of folk linguistics (Preston 2000), linked to earlier proposals such as one by Hoenigswald (1966), is entirely in line with this interest, though formulated outside the context of a theory of pragmatics.

8.   In his theory of "pragmatics as implicitness" Östman (1986) excludes deixis from the realm of pragmatics (and includes it in semantics) because it represents a form of explicit rather than implicit meaning. Leaving aside the issue of the line that is drawn between semantics and pragmatics, there is no contradiction between that stance and the treatment of deictic expressions as types of *implicit **metalanguage***: saying that their metalinguistic functioning is more implicit (even though it leaves a "trace") does not amount to saying that their meaning, in general, is implicit.

9.   For remarks on the pragmatics of ideology research, see Verschueren (1995a) and (1996); for an extensive exercise, see Blommaert and Verschueren (1998).

10. For an overview of research on language ideology, see Woolard and Schieffelin (1994); for some recent contributions to this topic area, see Schieffelin, Woolard and Kroskrity (1998) and Blommaert (1999).

References

Antaki, Charles and Sue Widdicombe (eds.)
    1998   *Identities in Talk*. London: Sage.
Auer, Peter
    1998   *Code-switching in Conversation*. London: Routledge.
Blommaert, Jan
    1999   Investigating narrative inequality: "Home narratives" of African asylum seekers in Belgium. *Working Papers on Language, Power & Identity* 1 (http://bank.rug.ac.be/lpi/)
Blommaert, Jan (ed.)
    1999   *Language Ideological Debates*. Berlin: Mouton de Gruyter.
Blommaert, Jan and Jef Verschueren
    1998   *Debating Diversity: Analysing the Discourse of Tolerance*. London: Routledge.
Caffi, Claudia
    1998   Metapragmatics. In Mey, Jacob L. (ed.), *Concise Encyclopedia of Pragmatics*. Amsterdam: Elsevier, 581–586.
Caffi, Claudia (ed.)
    1984   Metapragmatics. Special issue of *Journal of Pragmatics* 8/4.
Carnap, Rudolph
    1937   *Logical Syntax of Language*. New York.
D'hondt, Sigurd
    1999   Conversation analysis and history: Practical and discursive understanding in quarrels among Dar es Salaam adolescents. Unpublished PhD thesis, University of Antwerp.

Eelen, Gino
  1999   Ideology in politeness: A critical analysis. Unpublished PhD thesis, University of Antwerp.
Errington, Joseph J.
  1988   *Structure and Style in Javanese.* Philadelphia: University of Pennsylvania Press.
Gumperz, John J.
  1982   *Discourse Strategies.* Cambridge: Cambridge University Press.
Gumperz, John J. and Stephen C. Levinson (eds.)
  1996   *Rethinking Linguistic Relativity.* Cambridge: Cambridge University Press.
Hickmann, Maya
  1993   The boundaries of reported speech in narrative discourse: Some developmental aspects. In Lucy, John A. (ed.), *Reflexive Language: Reported Speech and Metapragmatics.* Cambridge: Cambridge University Press, 63–90.
Hinnenkamp, Volker
  1991   Talking a person into interethnic distinction. In Blommaert, Jan and Jef Verschueren (eds.), *The Pragmatics of Intercultural and International Communication.* Amsterdam: John Benjamins, 91–110.
Hoenigswald, Hoenig
  1966   A proposal for the study of folk-linguistics. In Bright, William (ed.), *Sociolinguistics.* The Hague: Mouton, 16–26.
Jacobs, Geertz
  1999   *Preformulating the News: An Analysis of the Metapragmatics of Press Releases.* Amsterdam: John Benjamins.
Jakobson, Roman
  1960   Linguistics and poetics. In Sebeok, Thomas, A. (ed.), *Style in Language.* Cambridge, MA: MIT Press, 350–377.
  1971   Shifters, verbal categories, and the Russian verb. In *Selected writings II.* The Hague: Mouton, 130–147. [First published 1955.]
  1985   Metalanguage as a linguistic problem. In *Selected writings VII.* Berlin: Mouton de Gruyter, 113–121. [First published 1956.]
Jespersen, Otto
  1922   *Language: Its Nature, Development, and Origin.* New York: Henry Holt & Co.
Kiefer, Ferenc and Jef Verschueren (eds.)
  1988   Metapragmatic terms. Special issue of *Acta Linguistica Hungaricae* 38.
Lucy, John A. (ed.)
  1993   *Reflexive Language: Reported Speech and Metapragmatics.* Cambridge: Cambridge University Press.
Meeuwis, Michael
  1997   Constructing sociolinguistic consensus: A linguistic ethnography of the Zairian community in Antwerp, Belgium. Unpublished PhD thesis, University of Antwerp.

Mey, Jacob
    1993   *Pragmatics*. Oxford: Blackwell.
Östman, Jan-Ola
    1986   *Pragmatics as Implicitness*. UMI no. 8624885.
Preston, Dennis
    2000   A renewed proposal for the study of folk linguistics. In Griffen, Peg, Joy
            Kreeft Peyton, Walt Wolfram and Ralph Fasold (eds.), *Language in Action:
            New Studies of Language in Society. Papers Presented to Roger W. Shuy.*
            Creeskill, NY: Hampton Press, 113–138.
Schieffelin, Bambi, Kathryn Woolard and Paul Kroskrity (eds.)
    1998   *Language Ideologies: Practice and Theory*. Oxford: Oxford University
            Press.
Silverstein, Michael
    1976   Shifters, linguistic categories, and cultural description. In Basso, Keith and
            Henry Selby (eds.), *Meaning in Anthropology*. Albuquerque: University of
            New Mexico Press, 11–55.
    1979   Language structure and linguistic ideology. In Clyne, Paul R., William F.
            Hanks and C. L. Hofbauer (eds.), *The Elements: A Parasession on Linguis-
            tic Units and Levels*. Chicago: Chicago Linguistic Society, 193–247.
    1993   Metapragmatic discourse and metapragmatic function. In Lucy, John A.
            (ed.), *Reflexive Language*. Cambridge: Cambridge University Press, 33–
            58.
    2001   The limits of awareness. In Duranti, Alessandro (ed.), *Linguistic Anthro-
            pology: A Reader*. Malden, MA: Blackwell Publishers, 382–402. [First
            published 1981.]
Tomasello, Michael
    1999   *The Cultural Origins of Human Cognition*. Cambridge, MA: Harvard Uni-
            versity Press.
Verschueren, Jef
    1985a   *What People Say They Do with Words: Prolegomena to an Empirical-con-
            ceptual Approach to Linguistic Action*. Norwood, NJ: Ablex.
    1985b   *International News Reporting: Metapragmatic Metaphors and the U-2*.
            Amsterdam: John Benjamins.
    1989a   English as object and medium of (mis)understanding. In García, Ofelia
            and Ricardo Otheguy (eds.), *English Across Cultures – Cultures Across
            English: A Reader in Cross-Cultural Communication*. Berlin: Mouton de
            Gruyter, 31–53.
    1989b   Language on language: Toward metapragmatic universals. *Papers in Prag-
            matics* 3, 1–14.
    1995a   The pragmatic return to meaning: Notes on the dynamics of communi-
            cation, degrees of salience, and communicative transparency. *Journal of
            Linguistic Anthropology* 5, 127–156.

1995b   Metapragmatics. In Verschueren, Jef, Jan-Ola Östman and Jan Blommaert (eds.), *Handbook of Pragmatics: Manual.* Amsterdam: John Benjamins, 367–371.

1995c   The conceptual basis of performativity. In Shibatani, Masayoshi and Sandra A. Thompson (eds.), *Essays in Semantics and Pragmatics.* Amsterdam: John Benjamins, 299–321.

1996   Contrastive ideology research: Aspects of a pragmatic methodology. *Language Sciences* 18, 589–603.

1999   *Understanding Pragmatics.* London: Edward Arnold.

Verschueren, Jef (ed.)

1987   *Linguistic Action: Some Empirical-conceptual Studies.* Norwood, NJ: Ablex.

Vološinov, Valentin Nikolaevic

1930   *Marksizm i filosofija jazyka* [Marxism and the philosophy of language]. Leningrad: Priboj.

Vygotsky, Lev S.

1978   *Mind in Society: The Development of Higher Psychological Processes.* Cambridge, MA: Harvard University Press.

Woolard, Kathryn A. and Bambi B. Schieffelin

1994   Language ideology. *Annual Review of Anthropology* 23, 55–82.

Folk metalanguage

Dennis R. Preston

1. Metalanguage 1

In the world outside of linguistics, people who are not professional students of language nevertheless talk about it. Such overt knowledge of and comment about language by nonlinguists is the subject matter of *folk linguistics*. In the following conversational extract from southeastern Michigan, for example, the respondent (M) tells the fieldworker (N) about an odd pronunciation:

M: The girl that just started working with us this summer, there are some words that she says (0.5) you know when she pronounces the words=I forget what they are- Oh (1.25) Monroe [mən'ɹo]. The city of Monroe. We have a rental office in Monroe. She calls it ['manɹo].
N: Oh really?
M: And we laugh every time she says it. We say "Oh, MONroe is on the phone" and- and you know, she laughs right along with us-and I said "Why do you say MONroe instead of monROE" and she said (1.75) "I don't know. That's just the way people around" – She's from Cl- the Cleveland area and she said people a lot of people just pronounce it that way.[1]

This is language about language, and it is just as much a metalanguage as the linguist's which refers to the same phenomenon (e.g., some US speakers have a tendency to place primary word stress on initial syllables when it is placed elsewhere by others).

Of course, one would have to dig deeper to see if M really meant to refer to the same phenomenon described by the scientific characterization (i.e., to such stress placement in general, so that, for example, M would recognize that pronunciations of *POlice* or *TENnessee*, rather than *poLICE* or *tennesSEE*, are examples of the same phenomenon). Regardless of the correspondence between the folk and scientific accounts of language (or lack thereof), I will refer to such overt comment about language as *Metalanguage 1*. Like the linguist's metalanguage, folk metalanguage is conscious. That is, it is not directed to a phenomenon which a speaker is unaware of, but to one which he or she has focused on in some way. Schmidt (1993: 36–37) summarizes Bowers' (1984) account of the conscious awareness of information as that which "… is processed to the level of short-term memory and selectively attended to".

At the outset, this consciousness requirement causes severe difficulty in the search for the nonlinguists' representation of some linguistic facts, because language use itself is largely automatic (and therefore unconscious) behavior.

> An automatic process is characterized by the following properties. It occurs (a) without intention (and is therefore unavoidable), (b) without giving rise to any conscious awareness, and (c) without producing interference with other ongoing mental activities.
>
> (Flores d'Arcais 1988: 117)

One might argue, however, that there are, on the one hand, many occurrences of deliberate (or even contrived) language use which are the result of conscious, on-line planning (or "monitoring") and that, on the other, there is the possibility of introspection which would allow for retrieval of linguistic material, however efficiently (and unconsciously) it is usually realized. Under these monitoring or introspective conditions, ordinary speakers ought to be able to provide linguistic commentary. Commentary about what? Well, at first glance, language seems pretty simple; there are only three parts to it:

> Broadly speaking, three things determine the form of a message's expression: (1) The content the speaker wishes to convey, (2) the effect the speaker wishes to produce in his or her auditors, and (3) the forms permitted by the language being spoken.
>
> (Garrett 1988:70)

One may certainly give a fully conscious report about what content they intended to convey (or what one believes someone else intended to convey to them). One may even report on what effect they intended to produce in the hearer or what effect a speaker apparently intended to produce in them (ranging all the way from the blandly illocutionary – *I was asking a question* – to the complexity of perlocution – *I was trying to impress them with how responsible I was*). When we ask nonlinguists to reflect on Garrett's third characteristic of message expression (*the forms permitted by the language*), however, we run into trouble. Récanati (1991 [1989]) states explicitly that the levels of language below what is *said* and *communicated* (his terms for what we might call the "literal" and "conversational" meanings) are not available to consciousness:

> In the case of sentence meaning [i.e., the result of semantic but not pragmatic processes], abstractness and cognitive depth go hand in hand with a further property, that of conscious unavailability. Of sentence meaning we can assume only tacit (unconscious) knowledge on the part of the speaker who utters the sentence. To be sure, users of language claim to have intuitions concerning what the sentences in their language mean; but these intuitions are not about their purported objects

– linguistic meanings. They do not bear on the linguistic meanings of sentences, which are very abstract and unaccesible to consciousness, but on what would be said or communicated were it uttered in a standard or easily accessible context.

(Récanati 1991 [1989]: 106)

This inaccessibility is not just due to the fact that the production and reception of such forms is automatic and therefore unconscious. It is because there is, at least from one point of view, simply nothing there to report on.

[I]t does not make much sense to say that a model "uses" the passive rule because the rule does not really exist. What does exist is a system of constraints and principles. To use this kind of system all that the computational model must do is operate according to these constraints.

(Berwick and Weinberg 1986: 198)

Many modern scientific approaches share this view. Linguistic well-formedness emerges from the interaction of very general principles, but these principles are not obvious in the constructions they authorize. In the above example, the general principles which combine to allow initial syllable stress in MONroe and POlice in some (generally southern) varieties of US English and the different combination of such general principles which produces monROE and poLICE (generally in northern varieties) are completely hidden from native speakers. Similarly, passive constructions exist in many languages because of the incidence (or "cooperation") of a number of underlying linguistic principles, none of which, in itself, has anything to do with passives (or could be construed as a passive rule). These parts of the linguistic system belong to what Jackendoff (1997) has called the "computational" mind and, as such, are outside consciousness. What we are conscious of is the *result* of computations rather than the computations themselves.[2]

One might argue, therefore, that folk linguists are interested in only the superficial results of deeper operations. That is, a passive construction has a patient-as-subject (*The house*), a specific verb form (*was burned down*) and an (optional) agent-as-object-of-preposition (*by the arsonist*), and all that (identified with whatever folk terminology might be used to express it) is available to conscious representation by nonspecialists. Perhaps, but those are not the usual things people discuss (even when asked to focus on particular constructions). When asked about the passive, the first facts G (another respondent from southeastern Michigan) mentions in the following are those of proscription and rhetorical effect.

G: It's not supposed to be a good uh – way of writing or speaking because it takes – (.hhh) uh because the speaker doesn't have responsi- he [sic] takes responsibility away from the uh – from the action. It's uh supposed to be a bad style of writing. It's very weak.

One may suggest (as we have in Niedzielski and Preston 1999) that G's ... *takes responsibility away from ... the action ...* is an indication of her knowledge of a structural-semantic element of the passive (the "demotion" – or even dele-tion – of agent), but it is also possible that it is nothing more than an echo of a proscription from writing classes she has taken (which she mentions explicitly in a later segment of this same conversation). No matter what detail(s) she has in mind about the structure of passives, it seems fairly clear that her motivation for noticing them at all (i.e., the source of her metalinguistic comment on pas-sives) comes from some sort of stylistic *rule* which suggests that passives are "weak".

In other words, even the functional correlates of form are not usually noticed by nonspecialists unless some other factor brings them into focus. One may argue, I believe, that the automatic processes outlined above have the effect of allowing communicators to focus on messages rather than on form. This is clearly the idea Sibata has in mind when he notes that "... the average language user is so involved with communicating that he [sic] is usually not conscious of the words he [sic] uses" (1971: 375). It remains, therefore, to be seen what sorts of social and/or psychological incidents divert speakers and hearers from their conscious attention to message and cause them to focus on form.

M's notice of "MONroe's" stress placement is pretty obviously contrastive. That is, "MONroe" has a rule which is different from hers, and M notices the different performance which arises from the application of this rule and pro-vides a folk linguistic, *Metalanguage 1* comment on it. Sibata also notes the likelihood of this sort of overt awareness: "It appears to be natural for forms which differ from those which one usually uses to attract one's attention" (1971: 374). Let us call this the "internal" factor which motivates nonspecialist com-ment on language.

Such notice may be very general. That is, some nonspecialists may have a completely unspecified awareness of some general difference they encounter (in contrast to their own use) but are not able to characterize what it is that al-lows them to identify it as unusual. In the following exchange between a field-worker (F) and another southeastern Michigan respondent (K), the latter has indicated that many of her older relatives have a Polish accent, but she claims to have no knowledge of the specific features which make it up.

K: It's Slavic maybe? Influence? – Uh. Your- your Polish, and – your German, – and (I don't-) they all have- and your Russian, there's kind of a same: – accent, but it's a little different, (from where you came over).

F: Uh huh. Can you give me some examples.
K: ((very quietly)) No::.

In Preston (1996a) I referred to the fact that folk awareness of language may, in addition to having a cline of *availability*, range along a continuum of *detail*, from the *specific* (as in M's notice of stress placement) to the *global* (as in this example, in which a respondent is not able to characterize anything about a Polish accent). The latter's inability in no way negates her consciousness of the Polish accent she refers to but means only that some linguistic level (here, probably the phonetic detail) is not available. To believe otherwise would cause us to conclude that people who lack information about internal combustion engines are not aware of trucks bearing down on them. In spite of their lack of specificity, then, I shall also call these sorts of folk linguistic comments internally motivated ones, for they seem to be based on the respondent's awareness of a difference between his or her language use and that of some others.

G's comments on the passive, however, suggest that the major social-psychological factor which motivates this folk notice of language has its origins in institutionalized or conventionalized regulations. I will refer to such factors as "external" ones, and anyone who has been to school, listened to language pundits, or read books on how to speak or write better has certainly absorbed much of this information, and some of it has even filtered into oral tradition. For example, there is little doubt that the reportedly many calls to CBS after the initial appearance of Harry Reasoner and Barbara Walters as co-anchors of the evening news some years ago were motivated by Reasoner's closing line: *Good night from Barbara and me*. Perhaps the origins of this folk belief about correct language are based in school-years' proscriptions of such constructions as *Bill and me want to go out*, but knowledge of the proscription of "X and object pronoun" (regardless of the grammatical slot the coordinate structure fills) is widespread in US English. *Whom* occupies a similar position as a result of what must have begun as institutionalized instruction. Now, the more complex a construction, the more likely *whom* is to appear – again, regardless of case (e.g., *I don't know whom he said called*).

These two conditions, then, which might be paraphrased as the *You ain't from around here, are you?* and the *He don't talk so good, does he?* motivations for language notice seem to cover the territory fairly well. When might they fail to account for the presence (or absence) of *Metalanguage 1*?

First, of course, a broken prescriptive (or external) rule may fail to cause notice if the hearer has no knowledge of it. This is particularly the case, one suspects, when such rules have become so dusty that only the fussiest would notice them. For example, it was once the case that negative comparisons were thought to be better expressed with *so* than *as* – *He's not so tall as I*. Nowadays, at least in US English, even guardians of the tongue are likely to let deviation from this old dictum pass unnoticed, although, to my surprise, a recent survey of undergraduate Michigan students showed that there was considerable awareness of the old rule which requires nominatives in the object of comparison, as illustrated in the same sentence above (Albanyan and Preston 1998).

Second, a misunderstanding of a rule might cause actual rule-breaking to go unnoticed. CBS, for example, would have probably received many fewer calls if the newscaster had said *Good night from Barbara and I*.

I am more concerned, however, with the subtler ways in which a misfiring of difference perceptions may occur; there appear to be two possibilities: one may perceive a difference when there is none, and one may fail to perceive a difference when there is one.

Williams, Whitehead and Miller (1971) report on a study in which Texas schoolteacher respondents were given voice samples of typical Anglo (white, European-American) children, African-American children, and Mexican-American children. In semantic differential evaluations of these speech samples (using such adjectival pairs as "fast – slow"), the teachers found both ethnic minority groups decidedly disadvantaged, particularly along dimensions which have to do with standard language use. When respondents were exposed to another evaluation experiment, however, a visual cue was added. The respondents saw a side view (so that the speech would not have to be synchronized with lip movement) of a child's face which clearly revealed membership in one of the ethnic groups listed above. When a minority child's face was combined with an Anglo child's voice, the evaluation of the child (on features having to do with language use) was lower than when the same voice was combined with a view of the Anglo child's face. It is clear what these teacher respondents have done. On the basis of person (ethnicity) perception, they have attributed an expected linguistic difference (and even realized the evaluative norms associated with that difference) when, in fact, there was none.[3]

Even more subtle, I believe, is the case of a failure to perceive a difference when there is one. Of course, a construction may simply go unnoticed if it is un-remarkably different from the hearer's own system, especially if the hearer has no overt clue (e.g., ethnicity) that the speaker may have a different linguistic system. Since language users are focusing on messages rather than forms, that is not surprising. Other cases, however, are more peculiar.

I once knew a native speaker of US English who came from that part of the North Midland dialect area where the *need* + past participle construction (e.g., *My clothes need washed*) is common and does not act as a distinguishing feature among social classes. To his amazement, I told him where he was from (although I admit to using other features than just the one under consideration here). I did tell him, however, that that was one of the clues I had used in the identification. The speaker (himself a linguist, although obviously not a dialectologist) was amazed to hear this since this construction was, to paraphrase him, "what everybody said". I assured him that, in fact, it occupied a pretty narrow belt of US dialect territory and would be considered odd outside those confines. Disbelieving this, my friend went to check with other native speakers of US English (from a variety of locations) and found, to his horror, that he was the odd man out. Most of the people he spoke to (since we were in a university setting outside the US) asked if it was a construction he often encountered in non-native English speaker student writing.

How could my linguist friend get to be in his mid-thirties, go through formal US education (including linguistic training), hear speakers from all over the English-speaking world, and fail (and have others fail) to note that his norm was different from theirs?

Easy. He was a middle-class, well-educated European-American from that part of the US about which there are few folk caricatures in general and no negative linguistic caricatures in particular. He had every reason to believe that his use was the norm. In short, his personal identity made it possible for him and even others not to notice the difference until I was unkind enough to point it out.

Since norms and rules still lie at the basis of even these errors of identification, then, I continue to believe that they are the primary motivators of folk linguistic comment, although we should be careful to note the power of identity and caricature in their application. In a number of studies of folk comment on (and evaluation of) varieties, I believe I have shown that the idea of correctness is the dominating one in US folk linguistics (Niedzielski and Preston 1999; Preston 1981, 1982, 1985a, 1985b, 1986, 1988a, 1988b, 1988c, 1988d, 1988e, 1989a, 1989b, 1991, 1992, 1993a, 1993b, 1993c, 1993d, 1994, 1996a, 1996b, 1997, 2000; Preston and Howe 1987).

In Preston (1996a), I also suggested that folk awareness operated not only along continua of *availability* and *detail*; any folk representation is also *accurate* or *inaccurate* from a scientific point of view. Assuming that stress placement is the phenomenon which is being characterized in the first conversational extract given above, one would agree that the folk characterization is *accurate*. At the other end of the spectrum, one may find folk comment which is inaccurate, although one must be careful not to accuse folk comment of inaccuracy when, perhaps, different categorizations of the phenomenon in question are intended (or when vocabulary differences exist). For example, Labov suggests that the folk characterization of "nasal"[4] is inaccurate:

> Frequently, if you ask somebody what he [sic] thinks of this style of speech (na-
> salized), he'll [sic] say it's very "nasal"; and if you produce a speech of this sort
> (denasalized), he'll [sic] say that's very "nasal" too. In other words, the denasal-
> ized speech characteristics of some urban areas and extremely nasalized speech
> are treated in the same way.
>
> (Labov 1966: 23–24)

What Labov has uncovered here from the folk would appear to be straightforward – their characterization of both nasalized and denasalized speech is "nasal",
therefore inaccurate. In Preston (1996a) (and elsewhere), however, I have suggested that Labov has not taken the folk representation on its own terms. Suppose, for example, that the folk mean by "nasal" something like "inappropriately
nasal" or "not the degree of nasalization expected in ordinary (or even "good")
language"? If that is so (and, as I have already suggested, I have every reason
to believe that folk representations, perhaps especially those of US English, are
very often filtered through evaluative notions), then the folk characterization is
accurate, and there is only a trivial difference between what linguists and the folk
mean by "nasal". The real proof of my contention here, lies, I believe, in showing that Labov's claim that "denasalized ... and ... nasalized speech are treated
in the same way" is incorrect. I have asked many nonlinguists to characterize
performances of excessively nasalized and excessively denasalized speech. Although, like Labov's respondents, they agree that both are "nasal", they treat the
two performances in radically different ways. The folk regard excessively nasalized speech as "whining", "wimpy", "annoying", and so on; denasalized speech
is called "tough-guy", "stupid", "Sylvester Stallone-Rocky talk". In short, although the folk may use a cover term for inappropriately nasalized speech in
general, they very dramatically differ in their regard for the two styles and rather
obviously distinguish between them. I show the relationship between the folk
and linguistic representations of "nasal" in Figure 1.

I do not doubt, however, that the folk may be simply wrong. In the first
extract given above, M suggests that the stress shift in the town name *Monroe*
is due to the fact that the speaker is from Cleveland and that people there may
talk that way. Cleveland is, in fact, a northern US city, and people there would
not use the southern US stress placement which results in such pronunciations
as *MONroe* and *POlice*.[5]

Whatever the result of a comparison between folk and scientific categorization and labeling of linguistic phenomena (that is, whatever the level of scientific accuracy of the folk comment), the folk belief is by no means diminished
as an object of research.

One might argue that there is a large territory of overt notice of language
not covered by this definition of *Metalanguage 1* (conscious, overt reference to

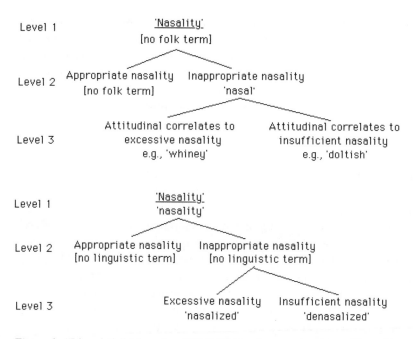

Figure 1. "Linguistic" (above) and "folk" (below) representations of "nasal"

language) and not motivated by the internal or external norm-oriented reasons offered above for instances of such use by nonlinguists. For example, let's take M at her word (from the first conversational sample offered above) and assume that when the girl in question calls on the phone, M may put her hand over the mouthpiece, turn to her office partners, and say "Oh, MONroe is on the phone". Unlike the entire conversational extract given above, this admittedly invented (but obviously inferable) situation might be said to contain no *Metalanguage 1* since there is no explicit reference to language itself in it.

I would claim, however, that all such performance speech (including even the most fleeting imitation of another's linguistic characteristics) requires a momentary focus on and hence reference to language itself, referring, perhaps, to a previously shared conversation if not a well-known cultural script. In this case, M and her co-workers share previous notice of MONroe's odd pronunciation, and imitation of it awakens (or is) a *Metalanguage 1* representation.

Similarly, when one embeds an imitation of a group or individual in an anecdote (or even in ordinary conversation), there is a dependence on the listener's recognition of the *Metalanguage 1* script (or common knowledge) which lies behind (and therefore need not be explicitly mentioned in) the performance. Needless to say, identities and associated stereotypes are also awakened by such performances. Coupland (this volume), for example, shows how a US television audience depends on clues of various performance voices by a television comedy series character (Sgt. Bilko) to detect the character's deception of others. Rampton (1995) shows how the performance of the voices of various ethnic groups is used by those who perform to establish an awareness in others of the performer's life style choices.

Notice, by the way, that an interesting problem remains in determining the *Metalanguage 1* status of the responses to many social psychological studies of language, particularly those classic experiments which submit regionally or ethnically different voice samples to respondents or evaluation, often by means of their placing the voices on a continuum of such paired opposites as "fast – slow" – the so-called matched guise model employing the semantic differential (e.g., Lambert et al. 1960). Some such experiments may use stimulus voices which do not awaken recognition of a caricaturistic sort on the basis of language form, but others may. In the latter case, I would say that covert *Metalanguage 1* forces were at work. For example, as I have suggested elsewhere (e.g., Preston 1992), many European-Americans regard any occurrence of African-American Vernacular English (AAVE) as a performance, even though for its native speakers its everyday use is ordinary. In other words, the mere occurrence of some varieties which have been caricatured and stereotyped is enough to count as a performance of them and qualifies any use of them whatsoever as a likely trigger of a *Metalanguage 1* response. I have suggested that language, therefore, among other social factors, may be one of the things which marks certain groups themselves (and their ordinary behavior) as folk objects in some cultural settings. It should be clear, therefore, that those surveys of language attitudes which respond to voices which awaken *Metalanguage 1* responses should not be simply compared to similar studies which use voices which awaken no such responses.

Whatever the complications, then, at least one approach to the study of folk linguistics is the collection and analysis (involving comparison to both professional accounts and other folk accounts) of such conscious metalanguage. It seems obvious that such work has relevance for both folklore and ethnography, assuming that there is considerable agreement that language plays an intimate and central role in culture, and that, therefore, folk characterizations of language are important to the general study of culture. Hoenigswald (1966) provides a justification of (and plea for) this sort of research, and there are many examples of the investigation of the folk notions of language in diverse cultures (e.g., Garner and Rubin 1986; Giles, Coupland, and Wiemann 1992; Goldman 1983; Gossen 1972; Heath 1983; Hill and Hill 1986; Kay 1987; Niedzielski and

Preston, to appear; Rumsey 1992; Sherzer 1974, 1983; Stross 1974). These folk notions have been elicited in various ways. In some cases, respondents have been led into discussions about language or language-related topics (e.g., Garner and Rubin 1986; Niedzielski and Preston 1999); in others, social psychological questionnaires or other instruments have been used (e.g., Giles, Coupland, and Wiemann 1992), while in others, respondents have simply been observed in natural, conversational settings by (participant-)observers (e.g., the anthropologically oriented investigations listed just above).

I might note that such study also enhances both theoretical and applied linguistics – the first by making linguists aware of categories and concepts which are real for the folk but perhaps not carefully attended to (if at all) in previous work by scientists; the latter by equipping applied linguists with a knowledge of the language beliefs of communities in which they work, a surely empowering knowledge (as would be, for example, a doctor's knowledge of folk beliefs about medicine in the community they hoped to serve).

In fact, for the purposes of applied linguistics, the greater the divide, perhaps the more important the folk notion is. The fact that some respondents call languages with frequent fortis velar fricatives *guttural* is perhaps trivial; the fact that some respondents believe that so-called primitive languages have only a few hundred words (even those strung together willy-nilly) and thus conclude that this reflects on the intellect and cultural complexity of the speakers has had and continues to have the most serious ramifications.

2. Metalanguage 2

Talk about language, however, is not the only use of *metalanguage*. Linguists more often use the term to refer simply to *mention of talk itself*. For example, the sentence *Bill said he was hungry* refers to what Bill *said*, and, by using that verb, encodes not just the content of what Bill said but also the (however trivially linguistic) fact that he *said* it. Even such expressions as *in other words, can you say that more clearly,* or *do you understand me?* could be said to be examples of metalanguage since they refer to the use of language.

These are examples of a metalanguage which is a normal part of everyday language use and understanding and does not appear to have the heavy consciousness requirement of *Metalanguage 1*. Although consciousness may be involved in some language use procedures (e.g., repair, as outlined in Levelt 1983), for the most part, production and processing strategies are automatic and unconscious, and these sorts of references to language use appear to operate at that level.

That is, one would not usually want to say that the utterer of *Bill said that he was hungry* was focusing on or even conscious of the "saying" as a complex, linguistic activity. (Even contrastive stress on *said* will result in a questioning of Bill's honesty or accuracy, not of his "saying" as a lingusitic act.) In short, *Metalanguage 1* talks about language *qua* language as opposed to the utterance content which is the subject matter of sentences which linguists usually intepret as displaying metalanguage (here, *Metalanguage 2*) properties.

Metalanguage 2 is, therefore, language use which refers to some property of language itself, but such reference does not focus the speaker's or listener's attention on those properties as ones of linguistic form.

In other words, the distinction between the two sorts of metalanguage suggested so far appears to be the relatively informal one of *topic*. In *Metalanguage 1* use, language is what the sentence (or conversation) is about (however briefly); in *Metalanguage 2* use, language is referred to, but it is not what the sentence or discourse is about. *Metalanguage 2*, therefore, will not play a role in folk linguistic accounts since it is language which refers to but is not about language. Of course, like every fact of language, *Metalanguage 2* use itself may be interesting from some sociocultural perspectives as it both varies in its uses from situation to situation and even varies in its shape and employment from one group to another (e.g., "So Bill says 'I'm out of here'" versus "So Bill goes 'I'm out of here'"), entailing, as usual, identification and associative factors both within and across group boundaries.

3.   Metalanguage 3

With these classificatory preliminaries in mind, we should be ready to "pick apart" the interesting *Metalanguage 1* content of exemplary discourses. Here is an obvious candidate, again quoted from a southeastern Michigan respondent.

M: Yeah, ah see that – that's what upsets me. You can see a really – an educated Black person, I mean I- you know I don't care what color a person is. It doesn't matter to me. – And you can underSTAND them and you can TALK to them and – Look at on the news, all the news broadcasters and everything. They're not talking ((lowered pitch)) "Hey man, ((imitating African-American speech)) hybyayhubyhuby". You can't understand what they're saying. And – I just don't think there's any excuse for it. It's laziness and probably – maybe it is you know, because they are low class and they don't know how to bring themselves up or they just don't want to.

This is very clearly a discourse which has language (the unintelligibility of AAVE and the irresponsibility of those who speak it) as its topic. M's notice of AAVE is very clearly motivated by both the conditions outlined above: AAVE is different from her own variety (the internal reason) and it is clearly not a prized or correct variety (the external reason). M also employs a performance to focus the listener's attention on the fact that AAVE is indeed unintelligible by providing a string of nonsense syllables, presumably an imitation of the acoustic affect AAVE has on M, but surely one she expects will ring true to her listener.

Doubtless all that is true, but for those who seek a revealing excursion into M's folk philosophy of language, it is pretty disappointing. We have only reported on M's *Metalanguage 1* commentary. Surely there is more to it. I believe there is, but we will have to dig out M's (and perhaps most) folk belief about language from resources other than the relatively rare occasions of such *Metalanguage 1* commentary.[6]

The richest territory to mine for folk belief about language may be the presuppositions which lie behind much *Metalanguage 1* use. They are, I believe, sorts of unasserted *Metalanguage 1* beliefs which members of speech communities share. I will call such shared folk knowledge about language *Metalanguage 3*, although I am aware that such underlying beliefs do not literally constitute even a specific kind of language use. Linguists and philosophers alike agree that presuppositions form the backbone of mutual understanding among conversational participants.

> Presuppositions are what is taken by the speaker to be the *common ground* of the participants in the conversation, which is treated as their *common knowledge* or *mutual knowledge*.
>
> (Stalnaker 1978: 320, emphasis in the original)

It should go without saying that the deeper the sense of community or shared culture among participants, the more likely that enormous amounts of presupposed (and therefore usually unstated) beliefs will play an important role.[7]

I have made earlier attempts to place the study of folk commentary on language within the general area of scientific studies of language by means of the graphic device shown in Figure 2 (Preston, to appear).

Perhaps reference to this research triangle will clarify the distinctions I am trying to make here. At the top of the triangle (at **a**) are the data of traditional linguistic research – human language output (and, one might add, intake). Of course, linguists are like all scientists; they do not seek only to collect and classify the facts of the data. As the **a'** above the top corner of the triangle suggests, they are also interested in the cognitive processes which lie behind language use – its organizing principles. *Metalanguage 2* facts lie in this top corner; they refer to language and, as I have suggested above, except for that fact, are unre-

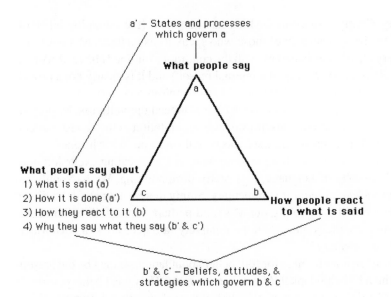

Figure 2. A "triangle" of language research areas

markable (although, of course, they require description and explanation from grammatical as well as sociolinguistic points of view).

Language use, however, triggers person and group identification and, as such, carries attitudinal as well as content messages, as the entire enterprise of the social psychology of language has shown. These data are represented in the **b** corner of the triangle, and when respondents rank a stimulus voice on such Likert scales as "fast" – "slow" or "educated" – "uneducated", they are providing *Metalanguage 1* commentary. Like the linguist, however, the social psychologist should seek out the underlying or organizing principles of these evaluations. Some will appear to be social rather than linguistic (e.g., "Southerners are not well-educated"), but, eventually, they will be connected to deeper *Metalanguage 3* beliefs (and even principles) – "Well-educated speakers will speak correctly". Such concerns are represented in Figure 2 at **b'**.

The **c** corner of the triangle in Figure 2 (the folk linguistic corner) shows an even more direct connection to the beliefs and organizing principles which underlie nonlinguist (*Metalinguistic 1*) commentary. Although the data from the **b** corner are acquired from covert responses to language samples and the ones from **c** are overt commentary, both have *Metalinguistic 3* beliefs (represented at **b'** and **c'**) in their background. These are the data which are the concern of the remainder of this paper.

Of course, all professional students of language use a scientifically-based *Metalanguage 1* when discussing any of the above facts, and one might even use a *Metalanguage 1* language to discuss that language (i.e., professional language), but that concern (and the underlying principles which lie behind professional language, perhaps only naively thought to be exclusively scientific) go beyond the concerns of this paper.

Such deeply-rooted folk beliefs about language as those represented in *Metalanguage 3* may also be thought of as forming a *cultural model*, and there is no doubt among culture theorists that they correspond closely to what I have characterized as underlying presuppositions.

> A cultural model is a cognitive schema that is intersubjectively shared by a social group. ... One result of intersubjective sharing is that interpretations made about the world on the basis of the folk model are treated as if they were obvious facts of the world. ... A second consequence of the intersubjective nature of folk models is that a great deal of information related to the folk model need not be made explicit.
>
> (D'Andrade 1987: 112–113)

Oddly enough, this most important of the investigations of metalanguage, the determination of the underlying folk theory (or theories) of language, has not received very much attention except in anthropological investigations, usually of cultures rather distant from modern industrial and technologically oriented ones (see the list of anthropologically-oriented studies of folk linguistics given above). That is too bad for two reasons. First, we ought to know the folk theories of language of all societies, not just for scientific completeness but also to avoid any accusations that scholars believe that folk notions abound only among cultures different from their own (usually industrial-technological ones where so little of this work has been done). Second, however, when work is done across cultures, the discussion is often contrastive. That is, readers are expected to be familiar with patterns of behavior and belief in their own culture (or to recognize them easily), and these are often the jumping-off spot in a scholarly characterization of behavior and belief in a less familiar setting. (Of course, I do not mean that the other culture's behaviors and beliefs are not taken on their own terms or have the meanings of the more familiar culture imposed on them. It is simply an anthropological convenience to provide a contrastive setting for many such discussions.) Unfortunately, a contrastive discussion cannot occur unless the knowledge of linguistic folk belief is rich on both sides. Some anthropologists seem to have studied their target culture very well but assumed (without investigation) the details of their own.

Rumsey (1992) is an example of such work, and I believe that he is nearly correct about the western languages (including English) which he contrasts with Ungarinyin (an aboriginal language in northwestern Australia). Roughly, his argument is as follows: English contrasts direct (*She said "I'm going to Osaka"*) and indirect (*She said she was going to Osaka*) reported speech. In Ungarinyin there is no indirect reported speech, and Rumsey concludes that a Western ideology of language – that language and use are not one and the same – is not viable for speakers of Ungarinyin. Westerners, he contends, believe that language items (vocabulary, for example) have an out-of-context existence which is somehow separate from its use. For speakers of Ungarinyin, language structure and use are inseparable, and language itself does not really exist except in use.

I am pretty sure that language, at least in the US, is indeed regarded as being separate from use, but I suspect it is not as abstract as Rumsey might seem to believe. Let me first represent that belief graphically (and contrast it with a general scientific conception of language) and then turn to an application of it to conversational data. Figure 3 contrasts the US folk and scientific views of language.

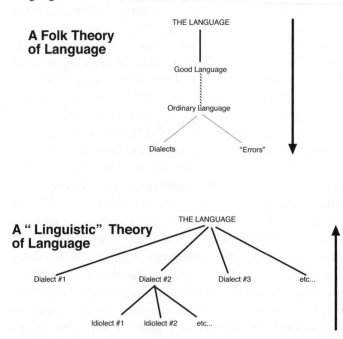

Figure 3. Folk (above) and linguistic (below) taxonomies of language

For the folk I have studied, language itself is the very real (although admittedly ideal) fact which dominates language use. (So far, Rumsey would appear to be right; the Ungarinyin apparently do not have this Platonic form lurking behind their usage.) For the folk, however, the only possible usage which derives from this ideal is good language, the forms enfranchised by the ideal itself. All other forms for them are deviations from what a language ought to be. In short, only language which derives its shape from the ideal is rule-governed; all other use deviates, and, to the extent to which such deviations do not make use of the rule-governed form as their basis, they are without rules.

Linguists, on the other hand, believe that a language is a very abstract notion. English, for example, is only a convenient fiction for the varieties which are its constitutive, not derivative, elements. (In Figure 3, I have limited detail at this level to dialectal variation, although, of course, other types could be mentioned, e.g., gender, age, ethnicity, even idiolect.)

With this understanding of the folk theory of language in mind, let us return to M, who states very directly why some African-Americans speak a variety which she cannot understand – they are "lazy". M may feel this is a little too blunt, for she goes on to excuse this behavior by noting that such speakers are low class and don't know how to escape that situation, although she is also quick to add that it may be that "they just don't want to". I will leave to social scientists discussion of these latter claims and stick to the linguistic facts. Let's see what those are.

M notes that "an educated Black person" can be understood and can be talked to (after the disclaimer that she does not care what color a person is, another part of this conversation which I will leave for discussion by others), but she says she cannot understand other African-Americans (and she gives a little imitation of how they talk, which, except for "Hey, man", does not even consist of words).

Her first important folk claim is, therefore, that she cannot understand some varieties of African-American speech, but isn't this because M and speakers of AAVE do not, as I suggested earlier, share rule systems? Let's look at this more closely.

Remember, M claims that she can't understand speakers of AAVE because they are "lazy". For her, the proof of this lies in the fact that many of them have not made the effort to learn her variety. She says "I don't think there's any excuse for it". What is "it"? Of course, "it" can only be the use of a variety which M cannot understand (at least within a social setting in which she believes she has the right to understand). It might appear at first that she simply believes that speakers cannot be excused for using their native-language rule-system when there is another one around preferred by some.

How can M justify her belief that those who do not acquire another rule system are "lazy"? Isn't such acquisition difficult? In fact, we have already seen one reason why many nonlinguists believe that standard English can be almost effortlessly acquired. As Figure 3 suggests, many find the standard variety to be the only embodiment of rule-governed behavior. The idea that nonstandard varieties are also rule-governed is a very strange notion since they are most often described by nonlinguists as lacking rules. The relative ease with which speakers who have no rules should catch on to a system which has a grammar appears to be obvious to speakers like M.

I was wrong then, at first, to suggest that M's underlying belief was that people with different rule systems ought to acquire hers. In fact, her belief is that people who use non-rule-governed systems should make the minimal effort to acquire an orderly one.

This is, of course, the most serious linguistic misunderstanding. No matter what language system another person in the world shows up with, it is a system. And, equally important, for those who know its rule system, it is just as efficient a device for communication and/or the organization of thought as any other language system, as Labov has shown so convincingly in his 1969 article "The logic of nonstandard English".

There is, in fact, an alternative view of minority speakers which may cause even greater disparagement of them than the "lazy" interpretation we have just seen. In this view, they are plain old recalcitrant because they already know good English but simply refuse to use it:

J: And I used to teach Black children. And I had a difficult time understand-
      ing what they were saying. And I found out later though that they were
      – it was intentional, because they could speak – like we speak. And they
      wer- because: I – was having difficulty with this o(h)ne little bo(h)(h)y. He
      was twe(h)lve. (.hhh) And – I – was supposed to test him, for uh reading
      problems. And I couldn't understand what he was saying. And so I called
      uh the teacher next to me was Black. (   ) next to me. (.hhh) So I did go
      over and get her, and I asked if she would help me. (.hhh) And she came
      in and she- – just- said to him, she said "You straighten up and talk – the
      right way. She's trying to help you". ((laughs))

You can bet that M would be even madder if she thought that all those people who were saying "Hey man, hybyayhubyhuby" could speak better but just re-fused to do so, but this is clearly what J has learned from her experience with a stubborn elementary school pupil (and she has been aided in this interpretation by a Black teacher, whom she regards as authoritative on the matter).

G, another school teacher, also voices the opinion that (apparently) *all* speakers know (somehow) the rules of standard English.

G: The children themselves – all of us at time may say the improper endings. We may say it. (.hhh) But we recognize it is somebody says to us "Is it correct", you say "No", you know, "This is the correct way (to) speak". (.hhh) But- to sit and TEACH it incorrectly I don't think is right. Cause you DO say "I have gone", You do not say "I have went".

G seems to believe that nonstandard usage is somehow recognized by its speakers. Of course, to the extent that such speakers have been instructed on the details of the contrast between nonstandard and standard grammar or to the extent that they have constructed a contrastive grammatical analysis of their own on the basis of their exposure to both varieties, G may be in some small part right. But he appears to mean more than that. He appears to believe that there is some sort of innate recognition that nonstandard constructions are not right. Except for slips, then, which he recognizes, "there is no excuse" for the use of nonstandard varieties because we all "know better".

Of course, that is not so. We do not know the rules of a variety we do not know. For example, try to imagine a situation in which everything you say or write will be judged and graded by how accurately it conforms to the rules of AAVE (or Ebonics or whatever you choose to call this variety). After all, you have surely had a lot of exposure to it – from movies, TV programs, books, and even interpersonal communication. I suspect, however, that most of us would not fare very well. Among those who would get failing grades are those syndicated columnists in the US (both Black and white, by the way) who wrote about the 1996–1997 Ebonics controversy, attempting to include examples of the variety. In fact, they performed miserably in AAVE. Most of their sentences would fall into the category "not valid examples of the variety in question". Their pathetic attempts were perfect illustrations of the pervasive folk belief that AAVE (or any nonstandard variety) consists merely of breaking the rules of standard English (any of its rules, any way one chooses to break them). (Admittedly, they seemed to use some silly strategy such as "sprinkle uninflected *be* widely throughout the discourse", but that is simply further proof that nonstandard varieties in the minds of the folk are not really rule-governed.)

As Rumsey suggests, however, there is a dichotomy between use and language for westerners, but I believe he fails to see that that is a result of the westerner's faith in the Platonic ideal of the language itself, resulting in a second-class status for linguistic facts which can be discovered in mere usage. D, G, and U are all trying to explain to H (the fieldworker, who is not a native speaker of English) what the distinction is between "gift" and "present".

D: Oftentimes a gift is something like you you go to a Tupperware party and
      they're going to give you a gift, it's- I think it's more=

                                           [
H: Uh huh.
D: =impersonal, – than a present.
                        [
G: No, there's no difference.
                                           [
D: No? There's real- yeah there's really
                                           no difference.
      [
G: There is no difference.
D: That's true. Maybe the way we use it is though.
U: Maybe we could look it up and see what "gift" means.
                                           [
D: I mean technically there's
                                           no difference.
      ((They then look up *gift* and *present* in the dictionary.))

The telling lines here, of course, are those which say that there is "really no
difference" ("technically") but that there is a difference "in the way we use it".
Linguists (apparently just like the Ungarinyin) understand that the meaning of
a word is, in fact, something like the collection of all its uses – all its contextual
instantiations. Obviously, for the folk, words have a real meaning (separate
from use), and the dictionary is a guide (as are teachers and language pundits of
one sort or another) to that shadowy but for the folk very real authenticator of
all that in language is rule-governed.

4.   Conclusion

While I value the collecting of *Metalanguage 1* comments and attitudinal responses to language, I believe that such investigations ought to lead to the underlying folk beliefs speakers of a language have about the nature of the object
itself (what I am calling *Metalanguage 3*).

   From earlier work I have done on the perception of language variety in the
United States (cited above), I have little doubt that the principal folk belief that
speakers of US English have is the Platonic one of a rule-governed, correct system from which all good language use ensues.[8] We have not, however, subjected
conversations about language to the kind of scrutiny which would allow us to see

the full ramifications of this folk model of language and others in action. That is, in many of the anthropological and ethnographic investigations listed above, the analyst has reasoned back from language use (whether of structure, as in Rumsey, or of performance as in Sherzer and others) to the folk model of the speakers.

One way to uncover *Metalanguage 3* beliefs will require more principled approaches to the analysis of the content as well as the structure of discourse. That is, we need what I called in Preston (1994) a content-oriented discourse analysis. Although numerous advances to discourse from a variety of approaches have been made over the last several decades (many reviewed in Schiffrin 1994), few have even attempted to show how structure (at any level) is intimately related to content,[9] including the underlying presuppositions of speakers which must be taken into consideration if a full account of the content is to be given. In a few places, I have tried to show how the tracking of reference (particularly through anaphoric devices), the low-level semantic delimitation of discourse markers, the deployment of personal pronominal reference, and the foregrounding and backgrounding of elements contribute to an understanding of what is being said (as well as how it is said) (e.g., Preston 1993d). Kleiner and Preston (1997) is an attempt to relate an unusual occurrence of *do*-support (not previously described in either the grammatical or discoursal literature) to a fact related to the content of a number of related conversations about race on university campuses.

Perhaps a more intensive investigation of discourses about language itself will eventually allow us to expose the cognitive models the folk use in reasoning about language. We will need to look very carefully at many more *Metalanguage 1* conversations before we can hope to go on to these deeper and more revealing levels of *Metalanguage 3*. Language itself is surely as important an area as those Fodor apparently had in mind when he wrote the following:

> Much everyday conceptualization depends on the exploitation of theories and explanatory models in terms of which experience is integrated and understood. Such pre-scientific theories, far from being mere functionless "pictures", play an essential role in determining the sorts of perceptual and inductive expectations we form and the kinds of arguments and explanations we accept.
>
> (Fodor 1981: 62)

Notes

1. The conversational examples provided here are authentic and are all taken from folk linguistic investigations of a variety of southeastern Michigan respondents. A

complete description of those data and findings is given in Niedzielski and Preston (1999). The transcription system used here is generally that of Gail Jefferson (as outlined, for example, in Schenkein 1978), although interactive features (e.g., overlap, back-channel) have been deleted in several cases in this presentation to allow for easier reading of the content.

2.   I do not mean to suggest that a native speaker would not detect a sentence which illustrated the "breaking" of one of these underlying principles (e.g., subjacency), but they would certainly conceive of it as an error of some other sort than the failure to apply a universal (or perhaps even language specific) linguistic constraint on well-formedness. (See Niedzielski and Preston (1999) for an examination of folk responses to such ungrammatical sentences.)

3.   Of course, actual linguistic differences might also cause person perception to go astray. The dialectologist Raven I. McDavid, Jr. liked to tell the story of his inability to rent an apartment when he first moved to Chicago. His South Carolina accent was perceived as African-American by telephone, and racist landlords and landladies would not rent to him until he appeared in person.

4.   I mean by nasal here the degree of non-phonemic nasality associated with the stream of speech, not the use of nasalization for phonemic contrast as in the vowel systems of French and Polish (although it is interesting to note that some speakers of English consider at least French to be a nasal language, but it is not clear that French nasal vowels are the only source of that impression).

5.   Even here, however, linguistic truth lurks behind folk misunderstanding. Cleveland (and industrial areas in northeastern Ohio in general) afforded many employment opportunities to underemployed and out-of-work Appalachians during and after the Second World War. Many of these immigrant families retain southern speech and other cultural characteristics (e.g., religion, entertainment and sports) into the third generation. If "MONroe" is from such a family, that would explain her stress assignment (in spite of her being from Cleveland).

6.   *Metalanguage 1* comment is only relatively rare. Given proper (socially non-threatening, casual) situations, nonlinguists have a great deal to say about language.

7.   Not all presuppositions in a conversation come from the rock-bottom shared cultural knowledge of a speech community or society. Some are revealed (or even negotiated) on the spot and become part of the ongoing presuppositions of a particular conversation.

> Presuppositions can be created or destroyed in the course of a conversation. This change is rule-governed, up to a point. The presuppositions at time t' depend, in a way about which at least some general principles can be laid down, on the presuppositions at an earlier time t and the course of the conversation (and nearby events) between t and t'.
>
> (Lewis 1979: 339)

By and large, these are not the sorts of more deeply-seated presuppositions (about the nature, structure, function, and use of language) under consideration here.

8. Some of these underlying folk beliefs in the area of attitudes towards so-called correct use have been brought to light in previous sociolinguistic studies under the heading language ideology. Effective recent treatments include Bolinger (1980), Finegan (1980), Milroy and Milroy (1985), Cameron (1995), and Lippi-Green (1997).

9. Some might argue that critical discourse analysis (e.g., Kress 1990) is just such an approach. Like Widdowson (1998), I am personally sympathetic to the political stance of this approach, but I cannot find in it, as its proponents claim, any considerable dependence on linguistics, however socially sensitive and insightful their analyses might be.

References

Albanyan, Ahmed and Dennis R. Preston
  1998   What is standard American English? *Studia Anglica Posnaniensia* 33 (Festschrift for Kari Sajavaara on his sixtieth birthday), 29–46.
Berwick, Robert C. and Amy S. Weinberg
  1986   *The Grammatical Basis of Linguistic Performance: Language Use and Acquisition.* Cambridge, MA: MIT Press.
Bolinger, Dwight
  1980   *Language: The Loaded Weapon.* London: Longman.
Bowers, Kenneth
  1984   On being unconsciously influenced and motivated. In Bowers, Kenneth and Donald Meichenbaum (eds.), *The Unconscious Reconsidered.* New York: Wiley, 227–272.
Cameron, Deborah
  1995   *Verbal Hygiene.* London: Routledge.
D'Andrade, Roy
  1987   A folk model of the mind. In Holland, Dorothy and Naomi Quinn (eds.), *Cultural Models in Language and Thought.* Cambridge: Cambridge University Press, 112–148.
Finegan, Edward
  1980   *Attitudes toward English Usage: The History of a War of Words.* New York: Teachers College Press.
Flores d'Arcais, Giovanni B.
  1988   Language perception. In Newmeyer, Frederick J. (ed.), *Linguistics: The Cambridge Survey, III Language: Psychological and Biological Aspects.* Cambridge: Cambridge University Press, 97–123.
Fodor, Jerry A.
  1981   *Representations: Philosophical Essays on the Foundations of Cognitive Science.* Brighton: Harvester Press.

98   *Dennis R. Preston*

Garner, T. and D. L. Rubin
 1986   Middle class Blacks' perceptions of dialect and style shifting: The case
         of southern attorneys. *Journal of Language and Social Psychology* 5,
         33–48.
Garrett, Merrill F.
 1988   Processes in language production. In Newmeyer, Frederick J. (ed.), *Linguistics: The Cambridge Survey, III Language: Psychological and Biological Aspects.* Cambridge: Cambridge University Press, 69–96.
Giles, Howard, Nikolas Coupland and John M. Wiemann
 1992   "Talk is cheap" but "my word is my bond": Beliefs about talk. In Bolton,
         Kingsley and Helen Kwock (eds.), *Sociolinguistics Today: Eastern and
         Western Perspectives.* London: Routledge, 218–243.
Goldman, Lawrence
 1983   *Talk Never Dies: The Language of Huli Disputes.* London: Tavistock.
Heath, Shirley Brice
 1983   *Ways with Words.* Cambridge: Cambridge University Press.
Hill, Jane and Kenneth C. Hill
 1986   *Speaking Mexicano: Dynamics of a Syncretic Language in Central Mexico.*
         Tucson: University of Arizona Press.
Hoenigswald, Henry
 1966   A proposal for the study of folk-linguistics [followed by Discussion, see
         Labov 1996]. In Bright, William (ed.), *Sociolinguistics: Proceedings of the
         UCLA Sociolinguistics Conference, 1964.* The Hague: Mouton, 16–20.
Jackendoff, Ray S.
 1997   *Consciousness and the Computational Mind.* Cambridge, MA: MIT Press.
Kay, Paul
 1987   Linguistic competence and folk theories of language: Two English hedges.
         In Holland, Dorothy and Naomi Quinn (eds.), *Cultural Models in Language and Thought.* Cambridge: Cambridge University Press, 67–77.
Kleiner, Brian and Dennis R. Preston
 1997   Discourse disputes: How come you do do like you do. *Folia Linguistica* 31,
         105–131.
Kress, Gunter
 1990   Critical discourse analysis. In Grabe, William (ed.), *Annual Review of Applied Linguistics 11.* Cambridge: Cambridge University Press, 84–99.
Labov, William
 1966   Comment on Hoenigswald 1996. In Bright, William (ed.), *Sociolinguistics:
         Proceedings of the UCLA Sociolinguistics Conference, 1964.* The Hague:
         Mouton, 20–26.
 1969   The logic of nonstandard English. In Alatis, James E. (ed.), *Georgetown
         Monographs on Language and Linguistics* 22, 1–44.
Lambert, Wallace, R. Hodgson, Robert Gardner and S. Fillenbaum
 1960   Evaluational reactions to spoken languages. *Journal of Abnormal and Social Psychology* 60, 44–51.

Levelt, Willem J. M.
1983   Monitoring and self-repair in speech. *Cognition* 14, 41–104.
Lewis, David
1979   Scorekeeping in a language game. *Journal of Philosophical Logic* 8, 339–359.
Lippi-Green, Rosina
1997   *English with an Accent*. London: Routledge.
Milroy, James and Lesley Milroy
1985   *Authority in Language: Investigating Language Prescription and Standardisation*. 2nd edition. London: Routledge.
Niedzielski, Nancy and Dennis R. Preston
1999   *Folk Linguistics*. Berlin: Mouton de Gruyter.
Preston, Dennis R.
1981   Perceptual dialectology: Mental maps of United States dialects from a Hawaiian perspective (summary). In Warkentyne, Henry (ed.), *Methods IV/ Méthodes IV (Papers from the Fourth International Conference on Methods in Dialectology)*. University of Victoria, British Columbia, 192–198.

1982   Perceptual dialectology: Mental maps of United States dialects from a Hawaiian perspective. In Preston, Dennis R. (ed.), *Working Papers in Linguistics* 14, 5–49.

1985a   Mental maps of language distribution in Rio Grande do Sul (Brazil). *The Geographical Bulletin* 27, 46–64.

1985b   Southern Indiana perceptions of "correct" and "pleasant" speech. In Warkentyne, Henry (ed.), *Methods/Méthodes V (Papers from the Vth International Conference on Methods in Dialectology)*. University of Victoria, British Columbia, 387–411.

1986   Five visions of America. *Language in Society* 15, 221–240.

1988a   Methods in the study of dialect perception. In Thomas, Alan (ed.), *Methods in Dialectology*. Clevedon: Multilingual Matters, 373–395.

1988b   Sociolinguistic commonplaces in variety perception. In Ferrara, Kathleen et al. (eds.), *Language Change and Contact: NWAV–XVI*. Austin: University of Texas Press, 279–292.

1988c   Change in the perception of language varieties. In Fisiak, Jacek (ed.), *Historical Dialectology: Regional and Social*. Berlin: Mouton de Gruyter, 475–504.

1988d   The nicest English is in Indiana. *Studia Germanica Posnaniensia* 14, 169–193.

1988e   New trends in perceptual dialectology. Paper presented at the Hong Kong Conference on Language and Society, Hong Kong, April 1998.

1989a   *Perceptual Dialectology*. Dordrecht: Foris.

1989b   Standard English spoken here. In Ammon, Ulrich (ed.), *Status and Function of Languages and Language Varieties*. Berlin: Walter de Gruyter, 324–354.

100   *Dennis R. Preston*

1991   Point of view in folk linguistics. A vantage theory perspective. Paper presented at NWAVE 20, Georgetown University, Washington, D.C., October 1991.

1992   Talking black and talking white: A study in variety imitation. In Hall, Joan, N. Doane and D. Ringler (eds.), *Old English and New: Studies in Language and Linguistics. In Honor of Frederic G. Cassidy*. New York: Garland, 326–355.

1993a   Folk dialectology. In Preston, Dennis R. (ed.), *American Dialect Research*. Amsterdam: John Benjamins, 333–377.

1993b   Folk dialect maps. In Glowka, Wayne and Donald M. Lance (eds.), *Language Variation in North American English: Research and Teaching*. New York: Modern Language Association of America, 105–118.

1993c   Two heartland perceptions of language variety. In Frazer, Timothy C. (ed.), *"Heartland" English*. Tuscaloosa: University of Alabama Press, 23–47.

1993d   The uses of folk linguistics. *International Journal of Applied Linguistics* 3, 181–259.

1994   Content-oriented discourse analysis and folk linguistics. *Language Sciences* 16, 285–331.

1996a   Whaddyaknow? The modes of folk linguistic awareness. *Language Awareness* 5, 40–74.

1996b   Where the worst English is spoken. In Schneider, Edgar (ed.), *Focus on the USA*. Amsterdam: John Benjamins, 297–360.

1997   The South: The touchstone. In Bernstein, Cynthia, Tom Nunnally and Robin Sabino (eds.), *Language Variety in the South Revisited*. Alabama: University of Alabama Press, 311–351.

2000   A renewed proposal for the study of folk linguistics. In Griffen, Peg, Joy Kreeft Peyton, Walt Wolfram and Ralph Fasold (eds.), *Language in Action: New Studies of Language in Society. Papers presented to Roger W. Shuy*. Creeskill, NY: Hampton Press, 113–138.

Preston, Dennis R. and George M. Howe
1987   Computerized studies of mental dialect maps. In Denning, Keith et al. (eds.), *Variation in Language: NWAV–XV*. Palo Alto: Stanford University Press, 361–378.

Rampton, Ben
1995   *Crossing: Language and Ethnicity among Adolescents*. London: Longman.

Récanati, François
1991   The pragmatics of what is said. In Davis, Steven (ed.), *Pragmatics: A Reader*. Oxford: Oxford University Press, 97–120. [First published 1989.]

Rumsey, Alan
1992   Wording, meaning, and linguistic ideology. *American Anthropologist* 92, 346–361.

Schenkein, John
1978   Explanation of transcript notation. In Schenkein, John (ed.), *Studies in the Organization of Conversational Interaction*. New York: Academic Press, xi–xvi.

Schmidt, Richard
1986   Consciousness, learning, and interlanguage pragmatics. In Kasper, Gabriele and Shoshana Blum-Kulka (eds.), *Interlanguage Pragmatics*. Oxford: Oxford University Press, 21–42.

Sherzer, Joel
1974   Namakke, Sunmakke, Kormakke: Three types of Cuna speech event. In Bauman, Richard and Joel Sherzer (eds.), *Explorations in the Ethnography of Speaking*. Cambridge: Cambridge University Press, 263–282.
1983   *Kuna Ways of Speaking*. Austin: University of Texas Press.

Sibata, Takesi
1971   Kotoba no kihan ishiki. In Words that bother us. Special issue of *Gengo Seikatsu* 236: 14–21. (English quotations and page references are taken from this article translated as "Consciousness of language norms". In Kunihiro, Tetsuya, Fumio Inoue and Daniel Long (eds.), *The Collected Sociolinguistic Works of Takesi Sibata, Sociolinguistics in Japanese Contexts*. Berlin: Mouton de Gruyter, 373–379.)

Stalnaker, Robert
1978   Assertion. In Cole, Peter (ed.), *Syntax and Semantics. Volume 9: Pragmatics*. New York: Academic Press, 315–332.

Stross, Brian
1974   Speaking of speaking: Tenejapa Tzeltal metalinguistics. In Bauman, Richard and Joel Sherzer (eds.), *Explorations in the Ethnography of Speaking*. Cambridge: Cambridge University Press, 213–239.

Widdowson, Henry
1998   The theory and practice of critical discourse analysis. *Applied Linguistics* 19, 136–151.

Williams, F., J. L. Whitehead, and L. Miller.
1971   Ethnic stereotyping and judgments of children's speech. *Speech Monographs* 38, 166–170.

Part 2. Metalanguage and ideological construction

Introduction to Part 2

Adam Jaworski and Nikolas Coupland

Part 2 of the book is entitled "Metalanguage and ideological construction". Three chapters deal with the ideological consequences of how media and political language is multiply layered. This is most explicit in the first chapter, by Theo van Leeuwen, who examines linguistic representations of political interviews in selected discourse analytic studies. The second chapter, by Dariusz Galasiński, examines the press coverage and representation of a celebrity television interview. The third, by John Wilson, focuses on interaction between British Members of Parliament in the House of Commons as recorded in Hansard (the official record of the Westminster Parliament).

Van Leeuwen's starting point in "Metalanguage in social life" is the distinction between metalanguage as a discrete, scientific register used to describe the "object language", and metalanguage in Jakobsonian terms, i.e. as fulfilling one of many functions of language. Van Leeuwen goes on to analyse extracts from three studies of political discourse in an attempt to demonstrate how linguists represent the object of their study – in this case the discourse of political interviews – and how this representation recontextualises language and ultimately the social practices originally enacted by this language. The analysis deals with the earlier analysts' (meta)linguistic or (meta)semiotic manipulation of such categories as the representations of social actors in the interviews and their verbal acts. In his conclusion, Van Leeuwen returns to the bi-polar view of metalanguage and argues for the adoption of a non-discrete view of metalanguage as a unique register (cf. chapters by Verschueren and Cameron). He argues that the analytic practices of different analysts yield different representations of "the same" type or instance of data. In this sense, linguists' metalanguage is not an objective, scientifically pure tool of description and interpretation. This is further evidence of the need to integrate metalanguage (or metacommunication) into first-order linguistic/semiotic descriptions. The principal argument is that linguists and lay people alike ideologise language by the unavoidable "meta" subtext of all their communication. As Preston (this volume) also argues, linguistic and folk metalanguages can produce different ideologies of language, even though the social mechanisms of their production are not dissimilar.

In "Sensationally frank revelations: Metalinguistic constructions of extralinguistic reality", Galasiński deals with the newspaper coverage of the BBC interview of Diana, Princess of Wales by Martin Bashir in November 1995. Galasiński demonstrates that the accuracy of the representation of the *exact* words from the interview is overridden by the journalists' attempts to create a certain version or image of the interview to suit their ideologically preferred reality. This chapter, then, offers new data to support Van Leeuwen's theoretical position. Metalanguage is an omnipresent component of all linguistic communication, and "lay" and "expert" metalanguages are inevitably ideologically charged; but also, metapragmatic processes can be used strategically to fabricate new stories out of old ones.

Wilson's chapter, "Lies, politics, and the metalinguistics of truth", addresses another form of multi-layering of metalinguistic processes. He examines the Hansard record of a parliamentary debate in which a cabinet minister uses certain metalinguistic descriptors of his government's communications with a political adversary, the IRA, which the government had earlier denied having. The MP is then accused of lying. In order to account for this situation, and in fact give his own verdict on whether the cabinet minister was lying or not, Wilson first engages in a discussion of the pragmatics of lying – a multi-layered metapragmatic act in itself. Then, he analyses the text of the MP's comments, as recorded in Hansard, and the conversational implicatures that these words invited. What is interesting here is not only the theoretical discussion of how multi-layered political talk can be, but also the implication that metalanguage is an indispensable element of linguistic production. This is clearly illustrated by the politicians choosing to say only what is likely to invite inferences favourable for them at the time, with the possibility of denying them later.

Metalanguage in social life

Theo van Leeuwen

1.   Introduction

There are, broadly, two approaches to the idea of metalanguage. The first is oriented towards representation. Here, metalanguage is a specialised scientific register, which, because of its unique object, transcends all other scientific registers: it does not represent the world directly, it represents representations of the world, and so, in a sense, places itself above other representations and becomes the ultimate arbiter of their signification. In Carnap's philosophical theory of language "the language which is the object of study is the object language" and "the language we use in speaking about that object language is called metalanguage". The metalanguage then serves to formulate the *theory* of the object language (Carnap 1958: 78–79). In Hjelmslev's "glossematics", the signs of denotative semiotics form the content of metalanguages. A new expression form is then superimposed on that content to create the metalanguage. Hjelmslev stresses the scientific nature of metalanguage, calling it "a metasemiotic with a nonscientific semiotic as an object semiotic" (1961: 120). In practice, metalanguage has often been form-oriented. Moving from "object language" to "metalanguage", or, in Hjelmslev's terms, from "denotative semiotic" to "metasemiotic", has also been moving from an emphasis on the signified to an emphasis on the signifier, from thinking of language as meaning, or as communication, to thinking of language as form. This move was not restricted to the field of language. It was a major mode of twentieth century thought. In other areas of theory (e.g. philosophy and mathematics) devising formal terminologies and formulating formal rules was also regarded as the highest form of theorising. In the domain of the arts, emphasis on form was, and often still is, a mark of cultural distinction (cf., e.g. Adorno 1976; Bourdieu 1986). And in society's major institutions, devising and perfecting content-free procedures became the highest form of social organisation (and today especially of management).

In the other approach, metalanguage is oriented towards communication and seen as part and parcel of everyday communication, hence also as part and parcel of the so-called "object languages". Here the emphasis is on function rather than form, and the "metalinguistic function" is seen as one of several simultaneous functions of linguistic communication (Jakobson 1960). As a result, metalanguage is here not a scientific register. No special training is needed to communicate about communication, nor does it afford any special distinction. Every time we say "What do you mean?" we use language in its metalinguistic function. The ability to communicate metalinguistically is one of the key characteristics of all human language, setting it apart from animal communication (cf. Hockett 1977, who calls it "reflexivity"). Its origins may even be situated before human language, in play, with its possibilities of "framing" actions in different ways (Bateson 1973).

Today the idea of metalanguage acquires new relevance in relation to databases, a field in which there is an urgent need for a theory and practice of the "meta-data" which will help us organise the mass of information in databases, and allow us to find more easily what we are looking for. Again this requires superimposing a layer of information on top of already formulated information – "information about information" – and again it could be argued that meta-data are already part and parcel of the way we organise, store and retrieve information.

I want to say something about metalanguage in this chapter, but not by further developing the contrast between these two approaches, however much it is, unavoidably, the backdrop of anything we can say about metalanguage. Instead, I want to take a fresh look at how contemporary linguists actually write about language – to then eventually return to the question of the possible special status of metalanguage and to the tension between the formal and the functional which metalanguage (and, indeed, linguistics as a whole) inevitably entails.

I will compare aspects of the way three linguistic texts describe and interpret the language of political interviews. The first is pp. 78–92 of Sandra Harris' paper "Evasive action: How politicians respond to questions in political interviews" (1991). The paper can be situated more or less in the tradition of pragmatics. It is based on a corpus of political interviews, and essentially seeks to investigate what causes politicians to come across as "evasive" in interviews, hence also what constitutes "proper" (non-evasive) answers to specific kinds of question. The second is pp. 178–192 from a foundational text in critical discourse analysis, Norman Fairclough's *Language and Power* (1989). The extract analyses an interview with Margaret Thatcher, aiming to reconstruct how she represents (and at the same time enacts) the relationship between the Government and the people. The discourse reconstructed in this way is not necessarily specific to the genre of political interviews, as a range of intertextual references suggests. Fairclough's emphasis is on using methods of critical discourse analysis to analyse the political content of the interview, rather than the interview as such, but he also shows that these two aspects cannot, in the end, really be separated. The third is pp. 136–157 of *The Media Interview – Confession, Contest, Conversation*, by Philip Bell and myself (1994), a section in which we describe the genre of the adversarial political interview. Though containing a fair amount of linguistic analysis, the book was primarily aimed at a media studies readership and my co-author is a media sociologist. We used Hallidayan systemic-functional linguistics and "Sydney School" genre analysis and hence concentrated very much on the flow of the political interview, and on constructing a rationale for the way its characteristic mode of questioning develops. The inclusion of this extract will add an element of self-reflexivity and hopefully make clear that it is not my intention to criticise any of these authors "from the outside". I am not on the outside in this matter. These are the writings of my colleagues, of people involved in the same endeavour, writing about language and the media, analysing texts, trying to gain from language description some purchase on important social issues and events. How do we write our "language about language"? How do we negotiate the tension between form and function it inevitably involves? Those are the questions I seek to explore.

2. Metalanguage as the recontextualisation of linguistic practice

Elsewhere (1993a, 1993b, 1999) I have argued the social semiotic point of view that all representation ultimately recontextualises social practices, that all our knowledge of "what is" ultimately derives from and is grounded in "what we do". Indeed, I see changing "what we do" into "what is", and so legitimating social practices and creating stability for social life (or delegitimating and destabilising social practices when they do not or no longer serve people's interests) as one of the key functions of all human communication, whether linguistically or otherwise. This may at first seem an extreme point of view. Do *all* representations represent social practices? What about representing natural processes? Yet think for instance of the weather. The weather itself is not a social practice. But when reference is made to it in texts, it will usually be through social practices or elements thereof, either because we have incorporated the natural processes into our social practices, or because we use social practices to understand natural processes. Weather reports, for instance, objectivate the social practices of meteorologists – practices of observation, of recording, and of performing mathematical and linguistic operations on these recordings. They seem like natural events only because they exclude both the observers and their practices of observation from the recontextualisation (cf. Van Leeuwen 1995):

> Even in the most abstract and theoretical aspects of human thought and verbal usage, the real understanding of words ultimately derived from active experience of those aspects of reality to which the words belong. The chemist or physicist understands the meaning of his most abstract concepts ultimately on the basis of his acquaintance with the chemical and physical processes in the laboratory. Even the pure mathematician, dealing with that most useless and arrogant branch of his learning, the theory of numbers, has probably had some experience of counting his pennies and shillings or his boots and buns. In short, there is no science whose conceptual, hence verbal, outfit is not ultimately derived from the practical handling of matter.
>
> (Malinowski 1935: 58)

Outside of science, reference to the weather will relate to social practices also. In literary stories, for instance, the weather may exteriorise participants' reactions to activities or other aspects of social practices, as in this example from a Simenon detective novel where 'the rain' substitutes for the hero whose enquiry is not progressing well:

(1)   It was still raining the following day. The rain was soft, cheerless and hopeless…

The other case, using social practices to understand natural processes, is well illustrated by this quote from Susan Sontag's *Illness as Metaphor* (1979: 64):

> Cancer cells do not simply multiply, they are 'invasive'. … They 'colonise' from the original tumour to far sites in the body, first setting up tiny outposts ("metastates") …

Accordingly, when exploring how linguists recontextualise language, I will explore how they move from "what we do" (in this case, "what interviewers do with language") to "what is" (in this case, "what 'interview language' *is* like") – but at the same time also try to understand how and why this transformation from "what we do" to "what is" was achieved.

To start with the former, finding the way back to "what we do" involves taking at least the following aspects of concrete social practices into account (for a fuller discussion, see Van Leeuwen 1993a, 1993b):

– *Participants*

Who are involved, in which roles?

– *Activities*

What do they do, and how do they react to what is going on?

– *Time*

When do they do it (and for how long, and how often)?

– *Place*

In what (kind of) place(s) do the activities take place?

– *Resources*

What tools and materials do the activities require?

In any given representation several of these may be left out. It is perfectly possible to talk about interviewers without referring to their interviewing activities, or to talk about interviewing without ever mentioning interviewers and interviewees. Again, the activities of the social practices may be represented extensively, or only referred to by a handful of very general nominalisations or process nouns ("the interview", "questions"). And apart from representing the participants, activities, times, places, resources and so on, representations will also *add* elements: evaluations, purposes, legitimations (cf. Van Leeuwen 1993a, 1993b, 1999). Rather than discussing all these elements and their possible discursive realisations at length, I would like to give an example, a single sentence from Saussure's *Course in General Linguistics* (1974 [1916]: 11):

(2)   The brain transmits an impulse corresponding to the image to the organs used in producing sounds

This sentence contains four activities:

transmit an impulse
(make) correspond to an image
use organs
produce sound

Two of these, "use organs" and "produce sound" recontextualise the act of speaking, but without including the speaker (a few sentences earlier Saussure has introduced "two people, A and B", so the speaker is not so much totally excluded as "backgrounded", cf. Van Leeuwen 1996). How do "use organs" and "produce sound" represent speaking? They represent it, not as a semiotic and social activity, but as a material activity. The crucial aspect of the semiotic activity, that it has content, that it is *about* something, or, in Halliday's terms, that it "projects" something, is absent. Elsewhere I have called this transformation "instrumentalisation" (Van Leeuwen 1995). Taken together, the two activity representations in fact represent speaking in economic terms, as the *use* of resources for the *production* of goods and services. However much we are used to this mode of representation, however much it has become the unthinking coinage of everyday communication, it still recontextualises a natural and universal human faculty in terms of a historically and culturally specific social practice. It is still a metaphor "we live by" (Lakoff and Johnson 1981).

Then there is the main clause, representing the cause and origin of speech production: "the brain transmits an impulse". Here the speaker ("person A") is included, but he/she is represented as a body part rather than a whole person, a transformation which I have called somatisation (Van Leeuwen 1996), and which often has the effect of demeaning or de-humanising the participants who are referred to in this way (e.g. women, the physically handicapped, medical patients). Here it represents the origin of the production process as not the speaker deciding to say something (a *mental* process), but the brain transmitting an impulse, a material process. This way of representing mental processes relates to issues of social control. What goes on in the mind is normally not part of the social practice, simply because it cannot be seen and hence it cannot be subjected to social control either. But if we can deal with it in the way we deal with physical processes, if we can record it and measure it in some form (recordings and measurements which will then require interpretation through some expert discourse) it becomes accessible and controllable. Secondly, the process is, again, interpreted through a social practice, this time a technical practice, the practice of telecommunication ("transmit an impulse to").

Thirdly, there is the "impulse corresponding to the image" (by "image" Saussure means the "sound image", the mental representation of the sound). Again the social practice on which this draws is telecommunication, the encoding of one signifier into another signifier (e.g. "morse code") able to be transmitted by technical means. But it is objectivated (Van Leeuwen 1996). All agency has been deleted from the act of encoding. It therefore remains, in the end, a mystery how the sound image is transformed into an impulse.

Finally, the social practice is thoroughly de-contextualised. There is no setting, no time and place, no context in terms of any kind of broader activity sequence of which the speaking forms part. For Saussure, this is, of course, because what he is describing here is the "individual" and "physical" side of language (but then, "langue", the social side, the "system", is also decontextualised in Saussure).

The three texts I will analyse below of course represent more than one social practice. All three represent (a) their own practice, the practice of analysing texts, (b) the practice of the political interview, and (c) the practices which the interviews are about, the practices that constitute political life. The following sentence from Fairclough (1989:188) is an example:

(3)   In the text we are looking at there are no overt references at all to opponents

The sentence represents (a) the process of analysing an interview ("we are looking at a text"), (b) the activities of the interviewee ("there are no overt references to opponents") and (c) at least a participant from political life ("opponents"). The structure of the clause then creates the relation between these three practices. The interview ("the text") forms the main clause, and political life is its content. But the critical discourse analyst and his readers (the "we" is inclusive here) and the process of analysis ("looking at") are embedded in the nominal group of which "text" is the head, so that text and "reading" are grammatically welded into a single unit. The act of reading literally and figuratively post-modifies the text.

3.   Recontextualising linguistic agents

If linguistics recontextualises social practices of "languaging", it is perhaps fair to say that more effort has gone into devising metalanguage about linguistic *activities* than about their agents and patients. Goffman's theory of "footing" (1981) remains an exception here. For the most part speakers and hearers have been generalised and idealised. Chapter 1.1 of Chomsky's *Aspects of the Theory of Syntax* (1965) contains 13 references to speakers and/or hearers, and one to the "speech community", but the vocabulary is limited:

> speaker
> hearer
> speaker/hearer
> idealised speaker-hearer
> idealised speaker-listener
> the child learning the language
> homogeneous speech community

Chapters 1.2 and 1.3 contain no references to speakers and/or hearers at all (I stopped counting after page 18) and none of the terms listed above are included in the otherwise quite extensive index. Almost forty years later linguistics has changed. It has become more text-oriented, and more interdisciplinary. As a consequence, the texts I am looking at here contain more, and more varied references to the participants involved in the "languaging". The tables below list the terms they use for "interviewer", "interviewee", and "audience". I include instances in which participants are replaced by their utterances, as in this example from Bell and Van Leeuwen:

(4)   Entrapment questions seek to drive the interviewee into a corner.

This could also have been "The interviewer seeks to drive the interviewee into a corner".

A number of points emerge.

First, all three writers "functionalise" participants, that is, they refer to participants in terms of their function or role in a specific institution, (cf. Van Leeuwen 1996). The relevant institutions here are (a) the media (e.g. "host", "interviewee", "audience"), (b) political life (e.g. "politician", "opponent", "voters", "the people"), and (c) linguistics/semiotics (e.g. "speaker", "addressee", "typified ideal hearer", etc.). All three texts refer to the participants in terms of both the media and political life, with some of the terms indicating that the political interview belongs to both these institutions ("political interviewer", "interviewed politician"). But the texts vary in the

Table 1. "Interviewee" vocabulary in three texts about the language of the political interview (*includes quotes)

	Harris	Fairclough	Bell/Van Leeuwen
(1)	interviewee	interviewee	interviewee interviewed politicians experienced interviewees guests
(2)	James Callaghan Peter Biffin Bernie Grant Margaret Thatcher Neil Kinnock	Margaret Thatcher	Andrew Peacock Paul Keating Bob Hawke John Hewson
(3)	politician	political leader	politician interviewed politicians politics leader of the opposition federal treasurer prime minister
(4)	participant	speaker addressee producer	

Table 1. (continued)

	Harris	Fairclough	Bell/Van Leeuwen
(5)			contestants 'bastards' batsman

(6)	agenda-shifting
	    manoeuvre
	responses
	answer
	elaboration
	en explicit "yes"
		*utterance**
		    (e.g. 'lines 7-12)
		textual features
		"we'"
		the pronoun "you"
		answer
		selection of vocabulary
		wording
		assertions
		modalities
		turntaking
		claim
		co-ordinate structures
		strategic purpose
			statements
			position
			facts

amount of emphasis they place on politics and the media. Fairclough clearly has a more varied vocabulary in the political field (and a greater interest in the audience), while Bell and Van Leeuwen have a few more media oriented terms, and less of an interest in the audience. By comparison, Harris remains a little more traditionally "linguistic" in this regard. All three authors must also negotiate between looking at language in the context of specific social practices and looking at language in general: they also use the kind of terms we can immediately place as part of the fields of linguistics and semiotics. Thus the language of these contemporary linguists has become more hybrid, more interdisciplinary, on the one hand retaining its connection with the generalising and de-contextualising vocabulary of the linguistic tradition, on the other hand introducing contextually specific (and "non-linguistic") elements. The question is, are these more traditional ways of representing language "metalinguistic", or are they merely more generalised, in the same way other scientific registers (e.g. psychology and biology) might also refer to participants in highly generalised ways?

Table 2. "Interviewer" vocabulary in three texts about the language of the political interview

	Harris	Fairclough	Bell/Van Leeuwen
(1)	interviewee	interviewer journalist	interviewer political interviewers media host host
(2)	Brian Walden Fred Emery Peter Jay John Tusa Jimmy Young	Michael Charlton	Paul Lyneham Jana Wendt Mike Gibson Richard Carleton
(3)	participant	speaker addressee participant	
(4)		"courtesans" home team bowler	
(5)	question reformulation turn illocutionary force utterances		question the first question the final question a series of Socratic checks relatively open question statements challenges cooperative solicitations accusation entrapment entrapment question checking conjunctions the WH-word adverbs the references elements the facts a berating tone the way he asks the question irony manner of delivery

Table 2. (continued)

Harris	Fairclough	Bell/Van Leeuwen
		the exchange the interview format the interview the adversarial interview the interviewer's moves the game
		the media

Table 3. "Audience" vocabulary in three texts about the language of the political interview

	Harris	Fairclough	Bell/Van Leeuwen
(1)	the audience the public the listening public	the audience the public members of the audience members of the public a mixed audience a diverse audience the radio audience mass audiences	the audience the public
(2)	we	the people the British people the ordinary person the working class the affluent "ordinary person" the people in general a collective we	the people the voters "us"
(3)	the hearer the overhearing audience	the hearer a typified "ideal hearer" on-lookers addressees	

All three authors refer to interviewers and interviewees by name, which is somewhat of a departure from the generalised and decontextualised way in which linguists have usually eliminated the social specifics of "speakers" and "hearers". Whether or not they explicitly aim at providing social and political comment (as in the case of critical discourse analysis), the writers all comment on specific events of political significance and all evaluate the conduct of the media as well as of the Prime Ministers and Opposition Leaders they mention by name.

Bell and Van Leeuwen invoke still further social practices. They quote a writer who calls the political journalists in Canberra "courtesans" who, rather than challenging the politicians on behalf of the audience, rely on them for handouts of news and in turn provide them with the electronic platform they need. Bell and Van Leeuwen also invoke the kind of sports and combat metaphors which the media themselves often apply to politics and politicians ("batsman", "bowler", "contestant"). Such comparisons almost always involve legitimation or delegitimation. Comparing politics to sport and combat reinforces a cynical interpretation of politics as being about personal ambition, winning office, votes, influence, etc., rather than about, for instance, "serving" the public. Bell and Van Leeuwen use these comparisons as part of their argument that the very way in which political interviews are conducted reinforces and enacts such a cynical interpretation of politics. But at the same time it makes their own language more like that of the media they criticise than the language of the other two authors.

Finally, all three texts contain many instances of "impersonalisation". For the most part these are instances of what I have called "utterance autonomisation" (1996), cases where the writer or speaker is replaced by his or her utterance, something which is often done to lend a kind of impersonal authority to the utterance (as in "The Bible says"). Formal and functional terms are not always easily separated in linguistics, but the tables show that functional terms (e.g. speech act terms such as "entrapment", "challenge", "accusation") and formal terms (e.g. "the pronoun 'you'", "co-ordinate structures", "adverbs") exist side by side, with Harris oriented somewhat more than the others towards functional, and Fairclough somewhat more towards formal terms. However, when formal terms are used as utterance autonomisations, the effect is to functionalise them, to represent them as agentive, capable of having an effect independent of who utters them:

(5)   Negative assertions evoke and reject corresponding positive assertions in the intertextual context.

(Fairclough)

(6)   ... responses which maintain cohesion, topic coherence, presuppositional framework and illocutionary cohesion.

(Harris)

(7)   The relatively open question which begins the interview establishes the cooperation necessary.

(Bell and Van Leeuwen)

This is not the case when the same terms are used in more descriptive ways – something which is relatively rare in these texts, but does occur, mostly in Harris and Bell and Van Leeuwen:

(8)   Responses may vary from a few words to a lengthy series of utterances.

(Harris)

(9)   [The relatively open question...] is a WH-question, using the WH-word "what"; it has second person address ("you") coupled with a cognitive mental process verb ("think") ...

(Bell and Van Leeuwen)

In one sense, such use of formal terms and such emphasis on how linguistic communication has its effect, is clearly metalinguistic, language about language, but on the other hand, how different is this kind of abstraction from abstracting other aspects from activities, e.g. from abstracting their mode of purposefulness, instead of their form, through the use of terms like "strategy", "manoeuvre", etc. Such terms, too, do not specify content, do not tell us, either in general or in specific terms what the activity actually is. Again, formalism is not restricted to linguistics.

A further aspect of the representation of participants is of interest, the question of whether the participants are represented in active or passive roles. The table below shows that Fairclough gives the interviewee a much more active role than Bell and Van Leeuwen, while Bell and Van Leeuwen give the interviewer a much more active role.

Table 4. Active and passive roles of interviewers, interviewees and audience in three texts about political interviews

	Harris n=306	Fairclough n=376	Bell/Van Leeuwen n=435
interviewer active	81 %	82 %	98 %
interviewer passive	19 %	18 %	2 %
interviewee active	84 %	95 %	71 %
interviewee passive	16 %	5 %	29 %
audience active	85 %	92 %	29 %
audience passive	15 %	8 %	71 %

Also of interest are expressions in which agency lies with some unnamed exterior force, as in the following two examples, where we do not learn who or what does the "pre-allocating" and who or what defines the "role of questioner":

(10) Turns are largely pre-allocated

(Harris)

(11) Control over the management and organisation of topics is afforded to the interviewer by virtue of the role as questioner

(Greatbatch, cited in Harris)

Such expressions may be fairly common in traditional linguistic discourse, but there are only a few instances in the three texts analysed here.

4.   Recontextualising linguistic activities

The amount of different terms for the activities of the participants is so large that it is impractical to list them in the kind of tables I used in the previous section. Harris' paper has 36 different expressions for what interviewers do and 47 different expressions for what interviewees do. Fairclough has 14 expressions for the activities of the interviewers and 105 for those of the interviewee (Mrs. Thatcher). Bell and Van Leeuwen have 143 different expressions for the interviewer's activities and 83 for those of the interviewee. Instead of listing them all, I will attempt to describe some of the key characteristics of these vocabularies.

Interviews are a particular kind of social practice, a *semiotic* practice, that is, a social practice which recontextualises one or more other social practices and makes meaning both through the way it presents itself and through the way it represents other practices. The question is, to which degree is this practice actually represented as semiotic? After all, it is possible to represent semiotic activities with (12) or without (13 and 14) inclusion of what they represent:

(12) The question lists desirable qualities for a people.

(Fairclough)

(13) The question requires the interviewee to be on the defensive.

(Bell and Van Leeuwen)

(14) The trap doesn't quite close.

(Bell and Van Leeuwen)

In the first example the interviewer's activity, questioning, is represented as a semiotic act: we learn what the question is about ("desirable qualities for a people"). In the other two examples, this is not the case. The activities are "materialised" (cf. Van Leeuwen 1995), represented as quasi-physical behaviour, or even as an event rather than an action ("the trap doesn't quite close" instead of "he doesn't quite close the trap"). The content "projected" by the activity, to use Halliday's terms, is not included. The semiotic act is represented as behaviour ("drive into a corner", "attack", "defend oneself") or as an instrumental act in which the semiotic dimension is objectivated and represented as a kind of tool or commodity ("use questions", "provide information", "employ various syntactic and semantic types").

Bell and Van Leeuwen represent the activities of interviewer and interviewee overwhelmingly in such "materialised" terms. 84% of interviewer activities and 89% of interviewee activities are materialised. While they use a wide range of terms for types of speech acts and types of questions, they have very few terms for specifying aspects of the content, and those they do use tend to be highly general ("issues", "topics", "view", "position"). Such more specific description of the content as does occur is bracketed or added as an apposition, rather than projected by the activities, as with "home buyers" in the following example:

(15) When Lyneham introduces a new element, "home buyers", this element, too, is picked up by Peacock in his answer.

(Bell and Van Leeuwen)

In Harris, too, the vast majority of activities is materialised (88% of interviewee and 97% of interviewer activities). But by using verbs like "use" and "employ", she instrumentalises terms which in themselves are semiotic and by themselves *could* project. "Questioning", for instance, *could* project ("questioning whether..."). "Employing questions" no longer can – "employing questions whether..." is not likely to occur. In Harris such instrumentalisations still use terms which are recognisably semiotic (e.g. "question"). In Bell and Van Leeuwen, on the other hand, the processes themselves often have a more material flavour – they are verbs which could either take a material or a semiotic object.

(16) Interviewers employ polar questions when they are attempting to force a politician to commit him/herself on a particular issue.

(Harris)

(17) Checking commits interviewees to positions from which they cannot easily retreat.

(Bell and Van Leeuwen)

All this contrasts strongly with Fairclough's text, in which only 54% of interviewer and 38% of interviewee activities are materialised. Fairclough, in this extract, makes relatively little use of functional, "speech act" type terms. For him, words and grammatical structures first of all *represent* relationships and identities (the relationship between Mrs. Thatcher and her audience, Mrs. Thatcher's identity as Prime Minister and woman) and only secondarily also enact, or "construct" these relationships and identities. Thus Fairclough represents the activities of the interviewer and interviewee as what they are, semiotic, rather than as actions which might as well not represent anything since all their meaning comes from what they do to the addressee (as in example 20) rather than from what they represent:

(18) This inclusive use [of "we"...] represents MT, her audience, and everyone else as in the same boat.

(Fairclough)

(19) Some of the coordinate structures in the text explicitly attribute properties to "the British people"...

(Fairclough)

(20) Frequent use of vocatives may enhance the confronting nature of the challenge.

(Bell and Van Leeuwen)

As a result of his emphasis on the semiotic dimension, Fairclough has a much wider range of terms for the act of representation: "represent", "reflect", "construct", "articulate", "refer to", "project", "list", "attribute to", "tell", "express", "make assertions about", "put across", and more. Harris has only three terms of this kind ("constructs", "projects", "gets across"). On the other hand, she uses a wide range of terms for the strategic aspects of the interviewer's and interviewee's activities: "apply strategies", "evade", "give indirect answers", "agenda shift", "refuse to answer", "avoid supplying the requested agreement-disagreement", "avoid giving a direct answer", "fail to answer", "challenge the illocutionary force of the question", "challenge the presuppositions of the question", "disagree with the interviewer's proposition", and more. Fairclough has only six expressions of this kind: "control interview", "be non-compliant", "reject interviewer control", "put interviewer in his place", "correct interviewer" and "steer away from question".

All three writers mostly use linguistic and pragmatic terms to represent the activities of interviewers and interviewees. But in Fairclough and Bell and Van Leeuwen there are also terms that are reminiscent of other fields. In Fairclough these come predominantly from the domain of politics, e.g.:

represent the people
express values of solidarity

convey nationalistic sentimentality
assimilate the leader to the people

In Bell and Van Leeuwen they come predominantly from the domain of the media, e.g.:

expose evidence of duplicity
use populist-consumerist approaches
canvass soft, human interest issues
investigate

In Harris, finally, quite a few of the activities are represented as mental activities, e.g. "inferring", "presupposing", "expecting", "rate responses", "judge supportiveness", etc. This is because she uses a pragmatic approach in which such cognitive terms play an important role, whereas Fairclough and Bell and Van Leeuwen use a more lexicogrammatical approach.

All three writers use both formal and functional linguistic and pragmatic terms. Bell and Van Leeuwen, for instance, use speech act terms like "contradict", "accuse", "challenge", "solicit opinion", "seek information", "comment", and so on, but also describe the activities of the interviewer and the interviewee in formal terms: "use honorific", "use vocatives frequently", "use adversative conjunction", "involve a 'but'", "use 'Yiddish rise-fall intonation'", "intensify adversatives with adverbs", and so on. What is of interest is how such formal and functional terms are brought together. Two methods are most common, in all three writers, and no doubt elsewhere too. Both could be said to express, by means of specific grammatical constructions, a view of the semiotic process. The first includes the human agent, the sign producer who *uses* the formal elements of language, the linguistic signifiers, as a resource for 'doing something with words', where 'doing' includes, of course, representation. This is the social semiotic theory elaborated, for instance, in Kress (1993) and also in this paper. But it is not only a theory, it is also routinely expressed in the grammar of clauses in texts which recontextualise semiotic practices, and not only in texts written by linguists. This grammar works as follows. The functional element is the main process of the clause, and the formal element a circumstance of means, as in 21, or the formal element, in nominalised form, is the object of verbs like "use" and "employ", with the functional element realised as a circumstance or purpose, as in 22, or, sometimes, a circumstance of time, as in 23 (where the meaning expressed, "incredulity", is "descriptivised").

(21) Both politicians attempt to agenda shift by means of elaboration.

(Harris)

(22) "*You*" is used to register solidarity and commonality of experience in workingclass speech.

(Fairclough)

(23) Jana Wendt uses it [the "Yiddish rise-fall intonation"] when incredulously repeating a phrase from an answer Peacock has just given.

(Bell and Van Leeuwen)

It is of course also possible to have form without function, as in 24, or function without form, as in 25 (in interpreting such cases we ought to follow one of the ground rules of critical discourse analysis: when something is deleted from a representation, look for the way in which this deletion serves the interests of the person and/or institution producing and distributing the representation – but this I will not pursue further here).

(24) ...the various syntactic and semantic types of utterances which are employed by interviewers...

(Harris)

(25) Interviewers seek to pin down interviewees on specifics.

(Bell and Van Leeuwen)

In the second method human agency is deleted, and the formal element, the linguistic resource, becomes itself agentive. The functional element is then represented as the process, as what the formal element *does*, whether this is an act of "expressing" or "representing" or some other kind of speech act.

(26) Both types of modality place MT in an authoritative position.

(Fairclough)

(27) 'We' refers to a collective like the British people.

(Fairclough)

While in theoretical discourses this view is often opposed to the previous one (debates on whether meanings are "in texts" or "in people"), in the practice of writing, the two views can live side by side. Take one of the sentences I have just written (and which I will now not change): "The first [method] includes a human agent". By putting it this way I have in fact made my "human agent" into a patient, and assigned agency to "the first method". My grammar contradicts my meaning. But maybe there is no contradiction. Maybe the two views express different aspects of or viewpoints on a complex truth, certainly in a culture where writing and other linguistic technologies *do* allow texts to become detached from their producers – and interviews combine the two aspects – they are both interactive events and, once recorded or broadcast, "texts" that can be transported into many contexts other than the interview itself.

It also possible to use functional elements as agents. In that case, however, the formal aspect need not be represented, and the process, "what the speech acts do", will be a more broadly formulated social aim or meaning, dynamically linking (meta)language and social life.

(28) The politicians are interrogated (...) in order to expose evidence of duplicity and to make public hidden schemes and self-serving motives.

(Bell and Van Leeuwen)

(29) How a politician manages his/her responses to "yes/no" questions may conceivably play a part in constructing a political style, and in projecting the public perception of that politician...

(Harris)

Other expressions lack the functional element altogether and transform linguistic activities into static descriptions of structures. This does not occur in the Fairclough extract I have analysed, because Fairclough explains the formal characteristics of textual features in an earlier, methodological chapter (e.g. 4.19)

(30) An *event* involves just one participant, which may be animate (*many peasants* in the SV examples above) or inanimate (*a black township*)

(Fairclough)

Combining such descriptions of formal elements and their functions or uses, then, tends to happen at the textual level, rather than through the structure of clauses and clause complexes. In Fairclough it happens, first of all, through the structure of the book as a whole, but in his analyses, too, he moves from form classes ("the pronoun '*you*'") or speech act types ("negative assertions") to what these form classes or speech act types *do* (e.g. "evoke and reject corresponding positive assertions"), and from there to what human agents do with that (e.g. "reformulate") – and the latter is represented as not totally predictable by the former, as "rather more complicated" than a decontextualised statement of linguistic function suggests. In other words, there is the system, and the semiotic potential of the textual features, and there are the things people do with that potential, the way they put it to work.

(31) Negative assertions. Negative assertions evoke and reject corresponding positive assertions in the intertextual context. But the picture is rather more complicated than this suggests in the case of the negative assertions of lines (29) – (30), because it is hardly credible to attribute the positive

assertions *they do have to be told* and *they do like to be (are willing to be) pushed around* to MT's political opponents. The point is that in alluding to opposition texts in the intertextual context, producers standardly reformulate them, substituting for the wording of their opponents an ideologically contrastive wording of their own. In this case, for instance, MT is alluding to and arguing against positive assertions which are more likely to be worded as something like *people need guidance* or *people are quite willing to accept guidance (from welfare agencies)*.

(Fairclough)

Bell and Van Leeuwen, in their chapter on political interviews, first describe the interview in functional terms, and then start again, first recapitulating the functional analysis ("the interviewer offers information that could … weaken the interviewee's position") and then describing the formal structures that realise the functions ("these statements incorporate adversative conjunctions…" etc.):

(32) Although we tend to call all the interviewer's contributions "questions", most challenges are not in fact questions. Rather they are statements in which the interviewer offers information that could, if not adequately countered by the interviewee, weaken the interviewer's position. Usually these statements incorporate adversative conjunctions such as "but", "(al)though", "on the other hand" (a variant is: "Let me put this to you…") to indicate their nature as objections to the interviewee's position. The adversative aspect may be intensified by adverbs such as "surely" ("but surely…") and frequent use of vocatives ("Mr Peacock…") and a berating tone ("you should be streets ahead, surely…" may enhance the confronting nature of the challenge

(Bell and Van Leeuwen)

Harris, finally, alternates between linguistic description and discussion and "case studies" or examples. This example shows the transition between the two, and the shift in voice it entails:

(33) It is probably simplest to define questions pragmatically as requests to provide information rather than syntactically as interrogatives, though most interviewer turns in my data (77%) do involve some form of interrogative. But, as Jucker suggests, it is useful to regard the various syntactic and semantic types of utterances which are employed by interviewers as pragmatic acts directed at eliciting information and, as such, the majority can be identified as 'questions' for all practical purposes. This is not to suggest that the question/answer framework in political interviews is never problematic or that breaches do not occur, as the following example

illustrates [*example omitted*] although Brian Walden's first two utterances are interrogative in form, their primary illocutionary force is not to elicit information but to act as an accusation that James Callaghan is refusing to provide an answer.

(Harris)

This passage first chooses a functional definition of the question over a formal one ("It is probably easiest to define questions pragmatically") while yet taking care to retain the link with the formal dimension which is the hallmark of linguistic discourse ("though most interviewer turns in my data do involve some form of interrogative"). In doing so it recontextualises in the first place the activities of linguistic analysts ("define", "identify", "suggest") and only secondarily those of interviewers and interviewees. But then the focus changes, and the data begin to speak for themselves, shifting between "function"-oriented formulations, in which the language does the work ("…two utterances … act as an accusation") and "use"-oriented formulations in which human agents do the work, as in 34.

(34) The interviewer elects to utilise highly restrictive forms of "yes/no" questions so that the failure of the politician to produce an explicit "yes" or "no" … will create a "noticeable absence"

(Harris)

5.   Conclusion

How does all this relate to metalanguage? Four points emerge:

– Meta-communication is part and parcel of everyday communication and not restricted to the discourses of linguists and semioticians. Metalanguage, the resource needed for meta-communication, therefore permeates the language as a whole and should not be conceived of as a specialised register used only by linguists.

If metalanguage is still a viable concept, then no longer in terms of formalism, no longer as a decontextualised and purely formal "mathematics of language". It has to be in terms of the second of the two approaches I started out with, a linguistic function intermingling with other linguistic functions, something we do with language – and therefore something for which language also furnishes the metalinguistic tools, such as we have been describing them in this paper.

– Formal terms are an important part (but not the whole) of metalanguage, provided they are linked with functional, content-oriented, and context-oriented terms. The way in which they are linked up defines metalanguage and the necessity to link up with context-oriented terms guarantees the transdisciplinarity of metalanguage, its ability to permeate the language as a whole.

Centering on linguistic form is not, as I have perhaps suggested earlier, a hangover from earlier forms of linguistics, but instead an indispensable tool for using language in its metalinguistic function. The ubiquity of metalinguistic communication suggests that we cannot get by without being able to ask, from time to time "what exactly is it we are doing when we use this or that speech act?" or "what exactly do we mean when we use this or that word or expression?" To do that, we need to represent those terms and expressions *as* terms and expressions, and that means: metalanguage. One of the useful things linguists can do is to provide tools that can actually be useful for the very practical things metalinguistic communication has to achieve. But metalanguage is not, and should not remain restricted to formal description. The metalinguistic function cannot be fulfilled by representing the form of language alone. Function and meaning must also be represented, and the language about language must be closely tied up, often by grammatical means, with language about the social practices in which that language is embedded and of which it forms part.

– Meta-communication is not restricted to language, but can be realised in other semiotic modes also.

In this paper I have concentrated on meta-language. But I was tempted to use the word "meta-semiotic" throughout. It is not the case that only language can speak of itself – think of the way contemporary computer icons can label classes of visual signifiers such as fonts, colours, grids, etc. But a fuller discussion of this will have to wait for another occasion.

– In everyday communication meta-communication accompanies communication. It is called upon in cases of special communicative needs or problems. Linguists, similarly, should be situated in the middle of social life, to be called upon, as creative consultants and constructive critics, when communicative needs and problems arise.

Just as the metalinguistic function cannot be separated from the rest of language, so the work of metalinguistic specialists cannot be separated from the rest of social life. Linguistics of the kind I have discussed here, does that. It aims, not just to write about language in social life, but to write as part of language in social life, to play a role in it. The more this is geared towards real communicative needs and problems of social life, the more the kind of metalanguage we have seen in action here can become "metalanguage in social life".

References

Adorno, Theodor
1976 *Introduction to the Sociology of Music.* New York: Seabury Press.
Bateson, Gregory
1972 *Steps to an Ecology of Mind.* New York: Ballantine.
Bell, Philip and Theo Van Leeuwen
1994 *The Media Interview – Confession, Contest, Conversation.* Sydney: University of New South Wales Press.
Bourdieu, Pierre
1986 *Distinction: A Social Critique of the Judgement of Taste.* London: Routledge.
Carnap, Rudolf
1958 *Introduction to Symbolic Logic and its Applications.* New York: Dover.
Chomsky, Noam
1965 *Aspects of the Theory of Syntax.* Cambridge, MA: MIT Press.
Fairclough, Norman
1989 *Language and Power.* London: Longman.
Goffman, Erving
1981 *Forms of Talk.* Oxford: Blackwell.
Halliday, M. A. K.
1985 *Introduction to Functional Linguistics.* London: Arnold.
Halliday, M. A. K. and James R. Martin
1993 *Writing Science: Literacy and Discursive Power.* London: Falmer Press.
Harris, Sandra
1991 Evasive action: How politicians respond to questions in political interviews. In Scannell, Paddy (ed.), *Broadcast Talk.* London: Sage, 76–99.
Hjelmslev, Louis
1961 *Prolegomena to a Theory of Language.* Madison: University of Wisconsin Press.
Hockett, Charles F.
1977 *The View from Language.* Athens: University of Georgia Press.
Jakobson, Roman
1960 Closing statement: Linguistics and poetics. In Sebeok, Thomas A. (ed.), *Style in Language.* Cambridge, MA: MIT Press, 350–377.

Kress, Gunther
    1993   Against arbitrariness: The social production of the sign as a foundational issue in critical discourse analysis. *Discourse & Society* 4, 169–193.
Kress, Gunther and Theo van Leeuwen
    1996   *Reading Images: The Grammar of Visual Design.* London: Routledge.
Lakoff, George and Mark Johnson
    1981   *Metaphors We Live By.* Chicago: University of Chicago Press.
Malinowski, Bronislaw
    1935   *Coral Gardens and their Magic,* vol. 2. London: Allen and Unwin.
Saussure, Ferdinand de
    1974   *Course in General Linguistics.* London: Peter Owen. [First published 1916.]
Sontag, Susan
    1979   *Illness as Metaphor.* London: Allen Lane.
Van Leeuwen, Theo
    1993a   Language and representation: The recontextualisation of participants, activities and reactions. Unpublished PhD thesis, University of Sydney.
    1993b   Genre and field in Critical Discourse Analysis: A synopsis. *Discourse & Society* 4, 193–225.
    1995   Representing social action. *Discourse & Society* 6, 81–107.
    1996   The representation of social actors. In Caldas-Coulthard, Carmen Rosa and Malcolm Coulthard (eds.), *Texts and Practices: Readings in Critical Discourse Analysis.* London: Routledge, 32–70.
Van Leeuwen, Theo and Ruth Wodak
    1999   Legitimizing immigration control: A discourse-historical analysis. *Discourse Studies* 1, 83–119.

Restoring the order: Metalanguage in the press coverage of Princess Diana's *Panorama* interview

Dariusz Galasiński

1. Introduction

On Monday, 20 November 1995, BBC 1 broadcast an interview between Diana, Princess of Wales and Martin Bashir. The interview was one of the most watched programmes in the history of the BBC. The interest in the interview was caused by the unwavering popularity of the Princess as well as her troubled relationship with her husband, reaching its peak in the ITV extended interview (June 1994) in which Prince Charles admitted to an extra-marital relationship. The interview also attracted record levels of interest world-wide with its audiences reaching beyond 200 million people. (Kurzon 1996: 217).

The event also attracted extensive press coverage. It was front-page news in all national British newspapers, which either devoted entire pages to the coverage, or, as the broadsheets did, placed it in their top parts, thus positioning it as the news of the day (cf. Kress and Van Leeuwen 1998). In this paper, I am interested in the ways the metalinguistic expressions referring to Princess Diana's contributions to the interview were used in the reports of the event. The data analysed here come from Tuesday's (21 November) English editions of the nine national British newspapers, 5 tabloids (*Daily Express*, *Daily Mail*, *Daily Mirror*, *Daily Star*, *The Sun*) and 4 broadsheets (*The Daily Telegraph*, *The Guardian*, *The Independent*, *The Times*).

2. The metalinguistic point of view

Introducing his model of communication, Jakobson (1960) proposed that one of the functions performed by language is focused on the code itself. Language can refer to itself, and thus perform the metalinguistic function. It is accepted, however, that metalinguistic expressions do not *merely* refer to language. They can, and do, introduce the speaker's point of view both on the expression itself and, at the same time, on all sorts of other aspects of extralinguistic reality, such as the speaker, the relationships the speaker enters with her/his interlocutors and others (see, e.g. Caldas-Coulthard 1994; Short 1989).

The reporting of someone's words is not merely a "neutral" account of what s/he said. The act of retelling something involves the speaker's control both of what is being retold as well as how the retelling is structured and organised, depending on the speaker's view of the world (Caldas-Coulthard 1994: 295). Furthermore, the reporting voice (Cook 1992: 184) may not be one which co-exists with the reported one, it may dominate it and, in the process, distort it. Indeed, in his account of voices in media discourse, Fairclough (1995: 81) argues that

> [o]ne feature of indirect speech is that although it is expected to be accurate about the propositional content of what was said, it is ambivalent about the actual words that were used – it may simply reproduce them, or it may transform and translate them into discourses which fit more easily with the reporter's voice. An interesting example is: *Libyan officials at the UN, faced by the threat of more sanctions, said they wanted more time to sort out the details of the handover.* Is *the handover* the Libyan formulation, or a translation of what the Libyans actually said into another discourse?

The question Fairclough asks is not one of the metalinguistic function of the sentence, but, rather, of the ideational, or representational function which is concealed in the metalinguistic expression. Caldas-Coulthard (1994: 305–306) seconds such views arguing that such *verba dicendi* as *urge*, *declare* or *complain* are not merely metalinguistic, but also metapropositional in that they label and categorise the reported speaker's contribution and as such are highly interpretative.

But metalanguage does not only introduce the reporting speaker's point of view on the utterance surface. Just like any other linguistic choice, metalanguage is also subject to carrying the ideology-laden set of assumptions. Just as through discourse in general (e.g. Fairclough; 1992; Fowler 1996; Fowler et al. 1979; Hodge and Kress 1993; Van Dijk 1993, 1998), it is also through metalanguage that ideologies are formulated, reproduced and reinforced. Furthermore, in the act of representing representation, the ideologies accomplished by metalanguage have the capacity to reinforce but also to subvert those carried by the discursive structures represented.

Finally, ideologies are representations that are deployed by social classes and other groups "in order to make sense of, figure out and render intelligible the way society works" (Hall 1996: 26). Thus, given that the very nature of metalanguage is to make sense of a particular part of reality – discourse – such interpretation must always be ideological.

Consequently, I shall argue in this chapter that metalanguage in the coverage of the interview was aimed not merely to refer to what was said, but, even more importantly, to construct an ideologically preferred version of the extralinguistic reality associated with the Princess of Wales and the event. The two main areas on which metalinguistic expressions focused were:

construction of Diana and her relationships with others;
construction of the interview.

Finally I shall argue that apart from explicit metalinguistic expressions, unambiguously referring to what Princess Diana said, the newspapers used implicit ways of referring to what was said using expressions that pretended to be direct quotations from the interview. These expressions, in turn, were used primarily to construct the very story that covered the interview.

3. "Metalinguistics of Diana"

3.1. The Princess of the nation

As I indicated above, the expressions referring to Diana's contributions to the *Panorama* interview serve in the press coverage of the interview not only to metalinguistically refer to what was said, but also to construct a certain image of the Princess and position her in relation to others. Witness the following excerpts under (1) and (2) below:

(1) Princess of Wales last night insisted that she would not abandon her public role. (*The Times*)

Princess Diana described her hurt at her husband's relationship with another woman, admitted that she herself had been in love with another man, but said she did not want to divorce. (*The Independent*)

She described her disappointment as the way the "fairytale" of her marriage to the Prince of Wales went wrong. (*The Times*)

(2) The princess of Wales spoke frankly about her bitter marital break-up and the future of the monarchy. (*The Guardian*)

She spoke with winning honesty about her bulimia and unflinchingly told the truth about her affair with Hewitt. (*The Independent*)

As might have been expected, Diana, by far the most popular member of the Royal Family, and one of the most popular persons in the United Kingdom, cannot have been constructed in negative light. The quotations above represent the two most prominent traits in the image constructed for Diana by the press. On the one hand (as in [1]), it is an image of a woman, and indeed, in line with the popular expectations of the Royal Family (see Billig 1992), a wife, who wants to carry out her duties. On the other hand (as in [2]), it is an image of a person who speaks the "truth". Verbs such as *describe*, *admit*, *speak* consistently used in the reports of the Princess speaking of herself, either presuppose the truthfulness of what is said, or are neutral with regard to it.

Moreover, while her husband is described as "having a relationship" with another woman, she was merely "in love" with another man. She also seems to be exonerating herself by *admitting* it. The *Daily Star* went as far as to describe her truthfulness as "opening her heart to the nation", which has the powers to relieve Diana of her sins and return her to the state of morality (cf. also Billig 1990a, 1992). Interestingly, this last quote was also used to position Diana on a continuum between the nation and the Royals who "have been stunned into an icy reservation" (*Daily Star*) by her decision to speak. Diana appears to be somewhere between the two poles of the society; although she is a Princess, she speaks to the nation.

The "neutral" reporting tone changes when Diana is described as speaking to or of the Royal Family. This time she no longer merely "says" things, but, rather, *blames* or *lashes out*. Witness the following excerpts:

(3)   She blamed an unsympathetic Royal Family for her eating disorder telling how she was accused of wasting food by eating and then being sick later. (*Daily Express*)

Diana blamed Charles's camp for mounting a campaign to discredit her with both the Gilbey and the Hoare stories to try to give the Prince the upper hand in any divorce discussions. (*The Sun*)

She lashed out at the Royal Family for not preparing her for her role as Princess of Wales and attacked Charles for not supporting her in her hour of need. (*The Sun*)

Furthermore, on occasions when the reporting verb was "neutral" when her relationship with the members of the Royal Family was referred to, what she is constructed as saying is unambiguously negative. Consider:

(4)   The Princess described her husband's closest aides as the "enemy", a group of people causing her grief. (*The Independent*)

The Royal Household was depicted as a vengeful mafia mob, Charles as a cold and grievously unsupportive husband, the Royal Family as rule-bound and unfeeling – all with barely a harsh word spoken. (*The Independent*)

The Princess said her husband's affair with Camilla left her "devastated". (*Daily Express*)

Not only is Diana closer to the nation than the rest of the Royal Family, who cannot bear her honesty and openness, but she does not even simply "slag them off", even though they are so bad. The relationship the metalinguistic expressions construct is predominantly that of fault on the part of the Royals. Interestingly, the unambiguously negative image of the Royal Family and the Household presented in the coverage stands somewhat at odds with the interview itself. Bull (1997; see also Abell and Stokoe 1999), analysing Diana's responses to Martin Bashir's questions, concludes that Diana's criticisms of the members of the Royal Family and Camilla Parker-Bowles were invariably implicit.

What is also noteworthy is that the press hardly ever attempts to distance itself from what Diana says, for example by using the verb *claim* (see, e.g. Caldas-Coulthard 1994). In fact, the verb is used only once, in an article in the *Daily Mirror*:

(5) Diana also claimed that after their separation Palace officials tried to write her off as a "basket case" and wanted her "in some sort of home".

It seems that the *Daily Mirror*'s distancing results from the seriousness of the charge Diana is constructed to be making against the Palace. However, it is only the newspaper's interpretation of what was actually said, in line with the positioning of Diana and the Royal Family in the coverage. The Princess of Wales is the one on the receiving end of the Royal Household's negatively perceived actions. Interestingly, the construction of a version of the reality preferred by the newspaper is effected by conflating two fragments of the interview separated by 22 turns:

(6) **116. Princess of Wales:** Well people were when I say people I mean friends on my husband's side were indicating that I was again unstable ermm sick and I should be put in an a home of some sort in order to get better. I was almost an embarrassment.

138. Princess of Wales: I was at the end of my tether I was desperate. I think I was so fed up with being seen as someone who was a basket case, 'cause I am a very strong person and I know that causes complications in the system that I live in.

In sum, Diana is constructed as standing in opposition to those who surrounded her. She is juxtaposed with the Royal Family in general and with Prince Charles and his staff in particular. The bi-polarity of the construction, however, goes further than the chasm within the Royal Family. It is also an opposition between the nation and the Royals. Diana is often positioned as one of the nation, or at least one communicatively interacting with it. Something other members of the Royal Family would probably not do.[2]

3.2. The Princess speaking to the nation

The interview itself was the other element of reality constructed by the expressions referring to what Princess Diana said. In addition to the references to Diana's frankness and honesty, the event was constructed as, firstly, extraordinary (see [7] below), and secondly, one that would have an impact upon the monarchy and Diana within it (see [8] below):

(7)   The Princess of Wales last night admitted before a nation-wide television audience that she has had an adulterous affair (*The Independent*)

In the most astonishing interview ever Diana confessed when asked if she had been unfaithful to Charles with Hewitt. (*Daily Mirror*)

Princess Diana last night sensationally confessed that she DID have an affair with dashing James Hewitt. She told millions of viewers: "Yes, I adored James Hewitt. Yes, I was in love with him." ... Her bombshell admission came during an astonishing hour-long interview on BBC 1. (*The Sun*)

(8)   Princess Diana last night rocked the monarchy with the most extraordinary public attack ever on the Royal Family ... And in her unprecedented interview with BBC's Panorama, she went on to criticise the royals and the palace staff. (*Daily Express*)

Diana made a series of damaging allegations which put her position in the Royal Family at serious risk. (*The Sun*)

Revelations that raise the stakes for Diana. (*The Independent*)

While the *Daily Express* and *The Sun* place Diana in agentive position, giving her the power to *rock the monarchy*, *The Independent* positions Diana as the goal of her own revelations. Diana is still, as in her relationships with others, on the receiving end of potentially harmful (and backgrounded here; Van Leeuwen

1996) actions of other agents. In either version, however, the press seem to agree that Diana is in one way or another contributing to the tensions within and the problems for the monarchy. Indeed a separate story in *The Independent* is entitled "Establishment moves to close ranks", a headline that positions Diana outside the establishment, once again showing her as someone ambiguous with respect to power.

3.3. The communicative situation

The metalinguistic expressions used in the press construct the interview in terms of a communicative situation focusing on its most important aspects: the speaker, the addressee, and the message.

Diana is the speaker who remains unchallenged in what she says. The references to what she says, apart from one (see [5]), do not show the reporters' detachment from the version she is constructed as offering. She is a credible speaker, one who *opens her heart*.

The problem of who is the addressee is more complicated. Superficially, it is Martin Bashir, who is the immediate addressee in the interview. And yet, as Clark and Carlson (1982) point out, the interview is carried out in the presupposed presence of the on-looking audience, who are the prime reason for the interview. And it is precisely the side participants (those who do not take part in the conversation, but are ratified listeners, Clark 1987) who are the intended target of what is being said.

It seems there are two such audiences. On the one hand, it is the nation, the usual audience for the reception of news about the Royal Family (Billig 1990a: 30–31), the millions she is said to confess to, or admit things to. On the other hand, it is also the Royal Family, who, apart from being the target of Diana's criticisms or blame, are also positioned as those upon whom the message will have a profound effect.

The newspapers endow Diana with the power that the Royal Family have apparently taken away from her. She is now in a position to present her version of the events and, ironically, it is the media that help her out.

4.   Diana disambiguated

As has been mentioned earlier, one of the traits that can be observed in the press coverage of the Diana interview is that while analysis of Princess Diana's responses indicates that her criticism of the members of the Royal Family is invariably implicit (Bull 1997), the press does not render the nuances of Diana's words. Rather, they disambiguate what she said and position her against the other Royals in clear and unambiguous terms. Diana and the rest of the Family are put on opposing poles: Diana – positive and the Royal Family – negative.

Diana's disambiguation can also be observed in the overall positioning of the story: the headlines. With the exception of two newspapers (the tabloids *Daily Star* and *Daily Mail*), all newspapers put what appeared to be a quote from the interview in the main headline. They either put the headline in quotation marks, or preceded it by an unequivocal attribution of voice: "Diana:". Only two merely implied a quote by using the first person singular. There were two groups of headlines. Three newspapers focused on what appeared to be Diana's insistence upon staying within the ranks of the Royal Family, another three chose to flag Diana's apparent admission of adultery.

Even though the disparities between the headline and the original were of varying strengths, none of what the newspapers presented as quotes were accurate excerpts from the interview. Witness the following (the excerpts contain the exact rendering of the punctuation used in the headline):

(9)   "I shall fight to the end, I will not go quietly" (*Daily Telegraph*)

I will not go quietly, says the Princess (*The Times*)

Diana: "I will not go quietly" (*The Guardian*)

What Diana did say, however, was the following:

(10)   **196. Princess of Wales:** I was a separated wife of the Prince of Wales I was a problem full stop. Never happened before what do we do with her?

197. Martin Bashir: Can't we pack her off to somewhere quietly rather than campaign against her?

198. Princess of Wales: Mm she won't go quietly that's the problem. I'll fight to the end because I believe that I have a role to fulfil and I've got two children to bring up.

Not only has Diana not said what is attributed to her, but, in move 198 she is merely echoing what was apparently said about her by the people in the Royal Household. The change of the nature of Diana's participant role or production format (Goffman 1981; see also Levinson 1988) starts in move 196. Marked by the self-reference in the third person singular, Diana switches her role from the author to the animator, or, as Levinson (1988: 171) proposes, the relayer. It is no longer the Princess of Wales speaking, but, rather, the Royal Household through a mouthpiece. In move 197, Martin Bashir parallels the shift and continues, only for Diana to finish it off in move 198. The change is again marked by the shift in pronominal self-reference – back to "I".

And yet the headlines, as abstracts of a story (Bell 1991), do not seem to take note of the authorship of the quoted words. They reinforce the overall positioning of Diana – one in a conflict, or a feud. The assertiveness of what is shown as her words is one *against* someone. Any implicitness in the interview is dispersed right at the beginning of the coverage.

Alternatively, *The Independent*, *The Sun*, and *Daily Mirror* focus their stories on Diana's admission of being involved in an extramarital affair. Their headlines state:

(11) Diana: "I have been unfaithful" (*The Independent*)

Diana: I had an affair with Hewitt (*The Sun*)

I loved James Hewitt (*Daily Mirror*)

The fragment of the interview these headlines refer to is in fact as follows:

(12) **223. Martin Bashir**: Did your relationship go beyond a close friendship?

224. Princess of Wales: Yes it did yes.

225. Martin Bashir: Were you unfaithful?

226. Princess of Wales: Yes I adored him yes I was in love with him. But I was very let down.

Note, firstly, that Diana's response in move 226 is evasive. As I have suggested elsewhere (Galasiński 1996a; 2000), an evasive answer is one which is semantically irrelevant to the question it answers. In other words, an evasive response does not satisfy the conversational demand (Dascal 1977; Holdcroft 1987) put forward by the question's propositional content. In the particular instance of the interview, the question demands that Diana say whether or not she was unfaithful to her husband. Diana, however, fails to answer that question, even though she does address its focus (cf. Kreuz and Graesser 1993; Graesser and Franklin 1990) and speaks of herself, attempting to conceal the fact that she is not answering the question (cf. Galasiński 1996b). Furthermore, the initial "yes" in the response was not followed by a falling intonation signifying that the rest of the response was an elaboration of the unambiguous answer. The initial "yes" is, in fact, qualified and explicated. Diana explains what she means by it. If anything, therefore, the unfaithfulness is constituted by the adoration or being in love.

Thus Princess Diana's answer leaves it open to interpretation what exactly she means by adoring or being in love with another man and what kind of unfaithfulness she means. Moreover, Martin Bashir does not press for more information and changes the topic. It seems that the ambiguity and evasiveness do not have to be resolved within the interaction – the interlocutors seem to share an understanding that no more will be said on the matter. Of course any follow-up would have been too costly socially and face-threatening in the extreme. The taboo on discussing an adulterous sex-life is dramatically increased by the fact that the interlocutor is the wife of the next British monarch. Furthermore, the exact form of the exchange (with all its ambiguities) is likely to have been negotiated and agreed in advance, leaving no room for spontaneity or an embarrassing question.

And yet, the newspapers dispose of any ambiguity or evasiveness on the part of Diana. Their headlines suggest unambiguously what she "must have meant" and propose only one interpretation of her response. Misquoting, it seems, enables journalists to present to their readers what might be the intended meaning of Diana's words. The press, while providing, in most cases, extracts from the transcripts of the interview and thus openly disavowing their potential claims to quoting accuracy, propose a certain view or interpretation of the reality.

Apart from the unambiguous conflict with the Royal Family, the headlines unambiguously construct what Diana said as admission of adultery, or an extramarital relationship. Also this disambiguation is in line with the overall coverage of what she said. As suggested above, Diana is constructed as truthful and heart-opening. Just as in a confessional she cannot beat around the bush, but be open and honest. Only in such a way will she win exoneration.

The headlines serve as implicit metalinguistic expressions. By pretending to be exact quotations from the interview, implicitly they serve as metapropositional expressions (Caldas-Coulthard 1994) and as such interpret what was said during the event from a particular point of view. They also seem to enhance the credibility and objectivity of the report (cf. Van Dijk 1991; Wooffitt 1992) while, on the other hand, they introduce an ideologically preferred view (Zelizer 1989; also Roeh and Nir 1990), an image of Diana that is consistent with the rest of their stories.

5.   The world according to Diana

I have argued here that the metalinguistic expressions used by the press function not only as references to what was said, but also as a means of constructing extralinguistic reality. Firstly, they are used by the press to construct an image of Diana herself, mainly in terms of a person with a sense of duty, and one able to speak the truth to the entire nation. Secondly, these expressions are used to position the Princess in relation to others. It is a relationship of blaming, of Diana's having been harmed by her family or her staff. Another set of these expressions was used to position the interview itself. The event is constructed as something extraordinary and at the same time an event which shook the monarchy, something that would cause *the establishment to close ranks*.

It seems, however, that there is a further aspect of the metalinguistic coverage of the interview. The largely interpretative, almost universally non-detached, way of reporting of what Diana said, gives the coverage a point of view parallel to that of the Princess. This is reinforced by the placing of implicit metalinguistic expressions in the headlines of the stories. Invariably, in broadsheets they are also placed in vertically polarised compositions, also visually indicating their importance as the "essence" of what happened, or, as in tabloid newspapers, the story's salience is established by its being the only one on the front page.

This essence is constructed as Diana's words, emphasising the Diana perspective on reality. For quotes, as Van Dijk (1991: 152) argues, allow the inclusion of a subjective interpretation of reality, a personal perspective through which the events are seen. Ideologically, therefore, it is Diana through whom the world is made sense of. If ideology can be understood as

> the mental frameworks – the languages, the concepts, categories, imagery of thought and the systems of representation – which different classes and social groups deploy in order to make sense of, figure out and render intelligible the way the society works.
>
> (Hall 1996: 26)

then Diana's perspective is placed at the level of ideological "shared social representations" (Van Dijk 1998). The most popular person in Britain is given the status and the power to define reality for us, the recipients of media discourse.

This is not to say, however, that the coverage of the Diana interview does not present itself with a number of ideological dilemmas (see Billig 1990b; Billig et al. 1988) – the texts accomplishing the ideological stances are not free from contradictory themes. Thus, while giving Diana the power to define the world, the coverage of the interview does not challenge the ideological principles of the establishment, or proposes a new morality that would license extra-marital affairs. Firstly, the press is careful not to position the Queen in relation to Diana, secondly, through the references to Diana's heart-opening and truthfulness, the interview is implicitly positioned as some sort of expiation, confession of "sins" through which morality can be restored (see also Billig's (1990a) discussion of the moral powers of the nation).

Thus, even though her actions and relationship towards the Royal Family are disambiguated, culturally, Diana is given the ambivalent position of the mediator (Leach 1982). She is the element between the "nation" and the monarchy, partaking in both of the opposing poles of society and getting them closer to each other. She has the power to rock the monarchy, to criticise it in front of millions, but at the same time she retains the title of the Princess of Wales, a princess, however, who seeks forgiveness from the nation. This particular role given to the Princess by the press seems to continue up until her death, whose coverage was so overwhelming in the United Kingdom that one might have assumed that not only nothing of comparable scale, but in fact nothing at all happened on the day Diana was killed in a car crash. But then she was the most important person in British society and by its coverage the press kept restoring and reinforcing the social order wished by its readers.

Notes

1.   I would like to express my indebtedness to Peter Bull, who made the transcript of the interview available to me. I am also indebted to Adam Jaworski, Nik Coupland and Kristina Bennert for their comments on an earlier version of the paper.
2.   Note that after the Princess' death in August 1997, one of the most vocal demands of the Royal Family and particularly of the Queen herself, was to speak to the nation, to communicate with the subjects in the wake of what was constructed as a national tragedy.

References

Abell, Jackie and Elizabeth H. Stokoe
    1999   "I take full responsibility, I take some responsibility, I'll take half of it, but no more than that": Princes Diana and the negotiation of blame in the "Panorama" interview. *Discourse Studies* 1, 297–319.
Bell, Allan
    1991   *The Language of the News Media.* Oxford: Blackwell.
Billig, Michael, Susan Condor, Derek Edwards, Mike Gane, David Middleton and Alan Radley
    1988   *Ideological Dilemmas.* London: Sage.
Billig, Michael
    1990a   Stacking the cards of ideology: The history of the *Sun Royal Album.* *Discourse & Society* 1, 17–37.

Billig, Michael
    1990b   Collective memory, ideology and the British Royal Family. In Middleton, David and Derek Edwards (eds.), *Collective Remembering*. London: Sage, 60–80.

Billig, Michael
    1992   *Talking of the Royal Family*. London: Routledge.

Bull, Peter
    1997   Queen of hearts or queen of the arts of implication? *Social Psychological Review* 1, 21–36.

Caldas-Coulthard, Carmen Rosa
    1994   On reporting reporting: The representation of speech in factual and factional narratives. In Coulthard, Malcolm (ed.), *Advances in Written Text Analysis*. London: Routledge, 295–308.

Clark, Herebert H.
    1987   Four dimensions of language use. In Verschueren, Jef and Marcella Bertucelli-Papi (eds.), *The Pragmatic Perspective*. Amsterdam: John Benjamins, 9–25.

Clark, Herbert H. and Thomas B. Carlson
    1982   Hearers and speech acts. *Language* 58, 332–373.

Cook, Guy
    1992   *The Discourse of Advertising*. London: Routledge.

Dascal, Marcelo
    1977   Conversational relevance. *Journal of Pragmatics* 1, 309–328.

Fairclough, Norman
    1992   *Discourse and Social Change*. Cambridge: Polity Press.
    1995   *Media Discourse*. London: Edward Arnold.

Fowler, Roger
    1991   *Language in the News*. London: Routledge.

Fowler, Roger, Bob Hodge, Gunther Kress and Tony Trew (eds.)
    1979   *Language and Control*. London: Routledge and Kegan Paul.

Galasiński, Dariusz
    1996a   Deceptiveness of evasion. *TEXT* 16, 1–22.
    1996b   Pretending to cooperate. How speakers hide evasive actions. *Argumentation* 10, 375–388.
    2000   *The Language of Deception*. Thousand Oaks, CA: Sage.

Goffman, Erving
    1981   *Forms of Talk*. Philadelphia: University of Pennsylvania Press.

Graesser, Arthur C. and Stanley P. Franklin
    1990   QUEST: A cognitive model of question answering. *Discourse Processes* 13, 279–303.

Hall, Stuart
    1996   The problem of ideology: Marxism without guarantees. In David Morley and Kuang-Hsing Chen (eds.), *Stuart Hall: Critical Dialogues in Cultural Studies*. London: Routledge, 25–46.

Hodge, Robert and Gunther Kress
    1993   *Language as Ideology.* 2nd edition. London: Routledge.
Holdcroft, D.
    1987   Conversational relevance. In Jef Verschueren and M. Bertucelli-Papi (eds.), *The Pragmatic Perspective.* Amsterdam: John Benjamins, 477–495.
Jakobson, Roman
    1960   Closing statement: Linguistics and poetics. In Sebeok, Thomas A. (ed.), *Style in Language.* Cambridge, MA: MIT Press, 350–377.
Kowal, Sabine and Daniel C. O'Connell
    1997   Theoretical ideals and their violation: Princess Diana and Martin Bashir in the BBC interview. *Pragmatics* 7, 309–323.
Kress, Gunther and Theo van Leeuwen
    1998   Front pages: (The critical) Analysis of newspaper layout. In Bell, Allan and Peter Garrett (eds.), *Approaches to Media Discourse.* Oxford: Blackwell, 186–219.
Kreuz, Roger J. and Arthur C. Graesser
    1993   The assumptions behind questions in letters to advice columnists. *TEXT* 13, 65–89.
Kurzon, Dan
    1996   The maxim of quantity, hyponymy and Princess Diana. *Pragmatics* 6, 217–227.
Leach, Edmund
    1982   *Social Anthropology.* Oxford: Oxford University Press.
Levinson, Stephen C.
    1988   Putting linguistics on a proper footing. In Drew, Paul and Anthony Wooton (eds.), *Exploring the Interaction Order.* Cambridge: Polity Press, 161–227.
Roeh, Itzhak and Nir, Raphael
    1990   Speech presentation in the Israel radio new: Ideological constraints and rhetorical strategies. *TEXT* 10, 225–244.
Short, Michael
    1989   Speech presentation, the novel and the press. In Van Peer, Willie (ed.), *The Taming of the Text.* London: Routledge, 61–81.
Van Dijk, Teun A.
    1991   *Racism in the Press.* London: Routledge.
    1998   *Ideology.* London: Sage.
Van Dijk, Teun A. (ed.)
    1993   Critical Discourse Analysis. Special issue of *Discourse & Society* 4/2.
Van Leeuwen, Theo
    1996   The representation of social actors. In Caldas-Coulthard, Carmen Rosa and Malcolm Coulthard (eds.), *Texts and Practices: Readings in Critical Discourse Analysis.* London: Routledge, 32–70.

Wooffitt, Robin
    1992   *Telling Tales of the Unexpected.* Hemel Hempstead: Harvester Wheat-
            sheaf.
Zelizer, Barbie
    1989   "Saying" as collective practice: Quoting and differential address in the
            news. *TEXT* 9, 369–388.

Lying, politics and the metalinguistics of truth

John Wilson

A great man – what is he? He rather lies than tells the truth…

Nietzsche (1968)

1. Introduction

Nietzsche thought long and hard about truth and its consequences. His famous "will to truth" has been much debated, and his overall views on truth remain somewhat ambiguous.

> The unconditional will to truth – what is it? Is it the will not to let one be deceived? Is it the will not to deceive? … But why not deceive? Why not allow oneself to be deceived?

(cited in Williams 2002: 16)

As Williams (2002: 15) notes, Nietzsche understood the value of truth, but also understood that truth could be "… unhelpful and destructive", and that in some cases perhaps falsehoods could be necessities for some greater purpose or value or good. So here is the puzzle, how does one maintain the truth for oneself and others and maintain at the same time progress, development, and change, when so often these things have progressed without truth. Although this has hints of a position of pragmatism, this was not the aim; the aim was not to give up on truthfulness.

This is, at one level, the aim of this chapter. We want to adhere to the concept of truthfulness by proposing that we push harder at the boundaries of what we define as "lies". Truth, it will be argued, involves much more than a correspondence of facts to the world. Williams (2002) links his theory of truth with such concepts as "trustworthiness" and "sincerity" (see also Habermas 1984). Similarly, although more implicitly, Bolinger (1973) suggested "truth" was an issue of language in its context of use. Truth, for Bolinger, was the relationship between "facts and sentences plus their contexts", and he added here "and contexts include intentions" (Bolinger 1973: 542). Consider the case of a politician asked during an election interview whether he or his government would raise taxes. Imagine the following response: "I have no intention of raising taxes".

Once elected taxes are raised. Has the politician lied? Here is a possible response to such an accusation: "At the time I spoke I had no intention of raising taxes, the context has changed since then and raising taxes is now necessary". So at time X, statement P was true, but at time Y it would be false. This seems reasonable enough, except that at time X those who heard the response would not necessarily have marked it with any time based constraints, and the politician could very well have known this. If he did, it could be said he had an intention to deceive the public, but that what he said was nevertheless, at the time of making the statement, true. This ignores Bolinger's sentence/intention/context view of truth. Taking this perspective I want to argue that if the politician had an intention to deceive, and this led the public to believe X was true in general, not time/context constrained, and he in fact did not believe X was true in general but was time/context constrained, I want to call this a lie.

2.   Where have all the lies gone?

There is a sense in which the general public view politicians as untrustworthy, untruthful, and perhaps, in extreme cases, liars. But when is one lying and when is one telling the truth? This is a complex moral and philosophical question, and one where it is difficult to draw clear boundaries. Consider the famous *Spycatcher* court case, when Sir Robert Armstrong, the government's representative, was accused of being "less than honest" (in itself, perhaps, a polite way of saying he was lying). In a response during cross-examination he noted that in a previous statement he had been "…economical with the truth". This phrase has now found its way into everyday use as an ironic and formulaic phrase. It has passed into folklore not only as a clever response to accusations of dishonesty, but also as a further example of politicians' manipulative (in this case linguistic) behaviour. Equally, consider the following comment made about the ex-President of the United States Richard Nixon:

> He has lied to the American people time and time again and has betrayed their trust. Since he has admitted guilt, there is no reason to put the American people through the impeachment process. It will serve absolutely no purpose. The only possible solution is for the President to save dignity and resign.
>
> (Video Box cover: The Clinton Affair. VIC productions)

This advice was offered in 1974 following the Watergate scandal. Most interestingly, however, it is advice which was offered by Bill Clinton, who was subsequently to become President himself, and, ironically, to become only the second president in the history of the United States to be tried for impeachment.

And for which crime was Clinton to be impeached if found guilty? Perjury, or more simply *lying*. There were two main accusations levelled against President Clinton; the first was that he had lied, and the second was that he had used his political influence in an inappropriate manner. Clinton was found not guilty in each case by a majority vote of the House of Representatives; but the vote was far from unanimous in each case, and it was clear that there were many who believed the President had lied.

The accusation of Clinton's perjury was based on whether he had told the Grand Jury the truth when he said he had not had "sexual relations" with Monica Lewinsky. What he did admit to was that he had had an "inappropriate relationship". As the evidence emerged it was clear that Clinton had had a number of sexual encounters with Miss Lewinsky, but not full intercourse – *full sexual relations*. In this context, and if one reads *sexual relations* as meaning sexual intercourse, Clinton was telling the truth. But if one reads *sexual relations* as any kind of sexual encounter then he was not telling the truth. Is there ambiguity in these statements or not? On such an issue was to hang the fate of the most powerful man in the western world – a fact indicating the force of language in the real life of politics.

But consider the fact that none of us tells the truth on every occasion. From the example of a doctor hiding the horror of a patient's disease, to a confirmation that we are enjoying our host's meal when in fact we are not. When my daughter was four I asked her, on noting all of the biscuits had disappeared, "Did you eat some of the biscuits from this biscuit tin?" She said, "No". I noted she seemed somewhat uneasy, however, so I pressed her. She then said, "No I didn't eat some of the biscuits, *I ate all of them.*" A politician in the making perhaps, but she could not be said to have been lying, or even untruthful, in her initial response – at least not in terms of how we normally understand these terms. What has happened here is that at an early stage she has understood the pragmatic principle of inference from quantification. In this case when we say *some* we imply *not all*. As Gazdar (1979) has argued, quantifiers such as *some* imply the negation of the next highest quantifier, in this case *all*. On the other hand when we choose *all* we entail the positive form of the next lowest quantifier (and subsequent lower quantifiers). For example, (a) would be a contradiction, whilst, (b) is perfectly acceptable:

(a)   I ate all but not some of the biscuits
(b)   I ate some if not all of the biscuits

In this context then, when I asked my daughter did you eat *some* of the biscuits, if she had said yes this would have been propositionally true, but it might have led me to believe she did not eat *all* the biscuits. Of two possibilities she decided (for good reasons of course) to deny that she had not eaten *some* of the biscuits, but rather she had eaten all of them. But we might forgive a four-year-old for perhaps confusing linguistics, context and responsibility. We could not, however, do this as easily for mature politicians. Indeed, Clinton argued that when he was being questioned by the Grand Jury it was the job of the prosecution to "get him", it was only fair, therefore that he carefully phrase anything he had to say. Nevertheless, this argument notwithstanding, in the case of Armstrong and Clinton there is something not quite right here in two senses. In the first sense our expectations of politicians may, indeed should, be higher than our expectations of ourselves, but they should be realistic not idealistic. Second, the limits of linguistic inferences may mask levels of responsibility. Nevertheless, utilising linguistic inferences should not be an excuse for the failure to exercise such responsibility.

These are the broad themes to be taken up in this chapter. We will consider a specific case study of lying in politics – or rather the accusation of lying in politics. We then explore in what ways inferences may seemingly subvert truth, and reflect on where responsibility lies – or alternatively who has responsibility for lies.

3.   Lies damned lies and politicians

In November 1993, following a series of remarks from both the then British Prime Minister, John Major, and his Secretary of State for Northern Ireland, Sir Patrick Mayhew, it became clear that there was a clash between their claims that they would not talk with the IRA, or its political wing Sinn Fein (both are often combined together as Sinn Fein/IRA, but in this chapter we will simply refer to the IRA), and the claims of the IRA that the British Government had been talking to them for some time (Belfast Telegraph, 29 November 1993; 15 December 1993). This clash was eventually resolved when the British government finally admitted, on 28 November, that they had indeed been in contact with IRA, and this contact had been ongoing for more than three years. This remarkable situation led to a speech in the House of Commons by Sir Patrick Mayhew in which he attempted to explain what had taken place (Hansard, Offical Reports, 1 and 29 November 1993). What he said is reported in some detail in Wilson (1997) and will not detain us here, other than to note that the explanation rested on two different types of metalingusitic act. The first, was to distinguish between what Mayhew called "channels of communication" and the act of *talking*; and the second rested on the use of presuppositional negation as found in Mayhew's phrase "no one was authorised to talk with the IRA".

In the first instance the government attempted to avoid any claims that they had either contradicted themselves or deceived the public when they said they would not *talk* to the IRA (John Major went as far as to say it "... would turn my stomach"). This move rested on a distinction between *talking* and *channels of communication*. Yes, the government *had channels of communication* which they used with the IRA, but this was not talking to them. After all, *channels of communication* come in many forms, writing, non-verbal signalling, Morse code, and so on. Further, Sir Patrick argued, such channels had to remain secret for the benefit of the public, since it was through such channels that information such as "bomb warnings" were passed. The second move of the government involved an ambiguous claim that *no one was authorised to talk with the IRA*. As I argue elsewhere (see Wilson 1997) this is a presuppositional phrase, and as such it presupposes the truth of its complement in both positive and negative forms (Burton-Roberts 1989; Gazdar 1979; Taylor 1997; Carston 1996). Both *someone was authorised to talk to the IRA* and *no one was authorised to talk to the IRA* allow for the possibility that talks have taken place with the IRA: in the first case authorised and in the second case unauthorised.

Now in the context of Sir Patrick's speech, which included these specific types of rhetorical explanation, the members of the House of Commons seemed, in general, to be satisfied with the argument. Both main opposition parties at that time, the Liberals and the Labour Party, noted that Sir Patrick had done his "duty" and was an "honourable man". From the Northern Ireland Unionist back-benches, however, Sir Patrick's explanation was not as readily accepted. The seemingly more extreme reaction being that of Ian Paisley when he noted:

> Rev. I Paisley: It is not a matter of whether there is a channel conveying mes-sages to the provisional IRA or whether the government have had contacts in the past, or have in the present, but that those statements have been denied by the Secretary of State ...The people of Northern Ireland demand that the Secretary of State explains why he issued falsehoods ...Why did he not stand by what he said outside the House, and I stand by what I said. It was a falsehood, it was worse it was **a lie**.

> (Hansard 1993: 790)

In the British House of Commons you may not call other honourable members *liars*, and in this context the Rev. I. Paisley was requested to withdraw his ac-cusation. This he refused to do, and as a consequence he was removed from the chamber. He might have been allowed to stay in the chamber had he simply said he believed what Sir Patrick Mayhew said to be false. However, as Ian Paisley himself makes clear, there are falsehoods and there are "lies", and in his view one is "worse" than the other.

We will return to the distinction between these in a moment. But let us just pause to consider what has actually happened here? Is it the case that the government has simply clarified an earlier presentation of the facts with a later one, in which *channels of communication* are substituted for *talk*, and in which if someone did talk to the IRA it was probably in an *unauthorised position*, and in such a position they must have been acting without the government's direct knowledge? Or is it that the Rev. Ian Paisley might be right, that what has happened here is that our elected leaders have lied? But if we have been lied to, how would we know? This is a core question for this chapter. In what follows we consider what it means to lie, and contrast this with the possible set of options adopted by the government in the case outlined above.

While it is difficult to define lies within the complex flow of normal everyday interaction (or political interaction), nevertheless we are believed to operate with an assumed level of pragmatic trust (Habermas 1984; Williams 2002). In this respect while it might be difficult to prove the government lied, what we can show is that they strategically manipulated the metalinguistics of truth, i.e. using language to comment on language, and in some cases the outcomes of this can look remarkably like lying.

4. To tell a lie

In his paper "The grammar of a lie", Epstein (1982) offers one of the few linguistic accounts of lying within a general political context (for more general overview see Bok 1978; Williams 2002; Bolinger 1973). The analysis operates, however, with a simple view of lying: one in which the participants in the Watergate trials are shown to be liars, if, after a specific incident or claim, what they said does not match with some state of affairs in the world. This seems perfectly reasonable, and would sit well with our common sense view of lying (see Williams 2002), but there are many complications here which are not considered by Epstein. Sometimes we may say something which does not match the facts of the world, and we may simply be mistaken; or sometimes we may say that which it turns out *does* match the world when we believed it did not. I might say, for example, that you should look in your back pocket and you will find some money, and I might believe this to be false. If, however, on checking your pocket you find money, then you will believe what I have said to be true, even though I might have intended it as a lie. The main problem is that we have, in general, given more attention to truth than to lies. In the Encyclopaedia of Philosophy there are over 200 references to truth and almost none to lying. The reason for this is that truth is often defined within formal models of meaning. In a formal model of meaning (such as that of Davidson 1984, for example), truth is defined as a set of conditions which must match in a direct way the propositional expression of a state of affairs in some possible world (including the actual world of course: see also Lewis 1969). Where statements do not match the facts in some possible world, they are said to be false in that world. Making a false statement is not the same as lying. In lying we try to distinguish between saying what is false and doing so intentionally. Here we assume a lie arises where a speaker X makes a statement Y knowing Y to be false, in a context where listener P does not know either that Y is false or that Y is true. Further, it is by virtue of X producing Y that P comes to believe that Y is true, and P also believes that X believes Y to be true. This can seem a bit complicated, but basically, in common sense terms, we lie when we intend to produce false statements and have others believe those statements are true. But, as is often the case, things are never as simple as we think.

Imagine that I want you to believe that the steak you are about to eat may be contaminated. I do not know this, and have no evidence for such a possibility. But suppose it would benefit me if I get you to believe what I say, I might want the steak myself. If I am successful in getting you to believe such a falsehood, I may have deceived you, but I did not know the information was false. Or consider the case where my recommendation for your promotion would normally guarantee the promotion, and I put forward such a recommendation. However, I want you to believe that I have not done so. Since I also know that you do not believe anything I say, by telling you that I have recommended you for promotion I will get you to believe that you will not be promoted. Now assume that for whatever reason my recommendation is rejected. In this case I will have got you to believe that I have not recommended you for promotion is true. Consider one final case that of Pablo Ibbieta in Sartre's story *The Wall*. Pablo was asked where Ramon Gris was hiding and Pablo, in an attempt to deceive the authorities told them that Gris was hiding in the cemetery. He was quite certain that Gris was hiding somewhere else. Ramon Gris, by chance, and completely unknown to Pablo, was hiding in the cemetery.

What these examples show is that our initial and common sense view of lying is difficult to pin down. You may know something to be true but lead others to believe it is false, or vice versa, or fail in both since there may be information outside your available knowledge which makes what you believe to be true, false, and what you believe to be false, true. But perhaps lying is not in the matching of content to thought or world, but rather only to thought and intention, as St. Thomas put it:

> ... if one says what is false, thinking it to be true, it is false, materially, but not formally, because the falseness is beside the intention of the speaker;

so that it is not a perfect lie, since what is beside the speaker's intention is accidental, for which reason it cannot be a specific difference. If on the other hand one utters a falsehood formally, through having the will to enunciate what is false, even if what one says is true, yet in as much as this is a voluntary and moral act, it contains falseness essentially and truth accidentally, and attains the specific nature of a lie.

So it is through our willingness to deceive that lies emerge; it does not matter what the subsequent outcomes may be in this or any other possible world which makes what we say either false or true. It is not truth or falsehood which matters, but rather our intentions to deceive.

Now let us consider a different kind of example. Suppose Peter wants to watch the World Cup final on television, and Peter asks Quentin whether he owns a television set, and Quentin says "no". But Quentin is also aware of the context in which the question has been asked, that is Quentin fully understands that Peter simply wants to gain access to a television so that he (Peter) can watch the World Cup final. Let us further suppose that Quentin rents a television, but does not own one. Given this context, Quentin's response seems in some way inappropriate, although formally the response he provided is true, i.e. Quentin does not own a television set. In the strictest sense of the above, therefore, Quentin could not have been said to be lying, although one might want to argue that Quentin has, in some way, deceived Peter. But above we said that the nature of lies resides in the intention to deceive. If that is the case then what is the difference here? The difference is between a context where one is referring to an intention to produce false statements (in the sense of St. Thomas) and a context where one produces true and appropriate statements but intentionally ignores legitimate contextual implications/inferences, which, as a result, lead to specific interpretations which are inconsistent with facts of the world. In our case Quentin allows Peter to believe that he, Quentin, not only does not own a television, but also does not have access to one. But why should we say that in one context we have a lie, while in another context it is merely a deception? This seems to result from saying that in the first case the speaker produces a statement which they believe to be false, but in the second case the speaker's statement is directly in line with what they believe true. Quentin believes, indeed knows, he does not own a television set. Nevertheless, there is something not quite right here. In the above context most normal speakers of English realise that Peter will interpret the negative answer to the question "Do you own a television set?", as also meaning the respondent does *not have* a television set, and further, that they do not have access to a television set. Now in such a context if one says simply "No", they know their listener will work out, or infer, that they do not have one available on which one could watch the World Cup final. In this case Quentin will have intentionally induced in Peter a number of false beliefs which are inferred rather than stated. But if one could show that Quentin was perfectly aware of such possible false inferences, why should we not say Quentin was lying as opposed to simply saying that he was deceiving Peter? The answer seems to be merely a difference between statements which may be shown to be false and inferences which may be shown to be false. The difficulty is that inferences are not normally thought of in this way (although see Bolinger 1973 for a different view). By the very nature of being inferences they represent information which has been worked out or calculated, as opposed to stated. In the formal theory of truth, noted above, some inferences are said to fall somewhere between being true or false, indeed arguments have been made for certain types of inference, such as presuppositions, to be coded as neither true nor false (Strawson 1964). For example, (1) can be said to be neither true nor false since Hitler was dead in 1979, and therefore any speculation on the regrets of Margaret Thatcher are irrelevant.

(1)   Margaret Thatcher does not regret having dinner with Hitler in 1979.

This is typical of the outcomes of formal arguments, they are divorced from the real world of interaction. The question is not whether (1) may be assessed as true or false in some theory of truth, but whether less exaggerated sentence forms might be used by a speaker to adjust a listener's view of the world in a direction different than their own. Consider (2)

(2)   Margaret Thatcher does not regret having dinner with Norman Tebbit in 1979.

For all I know the inference that *Margaret Thatcher had dinner with Norman Tebbit* may be true. However, let's say I believe that Norman Tebbit never had dinner with Margaret Thatcher, but that I wish some listener to believe it is true. If the listener trusts me and accepts the presupposition that *Margaret Thatcher had dinner with Norman Tebbit in 1979*, then they will add this inference to their stock of knowledge; i.e. they will come to believe X is true while I believe X to be false. And they will come to believe this explicitly as a result of my intentions in producing the utterance in the first place. Now this looks remarkably similar to how we might describe a lie in the case of statements.

Recall, as we have already shown above, it is not whether statements are true or false that is the issue, but rather whether the statements are presented in relation to some specific intention. If it should turn out that Margaret Thatcher did not have dinner with Norman Tebbit, or that she did but she did not regret it, or whatever, it doesn't really matter, since my goal of having my listener believe X was true while I believed X was false would still stand. It seems to me, therefore, if one treats lies as intentions to deceive, then it may be argued that one lies where one intentionally allows one's interlocutors to proceed with a set of false inferences intentionally induced by what one has said. Specifically, when it can be shown that the speaker believed the false inferences to be true or the true inferences to be false.

Turing back to our specific example, how can I say Quentin is lying when he says he does not own a television set, when this statement is materially true? The answer here is that in the specific context above the question was not simply *Do you own a television set*? even if these were the very words uttered, but rather *Do you know where I could get access to a television set, for example do you own one*? Now this is not an over-interpretation, any more than interpreting, *Can you pass the salt*? as a request for action and not specifically (or not only) as a question (Searle 1969). Many utterances in everyday interaction carry more information than is contained in the words themselves; this is the core of the emergent discipline of pragmatics (see Grice 1975; Wilson and Sperber 1996). The question is, who has responsibility for those implications and inferences which are contained in utterances, the speaker or the hearer. The answer is that it is a joint effort born of co-operation in a Gricean sense, and of a need to maintain communication and relevance in Sperber and Wilson's (1996) sense. Where, in any specific context, potential and legitimate inferences may follow from what we say, and we are perfectly aware of these, I want to suggest we have a responsibility for such inferences. Where such inferences lead to an interpretation distinct from that which we intend, for example, a belief which we might later want to claim is false, then if we intentionally let such inferences progress I want to suggest that this is similar to lying.

5.   Pragmatics, lying and politics

Let us return now to Sir Patrick Mayhew and look at what he did say (all the emphases in the following quotes have been added):

> It has always been perfectly clear that the British government has never authorised anyone to enter into *talks or negotiations* on their behalf.
>
> (Hansard Nov 1993: 796

> ... nobody has been authorised and nobody will be authorised to enter into *talks or discussions* with people who are responsible for violence or who justify the use of violence.
>
> (Hansard Nov 1993: 798)

there have been no *negotiations*, none have been offered and there will be none unless and until the IRA gives up violence and Sinn Fein gives up justifying it.

(Hansard 797)

... nobody has been authorised to undertake *talks* or *negotiations* on behalf of the government.

(Hansard 799)

All that there has been are *channels of communication*.

(Hansard 786)

... a *channel of communication* which was one whose value has been maintained for, as has been clear, many years – 20 years ... am I to have supposed that the public would have been better served if there had been no such channel – if there had been no means by which the IRA could send a message.

(Hansard 796)

As we noted above there are two main forms of rhetorical response involved in all this; first, a denial of talks but an acceptance that there were channels of communication; and second, a specific use of presuppositional negation to create a context of ambiguity. The first of these is a form of denial that there have been talks with the IRA. This is based on the use of a metalinguisic form of negation linked to the semantic concept of hyponymy. Hyponymy refers to hierarchical relations such as Rose–flower, Husky–dog. While all Roses are flowers, not all flowers are Roses, and while all Huskies are dogs not all dogs are Huskies. Equally, while talk is a channel of communication, not all channels of communication involve talk.

This is all fine. But what we are being asked to accept is that when a government says *we will not talk with X*, we are to take what they say literally, and not assume that other forms of contact have been made. In normal interaction phases such as *I am not talking to you* or *I will never speak to you again*, do not normally mean that other forms of communication will be chosen. Of course politics is a very specific kind of communicative context. But even here we must decide whether it is legitimate to assume that *will not talk to X, in fact it would turn my stomach to talk to X*, was meant to mean that other forms (channels) of communication were to be maintained.

Equally when we turn to the case of utterances such as "no one was authorised to talk to the IRA"; such an utterance leaves it unclear whether someone may have talked with the IRA, but in an unauthorised position, or whether no one talked to the IRA, as in a possible cancellation clause (Wilson 1997):

(3)   No one was authorised to talk with the IRA – *but someone did*
       No one was authorised to talk to the IRA – *and no one did.*

If one leaves an utterance such as "no one was authorised to talk with the IRA" as vague and open in terms of possible interpretation, and one does this intentionally, assessing specific audience interpretations in their favour, then one is again, at least potentially, being deceitful. But are they lying? Well, let's say yes, for the moment. In this case, we can argue that inferences (as implicatures or whatever) are legitimate forms of knowledge, and inform our behaviour in as much as true or false statements. This being the case, if a speaker knowingly guides their hearer to an inference which represents a state of affairs in the world which is false, and if the speaker knows that acceptance of this inference as representing a true state of affairs is in their favour, then they may be, in our terms, lying. The reason for this is that where one can show the speaker is aware of both the content and contextual implications of what they said, then they are responsible for both. What I am suggesting is that where this responsibility is subverted through the production of false statements, or through allowing incorrect inferences to proceed, the speaker is lying.

To many this will seem incorrect; both in an intuitive sense, in that in the case of inferences speakers have not said what is false, and in a more technical sense, since speakers cannot control the interpretations of listeners, they cannot be held responsible for these. In the first case the objection is merely an assertion regarding our intuitive views of lying, and we have already outlined the difficulties of tying down this intuitive perspective. In the second case we have the basic problem faced in dealing with the pragmatics of communication. As Sperber and Wilson (1996) note, successful communication is not guaranteed, on the other hand it is generally the norm, and there are clearly strong guidelines which we all draw upon: Sperber and Wilson's *Principle of Relevance* being a case in point.

Let us return here to our television example. Remember that Peter wanted to watch a football match and asked Quentin if he owned a television. Peter said "no", even though he rented one. It was suggested that this was a context of deceit, but not of lying, because what Quentin said was not false. But this assumes it is agreed that all lies must simply be false in terms of matching the facts of the world. On the other hand, what we are suggesting is that in terms of available knowledge, as generated by both what has been said and what has been inferred, that some aspect of knowledge is intentionally represented as true, but which is in fact false, either in relation to a representation of the actual world, or of the world as represented by legitimate inferences. This additional inclusion of inferential knowledge allows us to conclude that Quentin is being deceitful, but further, since he has allowed an inference to proceed (i.e. he does not have a television) which is in fact false, this inference now forms part of Peter's local belief set, i.e. of his shared knowledge with Quentin. Peter now believes that Quentin does not own a television set (which is true), but further Peter also now believes that Quentin does not have access to a television set (which is false). I am suggesting that because Quentin has now generated in the mind of Peter that which is false, he could be said to have lied to Peter as much as if he had produced a statement which could be shown to be false, and intentionally produced as such. The reason here is that the outcome is the same. If Quentin had said he did own a television when he did not, and he did so intentionally in the sense of St. Thomas, then he has led A to believe something which is false and he has lied. Equally, it seems to me, and given our present knowledge of pragmatics, we can say that Quentin has also led Peter to believe something which is false: so it seems possible also to call this a lie.

The difference is that in one case Quentin said something which was false, and in the other he has implied that which is false. So what's the difference if the outcome can be shown to be the same? The obvious difference is between what is said and what is implied. I prefer Grice's (1975) interpretation between what is said and what is meant. Grice's point was that what we say and what we mean are not the same, and pragmatics has been focusing on this difference ever since. Therefore, sometimes what we say and what we mean are the same, and sometimes they are not. In this second case we are called upon to do more work in order to achieve meaning. In both cases if we give meaning the primacy, as opposed to the utterance of specific words themselves, then the difference between saying what is false and implying what is false seems less distinct. In both cases we are focusing on what is meant; it is just in one case the content of the words themselves will suffice, but in the other we have to take account of such things as context and shared knowledge. However, if we say we are interested in what is meant, as opposed to what is said, and argue that where what is meant is shown to be false, and intentionally projected as such, then whatever the state of the actual or any other possible world, we could be said to have a lie, and it follows in this sense that Quentin has lied.

Returning to the case of the claims of the British government, can we say they have lied? First, we must ask not whether what they said was false in the world, but rather what was it they meant by what they said, and was this false in the world. Here, admittedly, the proof can never be exact, since at the time of their statements we do not have direct access to their intentions. We do not have this either in the case of statements, of course, and mistakes do occur as much as lies. But the lack of direct access to intentions is not unusual in pragmatics, and all we can offer are arguments based on pragmatic theories of the way language operates. As we noted above, given the strength and context of the statements made by Sir Patrick Mayhew and John Major, when they said they would not talk with the IRA, were we to assume they only meant they would not have any oral articulate contact? Given previous arguments this is a bit disingenuous. Recall that Sir Patrick himself admitted (repeated from above):

> ... a *channel of communication* which was one whose value has been maintained for, as has been clear, many years – 20 years ... am I to have supposed that the public would have been better served if there had been no such channel – if there had been no means by which the IRA could send a message.
>
> (Hansard 796)

Now are we to assume that whenever it was stated that "no one would talk to the IRA" we were to have worked out the existence of other potential communication channels distinct from talk? This wouldn't make any sense since these links were to have been considered necessary, but most importantly of all *secret*. Is Sir Patrick now saying that they were only an inference away?

Overall, and given the general pragmatic context in which the original statements where made, was it legitimate to infer from what the government said that they would have no contact with the IRA – I believe this is a legitimate inference. Unfortunately, like all inferences, they may be denied at a later date, or treated as over active interpretations on the interpreter's part. The view of this chapter, however, is that where one can present a case that specific inferences worked in favour of the speaker at time X, and at that time they were readily available to both the speaker and audience, for the speaker at a later date to deny the validity of the inferences drawn by the audience, while at time X letting these proceed, indicates either an error on their part, or if the inferences where intentionally generated, then it is possible to call this a lie. Perhaps I'd better leave the chamber.

References

Aquinas, Thomas
　　1922   *Summa Theologica* 2.2 ques.109,110. Literally translated by the Fathers of the English Dominican Provina. London: Burns, Oates and Washbourne Ltd.
Belfast Telegraph, 29 November 1993.
Belfast Telegraph, 15 December 1993.
Bolinger, Dwight
　　1973   Truth is a linguistic issue. *Language* 49, 539–550.
Bok, Sissela.
　　1978   *Lying – Moral Choice in Public and Private Life*. Sussex: Harvester Press.

Burton Roberts, Noël
  1989   *The Limits to Debate: A Revised Theory of Semantic Presupposition.* Cambridge: Cambridge University Press.
Carston, Robyn
  1996   Metalinguistic negation and echoic use. *Journal of Pragmatics* 25, 309–330.
Davidson, Donald
  1984   *Inquiries into Truth and Interpretation.* Oxford: Clarendon Press.
Epstein, Judith P.
  1982   The grammar of a lie: Its legal implications. In DiPietro, Robert J. (ed.), *Linguistics and the Professions.* Norwood, NJ: Ablex, 133–142.
Gazdar, Gerald
  1979   *Pragmatics: Implicature, Presupposition and Logical Form.* New York: Academic Press.
Grice, H. P.
  1975   William James Lectures. Logic and conversation. In Cole, Peter and Jerry L. Morgan (eds.), *Syntax and Semantics. Volume 3: Speech Acts.* New York. Academic Press, 41–58.
Habermas, Jürgen
  1984   *Theory of Communicative Action*, vol. 1. Translated by T. McCarthy. Cambridge: Polity.
Hansard Official Report, 1 November 1993.
Hansard Official Report, 29 November 1993.
Horn, Lawrence
  1985   Metalinguistic negation and pragmatic ambiguity. *Language* 61, 121–174.
Lewis, David K.
  1969   *Convention.* Cambridge, MA: Harvard University Press.
Nietzsche, Friedrich W.
  1968   *The Will to Power.* Translated and edited by Walter Kaufmann. New York: Vintage Books.
Searle, John R.
  1969   *Speech Acts.* Cambridge: Cambridge University Press.
Sperber, Dan and Deirdre Wilson
  1996   *Relevance: Communication and Cognition.* Oxford. Blackwell.
Strawson, P. F.
  1964   Identifying reference and truth values. *Theoria* 30, 96–118.
VIC productions
  1998   *The Clinton Affair.* Video box cover.
Taylor, Kenneth
  1999   *The Philosophy of Language.* Oxford. Blackwell.
Williams, Bernard
  2002   *Truth and Truthfulness.* Princeton: Princeton University Press.

Wilson, John
    1997   Metalinguistic negation and textual aspects of political discourse. In Blommaert, Jan and Chris Bulcaen (eds.), Political linguistics. Special issue of *The Belgian Journal of Linguistics* 11, 69–88.

Part 3. Metalanguage and social evaluation

Introduction to Part 3

Adam Jaworski and Nikolas Coupland

In Part 3 of the book, *Metalanguage and social evaluation*, two of the three chapters are in the theoretical and empirical traditions foregrounded in Preston's scene-setting chapter in Part 1. Tore Kristiansen's "Attitudes and values in representations of language: Their role in language variation and change", and Peter Garrett, Nikolas Coupland and Angie Williams's "Adolescents' lexical repertoires of peer evaluation: *Boring prats* and *English snobs*", report studies at the interface between dialect variation and social evaluation. The third chapter, Adam Jaworski and Itesh Sachdev's "Teachers' beliefs about students' talk and silence: Constructing academic success and failure through metapragmatic comments", combines attitudinal research with Critical Discourse Analysis.

Kristiansen reports on his work in the Næstved area of the island of Zealand in eastern Denmark. He explores the importance of metacommunicative data, in this case self-reports of different types (based on codings but also discursive representations) for the understanding of linguistic variation and change involving the Copenhagen, Standard and Zealand dialect varieties. Kristiansen appeals to the concept of a "social identity instinct" as the force driving sociolinguistic structure and change. Sociolinguistic norms and variation are the focus of explicitly evaluative responses by informants, who position themselves differently within a "three-pole normative field". As informants identify with or distance themselves from specific normative dialect forms, they construct allegiances, boundaries and socio-cultural identities, most sharply distinguished by age and geography. In a wide-ranging theoretical discussion, Kristiansen reconsiders the "evaluation problem" as defined by Labov, the role of cognitive factors in language variation and change, and the implications for sociolinguistic research methods.

Garrett, Coupland and Williams's study involves audio-recording of school students in six regions of Wales telling stories in their local English dialects. Some fragments of these narratives were used as samples representing the main dialect regions in Wales and were later played back to other teenagers across the country. The "judges" in this phase of the research wrote down their first impressions as sets of "keywords". The keywords prove to be richly indicative of the evaluative discourses they employ in the process of group formation, exploring available identities and intergroup relationships. As in the Kristiansen study, they provide insights into the social dimensions that are evaluatively salient among the kids' groups. Two broad metalinguistic dimensions are called into play in the responses: representations of the stereotyped meanings of, firstly, dialect forms and, secondly, narrative styles. In fact, the chapter illustrates how evaluative metalanguage conflates at least these two dimensions of spoken performance, suggesting that language attitudes research has abstracted too radically from considerations of genre and social context.

Explicit evaluation of communicative skills of students applying for entry to British universities is discussed by Jaworski and Sachdev. The authors analyse a number of school references written for such students, with a specific focus on the teachers' mention of students' "communication skills". These are construed in the references as a (good) ability to speak, to discuss academic topics, and to engage in other types of desirable verbal activities. That is, the references posit a view of "effective communication" in terms of *talk*, as opposed to *silence*, since relative reticence, withdrawal from group discussions, and so on are viewed negatively. The authors argue that the overwhelmingly positive treatment of talk and volubility, and the negative evaluation of silence, are deeply entrenched cultural traits in teachers' beliefs about communication, and form their implicitly shared metalanguage (cf. Preston, this volume). As Cameron argues in her chapter, metadiscourse on language presupposes certain ideological positions and points to a 'larger moral order', or it is constitutive of what Preston, this volume, refers to as *Metalanguage 3*. In the case of educators writing references' for their students, their orientation to *talk* and *silence* can be seen to presuppose tacitly shared notions of a "good" student and a "desirable" academic process.

Social meaning and norm-ideals for speech in a Danish community

Tore Kristiansen

1. Metacommunicative data in the study of language variation and change

This chapter deals with metalanguage, or more generally with metacommunicative data, from the perspective of language variation and change. By "metacommunicative data" I understand anything that can be seen as a *comment* on some aspect of human communication. Such comments can stem from many sources, including ordinary spoken discourse, written texts, questionnaires, experiments, and body language. The defining criterion is that the purpose is to give some kind of comment on some aspect of communication. Metacommunicative data have played an important role in many research projects since the very beginnings of modern sociolinguistic research into language variation and change. William Labov, for one, has always taken great care to gather metacommunicative data in his projects, by making language a topic at some point in the sociolinguistic interview and by carrying out what he calls field experiments, including self-report tests, subjective reactions tests, linguistic insecurity tests, and others (see, e.g. Labov 1984).

The resulting data inform us about how linguistic differences are perceived and evaluated by individuals and groups and have made a major contribution to our understanding of variation and change in general. As we all know, it has been common (and for some it may still be possible) to understand variation and change as something that goes on in "language in itself": language varies and changes "in itself" and "by itself". Labovian sociolinguistics, of course, developed in strong opposition to this "language in itself" conception. Labov's first study, at Martha's Vineyard (Labov 1963), already showed convincingly that language variation and change is to be explained in terms of socio-psychological processes of categorization, comparison and evaluation. In the words of Wolfram and Fasold, "... it is the perception of dialect differences and the evaluation of these differences by participating members of the society which is the real basis for the existence of social dialects" (1997 [1974]: 110). Or, in a more recent formulation by Chambers: "The underlying cause of sociolinguistic differences, largely beneath consciousness, is the human instinct to esta-

blish and maintain social identity" (1995: 250). In other words, and ontologically speaking, evaluation precedes variation.

This assumption has become so commonplace in sociolinguistics that it
is difficult, at least for me, to understand how anyone could ever believe that
language varies and changes "in itself" and "by itself". But if we have come to
see our perceptions and evaluations, and what we might call our social identity
instinct, as the *driving force*, it seems evident that we should try and shed light
on this force in our studies of language variation and change. So my starting
point is the importance of metacommunicative data: in order to deepen our
understanding of language variation and change processes, we need to collect
and analyse all kinds of "comments" which can inform us about people's perceptions and evaluations of aspects of their linguistic usage and environment.
If, ontologically speaking, evaluation precedes variation, there will always be
tensions and possible contrasts between what is going on at the level of social
identity formation and what is going on at the level of language use. These
tensions and contrasts are the hotbed of language variation and change and
should be studied in particular speech communities and addressed in multiple
ways, at the level of both social groups and individuals. I have adopted such an
approach in a long-term project researching language variation and change in a
particular Danish speech community. The following sections present analyses
of some metacommunicative data from this project. (Other reports in English
can be found in Kristiansen 1997, 1998, 2001, 2003; Kristiansen and Giles
1992.)

2.   Demographics and language usage in the Næstved area

The speech community under study is the town of Næstved and its surrounding area, situated on the island of Zealand some 80 kilometres to the south of
Copenhagen (see Map 1). Copenhagen is Denmark's capital and the only big
city in the country. Out of a national total of 5 million inhabitants, 1.5 million live in the conurbation of Copenhagen. Næstved itself has 38,000 inhabitants. An additional 45,000 live within Næstved's surrounding area, which in
the project is defined as a circle with a radius of 20 kilometres from the city
border, roughly speaking. Work-related commuting out of and into Næstved
is balanced, with around 6,000 people moving in each direction. Among the
out-commuters, some 2,600 go to Copenhagen. Overall, Næstved plays an increasingly important role as a regional centre, primarily in the domains of trade
and education, while at the same time being under heavy and general influence
from the capital city.

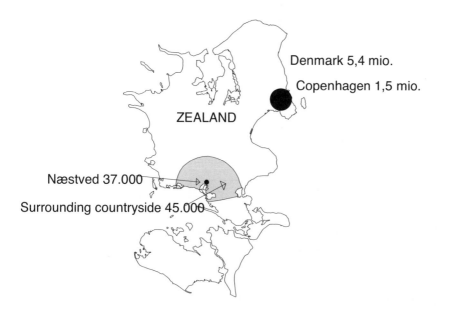

The traditional Zealand dialect has been described in works by dialectologists (see Ejskjær 1970). Quantitative variationist studies have shown that traditional dialect features are becoming rare in the speech of young people (Jørgensen and Kristensen 1994). This is the case not only in the Næstved area but in Denmark in general (Kristensen 2003; Pedersen 2003). Features from Copenhagen speech are taking over. In the Næstved area this process is so advanced that it has become rather meaningless to study language usage in the area as a matter of variation between local variants and Copenhagen variants. Few variables can be established to allow for such variation to be analyzed quantitatively.

In Figure 1, the "Zealand-Copenhagen variation" is represented in variables 7–10. The ending (*-et*) (variable 7) recurs frequently in all speech since it expresses grammatical functions like the definite form of neuter nouns (*huset* 'the house') and the past participle of most verbs (*malet* 'painted'). The variants are [ð] (Copenhagen) versus [e] or zero (Zealand). The same variation is present in the words *meget* 'much, very' and *noget* 'some, something' (variables 8a and 8b), which fulfill several grammatical functions and form part of frequently used pragmatic particles and stock phrases. Likewise, variable 9N *-ede* is a question of either presence or absence of [ð]. The variable is frequent as the preterite form of most verbs (*malede* 'painted') and as the definite and plural form of the past participle in adjectival usage (*den malede bænk* 'the painted bench', *de malede bænke* 'the painted benches').

VARIABLES		NON-STANDARD				STANDARD = high Cph
		0	25	50	75	100
low Copenhagen	1H		G C B	A		
	2G	C B A	G			
	2D	A	BC G			
	2V	G	CB	A		
	2N	CAB G				
	3H	A B G C				
	4H		BC AG			
	5	AC BG				
traditional dialect	7			B	G C A	
	8a				A GB C	
	8b			G AB	C	
	9N			B G	A C	
	10			CB A	G	

A = phase 1 of interview   C = reading
B =   -   2   -   G = group session

Figure 1. Language usage by adolescents (N = 48) (adapted from Jørgensen & Kristensen 1994)
     1st group of variables: low Copenhagen vs high Copenhagen
     2nd group of variables: traditional dialect vs high Copenhagen

Whereas the +/- [ð] variation goes largely unnoticed in the speech community, the *stød*-manifestation (variable 10) is a highly salient feature of Zealand speech – a strongly stigmatized stereotype. *Stød* is a prosodic feature which is linked to the syllable. In most Danish speech, including Copenhagen speech, *stød* is normally realized as a glottal constriction, but in Zealand speech the *stød* is often pronounced more vigorously, and often as a glottal stop with a re-duplication of the syllabic segment (vowel or postvocalic sonorous consonant) which "carries" the *stød*.

While variation of the "Zealand-Copenhagen" type is quite limited, Copenhagen speech itself is replete with variation, and much of this variation spreads to the rest of Denmark together with the general advance of Copenhagen speech. Variation in Copenhagen speech has been thoroughly described, both diachronically and synchronically (Brink and Lund 1975; Gregersen and Pedersen 1991), and is normally presented as variation between a high status variety and a low status variety. The "high Copenhagen" variety is commonly known as *rigsdansk* ("standard Danish", cf. German *Reichs-*), i.e. the "national" language taught in school, used in the media, etc. The "low Copenhagen" variety is commonly known as *københavnsk* 'Copenhagen dialect', i.e. the language spoken by the working class or more generally by the "people" of Copenhagen. I shall adopt this terminology for the time being and talk about *Standard* variants versus *Copenhagen* variants.

In Figure 1, Standard-Copenhagen variation is represented by variables 1H–5, all based on variation in vowel quality. In all linguistic contexts specified for short and long (a) (variables 1H–2N), Copenhagen variants are more fronted than Standard variants. In the (aj), (ræ) and (ær) variables (3H–5), the Standard vowels are the more fronted ones. Scales in Figure 1 go from 0% Standard variants on the left to 100% Standard variants on the right. The letters in the Figure represent percentages of Standard variants used by young people of the Næstved area in three different phases (A, B and C) of a sociolinguistic interview and in a group session (G). I do not elaborate on those differences here, but simply establish that these adolescents show an average of around 80% Standard variants on variables which include a traditional Zealand variant versus a Standard variant, and the same average of around 80% Copenhagen variants on variables which include a Copenhagen variant versus a Standard variant (Jørgensen and Kristensen 1994).

3.   Self-evaluation and norm-ideals in Næstved

According to the description above, the natives of the Næstved area speak a language which can be characterized as more or less Zealand, more or less Copenhagen, and more or less Standard. This seems to indicate that there are – at the level of representations, attitudes and values – three "target norms" which young people have to relate to as they grow up and (self-)categorize in relation to the speech and speakers of this speech community. I think of these targets, which I call *norm-ideals*, as representations/evaluations of particular ways of speaking, as focused combinations of language use and social values. Such norm-ideals will often be cognitively represented as a set of prototypical speakers. This section of the chapter, which presents results from a self-evaluation experiment, is an attempt at determining the actual status (existence and social meanings involved) of the three suggested norm-ideals in the Næstved speech community.

Three groups of informants were involved in the self-evaluation experiment, all natives of the Næstved area: children (aged 9–10), adolescents (most of them aged 16–18) and adults (aged 30–83). The samples were selected to be equally distributed as to sex and geographical affiliation (Næstved versus the surrounding countryside), and were broadly composed as to social status. Informants listened to three readings of the same text, which were performed to clearly represent the Copenhagen, Zealand and Standard varieties. The Copenhagen and Standard readings were performed by two 40-year-old women from Copenhagen, the Zealand reading by a 75-year-old woman from Næstved's surrounding area. Phonetic differences between these stimulus voices are given in Figure 2.

	Copenhagen	Zealand	Standard
STØD			
... with redublication of the 'stød-carrying' segment	no	yes	no
... on short vowels in words like			
fætter '(male) cousin', *katten* 'the cat'	no	yes	no
... in the second part of composita like			
borddamen lit. 'the table lady' (female) dinner partner	no	yes	no
køkkenhaven 'the kitchen garden'			
... in the word *nu* 'now'	no	yes	no
VOWEL QUALITY			
short (a) before dentals *katten* 'the cat'		æ	æ
... + /r/ in the following syllable *plaster* 'plaster'			æ
short (å) *Charlotte, kartoffel* 'potato'			
(aj) *spejlet* 'the mirror', *stegen* 'the roast'	j	j	aj
(øj) *røg* 'rushed', *høje* 'the elevated'	j	œj	j
(ræ) *skræmt* 'frightened', *revne* 'crack'	r	r /re	r
VOWEL QUANTITY			
lengthening of vowels in syllables without stød			
nakken 'the neck', *kaffe* 'coffee'	yes	yes	no

Figure 2. Phonetic characteristics of stimulus voices in the self-evaluation experiment

The *stød* feature is not only manifested more vigorously in the traditional Zealand dialect (see above), it is also present in more types of words. Several examples of this are present in the reading by the elderly Zealand woman. Among these, only *stød* in the word *nu* is relatively frequent in the speech of young people. Other features of the Zealand dialect which are not heard in young people's speech are the old woman's realizations of the (ai) and (øi) diphthongs, as well as the quality of her short /a/ before dentals when an /r/ follows in the next syllable. A traditional difference between the Standard and Copenhagen is the pronunciation of the short (å), a difference which is also found on the tape. Finally, lengthening of short vowels in syllables without *stød* is common in Copenhagen and Zealand speech and present in both stimulus voices.

The only information given in advance was that informants would be listening to three ways of pronouncing Danish, represented by numbered circles in the corners of a triangle, which they had in front of them on a piece of paper. Figures 3–5 on page 175 are scaled down examples of the triangle. (Notice that the circles were not labelled as in these Figures, just numbered 1, 2, 3). The informants' task was to place their own speech schematically in relation to the three voices, either as identical with one of the voices, or somewhere between them, wherever they judged to be the appropriate place. Afterwards, audio-recorded discussions were undertaken, in which the informants were asked questions about the kinds of Danish they had heard: could they recognize them? name them? how could they be recognized? what are their characteristic features? who talks like that? and so on.

The procedure is based on the assumption that linguistic self-evaluation involves relating one's own speech to a set of competing norm-ideals: if a voice is judged relevant as a point of reference, that judgement has both a linguistic and a social aspect to it. The informants' reactions to the voices (their self-evaluations and their comments in the subsequent discussion) tell us about their "knowledge" of the norm-ideals in the Næstved area. If significant correlations are found between self-evaluation patterns and social groups, this is an indication that several norm-ideals exist in the speech community. This is not to say that norm-ideals mean the same to all members of a social group, either in the experimental situation or in everyday life. (We return to the role of norm-ideals at the individual level in Section 4, below). But the very presence of competing norm-ideals in the speech community can only be recognized in patterns of representations/evaluations at the level of social groups.

On the assumption that social identifications (categorizations/evaluations of self and others) involve accentuation of resemblances and differences in relation to ingroups and outgroups, respectively (Hogg and Abrams 1988), the experimental situation here is assumed to provoke stereotyping processes such as: "I'm young, so my language is like ... and not like ...", or: "I'm from the town, so my language is like ... and not like ...", etc. In other words, the interesting question is not so much whether people assess their own speech correctly from a purely linguistic point of view, but rather which pattern of social meaning emerges (cf. Garrett et al., this volume).

On the basis of common knowledge and my own acquaintance with the Næstved speech community over many years, I find it legitimate to assume that evaluations like "urban", "modern", "correct", "educated" are associated with the Standard, whereas evaluations like "boorish", "old", "incorrect", "uneducated" are associated with the traditional local Zealand dialect. At the outset it is far less clear what a Copenhagen way of speaking might mean, evaluatively and stereotypically, to natives of the Næstved area. As already mentioned, speech dominated by Copenhagen variants has traditionally been associated with the working class of the capital city and strongly stigmatized as "bad" language. But against the background of the recent and rapid spread of Copenhagen variants among young people, all over Denmark, one must assume that Copenhagen speech is perceived and evaluated otherwise today. It may still be seen as a town variety, but it is probably associated more with youth than with working class.

Hence, we assume that the Næstved speech community can be seen as a normative field with three poles, and furthermore that these poles are "known" (recognized and evaluated) in the speech community as just described, i.e. these norm-ideals do play their role as presumed in processes of social identification. We can then propose some hypotheses as to how the natives of the area will self-evaluate relative to each other as *adolescents* versus *adults*, and as *Næstved* people versus *countryside* people. These hypotheses can be formalized, as follows:

Hypothesis 1: linguistic self-evaluation and age
1a   More adolescents than adults will self-evaluate as "Standard/urban ...".
1b   More adolescents than adults will self-evaluate as "Copenhagen/ young ...".
1c   More adults than adolescents will self-evaluate as "Zealand/boorish ...".

Hypothesis 2: linguistic self-evaluation and geographical affiliation
2a   More Næstved people than countryside people will self-evaluate as "Standard/urban ...".
2b   More Næstved people than countryside people will self-evaluate as "Copenhagen/young ...".
2c   More countryside people than Næstved people will self-evaluate as "Zealand/boorish ...".

The tape-recorded discussions following the self-evaluation experiment revealed that no-one in the group of *children* was able to recognize the Zealand voice, and only a few were able to recognize the Copenhagen voice. As for the Standard voice, the children did not know a name for that one either – as already mentioned it is rather commonly known as *rigsdansk* –but the great majority of them were certain that their own speech was like the Standard voice.

Figure 3 shows that the children were impressively consistent in sticking to the Standard-Copenhagen dimension of the triangle, i.e. acting in complete accordance with their not "knowing" the Zealand norm-ideal as relevant for (self-) identification in their speech community. As a consequence, the children's self-evaluations are not included in the analyses below. But before we leave them altogether, it should be mentioned that these children, aged 9–10, seemed not to have any experience with language variation, for example from being corrected,

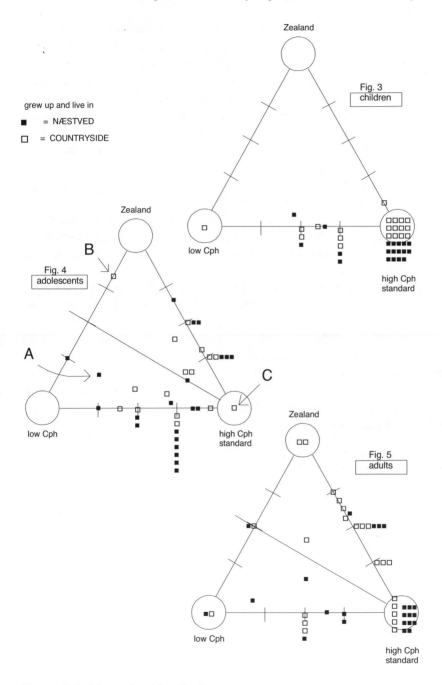

Figures 3–5. Linguistic self-evaluations

teased, and so on – at least not experiences that they were aware of and able to talk about. Attempts to discuss this with them proved completely fruitless.

In the group of *adolescents*, knowledge of the norm/variation complex was quite different. All three voices were easily recognized by all subjects, except for a very few who did not recognize the Zealand voice. Nor was it difficult to sustain talk with the adolescents on the topic; most of them had experiences and opinions to share. In other words, the preadolescents and adolescents of the Næstved area show a difference in sensibility to the linguistic variation and its social significance in their speech community which corresponds well with Labov's position on this issue (see Labov 1972; for further discussion of this issue and references, see Williams et al. 1999).

In the *adults* group, most subjects were able to name the three varieties correctly, but there was some uncertainty regarding the Copenhagen voice. Some adults perceived it as some kind of Zealand speech. At the same time, they had no doubts that the Zealand voice was very "Zealandish" indeed.

It is evident from a first glance at Figures 4 and 5 that there is a difference in how adolescents and adults self-evaluated in relation to the Standard pole. Only one of the adolescents identified completely with the Standard voice (3%), compared with 16 of the adults (35%) (cf. Table 1). The difference is highly significant, which means that Hypothesis 1a is not confirmed: adolescents are not more likely to identify with the Standard than adults. Actually it is the other way round: whereas a considerable number of adults indicate complete identification with the Standard voice, adolescents distance themselves more or less from the Standard pole.

Table 1. Self-evaluations by adolescents and adults (figures are percentages)

	STANDARD	direction COPENHAGEN	direction ZEALAND
ADOLESCENTS (n=37)	3	58	39
ADULTS (n=46)	35	25	39
	***	**	

*** p<.001   ** p<.01

If we make quantification possible by dividing the triangle into two (as has been done in Figures 4 and 5), and treat the Standard pole as the starting point in informants' self-evaluations, we can study differences in the data by comparing the numbers of adolescents and adults who "move" in the direction of the Copenhagen and Zealand poles, respectively. (The three informants on the dividing line, one adolescent and two adults, have been left out of the computations).

We then find, on the one hand, that more adolescents than adults move in the direction of the Copenhagen pole (Table 1) – a pattern which confirms our Hypothesis 1b about a Copenhagen norm-ideal playing a role in processes of social identifications involving age. On the other hand, Hypothesis 1c is not confirmed: there is no difference in the proportion of adolescents and adults who move in the Zealand direction (Table 1). This pattern must be taken to indicate that the traditional Zealand norm-ideal (as represented by the voice in this experiment) is so "old fashioned" and "distant" that it does not play any role in the construction of age categories in the Næstved speech community.[1]

As we move on to comparing the self-evaluations of the Næstved subjects with those of the countryside subjects, it becomes more difficult to spot directly from Figures 4 and 5 whether there are systematic differences or not. A quantification according to the same principles as before gives the results shown in Table 2.

Table 2. Self-evaluations by natives of Næstved and Countryside (figures are percentages)

	STANDARD	direction COPENHAGEN	direction ZEALAND
Adolescents			
NÆSTVED (n=21)		70	30
COUNTRYSIDE (n=16)		44	50
Adults			
NÆSTVED (n=23)	48	32	18
COUNTRYSIDE (n=23)	22	17	59
			**
Total			
NÆSTVED (n=44)	50		24
COUNTRYSIDE (n=39)	29		55
	*		**

** p<.01   * p<.05

If again we start by considering the Standard pole, a comparison is meaningful only within the group of adults (since only one adolescent has identified with the Standard): 48% Næstved adults versus 22% countryside adults identified with the Standard, which comes close to being a significant confirmation of our Hypothesis 2a (p=.06). At the same time Hypothesis 2b is confirmed: more Næstved people than countryside people moved in the Copenhagen direction, the difference being present in both age group samples, greatest in the sample of adolescents, and statistically significant in the total sample. As the other side of the coin, so to speak, Hypothesis 2c is also confirmed: in the total sample significantly more countryside subjects than Næstved subjects move in the Zealand direction. The difference is present in both age groups, but significantly so only with the adults.

Overall, the linguistic self-evaluation experiment was designed to test the conception that the Næstved speech community defines (or is defined by) a *three-pole normative field*. This would be taken to be the case if, and only if, different social groups produced significantly different self-evaluative patterns in reaction to what, from a dialectologist's point of view, were judged to be clear Copenhagen, Zealand and Standard readings of the same text. It turned out that social groupings according to *age* (adolescents/adults) self-categorize differently in the dimension defined by the Standard pole versus the Copenhagen pole. More adolescents than adults distance themselves from the Standard and move in the direction of Copenhagen. This "move" can be taken as a confirmation of the hypothesized youth-value attached to Copenhagen-accented speech. In addition, it can also be seen as an indication that Copenhagen-accented speech is increasingly being conceived of as the Standard language by young people, as I have argued on the basis of other metacommunicative data from the Næstved project (Kristiansen 2001, 2003).

Also, it turned out that social groupings according to *geographical affiliation* (Næstved/countryside) self-categorize differently in the dimension defined by the local (Zealand) pole versus the non-local (Standard and Copenhagen) poles. On the one hand, countryside people move in larger numbers than Næstved people in the Zealand direction, and more so among adults than among adolescents. This indicates that the traditional Zealand norm-ideal, while still playing a role among the adults in processes of social identification as either a "town person" or a "countryside person", may be losing its significance in such processes among the adolescents.[2] On the other hand, Næstved people identify in larger numbers than countryside people with the Standard and "move" in larger numbers in the direction of Copenhagen, thus indicating that both Standard and Copenhagen speech are conceived of and evaluated as "urban". But while it is Standard speech which (still?) plays the predominant part in the construction of the "urban/rural" opposition among adults, Copenhagen speech obviously plays a more important role in the construction of this opposition among adolescents.

This leads to the conclusion that it is indeed appropriate to conceive of the Næstved speech community as a three-pole normative field, which the natives of the area relate to (or operate within) in processes of social identification, at least when categories of age and urban/rural belonging are at stake.

4.   Norm-ideals and the discursive construction of selves

If the actual status of norm-ideals – their existence and the social meanings they involve – has to be established at the level of social groups, we need to focus on the individual if we want to appreciate how the norm-ideals function in the construction of selves, or (expressed the other way round) how the construction of selves is achieved in relation to norm-ideals.

In asking questions about how individuals relate to the norm-ideals they "know" in their speech community, and how these enter into the group-/identity formation processes going on in the individual's mind, we shift from a quantitative analysis to a qualitative approach, which forces us to pick out only a few informants for analyses. But who should we pick? An obvious possibility is to use the patterns of self-evaluation in Figures 4 and 5 as a guide to the most interesting cases. Of course, a case can be interesting because it is typical or because it is atypical. I have chosen here to look at the three most atypical males in the group of adolescents, i.e. the three young men who have self-evaluated as most Copenhagen, Zealand and Standard, respectively. They are identified as informants A, B and C in Figure 4.

The analyses are based on two types of information – firstly, relevant *information from their life stories* as told by the informants themselves in tape-recorded individual interviews, secondly, *what they say about language* in one way or another, either in the individual interview, or in the tape-recorded group discussion which followed the self-evaluation test, or in a questionnaire filled in at the end of the group discussion. All of this data was collected in 1986.

4.1. Informant C

Let us again start in the Standard corner of the triangle with informant C, a countryside informant, who at the time of the interview was aged 17 and in training to becoming a mechanic.

C is the only adolescent who has evaluated his own speech as being identical with the Standard voice. The analysis of his actual, tape-recorded speech reveals this evaluation to be fairly precise in the Standard-Copenhagen dimension. Referring to the variables in Figure 2, his speech can be characterized as showing no Copenhagen vowel qualities, and only 17% vowel lengthening. C's self-report is less precise in the Standard-Zealand dimension. In contrast to the Standard norm, his *stød* do often show the more vigorous Zealand realization, and he also has a few instances of non-Standard *stød* assignment in the word *nu* and in the second part of composita.

Over-reporting, i.e. reporting one's own language to be more standard than it actually is, is often interpreted as an indication of linguistic insecurity, and is commonly seen as an attempt at securing a more positive self-image, at strengthening one's social position, etc. (Labov 1972; Trudgill 1972). In the case of C, it may seem natural to follow this line of reasoning, the more so because C gives a general impression of subscribing to the "everyone is the architect of his/her own fortune" ideology. When he tells about his father, C presents him as a self-made man and an example to be followed. He has travelled as a salesman and mender in various service jobs for many years, has followed evening classes and improved his qualifications, and is now travelling for a firm in Copenhagen, *så det kører da meget godt for ham* 'so he has got it going for him'. At the time of the interview, C was in training as a mechanic and wanted to continue his training to become an electro-mechanic like his father, *for der er ikke så mange penge i at være mekaniker* 'because there is no big money in being a mechanic' and then leave for Copenhagen, where he thinks there are more opportunities for getting into the electro-mechanic trade and for earning money. To begin with, however, he has to find a place as a mechanic apprentice, which is not so easy, but C thinks that *man skal bare gide, man skal bare gøre en indsats selv også, så kan man sagtens* 'you just have to go for it, you have to work for it yourself, then it's easily done'.

Generally speaking, C presents himself as a young man who is on his way up in society, who knows the recipe to get there: leave for Copenhagen, improve your education, earn more money, make an effort! To the extent that "talk like a school teacher or a media news-reader" seems a natural continuation of this list, C's reporting his own speech as identical with the Standard can be seen as a natural part of the general self-presentation he produces in his meeting with a linguist from Copenhagen University.

However, in spite of his "individual social climber" ideology, we cannot interpret C's self-evaluation as a clear case of over-reporting. The tape-recorded discussion reveals that the line between Standard and Zealand in the triangle does not represent a linguistic continuum to his mind. Informants in the group of adolescents took part in the self-evaluation experiment in smaller groups of three to four persons. C was in the only one of these smaller groups of adolescents which was not able to determine voice number 2 (the Zealand voice).

They identified the Copenhagen voice correctly without hesitation (C was the first to say it), but they apparently had no notion of the traditional Zealand dialect. They proposed several other Danish provinces for the Zealand voice. C was the first to propose Lolland (an island to the south of Zealand), and he states that *Jylland er i hvert fald med* 'in any case, Jutland isn't it' (Jutland is far away, the western part of Denmark). He also says: *toeren ved jeg sgu ikke ja det er i hvert fald ikke dansk* 'number two I bloody don't know anyway it's not Danish'.

This shows that C does not distinguish between the Standard and his own way of speaking with a "mild" Zealand accent. It is just "Danish", in opposition to the Copenhagen dialect (which he recognizes) and the other dialects (which he evidently is rather unfamiliar with). Consequently, C says about the Standard voice that *det var ja sådan ligesom vi snakker her sådan* 'it was you know like we talk here you know'. And he sticks to *Næstved* when someone else in the group proposes *pænt sjællandsk sådan lidt op ad Ringsted* 'nice Zealandish something like around Ringsted' (Ringsted is a town between Næstved and Copenhagen).

Examples indicating a low linguistic awareness in C could be multiplied. However, the point here is clear enough. The traditional "broad" Zealand dialect is beyond his notion of possible language use in the Næstved area. And he has not developed any awareness that his own speech and "like we talk here" is not accepted everywhere and by everybody as *rigsdansk* 'Standard', or just *dansk* 'Danish', as he calls it. Neither does he seem to have developed any awareness of linguistic variation in the Næstved area, in spite of having lived in several places in the area while growing up (his parents divorced when he was 5 years old and he lived intermittently with both his father and mother). He answers negatively to questions about having felt ridiculed or having been teased because of his way of speaking.

Hence, if we consider C's self-evaluation on the basis of what *he* "knows" about his speech community and not on the basis of what linguists know, his identification with the Standard voice cannot be seen as a case of over-reporting in relation to the Zealand pole of reference (as an indication of linguistic insecurity, of social upwards striving, or whatever). It is not an act of dissociation from "Zealandishness" in any sense, since to his mind there is no distiction between "Zealandishness" and "Danishness". (This is a bit surprising, however, since he relates that both his parents grew up on farms in the area. So, unless he has had no contact with his grandparents, which is not evident from the interview, we might have expected him to say what some other adolescents said about the Zealand voice, "she talks like my grandmother".)

Also in relation to the Copenhagen voice – which he recognizes – C's sticking with the Standard might actually be seen as nothing more than an accurate evaluation of his own speech (and this time accurate also in relation to objective linguistic description). However, in view of his generally low linguistic awareness and strong individual climber ideology captured by the tape-recordings, C's locating himself at the opposite end of the scale may just as well be seen as an act of dissociation from the traditional representation and evaluation of the Copenhagen dialect as low status, working class language.

4.2. Informant A

The male adolescent who put his own speech closest to the Copenhagen corner of the triangle grew up in Næstved. He was 21 at the time of data collection and attended *enkeltfags-hf* (a general upper secondary education programme offering courses on a single-subject basis).

As can be seen in Figure 4, informant A has evaluated himself very much as Copenhagen-like, with some Zealand flavour added. The analysis of his speech shows this to be a very good evaluation. Referring to the variables in Figure 2, the tape-recorded interview with A shows the following percentages of Copenhagen variants: vowel lengthening 55%, short (a) 25%, (aj) 93%, short (å) 58%, (øj) 100%, (ræ) 93%. His *stød* never show the distinct Zealand realisation, but he does produce a couple of *stød* in the word *nu*, and also a few instances of *stød* in short vowels and in the second part of composita.

Like C, A is a child of divorced parents, but his years of growth were much more stormy. The parents divorced when he was 6 and he did not know his father for the following 12 years. His mother had been without work and on permanent relief for many years. She had been married five times and ... *rendte med en hel masse andre fyre ind imellem* 'ran away with a lot of other guys in between' who did not treat her too well *det var sgu lige før næsten lige før at det var en hverdagsbegivenhed altså at min mor fik klø ikke også* 'it was nearly every fucking it happened almost every day that my mother got beaten you know'. So A was taken away and put in a residential centre for young people when he was 14. At the time the data was gathered he was very active in a political youth organization on the far left wing:

den opfattelse jeg har i dag jeg har sgu ikke fået den gennem teoretiske studier eller noget vel, jeg har fået den primært gennem at opleve min mor som en udstødt ikke også og som en som ikke kunne klare sig, jeg er ikke jeg vil aldrig nogensinde give min mor skylden for det hun har gjort ved mig vel overhovedet ikke, tværtimod vil jeg give Formynderiet og systemet skylden ikke også, og så har jeg været ude og sejle i Afrika og Syd-Amerika og der har jeg sgu set elendighed nok og der er jeg jeg internationalist altså helt sikkert! 'the views I've got today I haven't bloody got them through theoretical studies or anything you know, I've got them mostly by seeing my mother as an outcast you know and as someone who couldn't cope, I am not I will never ever blame my mother for what she has done to me you know never, on the contrary I blame the caring arrangements and the system you know, and I've been out sailing in Africa and South-America and there I've seen enough bloody misery and there I'm an internationalist yeah no question!'

He also reports having served three years as an apprentice at an engine works in the countryside – *hos en forfærdelig mester* 'under a terrible boss'. In general, it seems to be an important trait that he has emerged from his formative years with strong attitudes towards the society around him, and quite different attitudes from those we found with C.

He has no personal ambitions beyond the solidarity with the weak, the oppressed and *den almindelige danske arbejder* 'the ordinary Danish worker': *jeg vil sgu ikke blive til noget altså jeg vil bare have det godt med mig selv og dem jeg kan lide det er sådan de krav jeg stiller så jeg har ikke nogen ide om hvad jeg vil være* 'I don't bloody want to become someone you know I just want to feel happy with myself and the people I like that's all I demand so I don't have any ideas about what to become'. He feels attached to Næstved *fordi det er nok den værste by jeg har hørt om at lave politisk arbejde i af de større byer i Danmark fordi det er virkelig en bondeby* 'because it's about the worst town I've heard about for political agitation among the greater towns in Denmark because it's really a peasants' town'. He repeatedly expresses negative attitudes towards peasants, the Zealand dialect and regional dialects in general. In general, A must be characterized as linguistically far more aware than C. His self-evaluation as Copenhagen-like with some Zealand flavour added is very accurate. He has no problems determining the voices in the experiment, is fully aware that language use varies, and is able to give examples of Zealand dialect (both from lexicon and prosody). As to attitudes, he expresses positivity towards the Copenhagen dialect and negativity towards the Standard and Zealand dialects. From his life-story we learn that he holds strong negative feelings against peasants, bosses and capitalists; solidarity with the working class is very central to him. In the case of A, then, it seems that both his way of speaking and his self-evaluation follow strightforwardly from his representations, attitudes and values in the domains of both language and society.

4.3. Informant B

Finally we can consider B, who has self-evaluated as very Zealand-like. He grew up in the countryside. When the data were collected he was 20 years-old and, like informant A, attended *enkeltfags-hf.*

If indeed B is the most Zealand-sounding of the three informants under study, this is mainly due to the fact that the traditional Zealand intonation is clearly present in his speech in quite a different way from A and C. In addition, many of his *stød* realizations are clearly of the Zealand type, and 50% of his vowels in syllables without *stød* are lengthened (which may be seen both as a Zealand and a Copenhagen feature). He shows Zealand *stød* assignment in *nu*, but no instances of this either in short vowels or in the second part of composita.

As to the "Standard-Copenhagen" variation, B's speech is largely dominated by the Standard variants for the vowel variables listed in Figure 2. More interesting in his case, however, is the fact that he produces quite a few very conservative, 'close to written form', Standard pronunciations. In several instances he gives a long vowel followed by [v] in words which are usually pronounced with a short vowel followed by an offglide [u] *liv* 'life', *greve* 'earl', *lave* 'make', *blive* 'become'. He even does this in the word *have* 'have', the Standard pronunciation of which is /ha'/ (where ' represents *stød*). Furthermore, B shows a high frequency of pronounced *-e* (schwa) before a pause. As a fairly general rule these are either assimilated (after voiced consonants, as in *drenge* 'boys', where *-ng-* represents a velar nasal) or dropped (after unvoiced consonants, as in *næste* 'next'). In the interview, B shows 85% schwa-pronunciation in both contexts. (For the sake of comparison, the figures for informant A are: 0% after voiced and 10% after unvoiced, and for informant C: 0% after voiced and 100% after unvoiced). Finally, B uses the "long forms" *moder* and *fader* several times when talking about his mother and father; these are relatively frequent in writing but practically never heard in modern Danish speech, which has pronunciations corresponding to the written short forms *mor* and *far*.

All in all, B's locating himself far up in the Zealand corner is quite inaccurate from a descriptive linguistic point of view. But as an "act of identity" it becomes an understandable, almost logical, response when we listen to what he has to tell about his life and experiences with language. In opposition to A and C, informant B gives us a good example of a stable, ingrained childhood and adolescence. He has really grown up in a close network, in a small village a few kilometres outside of Næstved, where the family has lived for generations. He has five brothers and sisters. As he says: *der er ligesom meget familie der bor rundt omkring os* 'there's kind of a lot of family that live around us'. His father, his mother, his uncle and his brother are the only workers at a small factory in a near-by village. The factory is owned, however, by *en mand i København* 'a man in Copenhagen'. In such an environment, people maintain their way of speaking, or as B says: *det gør man jo vel egentlig ubevidst gør man ikke, når man er i de der små miljøer, både her på Sjælland og i Jylland ikke også, taler man det sprog fordi familien og vennerne taler det ikke også* 'I suppose you do so unconsciously don't you, when you are in those kinds of close environments, both here on Zealand and in Jutland you know, you talk that language because the family and the friends talk it you know'.

However, he reports that the village idyll was broken: *ude hvor jeg bor kan man dele dem op i to grupper* 'out there where I live you can divide them into two groups'. There is the original, indigenous population, and then all the new-comers:

> *altså de der der har store stillinger og sådan noget de kom ud på landet der i 60'erne og 70'erne, så da jeg begyndte at gå i skole da var det ... vi var kun to altså min tvillingesøster og så mig ovre fra den gamle del og de resterende det var fra de der tilflytterkvarterer, så jeg tror helt givet at jeg nok har haft en mar-kant dialekt fordi jeg blev passet af min farmor – hun boede lige ved siden af jo – den halve dag jo så jeg tror helt givet at jeg har haft den* 'you know those who had those big positions and things they came out in the countryside in the sixties and seventies, so when I started to go to school then it was ... we were only two you know, my twin sister and myself from the old part and the rest that was from those newcomer areas, so I'm quite sure I had that marked dialect because I was taken care of by my grandmother – she lived next door you know – half of the day you know so I'm quite sure I must have had it'.

So B has no problems recognizing the Zealand voice: *det lyder lige som min farmor hun snakkede* 'it sounds like my grandmother like how she talked'. He thinks it's something of the same when his parents talk. And he is very cons-cious that he has dialect features in his own speech and is good at characterizing the dialect: *vi trækker ligesom ordene ud ikke også, det kan jeg også være slem til en gang imellem, at trække de der ord ud* 'we kind of draw out the words you know, I can be given to that myself from time to time, drawing those words out'.

If he is so aware of the dialect "colour" of his language, the reason is of course that others have been busy pointing out to him that his language is differ-ent. *Ja mon ikke* 'Yeah, you bet!' is his spontaneous answer when asked whether he has ever experienced teasing. At the time of participating in the study, he had a summer job in Copenhagen, where he often heard sarcastic comments. However, he does not think that this has made him try to change his language. On the contrary:

> *hvis de ikke synes jeg er god nok så kan det også gøre lige meget fordi jeg ændrer ikke mit sprog, hvis de siger at jeg skal sige* ånsdag *at jeg ikke må sige* o'onsdag *ikke også, men ved du det de får sgu fingeren du fordi at så siger man bare* oo'oonsdag *i steden for simpelthen du og slår i bordet du, ja men det kan du tro fordi mit sprog det er lige så meget berettiget som københavnsk eller der oppe på den anden side af Ringsted ikke også* 'if they don't think I'm good enough I

don't care because I don't change my language, if they say that I shall say *ånsdag* "Wednesday" that I may not say *o'onsdag* you know, do you know what I bloody give them the finger you know because then you just say *oo'oonsdag* instead definitely you know and thump the table, believe me because my language is just as justified as the language in Copenhagen or up there on the other side of Ringsted you know'.

Clearly his position is that teasing and sarcastic comments only lead to more use of dialect features, *i protest* 'in protest' as he puts it. In the questionnaire he states that his pronunciation has changed to become more Zealandish, in accordance with his own wishes.

This is in contradiction, however, to his own assumption that he must have started school with a language something like his grandmother's. And also of his own wording that: *der har været en påvirkning i skolen, en rettelse i sproget i løbet af skolegangen* 'there has been an influence in school, a correction of the language during the years of schooling'. He does not remember his pronunciation being plainly corrected in school, but he remembers being told to *tale tydeligt og klart og sådan nogle ting* 'speak distinctly and clearly and that sort of thing'. Elsewhere he reports, however, that it is a marked feature of the dialect that *vi skærer ordene af og forkorter ordet* 'we cut off the words and shorten the word', and that he was told, *også i skolen i hvert fald at endelserne ryger lige ud til siden* 'also in school you bet that the endings vanish into the blue'.

To conclude, then, B seems to provide us with a clear case of linguistic insecurity. His flaunting of solidarity with his background and local dialect – with all dialects in protest against Copenhagerners and their putting on airs – remains unconvincing in the light of his own language usage and the many contradictions in what he says about language. As mentioned earlier, insecure language users are normally supposed to be over-reporters in self-evaluation tests; they evaluate their own speech to be more like society's standard norm than it is in reality. Within such a model we would have to say that B under-reports; he presents his own language as less standard than it is in reality. Under-reporting is taken as an indication that non-standard ways of speaking can also be prestigious. They have so-called covert prestige. In the case of B, the prestige of the Zealand dialect is overt enough. But we do not really believe him when he tells us that he has changed his language to be more Zealandish – and has wanted to do so. His ideology and his under-reporting is more plausibly seen as a kind of defence in the interview situation, a consequence of his "knowledge" that he does not speak as Standard-like as he would wish to, if only he could. If B's self-evaluation is a clear misrepresentation from a purely linguistic point of view, it is at the same time and no less clearly a product of the processes through which

B creates his social identity, as a member of the Næstved area speech community in general and in his meeting with a dialectologist in particular.

5. Consciousness and salience

I focused above on the actual status (existence and social meanings) of three norm-ideals in the Næstved speech community, investigated at the level of social groups in patterns of metacommunicative data from a linguistic self-evaluation experiment. Then I considered the role of these norm-ideals in self-construction, studied in discourse data from individual adolescents. On the *theoretical* assumption that our "social identity instinct" is the critical factor underlying language variation and change, it is in the nature of things that the study of these phenomena must include an interest in the perceptions and evaluations which (re)create the "life" of language. However, recognizing socio-psychological processes as the "driving force" does not necessarily mean collecting and analyzing metacommunicative data. As a matter of fact many sociolinguists abstain from including metacommunicative data in their studies and only infer socio-psychological interpretations from patterns of usage. Reasons for this are rarely given, but some would argue that metacommunicative data are encumbered with methodological problems of validity and reliability which are too serious for these data to be of much interest (e.g. Milroy 1987a: 141, 1987b: 107). From this standpoint it might be argued that "In fact, statistical counts of variants actually used are probably the best way of assessing attitudes" (Milroy and Milroy 1985: 19). Since a social identity approach to language variation and change takes for granted that patterns of usage reflect (manifest, express) perceptions and values, it seems to go without saying that a way of assessing people's attitudes towards language is to count the variants they use. However, unless we are to be caught in circular reasoning I think we need to approach what Labov has called "the evaluation problem" by producing independent evidence to supplement our counts of variants actually used. As Labov puts it: "The *evaluation* problem is to find the subjective (or latent) correlates of the objective (or manifest) changes which have been observed" (Labov 1972: 162).

Validity and reliability problems certainly do arise with metacommunicative data. It is a well-established fact in sociolinguistics that we do not necessarily learn the truth about either language usage or attitudes by asking people to tell us how they speak and what they think about various ways of speaking. In fact, to the extent that Chambers is right in claiming that our social identity instinct operates "largely beneath consciousness", we should not expect consciously given comments to reveal anyone's "true linguistic self". A discussion of consciousness is clearly pertinent here. What does it mean for something to be beneath consciousness? As a first step, we need to distinguish between the subconscious and the unconscious. Distinctions which we are unconscious of do not play a part in our negotiations of social identity; we can only relate, affectively and behaviourly, to distinctions we perceive cognitively, to categories we know. This "knowing something", and thereby the possibility or necessity of relating to it, can be conscious – or subconscious. In this sense, I think we may accept the view that our creation and recreation of sociolinguistic differences, as part of our engagement in social identity processes, is something that goes on largely beneath consciousness, i.e. *sub*consciously.

But at the same time we should keep in mind that distinctions, including sociolinguistic differences, may well be subconsciously present to our minds in some situations, and consciously present in others. The salience of distinctions to our minds, and thereby our awareness of them, is not constant. In general social psychological terms, Hogg and Abrams (1988: 24) argue that "since social self-identifications are essentially social self-categorizations, it is not difficult to generate a *principle* governing their salience. Within any given social frame of reference that social categorization will become salient which best 'fits' ... the relevant information available to the individual". They go on to conclude that "there is a dialectical relationship between cognitive processes and motivations or goals. There is a dynamic negotiation of self-conceptualization" (ibid: 25). In the same vein it can be argued that the salience of language differences in negotiations of social identification will vary according to the social context (Giles and Coupland 1991). It is part of this picture that some sociolinguistic differences may become salient more easily than others, and more easily to some people than to others (for discussions of linguistic awareness and salience cf. Preston 1996, this volume; Auer et al. 1998).

No doubt, then, linguistic salience/consciousness is complex and indicative of the seriousness of the methodological problems potentially connected with metacommunicative data. To be sure, as Dennis Preston has repeatedly stressed, "folk" comments on language will always, whatever they are, be of value and interest from some sociolinguistic point of view. However, if we are out "to find the subjective (or latent) correlates of the objective (or manifest) changes which have been observed" – from the point of view that these subjective correlates, as integrated parts of identity formation processes, are the sine qua non of linguistic variation and change – then our main interest will be in tracing and picturing the attitudinal pattern which, in a given speech community at a given time, is responsible for reproducing/changing the usage pattern. Thus, from a variationist's perspective, representations and values which have consequences in terms of language usage are the "real" ones, the ones we should be looking for. The various methods used in the Næstved project show that people vary quite considerably in their attitudinal reactions, depending on whether language was salient or non-salient in the evaluative situation, i.e. on the difference of awareness involved. Comparisons of conscious and subconscious evaluative patterns with usage indicate a clear difference in the impact of these patterns on variation and change. In particular among adolescents, the conscious (overt) language attitudes are contradicted by the subconscious (covert) attitudes. So in the sense that they accord with the changes in language usage and, arguably, can be seen as governing these changes, I take the subconsciously displayed attitudes to be the more "real" ones (Kristiansen 1997).

Then, what about the value of the data obtained in situations where informants were encouraged to make comments by a researcher, as in the two approaches I have dealt with in this chapter? It is obvious that both in the interview situation and in the self-evaluation situation language was salient – and that overt attitudes and stereotypes were part of the game. I do not think, however, that this in itself make the resulting data worthless within a study of language variation and change. I have tried in this chapter to treat two kinds of consciously given comments from a discursive perspective (as advocated by Giles and Coupland 1991: 53). Not only what people say in an interview, but also what they do in an experimental task (like marking off one's own speech style schematically in a triangle) can be interpreted as constructive self-presentations within a social psychological framework. Analyzed in this perspective the informants' consciously given comments do shed valuable light on the "real" attitudinal situation in the Næstved speech community. More generally, analyses of tensions and contrasts between conscious and subconscious evaluations, in individuals as well as in social groups, do shed valuable light on the hotbed of language variation and change. So instead of refraining from confronting the "evaluation problem", we need to invest more energy in improving our methods of gathering and analyzing many kinds of metacommunicative data.

Notes

1.   Of course, the self-evaluation data in Figures 4 and 5 can be made the object of quantitative analyses in many ways. If we not only count the subjects who move in the Zealand direction, but also treat the sides of the triangle as scales (as they were in fact presented to subjects in the experiment, cf. Figures 3–5) and also consider *how far* they move, we find that the adults on average do locate themselves

190   *Tore Kristiansen*

closer to the Zealand pole than do the adolescents. So in that sense Hypothesis
1c is confirmed (p<.01, one-tailed Kruskal-Wallis). However, the interpretation
of this difference is complicated by the fact that the same picture appears also in
the Copenhagen direction. Here we expected, and found, more adolescents than
adults to be attracted by the Copenhagen pole, but at the same time it turns out
that those adults who do move in that direction do so more decidedly than do the
adolescents (p<.05, two-tailed Kruskal-Wallis). Clues to the best interpretation of
this difference in "step length" between adolescents and adults may possibly be
tracked in analyses of other data from the interviews. In the analysis here I shall
have to take the mere fact of "stepping away" from the Standard as the critical fact
and disregard the length of the step.

2.   It is possible that another, new Zealand norm-ideal exists or is in the process of
being born. A focusing process may be defining a set of language variants – probably a certain combination of mostly Copenhagen variants with a few Zealand
variants – which are used and positively valuated by adolescents from Næstved
town in particular. The data from the self-evaluation experiment do not inform us
about whether this is the case or not, but the question as such is being studied by
other means within the framework of the Næstved project (and is touched upon in
Kristiansen 1997, 1998).

References

Auer, Peter, Birgit Barden and Beate Grosskopf
    1998   Subjective and objective parameters determining "salience" in long-term
            dialect accommodation. *Journal of Sociolinguistics* 2, 163–187.
Brink, Lars and Jørn Lund
    1975   *Dansk Rigsmål 1–2. Lydudviklingen siden 1840 med særligt henblik på
            sociolekterne i København.* Copenhagen: Gyldendal.
Chambers, J. K.
    1995   *Sociolinguistic Theory. Linguistic Variation and its Social Significance.*
            Oxford: Blackwell.
Ejskjær, Inger
    1970   *Fonemsystemet i Østsjællandsk på grundlag af dialekten i Strøby sogn.* Co-
            penhagen: Akademisk Forlag.
Giles, Howard and Nikolas Coupland
    1991   *Language: Contexts and Consequences.* Milton Keynes: Open University
            Press.
Gregersen, Frans and Inge Lise Pedersen (eds.)
    1991   *The Copenhagen Study in Urban Sociolinguistics 1 –2 .* Copenhagen: C.A.
            Reitzels Forlag.

Hogg, Michael A. and Dominic Abrams
  1988   *Social Identifications: A Social Psychology of Intergroup Relations and Group Processes.* London: Routledge.
Jørgensen, J. Normann and Kjeld Kristensen
  1994   *Moderne sjællandsk. En undersøgelse af unge sjællænderes talesprog.* Copenhagen: C. A. Reitzels Forlag.
Kristensen, Kjeld
  2003   Standard Danish, Copenhagen sociolects, and regional varieties in the 1900s. *International Journal of the Sociology of Language* 159, 29–43.
Kristiansen, Tore
  1997   Language attitudes in a Danish cinema. In Coupland, Nikolas and Adam Jaworski (eds.), *Sociolinguistics: A Reader and Coursebook.* London: Macmillan, 291–305.
  1998   The role of standard ideology in the disappearance of the traditional Danish dialects. *Folia Linguistica* 32, 115–129.
  2001   Two Standards: One for the media and one for the school. *Language Awareness* 10, 9–24.
  2003   The youth and the gatekeepers: Reproduction and change in language norm and variation. In Androutsopoulos, Jannis K. and Alexandra Georgakopoulou (eds.), *Discourse Constructions of Youth Identities.* Amsterdam: John Benjamins, 279– 302.
Kristiansen, Tore and Howard Giles
  1992   Compliance-gaining as a function of accent: Public requests in varieties of Danish. *International Journal of Applied Linguistics* 2, 17–35.
Labov, William
  1963   The social motivation of a sound change. *Word* 19, 273–309.
  1972   *Sociolinguistic Patterns.* Oxford: Blackwell.
  1984   Field methods of the Project on Linguistic Change and Variation. In Baugh, John and Joel Scherzer (eds.), *Language in Use.* Englewood Cliffs, NJ: Prentice Hall, 28–53.
Milroy, Lesley
  1987a   *Language and Social Networks.* 2nd edition. Oxford: Blackwell.
  1987b   *Observing and Analysing Natural Language.* Oxford: Blackwell.
Milroy, Lesley and James Milroy
  1985   *Authority in Language: Investigating Language Prescription and Standardisation.* 2nd edition. London: Routledge.
Pedersen, Inge Lise
  2003   Traditional dialects of Danish and the de-dialectalization 1900–2000. *International Journal of the Sociology of Language* 159, 9–28.
Preston, Dennis R.
  1996   Whaddayaknow? The modes of folk linguistic awareness. *Language Awareness* 5, 40–74.

Trudgill, Peter
    1972   Sex, covert prestige and linguistic change in the urban British English of Norwich. *Language in Society* 1, 179–195.

Williams, Angie, Peter Garrett and Nikolas Coupland
    1999   Dialect recognition. In Preston, Dennis R. (ed.), *Handbook of Perceptual Dialectology*. Amsterdam: John Benjamins, 345–358.

Wolfram, Walt and Ralph W. Fashold
    1997   Field methods in the study of social dialects. In Coupland, Nikolas and Adam Jaworski (eds.), *Sociolinguistics. A Reader and Coursebook*. London: Macmillan, 89–115. [First published 1974.]

Adolescents' lexical repertoires of peer evaluation: *Boring prats* and *English snobs*[1]

Peter Garrett, Nikolas Coupland and Angie Williams

1. Introduction

1.1. Language and adolescent development

Young adults in their early to mid-teen years are an important age group in language attitudes research. In the Welsh context, for example, there are repeated findings that there is a critical period of decline in the supportive attitudes towards the Welsh language in this age group (e.g. Sharp et al. 1973; Baker 1992). It is frequently emphasised that this is a period of rapid change and development, with physical changes occurring alongside changes in self-concept, and a move away from family identity towards peer-group identity (Baker 1992).

Entry into secondary school (age 11 in the UK) leads to some abrupt and major transformations in peer relationships. Youngsters come into direct contact with a much larger population of peers, on account of both school size and the move away from the self-contained classrooms of primary school to the daily routine of moving from class to class for different subject lessons. Moreover, adults' overseeing of peer relationships diminishes, and youngsters negotiate this new and radically enlarged peer terrain relatively independently. Research has shown that more time is spent with other members of peer groups as children move into their early teens, and less time is spent with the family. As they progress through the teenage years, they are actively engaged in "progressive identity formation" (Waterman 1982), and peer groups become increasingly important as a "vehicle for social comparison" (Heaven 1994: 95), providing a niche for identity exploration, functioning as a source of companionship and social support and protecting them from adult authority (p. 79). The price of group membership is peer pressure to experiment with new roles and behaviour, a process that is implicit in identity formation (Newman and Newman 1988).

From the point of view of language, Bradford Brown, Mory and Kinney (1994) maintain that teenagers' images of identities available to them are formed and refined not simply through observation of peer groups, but also through evaluative conversations about them with their friends. Hence evaluative language and in particular the lexical typologies of these teenagers are an important part of this process of establishing identities. In addition, Rampton (1995) has demonstrated how teenagers experiment through language with these alternative identities that are available to them. His work focuses specifically on stylistic "crossing", in which for example young people of Asian descent might use stylised Asian voices to suggest they are less competent in spoken English than they in fact are. Language is shown to provide a means through which teenagers try out various identities to see how others react, and how these identities impact on their social relations with others.

Teenagers' metalinguistic awareness is important for a theory of human cultural development: that is, "knowing" cultural alternatives, exploring them evaluatively, on the way to (re)defining themselves. Such cultural alternatives are, partly, established sociolinguistically. Belonging to (or being perceived to belong to) a particular group of peers at school, or aligning oneself with a regional community, or projecting a professional identity, etc. relates partly to a way of talking, and partly perhaps to a thought style and set of attitudes that goes with it, or is implied by it. Hence evaluation of language variation has several potential functions. For example, it is where we are able to engage with a range of cultural identities and try them out (illustrated in Rampton's work), to help clarify the alternative identities that are available in the social system (perhaps accessed through interpersonal contact or the media), to boost the identity or identities one currently adopts and/or to establish the difficulty or ease with which one might switch to another. So, evaluating the identities of others is part of evaluating oneself. In addition, comment about language variation is where social evaluations are made, for example, among peers, as illustrated in the work reviewed by Bradford Brown et al. (1994). This latter function of metalanguage is the main focus of this chapter. And, insofar as evaluating oneself and one's peers contributes to a sense of individuality and sociality, it is part of the functioning of language *for* society (see Coupland and Jaworski, this volume).

1.2. Adolescents in language attitudes research

Perhaps paradoxically, while the somewhat fluid and experimental nature of adolescent evaluations is acknowledged, or indeed emphasised, in some language attitudes surveys (Baker 1992), other developmental language attitudes research has concluded that adolescents have developed relatively stable "adult-like" attitudes, and that children have gained an awareness of the social significance of language by the age of 10 or 11 (Day 1982). However, much of the work regarding the attitudinal development in such young people is concerned with the evaluative distinctions made between the prestige variety in the judge's own context and the judge's own non-standard variety (or some other variety which they are able to place in a broad undifferentiated "non-standard" category). This is only a first step towards an awareness of the differentiated social meanings of a whole range of non-standard varieties (consider the children and adolescent groups in Kristiansen, this volume). It is this latter degree of awareness that facilitates the experimentation, changes and re-orientations that Baker and Rampton (in different ways) point to in language behaviour during the mid-teens, and which is the basis of our own research in Wales.

Adolescent and pre-adolescent judges have frequently been employed in studies that have used the matched-guise technique (Lambert et al. 1960). The pre-adolescent judges in the studies by Price, Fluck and Giles (1983) were around 10 to 12. Giles (1970) and Paltridge and Giles (1983) each included one group around 12 years old. Some studies have used groups of teenagers including those in their mid-late teens, e.g. the 16 to 18 year-olds in Giles, Baker and Fielding (1976). For the most part, such studies have involved teenagers in evaluating adult speakers rather than teenagers. The study we report here involved mid-teenagers evaluating other mid-teenagers.

1.3. Semantic differential scales

Typically, matched-guise studies ask judges to listen to recordings of a series of apparently different people, when in fact they are listening to the speech of one person performing a range of language varieties or "guises". Again typically, judges then rate each speaker on a number of bipolar adjective (semantic differential) scales (e.g. sincere/insincere, rich/poor). The scale ratings are then factor-analysed in order to identify the broader evaluative dimensions that the judges are operating with. These dimensions are now generally considered to be well established in language attitudes research. Zahn and Hopper (1985) pooled scale adjectives from a large number of speech evaluation studies, and through factor analysis in a single study, involving nearly 600 judges, found that each of scales loaded into one of three differentiated factors, which they labelled "superiority" (e.g. educated / uneducated, rich / poor), "attractiveness" (e.g. friendly / unfriendly, honest / dishonest) and "dynamism" (e.g. energetic / lazy, enthusiastic / hesitant).

This well-documented pattern of evaluative dimensions has meant that many attitudes studies in language and communication have taken their scales from those used in previous studies. One disadvantage of this, however, is that some circularity may be induced, whereby the well-documented dimensions simply become better-documented, and so may be thought to be exhaustive, while others remain out of view. In our own earlier work on attitudes towards Welsh English dialects we found that "Welshness" did not correlate with any of the other scales, and so pointed to a quite distinct dimension, absent from previous summaries of dimensions such as Zahn and Hopper's (Garrett et al. 2003).

In other studies, researchers have felt it valuable to supplement scales from previous studies with scales from their own preliminary work with comparable judges (e.g. Nesdale and Rooney 1996). And in others, researchers have based all of their scales on those gathered in open-ended preliminary work (e.g. Price et al. 1983). From the pools of items gathered in this way, a number are selected for the main study. The intention is that this will ensure that the evaluative scales adopted are those which are evaluatively meaningful to the judges themselves rather than those merely considered appropriate by the experimenters.

The pools of items and the process of transforming them into the final set of scale labels are not detailed in such studies (beyond stating usually that selection is based on the most frequently occurring items in the pool). Our own experience, though, suggests that this is not necessarily a straightforward process, at least when working with young teenagers. The items finally arrived at (where reported) in such studies resemble something more akin to "tidied up" adult versions of the sorts of items that we ourselves have collected from teenagers. If this is how such items are arrived at, there is a risk of designing out the evaluations made within teenage culture and of eliciting relatively "overt" values, in line with the idea that teenagers of this age have developed "adult-like" attitudes.

Our argument in this chapter is that the value of preliminary collections of spontaneous items referred to above need not be limited to providing a basis for semantic differential labels. We maintain that they are also worthy of investigation in their own right as the *evaluative repertoires* of the groups we study, and that they also offer a depth and richness that usefully helps to offset the limitations of scale ratings alone. A more open-ended approach can help us understand not only the different profiles that speakers have, but also the process of evaluation itself and its own cultural constitution.

Our argument is also based on the way in which some of the key attributes – economy, measurement, and comparability – of semantic differential scales can also carry limitations. For a lexical item to be employed on such scales, it must have the quality of gradability and (usually) an antonym for directionality to be expressed. In other words, the two items used for the bipolar scale must be in a paradigmatic relationship of opposites in a paired system, with each member of the pair at opposite ends of a continuum. Hence, if, when conducting a preliminary study to collect spontaneous items from a group of judges for later use in the construction of semantic differential scales, a judge produces a response that has no antonym and/or is not gradable, this has to be discarded.[2] In addition to these issues of antonymy and gradability, it is also supposed that the evaluative adjectives on these scales are themselves "semantic primes", i.e. that they have the same meaning for all people in all circumstances. However, in some instances it might be unreasonable to make such assumptions. For example, for adolescents in the UK today, the most common use of the apparently unambiguous word "sad" is almost certainly used as a counter-empathetic response to another person's inadequacy rather than in its "overt" sense of an empathetic response to a state of event that might implicate another person. With judges of that age-group, one should arguably exercise some caution when employing such items on semantic differential scales.

The study we report in this chapter is part of our programme of language attitudes work investigating evaluations of English language speakers in Wales, and involving mid-teenagers in schools all over Wales judging speakers of their own age who are telling narratives in their dialects to their peers. Our goal here was to study the teenagers' evaluations that were firmly embedded in young people's own activities contained in these narratives, as well as relating (as we have established empirically – see Garrett et al. 1999, 2003) to sociolinguistic dialect variation. The narrative performances differ from the "speech stimuli" that are so often used in language attitudes research, in that they are instances not only of dialect, but also of contextually situated language use, or forms of cultural practice for these teenagers. In preparing the scales for our main questionnaire, we conducted a preliminary study to elicit a stock of terms the teenagers themselves used. As we examined these terms, we felt that they gave us crucial insights into the socio-cultural world inhabited by these teenagers, as well as into the "cultural functioning" (Urban 1993) that occurs between evaluative responses and narrative performances, and we felt that these terms deserved further study. We therefore included an item in the subsequent questionnaire to enable us to collect more of them. These data form the focus of this chapter.

2.   Method

2.1.   Preparation of audio-recorded materials

A large data-base of audio-recorded narratives by school students aged 15–16 was collected throughout Wales. To achieve this, from a comprehensive list of secondary schools throughout Wales, 40 were selected, based on the criteria of regional spread and lack of proximity to the borders between the six regions displayed in Figure 1. These schools were invited to participate in a study of regional variation in Welsh English. Of the schools who agreed to participate, two were initially selected from each of the six regions. These regions are listed below. We identified these regions in Figure 1 on the basis of (the limited amount of) available dialectal research on English in Wales (see Coupland 1990) and the data from our previous studies on perceptions of English dialects in Wales.

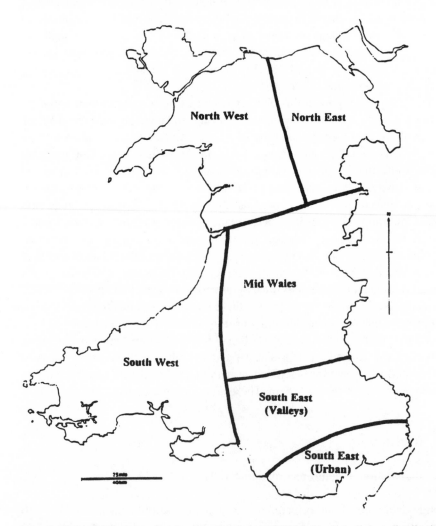

Map 1. Map of Wales showing the broad patterns of Welsh English dialect distribution

1. The Cardiff conurbation. Cardiff is the capital city of Wales. The region became established as an industrial urban centre during the 19th century, and

is historically very anglicised. Compared to other parts of Wales in recent years, Cardiff has benefited from a great deal of inward investment, and is economically stronger and more prosperous than the other regions. The English language variety in this area has been characterised in many studies (e.g. Coupland 1988; Mees 1983; Windsor Lewis 1990).

2. The south east Wales Valleys. From the 19th century until the 1980s, this was a heavy industrial zone producing coal and steel, but with the rapid disappearance of these industries, it is now marked by high levels of unemployment and social deprivation. The region has another broadly distinguishable regional variety of English (see Connolly 1990; Hughes and Trudgill 1979; Tench 1990 for descriptions of localities impinging on this region).

3. The south west, a rural, agricultural, and traditionally Welsh-speaking "heartland", now somewhat fragmenting in terms of its Welsh language speakers, according to the 1991 census data (Aitchison and Carter 1994). The English variety is more influenced by the Welsh language than the previous two regions (see Parry 1990).

4. Mid-Wales, a predominantly agricultural zone occupying the centre of Wales on a north-south axis, but excluding western coastal areas, which tend to be incorporated into the south west zone. Compared with the "heartlands" of the north west and south west, this region is largely non-Welsh-speaking. To our knowledge, there have been no sociolinguistic or dialectological studies of this region, but the eastern mid Wales English dialect is characteristically rhotic, and in some respects aligns with the features of the "upper south-west" dialect area of England (Trudgill 1990).

5. The north east, a comparatively urban industrial zone, and, like mid-Wales, relatively anglicised in contrast to the north west and south west regions. The English dialect is strongly influenced by the English of the nearby Liverpool conurbation.

6. The north west, a predominantly rural and agricultural zone, associated with sheep farming and slate quarrying, the latter of which has declined considerably over recent decades. The region is a key part of the Welsh language heartland "Y Fro Gymraeg", where Welsh language influence on English is stronger.

In each of the selected schools, we audio-recorded approximately fourteen 15 year olds, telling personal anecdotes which they judged newsworthy in some way in front of their peers in a classroom setting. They were told that we were interested in collecting "stories that young people your age tell". We supplemented this general request with the following prompt:

> All people are story tellers. You come to school every day and tell your
> mates about things that have happened to you. This is what I want you to
> do today. Think of something that has happened to you or someone you
> know and tell us about it. For example, a funny or embarrassing incident,
> a frightening story, accident or danger, or a time you got into trouble with
> your parents.

Since the students self-selected into the task and needed to survive the event in
front of their peers, we made the assumption that a degree of newsworthiness
was also an internally motivated requirement. There was only rarely any difficulty in eliciting a supply of volunteered narratives. The majority are based
around (actual or fictitious) events with a mildly anti-establishment character,
often involving personal and physical threats or accidents. Overall, 175 narratives were collected.

For the evaluative study, we selected two narratives from each of the six Welsh
regions. The six specific Welsh communities represented were Cardiff (urban
south east), Newtown (mid-Wales), Carmarthen (south west Wales), Merthyr
Tydfil (south east Wales Valleys), Mold (north east Wales), and Blaenau Ffestiniog (north west Wales). The selection criteria were that the speakers should
be representative of their particular dialect communities (confirmed by detailed
phonetic descriptions produced by independent experts), and that the narratives were reasonably successful (in the sense of being well-received by their
audiences). Regionally identifying references were also avoided. In addition
and for comparison, personal narratives of an identical sort were tape-recorded
from two Received Pronunciation (RP)-accented 15-year-old school students
from a private school across the English border in Gloucestershire. To control
for gender differences, we confined the study to evaluations of male speakers,
since they were the majority of story telling volunteers, and so gave us a larger
number of narratives from which to select.

We then selected an excerpt from each of the 14 narratives (see Appendix
A for transcriptions), as a reasonably self-contained episode lasting no more
than 50 seconds, in order to reduce possible fatigue effects, since, even with
only two representative dialect examples from each of the communities, each
group of listeners had to hear and respond to 14 extracts. To counter order effects, two audio-tapes were prepared, allowing the excerpts to be heard in a
different sequence by each half of the sets of students.[3] Our reasons for using such "authentic" narratives rather than more contrived matched guises or
"verbal guises" (Cooper and Fishman 1974) are set out elsewhere (Williams
et al. 1999; Garrett et al. 1999, 2003), but include the need to account for how
"dialect" in the narrow sense interacts with socio-culturally conditioned ways of

speaking (which we pointed to above in our discussion of teenagers caricaturing the groups around them).

2.2. Preparation of the questionnaire

A speaker evaluation questionnaire was prepared, containing a separate page of items to be completed for each voice heard. Each of these pages began with the open-ended instruction: "Write down your first impressions when you listen to this speaker". This allowed spontaneous cognitive and emotional responses free of the restrictions imposed by forced choice. The questionnaire indicated that they should write down three such items for each voice.

This preliminary task was followed by seven judgement scales selected after pilot work in which a comparable sample of mid-teenagers had been asked to listen to the stimulus tape and write a response to the same open-ended item as above. All seven resulting questions were formulated to be answered on a unidimensional 5-point scale where 1 = "not at all", and 5 = "very much". The questions were: "overall, do you like this speaker?"; "do you think this speaker does well at school?" (e.g. gets high marks in exams); "how much like you do you think this speaker is?"; "do you think you could make friends with this speaker?"; "how Welsh do you think this speaker sounds?"; "do you think this speaker is a good laugh?"; "how interesting does this story sound?" The "you like", "like you", "make friends", "good laugh", and "interesting story" scales connect with Zahn and Hopper's (1985) attractiveness dimension. "Good at school" indirectly reflects Zahn and Hopper's superiority dimension, viewed from within the educational establishment, to the extent that this is relevant in young people's judgements of each other. "How Welsh" measures a perceived ethnicity, and in some respects authenticity, criterion which emerged strongly in our previous work as a salient evaluative dimension of Welsh English dialect communities. The results of these scales data are reported in Garrett, Coupland and Williams (1999, 2003), and we do not dwell on them in this chapter. However, we do make reference to them, where useful, and so Appendix B contains a table of the mean scores.

2.3. Respondents

The evaluation phase of the study involved returning to each of the six regions to collect school students' responses. The risk that students would recognise individual speakers precluded using the same schools that provided the initial audio-recordings. However, the schools in the evaluation phase needed to be matched as far as possible with those from which the narratives had been collected. Teachers assisted us in the selection of schools that made a reasonable match. In the more rural locations, where few secondary schools exist, there were some difficulties in finding good matches nearby. Hence, in (relatively rural) mid-Wales, it was necessary to accept a school in Builth Wells as a match for the Newtown school, even though the schools were about 45 miles apart.

2.4. Procedure

In each school, the selected audio-recorded story extracts were played to a group of mixed-ability year ten (15 year-old) students, males and females. Mixed ability groups were achieved by drawing students from a number of classes, or, where numbers were smaller, taking all the pupils from a whole year. A total of 169 students filled in a questionnaire to evaluate each speaker in turn.

3.   Results and discussion

We restrict ourselves in this chapter to the responses to the open-ended item asking them to write down their first impressions of the speakers ("keywords"). We refer to the speakers/narratives by their dialect community followed by the speaker's randomly allocated number. The dialect community labels are NW (north west), NE (north east), SW (south west), Mid (Mid-Wales), Cardiff, Valleys, and RP.

It should be remembered that the teenagers were asked quickly to throw down first impressions, in order to elicit their immediate cognitive responses. In order to achieve this, it was necessarily the case that no time was permitted for the careful and thoughtful selection of terms that most accurately and unambiguously summed up their impressions. Moreover, as with any folk comments on language, responses range along a continuum of global to specific character (Preston 1996). Furthermore, since the teenagers were responding to audio-recordings of 14 different speakers, each presenting their own narrative, their keywords might refer to some quality of the speaker's narrative (content, performance, etc.) or to a quality of the English dialect of the speaker, or to the speaker himself. Inevitably, it was sometimes not clear quite which of these a keyword referred to. For example, one of the stories (Valleys5) related events leading to the speaker's father losing his foot in a traffic accident. Hence, the keyword *sad* was difficult to interpret. It might have referred to the accident in the story, a quality showing through in the boy's voice, or it could even have been intended as a negative evaluation of the speaker with its contemporary counter-empathetic use (in the UK, at least), as it most certainly was with other speakers. Such variabilities work very much against the convention of attempting to place all the data into rigorous categories for subsequent ease of analysis, a procedure which may also risk obscuring other interesting differences in the data (Potter and Wetherell 1987).

On the other hand, it was obviously not feasible or worthwhile to pursue all of the 5261 keywords individually. Some items grouped together very obviously, e.g. *not interesting* and *uninteresting*, and it would have made no sense to pursue them as separate items. There were, though, some isolated items which did seem interesting to check individually, some of which proved more illuminating (e.g. *boring*) than others. Due to space constraints, we are selective in the cases we consider below, taking just one or two of the most obvious and interesting groupings and single items in the responses. For groupings not discussed here (e.g. *bullshitter*, *troublemaker,* and items concerned with sexuality and drugs), we refer readers to Garrett, Coupland and Williams (2003).

Notwithstanding what has just been said about the data processing, two overall statements can certainly be made at the outset. One is that these young people's evaluations of their peers emphasised negativity. The second is that there was a considerable range of evaluative content in the keywords. One plausible explanation for these properties is that if 15 is an age at which teenagers are exploring a range of available identities, this may require an equivalent range of differentiating evaluative descriptors. And positioning themselves in relation to this range of identities will perhaps mean rejecting more than they find acceptable, and so lead to more negative than favourable reactions. This phase of experimentation with different roles and behaviours, which seems to prevail during middle adolescence, has been referred to by Marcia (1980) as "identity moratorium". Gavin and Furman (1989: 832) also draw attention to the high degree of negative or antagonistic interactions amongst adolescents at 14 to 16 years, and point to three important functions served by such antagonism at this age. One is that it boosts the adolescent's own self-worth. The other two operate more obviously at the group level. Antagonisms impose similarity among members, with non-conformity being punished. Then, antagonisms lead to greater within-group dominance hierarchies with confirmed leaders and followers, eventually reducing antagonism.

3.1. Taboo/pejorative items

Given the fact that the teenagers were encouraged to write down whatever their first impressions were of the speakers and narratives, it perhaps comes as no surprise that a large proportion of the items they wrote were what we have termed "taboo" items (e.g. *dickhead*, *twat*, *wanker*, *prat*, etc.). Also included in this group are items that are not strictly taboo, but pejorative, with similar albeit milder force (e.g. *wimp*, *drip*). These items warrant some discussion, since they accounted for 10.63% of all keywords, seemingly constituting a considerable proportion of the teenagers' evaluative lexical repertoires, and indeed forming a sizable repertoire in themselves of some 112 different items. Similarly, de Klerk (1997) found a rich variety of items in a study of expletives, but in that study respondents were specifically asked to produce expletives rather than linguistic evaluations of any nature – expletive or non-expletive. Interestingly, in published language attitudes studies where teenage judges have been trawled for evaluative terms prior to the main study, such taboo items are not given even a passing mention. Yet it is hard to imagine that they would not have featured at all. De Klerk (1997: 147) comments that one expects slang and expletives to be abundant amongst teenagers, since their functions include the reinforcement of group membership and the signalling of shared knowledge and interests. On the other hand, their omission is understandable, given that they are likely to be seen to be of no real value for the contruction of semantic differential scales, and given too the tendency for the messiness of the research process to be hidden from view in most published work (Holmes and Ainsworth 1997).

Identifying the specific semantic features of taboo words is problematic. As far as possible, items placed in this grouping were only those that could be reasonably regarded as not being intended by their users to carry any specific or literal meaning. Some items had some clear reference to another group of items, and so were not included in this general list. For example, it was clear from the juxtapositioning with other keywords that *sheepshagger* and *shitshoveller* referred to farming activity, and these were included with the other "farming" words. Hence not all taboo words were included in this taboo/pejorative grouping.

It is striking that some of the communities of judges have used these items far more than others. 25.78% of all the keywords produced by the Valleys judges fall into this category, and 20.14% of all those provided by the mid-Wales judges. In contrast, the other figures are the north-east (7.16%), the south-west (4.72%), Cardiff (4.54%), north-west (3.72%). However, the data were collected in one single session within each region, so these differences cannot be confidently attributed to significant cultural differences among the regions themselves. The effect of this large proportion produced by the Valleys, however, does mean that they produce fewer other items, as is evident below.

Interpretation of the way these items are aimed at the different speakers is not straightforward. Looking at the mean scores for our scales ratings data (set out in Appendix B), there is a striking general negativity in the teenagers' quantitative judgements, with scarcely any mean scores rising above the mid-point of the scale. It is tempting then to see this large group of taboo items as a reflection of these generally negative evaluations. But this interpretation does not hold, since the most popular and positively (or least negatively) rated speaker overall in our scales results is Cardiff11, who attracts the second largest proportion of these items (14.56% of all the keywords written about him). Nor is the opposite interpretation tenable that such items are meant favourably – e.g. that you have to be a *prat* to be liked – since the RP speakers are consistently downgraded on all but the "good at school" scale in our quantitative data, yet they too attract high proportions (RP3, 13.24%; RP12, 12.99%). The best interpretation is that many of these items (e.g. *prat*) have variable force, and others (e.g. *arsehole*) might invariably be meant negatively (but the rich assortment of 112 items were too thinly spread across the judges and speakers to tease out such distinctions). Notwithstanding the low numbers of instances, some support for this is found by just comparing RP3 and Cardiff11. They are labelled *prat* seven times and nine times respectively. *Knob* is used for Cardiff11 14 times and 4 times for RP3. Cardiff11 is seemingly "enjoyed" because he is seen to be an entertaining and amusing *prat* or *knob*, alongside other very positive evaluations about his association with pool halls, for example. RP3 is put down perhaps because he is perceived by these teenagers as a wimpish *prat* or *knob* and unable to manage without teacher's help.

For the most part, this group of labels can be regarded as offensive, at least in traditional terms. In addition to this, it is noteworthy that they are overwhelmingly nominal rather than adjectival. Furthermore, they are categorial nominals. Hence, coding a speaker as an *arsehole* relegates the speaker to a social category of *arseholes*. Many such items then are outgrouping. Thus these evaluative items are not only hanging an attribute on an individual, but also placing an individual in a social space, and indicating where the evaluator stands in relation to that space. This is an important and specific function of evaluation.

3.2. Boring

Recent UK media portrayals of adolescent characters (specifically, BBC television's "Harry Enfield and Chums") have generated a widespread and enduring association between the use of the word *boring* and (at least young and mid-) teenagers. This characterisation is amply supported by our keywords data, with *boring* being by far the most frequently used of all the items, even without taking into account the more specific collocations of *boring story*, *boring voice*, etc. The item *boring* accounts for 9.77% of all keywords, almost as many as the whole of the above taboo category.

It appears to convey a general sense of lack of engagement by the listener for some or other reason. The use of this item too can be seen in terms of out-grouping, though by a different route from the taboo items above. This time the speaker is not relegated to a named group or crowd, but is outgrouped through judges signalling that they are not engaged with the speakers or narratives currently. *Boring* is something of an umbrella response, in that the lack of engagement might be caused by a whole range of factors. This becomes particularly obvious when attempting to look for other items that it might be grouped with – hence it is considered alone here, in its own right. One might try to group it with an item such as *uninteresting*, or, equally, with *not exciting* or *not funny*, though from our data it would be impossible to justify grouping it with one rather than the other, and there are at the same time good reasons for wanting to make distinctions among *uninteresting* and *not exciting* and *not funny*. At times, the collocation with other keywords by the same judge suggests that a speaker or narrative might be boring because of slow delivery, or frequent pauses, or because he *goes on*.   For the judges, *boring* can usefully relate to some aspect of the narrative performance (dialect, tempo, monotone) or some component of the narrative content (an uninteresting story, lacking excitement, lacking humour), or both at once.

The item could present difficulties to a researcher collecting keywords solely to construct semantic differential scales. If *boring* were one end of a scale, what would go at the other end? The choice would be crucial to the interpretation the judge would most likely place upon *boring*. *Boring* would derive its more specific meaning from the other item, and in doing so would doubtless lose the sense in which it is used within the evaluative culture of these adolescents.

Its general meaning of lack of engagement turns out to be a very useful general measure for our present discussion. In contrast to the use of the taboo items, the negativity of this item can be asserted with more confidence. For example, a brief eyeballing of the data in Table 1 shows that the rank ordering of the speakers in terms of both "good laugh" and "interesting story" roughly reverses the rank ordering according to the number of mentions of the word *boring*. It is particularly noticeable that although the most popular of the speakers according to the scales (Cardiff11) attracted the second most taboo items (see above), he attracts almost no mentions at all of *boring* (a mere 1.21% of all his keywords).

Table 1. Keyword *boring* comments about speakers, compared to mean scores for "interesting story" and "good laugh" in the scales data.

Speaker	Boring as percentage of each speaker's comments	Interesting story	Good laugh
Mid14	16.76	1.86	1.98
Cardiff1	15.52	1.87	2.34
Mid6	15.01	1.89	1.99
Valleys8	14.13	1.79	2.16
RP3	14.05	1.78	1.70
RP12	13.97	1.99	1.88
SW13	13.60	1.89	2.16
Valleys5	10.79	2.58	2.16
NW7	7.53	2.52	2.27
NE9	5.60	2.71	3.24
NW10	4.13	3.28	2.97
SW4	4.00	2.60	3.17
NE2	2.15	2.87	2.97
Cardiff11	1.21	3.69	3.75

There are differences in the extent to which the different judging communities use *boring* (and confirm the Harry Enfield stereotype). The north-east (13.08%), Cardiff (12.84%) and the Valleys (12.43%) use the term markedly more than the south-west (8.53%), mid-Wales (5.58%) and the north-west (4.92%), suggesting a split between those living in relatively industrial areas and those living in rural communities. Possibly, the more rural communities are operating with higher thresholds of boredom, or at least may be less prone to downgrade speakers of their age for failing to engage them.

3.3. Welshness/Englishness

Of the keywords written by the entire sample of teenagers, 388 (7.37%) referred to the Welshness or Englishness of the speaker/narrative. This is again a sizable proportion. Following our earlier work on Welsh English (Coupland et al. 1994, 1999; Garrett et al. 1995, 1999; Williams et al. 1996, 1999), such data provide further confirmation that this is a particularly meaningful component of the evaluation of language in certain (especially post-colonial) contexts, and a particularly salient dimension for these young people in Wales. Ethnic or cultural provenance is overlooked in much earlier language attitudes work, and hence does not surface among the judgemental dimensions found by Zahn and Hopper (1985). Table 2 shows the distribution of these keywords (horizontally) across speakers and also (vertically) across the communities of judges.

Table 2. Numbers of keyword references to "Welshness" and "Englishness" used by teenage judges in the six communities for the fourteen speakers. (Figures in brackets are the numbers expressed as percentages of total of keywords produced by communities.)

Speakers		North-east	North-west	South-west	Cardiff	Mid-Wales	Valleys	Totals Eng. and Welsh	Totals Eng. PLUS Welsh
						Communities			
Cardiff1	Welsh	14 (17.07)	4 (9.30)	7 (8.64)	3 (3.74)	0	0	28 (8.36)	29
	Eng.	1 (1.22)	0	0	0	0	0	1 (0.30)	(8.66)
NE2	Welsh	0	0	0	0	0	0	0	12
	Eng.	1 (1.43)	5 (10.20)	6 (6.74)	0	0	0	12 (3.23)	(3.23)
RP3	Welsh	0	0	0	0	0	0	0	6
	Eng.	0	1 (2.00)	5 (5.95)	0	0	0	6 (1.62)	(1.62)
SW4	Welsh	12 (13.95)	11 (20.75)	4 (4.82)	10 (17.86)	10 (16.95)	5 (7.94)	52 (13.00)	52
	Eng.	0	0	0	0	0	0	0	(13.00)
Valley5	Welsh	10 (13.70)	13 (20.97)	1 (1.37)	2 (4.00)	2 (3.77)	1 (1.45)	29 (7.63)	29
	Eng.	0	0	0	0	0	0	0	(7.63)

Table 2. (continued)

Speakers		North-east	North-west	South-west	Cardiff	Mid-Wales	Valleys	Totals Eng. and Welsh	Totals Eng. PLUS Welsh
				Communities					
Mid6	Welsh	1 (1.43)	0	2 (2.63)	0	2 (3.28)	0	5 (1.34)	13
	Eng.	1 (1.43)	5 (9.62)	2 (2.63)	0	0	0	8 (2.14)	(3.49)
NW 7	Welsh	0	12 (20.69)	19 (23.75)	2 (2.90)	8 (12.50)	1 (1.45)	42 (9.88)	42
	Eng.	0	0	0	0	0	0	0	(9.88)
Valley8	Welsh	2 (2.78)	7 (14.29)	18 (24.66)	4 (8.16)	10 (14.93)	3 (4.62)	44 (11.73)	46
	Eng.	0	1 (2.04)	0	1 (2.04)	0	0	2 (0.53)	(12.27)
NE9	Welsh	0	0	0	0	0	0	0	23
	Eng.	0	6 (12.50)	16 (21.05)	1 (2.17)	0	0	23 (6.44)	(6.44)
NW10	Welsh	9 (13.85)	6 (9.84)	22 (30.99)	3 (6.12)	9 (21.95)	0	49 (14.45)	50
	Eng.	0	1 (1.64)	0	0	0	0	1 (0.29)	(14.75)
Cardiff11	Welsh	0	4 (7.14)	1 (1.14)	2 (3.23)	1 (1.64)	0	8 (1.94)	10
	Eng.	0	1 (1.76)	1 (1.14)	0	0	0	2 (0.49)	(2.43)
RP12	Welsh	0	0	0	0	1 (1.82)	0	1 (0.25)	23
	Eng.	0	6 (9.84)	13 (15.85)	0	1 (1.82)	2 (2.78)	22 (5.39)	(5.64)
SW13	Welsh	7 (10.45)	15 (26.32)	9 (11.84)	5 (8.06)	4 (7.41)	1 (1.69)	41 (10.93)	42
	Eng.	0	0	0	1 (1.61)	0	0	1 (0.27)	(11.2)

Table 2. (continued)

Speakers		North-east	North-west	South-west	Cardiff	Mid-Wales	Valleys	Totals Eng. and Welsh	Totals Eng. PLUS Welsh
							Communities		
Mid14	Welsh	0	1	5	0	0	0	6	
			(1.89)	(7.14)				(1.76)	11
	Eng.	0	3	1	1	0	0	5	(3.42)
			(5.66)	(1.43)	(1.79)			(1.47)	
Totals for Welsh		55	73	88	31	47	11		
		(5.29)	(9.71)	(7.99)	(4.03)	(6.39)	(1.28)		
Totals for English		3	29	44	4	1	2		
		(0.29)	(3.86)	(3.99)	(0.52)	(0.14)	(0.23)		
Totals for Eng. PLUS Welsh		58	102	132	35	48	13		388
		(5.58)	(13.56)	(11.98)	(4.55)	(6.53)	(1.51)		(7.37)

Overall, these frequencies are a good reflection of the results from the scaled items on the questionnaire, dividing the speakers into an *English* grouping of RP and NE, with the others more frequently attributed *Welsh* qualities. Mid-Wales finds a somewhat more ambiguous position in the keywords data than in the scales data, though the number of ethnicity comments for both the Mid speakers is low. Cardiff's dual image as on the one hand the capital city of Wales, and on the other, a somewhat anglicised urban centre, is reflected in the relatively mid position of these two speakers. Interestingly, they are divided here, with Cardiff11 (the most popular of all the speakers/narratives in our scales data) having a low proportion of items describing him as *Welsh* similar to *English* group. However, when we look at comments about Englishness, we see that Cardiff11 is here aligned with the *Welsh* group. So the most likely explanation for Cardiff11's lack of comments about Welshness is that, given the comparative success of this speaker, respondents may have found themselves with a far richer stock of other first impressions to jot down in the three keyword slots available, such that Welshness, while important, may have been washed aside.

    In terms of the number of comments about Welshness, the speakers from each dialect community tend to pair off, attracting similar numbers of comments about Welshness and Englishness. Despite the larger gaps in the numbers of Welshness comments between Cardiff1 and Cardiff11, and between Valleys5 and Valleys8 (29 and 46 comments respectively), the overall pattern does again appear to suggest that these judgements are based primarily on dialect features rather than on any other variables in the speakers or narratives.

If the proportion of comments about Welshness is compared with those about Englishness, we see that the proportion is comparatively low for Englishness. If all the Welshness and Englishness comments are collapsed into one "ethnicity" category, then the five speakers that attract most of these comments are NW10 (14.75%); SW4 (13.00%); Valleys8 (12.27%); SW13 (11.2%), and NW7 (9.88%). In all these cases, the comments are solely or mainly about Welshness. And taking all of the ethnicity words from the judges in all the communities about all of the speakers (388 words), it is striking that 78.6% of them are references to Welshness. So as a generalisation for the whole pan-Wales set of judges, then, it might be argued from the keywords data (insofar as they can be taken as a reflection of relative salience) that Welshness is a more salient characteristic in English than Englishness is for these teenagers.

This overall claim finds some support in the fact that those speakers attracting fewest comments about ethnicity (Cardiff11 aside) are RP3 (1.62%); NE2 (3.23%); Mid14 (3.42%); Mid6 (3.49%); RP12 (5.64%), and NE9 (6.44%), who are seen as mainly *English* or fairly balanced (the Mid speakers). Englishness does have some salience, of course, and it is noticeable that it appears to hold more salience for certain communities. Table 2 shows that almost all of the 83 comments about Englishness (mainly directed at the NE, RP, and Mid speakers) come from judges in the north-west (29 comments, or 3.86% of all their keywords) and the south-west (44 comments, or 3.99%).

However, these are still far fewer than the comments they make about Welshness, even allowing for the fact that there was a greater number of speakers remaining for whom Welsh labels might be used (the NW, SW, Valleys, and Cardiff speakers). The south-west judges make 88 comments about Welshness (7.99% of all their keywords), and the north-west judges make 73 (9.71%).

The above "pan-Wales" observation needs some qualification. Most of the comments rained upon RP3 and RP12 about Englishness come from the south-west. These are sometimes expressed simply as *English*, with the same judge using other keywords such as *posh* and *snob*, as if the term *English* itself carries a pejorative intensity rather than a mere factual force. Elsewhere, Englishness is expressed with more conspicuous hostility, e.g. *English, enough said!*, and the word *English* accompanied by a swastika and skull and crossbones. This is an illuminating supplement to the scales data. Here the teenagers are turning their attention to the outgroup, vividly elaborating on how they view Englishness. The inclusion of a "How English do you think this person sounds?" scale would not have made so clear the character of such hostility and intensity, nor the pragmatic force of "Englishness" for the south-west judges.

The south-west and the north-west are the communities that have most to say about ethnicity (11.98% and 13.56% of their comments respectively). These are the two heartlands of Welsh identity and areas where the Welsh language is still relatively strong (Aitchison and Carter 1994), and connotations of Welshness are high (Coupland et al. 1994; Williams et al. 1996, 1999). Those with by far the least to say about ethnicity are the Valleys judges (1.51%). However, even if one cannot describe the Valleys as a stronghold for the Welsh language, the region undoubtedly holds powerful connotations of Welshness, just as the north-west and south-west do (Coupland et al. 1994; Garrett et al. 1995; Williams et al. 1996, 1999), so one might expect to see more comments about ethnicity on the same sort of scale as from the south-west and north-west judges. It is possible that the reason for this lack of comment on ethnicity is caused by the exceptionally high proportion of their keywords that were "used up" in the taboo category (see above).

The "how Welsh" scale results also have further light cast on them from an examination of the comments made by the south-west and north-west judges about each other's speakers. Table 2 shows that this is in fact where the greatest exchange about Welshness takes place in our data. The south-west judges' comments about the NW speakers are arguably exclusionary. 16 of their 19 Welshness comments aimed at NW7 are accounted for by the items *gog*, from Welsh *gogledd* 'north' (12 occurrences), *North Wales* (2), and *North Walian* (2), indicating that the south-west see Welshness as having regional differentiation. Their 22 similar comments about NW10 include 6 *gog*, 4 *North Walian*, 4 *from North Wales*, and 3 *North Wales accent*. In contrast, of the north-west's 11 Welshness items about SW4, 9 are simply *Welsh*, as are 13 of their 15 comments about SW13, as if ingrouping their south-west neighbours. Although the idea of the north-west being perceived as "differently" Welsh is not new to us (it was evident in the multidimensional scaling we conducted on the scale ratings – see Garrett et al. 1999, 2003), the keywords suggest that this view may not be shared by the north-west (e.g. in a claim to be exclusive), and that the south-west plays a strong role in this dynamic. These issues warrant further research.

3.4.   Farming and other activities

Table 3 shows the results for a group of items exemplified by *farmer, country type, sheepshagger*, etc. These comments are made mainly about Valleys5

(10.26%), Mid6 (14.26%) and SW13 (9.87). The stories themselves are rural in content, each of them relating an event which happened to the speaker himself. There is one other unambiguously rural story involving the speaker (Valleys8) that does not attract so many comments of this type (1.6%), possibly because this one differs from the others in that it does not involve an accident (but, rather, fun), and there is no suggestion that the speaker himself actually lives on a farm.

Table 3. Number of references to *farmer*, *country-type*, *sheepshagger*, etc. in the six judging communities for the fourteen speakers. (Figures in brackets are the numbers expressed as percentages of total keywords produced by communities.)

	Communities						
Speaker	North-east	North-west	South-west	Cardiff	Mid-Wales	Valleys	Speaker total
Cardiff1	0	0	0	0	0	0	0
NE2	0	0	0	0	0	0	0
RP3	0	0	0	0	0	0	0
SW4	0	0	0	0	1	0	1 (0.25)
Valleys5	2	7	12	1	15	2	39 (10.26)
Mid6	6	10	18	2	17	1	54 (14.48)
NW7	2	1	0	0	0	0	3 (0.71)
Valleys8	0	0	1	1	4	0	6 (1.60)
NE9	0	0	0	0	0	0	0
NW10	2	0	0	0	0	0	2 (0.59)
Cardiff11	2	0	0	0	0	0	2 (0.49)
RP12	0	0	0	0	0	0	0
SW13	1	12	15	3	5	1	37 (9.87)
Mid14	0	1	0	0	0	0	1 (0.29)
Comm. Totals	15 (1.44)	31 (4.12)	46 (4.17)	7 (0.91)	42 (5.71)	4 (0.46)	145 (2.76)

It is also worth noting that most of these comments about farmers, farmers' boys, etc. are made by just three communities of judges: mid-Wales (5.71%); south-west (4.17%) and north-west (4.12%), the others making far fewer (NE, 1.44%; Cardiff, 0.91%; Valleys, 0.46%). These connotations of farming and rural life are strongest, then, for the judges from the first three communities, and this can be attributed to the rurality of the judges themselves. The salience is undoubtedly generated by the contact (for example, in rural market towns), throwing agricultural life into sharp contrast with the lure (perhaps especially for teenagers) of global culture and urban lifestyles. These rural stories were rated negatively on most of the scales in our data, so we are entitled to see these comments as a rejection of farming and country life.

With large areas of Wales still very much dependent on agriculture, and currently in crisis economically, the prospect of few obvious alternative local opportunities for their future may be making this evaluative factor a very sensitive one, in some regions in particular. For the teenagers in relatively urbanised industrialised regions, the lifestyles and social attributes of *farmers* are not an issue, of course. They do not come across them to the same extent (if at all).

In some ways, it might seem unremarkable that stories about farms should attract these sorts of comments. But the results take on more importance if considered alongside other keyword findings. It is notable that Cardiff11, though a city kid engaged in playing pool, does not attract lots of comment about the activity of playing pool. It is also worth noting that RP12 does not attract comment about going to funfairs. One might argue that the cases of Cardiff11 and RP12 are quite different in that they do not concern economic activities, but recreational ones, and that one would not expect recreational activities to attract the same level of comment. But SW4 attracts a great deal of comment about rugby, and, though a recreational activity, this again is an activity that goes right to the heart of Welsh cultural traditions and stereotypes. 11.25% of the comments about SW4 are connected with rugby and sport. (There are almost no other comments about sport for the other speakers, even for Cardiff11.) The evaluative profile of SW4 in the scales data is generally very favourable, so we are entitled to see these comments about rugby and sport in positive terms. This time, it is the Cardiff judges who make most comments about rugby and sport (21.43%). Though perceived as relatively anglicised, with relatively few Welsh language speakers, Cardiff has a jewel of Welsh culture embodied in its rugby playing and its national rugby stadium in the centre of the capital. Mid-Wales too attributes importance to this property (13.56%), along with the south-west itself (13.25%), and to a lesser extent, the north-east (9.30%). By comparison, the north-west (5.66%), along with the Valleys (4.76%) give little attention to this aspect of SW4. These data offer a clear illustration of how evaluations are made in terms of categories and qualities available in the culture, either locally (e.g. farming), or more widely (e.g. rugby), and that the loadings of such evaluations will vary accordingly.

3.5. Rich/posh

3.93% of all keywords referred to socio-economic factors: *posh, rich*. The RP speakers, predictably perhaps, attract most of these. 24.51% of the comments about RP12 fall into this group. The figure for RP3, though lower at 10.54%, is nevertheless way ahead of the others. The only others attracting numbers of such comments worthy of mention are Mid6 (6.97%), who probably projects an image of himself not as the son of a poor farmer, but as the offspring of a more affluent one, and who is allowed to drive his father's tractor to carry out farming tasks, and Cardiff1 (4.78%), who talks about events on his holiday in Spain. This dimension effectively separates out these four speakers from the rest. *Posh* is frequently found collocated with *snob*, pointing to outgrouping processes once again.

There are also differences in the degree to which the different judge communities focus on richness, poshness, etc. The dimension seems most salient for the mid-Wales judges (5.31%), the north-west (5.19%), Cardiff (4.80%) and the south-west (4.72%), and less so for the north-east (2.21%) and the Valleys (2.02%). A group of words relating to intelligence and braininess also separated out the RP speakers (this time, along with NE9) from the others, with the Valleys judges again hardly mentioning such attributes at all.

4.   Conclusions

We set out to argue that keywords can be of wider value than as merely a preliminary stage in designing language attitude measurement scales. They are informative both alongside such scales and also in their own right as evaluative data for investigating attitudes. We have attempted to demonstrate that keywords can give us deeper insights into data elicited from one-dimensional scales, allowing better access to the multidimensional character of attitudes. This multidimensional nature of language attitudes and of the semantic items that express them makes simple comparison more difficult, and indeed ease of comparison has always been one of the advantages claimed for such scales. But one-dimensional scales can only capture one-dimensional comparisons, which though simple, may at times not delve deep enough.

Even if examined without reference to accompanying scales, keywords do not necessarily altogether sacrifice qualities of intensity, direction or comparability. Many items do suggest directionality and at least some rough idea of intensity. For example, *English, enough said!* suggests negative directionality and strong intensity. But it also carries an emotional reaction that would be missed by a circle around "very English" on a 7-point scale. *Sheepshagger* also suggests these qualities, and also projects quite precise stereotypical imagery. Such items may form the basis of some useful qualitative comparison – e.g. of *sheepshagger* as an image of one community and *townie* for another.

Some caution is needed with this kind of data when making numerical and percentage comparisons, and it is possible that in some cases here, these have been stretched a little further than the data comfortably allow (especially by region). For example, a dearth of comments from one judging source might be attributable to their having "used up" their three keywords on other dimensions, thus making it less secure to compare percentages than it would be with forced-choice schemes. However, there is considerable value in being able to draw out some illuminating socio-semantic dimensions, which later studies can subject to more detailed analysis.

Discussion should not be restricted to the use of keywords against the background of using semantic differential scales in language attitudes research. Their value undoubtedly extends to other sociolinguistic traditions too. Keywords could usefully supplement the tradition in which correlations are explored between sociolinguistic variables and social groups to investigate in more depth the various motivations and social connotations with which language users are operating (see Kristiansen, this volume).

Keywords, then, offer a shorthand for evaluative discourses, and how they are structured within particular groups. We see how evaluative language does more than hang qualities or attributes on targets. For example, to return to our earlier mention of evaluation as a set of functional processes for group-formation, keywords can actively "promote" or "relegate" individuals to membership of ingroups and (especially here) outgroups. Keywords are often group labels (nominals) rather than just person attributes (adjectives).

They also allow access to a complex set of theoretical issues to do with salience (which are far from resolved in this study). The data show how unlikely it is that speaker/language evaluations can ultimately be captured via a universal set of dimensions. Specific groups (here, Welsh teenagers) have their own sociolinguistic repertoires for doing evaluation, just as specific targets are evaluated via attributes considered meaningful to assess them. The data have also suggested that salience is linked to the cultural constitution of judges' own communities, e.g. where farming is an experiential reality. But how a dimension is salient again depends on a local cultural process: being a farmer is only really attributable as undesirable by teenagers in rural communities who can conceive feasible and more attractive alternatives to farmers' lives.

These keywords, then, provide a window to these teenagers' aspirations, to their cultural and spatial outlooks, and to their assessments of the range and nature of the opportunities, relationships and identities that might be available to them. The general negativity in the evaluations is striking, and it is clear that they have multiple means of rejecting many of their Welsh peers. They may do this on personal criteria such as *boring*, and also on sociocultural criteria of being *farmers* or indeed *Welsh*. And while Welshness itself is seen from an English vantage point, Englishness too is strongly outgrouped and even pilloried, especially by the south-west. The processes operating to generate such negativity at this age have also been considered here: for example, the moratorium period in which there is a searching through the proliferation of potential identities at this age, and a concomitant need for teenagers to distance themselves from such a large number compared to those with which they wish to identify themselves more closely. But although moratorium is essential for identity achievement (Marcia 1980), there is no guarantee that all teenagers move into early adulthood having accomplished identity achievement (Heaven 1994: 33), and at worst our data arguably breed some concern that the evaluative patterns might not leave much space for positive and satisfying personal or sociocultural identities. That said, the study of the teenagers' evaluative repertoires shows itself to be of great value in pointing us towards a better understanding of the comparisons they are making and the stereotypical images they are working with, and better enables us to see their life-view and understand how they are negotiating their identities.

Appendix A. Transcripts of the 14 narrative excerpts

Transcription conventions

Bracketed numbers indicate pauses, timed in seconds (1.0). A brief pause is marked as (.). Unintelligible items are marked as (( )).
Incomplete words are included, e.g. "al" as a non-completed form of "albums".
"cos" is used for the conventionally reduced form of "because".
Punctuation is omitted because it typically misrepresents the grammatical and functional character of spontaneous talk.

Cardiff1
um (.) went on ho I went on holiday (.) to stay at my uncle's (2.0) cos he he's got a (.) he used to have a house in Spain until he came home and my cousin and my aunt used

to live over there as well (2.0) so we stayed over there (1.0) an um it was about the (.) second week cos we were over there for two weeks (.) and my cousin (.) cos at that time he couldn't really get a job over there (.) used to sell lighters for all to all the English bars cos there's all English bars along the beaches there's two beaches like (1.0) so we were coming back from selling all these lighters (1.0) and half way along then I said oh (.) Craig I think I'm gonna be sick (1.0) cos I really felt sick cos we'd been we'd been out in the sun all day and I really wasn't used to it (1.0) so (.) got back then (.) he said oh don't worry we'll get back in time.

NE2
I went to (.) tip it was the second time I'd ever been (.) was a couple of weeks ago (.) and um first time I (.) went I just walked straight in cos you had to be eighteen to get in and we got inside (.) and about half an hour after we got in they announced that MTV were gonna arrive nobody knew they were gonna be there an they all turned up and um (.) well I didn't know anyway (*laughs*) and they turned up and they started throwing t-shirts out and everything most of the big fellas there were already drunk (.) and I was just grabbing these t-shirts (.) and I was fighting the for them off people (.) six seven foot (.) easily an I was really amazed by this it was great (*laughs*) and it gave me a real big ego boost that did (2.0) and um got several autographs one off a band which I (.) been listening to an I've got a couple of their al got one of their albums I was rather chuffed with that.

RP3
and we were finishing off some (.) boxes alright they were something like that and there's a belt sander which has now been sort of stopped use (.) stopped the use of and uh I was just sanding something down and I was really tired and my fingers slipped off the box (.) and actually hit the belt sander just the ends of my fingers luckily it didn't hit I took it away in time (.) I I didn't think much had happened I thought I'd just sort of scraped the top (.) and um I I didn't feel that bad so I just sort of run it under some water (.) some cold water to try and to try and stop it bleeding but (.) uh it sort of about after two or three minutes I (.) I started feeling really bad I sort of felt really sick (.) so I told the teacher in charge of it (.) and he said oh well if you're feeling sick you'd better go go and sit outside and he said it's quite nasty.

SW4
I got a friend called [name] oh he's just massive I just got to say he's just massive (.) and he plays rugby with us (.) and he plays prop but oh one d time we were playing up at [place] (.) and he had to come on in the second half to substitute for a small chap (.) he came on the small chap pulled his jersey off (.) and then [name] literally attempted to put the jersey on (.) yeah he just got it on his (.) his (.) two arms and he tried to put his head in but he just couldn't get through (.) I was everybody was howling (.) his everything was wobbling his chest his belly his back his legs his oh it was disgusting and he's got oh ay I just everybody calls him Michelin man he's got to be he's got so many rolls of

fat so disgusting (1.0) and then (sigh) he came on (.) and he oh he can't run at all he's so unfit and it's a bit sad to tell you the truth.

Valleys5

one night it was raining heavily and as he was coming back (1.0) um (1.0) the farmers were fetching in in I fetching in the sheep cos of the thunder and lightning and that (.) and he didn't see em so as he come round the corner (.) as he swerved to miss em he hi he hit the lam he hit three lamp-posts bounced off (.) one hit another as he come off that one (.) um he w went head first into the third (.) and a a as as that happened (1.0) he went flying out through the window (.) th through the windscreen (.) we (.) when he went through the windscreen his foot had become left foot had become trapped in in the (.) in between the pedals so as he went through it tore his foot off (.) and (2.0) where if he had had his seatbelt on he would have been dead (.) completely otherwise (.) cos when when he had hit the engine (.) with the force come back and (.) when a when he when the fire brigade come um my father was laying on the floor and the engine was where he wa where the passenger and the driver's seat was.

Mid6

I was mucking out the shed I was and (1.0) in the (.) tractor (.) and I got one load in the front fork mm and (.) and I went in and I went into the mixen and what you do you just lift up the muck and put it on the top (1.0) so you dig in to a bit of the mixen and get a bit more in the front fork and lift it up into the top (.) and instead of when I put it into the mixer instead of the front end coming up with the muck the back w end wheels came up (.) cos there wasn't enough weight in the back so the back end came up (.) but the wheels still going round (.) but the front fork only goes so far up so the wheels stopped after a while (.) and the back wheels are (.) above the front ones (.) and the bonnet was on the front (.) so it was swaying about a bit like this and I (.) just about managed to get off half way up (1.0) so then dad came along after and stopped the tractor and put it down and I just (1.0) there's me standing there getting really worried (*laughs*) what am I going to do now (1.0) could have been dangerous.

NW7

um (.) I know this bloke (.) and he's well known of because (.) he's acting a bit weird (.) um there (.) quite a lot of stories going round about him (.) but (.) um (.) I think the best ones are (.) the one where he (.) went to buy a new helmet for his bike (.) and to see if this helmet worked and was unbreakable he found a brick (.) and threw the brick up in the air (.) and tried to make it land on top of the helmet but as the brick came down he put his hand on top of his head (.) and the brick landed on his hand and broke all his fingers.

Valleys8

I was ah me and my friend we decided ah go for a walk one day and there's this tunnel by his house (.) and it's like all sewage going into it there's like a walkway (.) in it so we had some torches and we went up it (1.0) and there's a like a bank s down there so we walked it it's about half mile long (.) and when we came out the end the it's like um workmen machines pumping (.) stuff out and pumping stuff in I don't know what (.) and um (.) you know we were just sort of mucking around with all if that see what they were doing and (2.0) my friend (.) he decided to turn it on to see what it done (.) so he turned it on on and and it was pumping a bit and he turned it off (.) and then he turned it on again and the pipe was starting to come off and it was squirting up in the air (.) like a a sprinkler.

NE9

then I so er (.) decided to cool down and go downstairs and have a meal in the restaurant and er (.) my feet were a bit tired and er (.) it was pretty pretty warm (.) and erm I felt this tickling in my feet and I thought it was just cos I'd been walking quite a bit and that but um (.) so I ignored it for a while and we ordered our food and (.) I I as I I finally go got tired of it and so I asked my mum if er (.) if she if she could feel the same thing and she said yeah and so did my dad so did my sister so we were getting a bit worried and just (.) slowly peered under the table and there was just a huge swarm of cockroaches they were just going everywhere all over the floor it was disgusting like.

NW10

he's done some pretty stupid things um (( )) as well he (.) stole a gate from the fire brigade place (.) and um cut the gate up and used the bars to um build a go-cart with a welder (.) and stuck a motorcycle engine on it and he got in some pretty deep trouble for that (1.0) um (.) he also about three years ago no about two years ago (.) he was o he was on a motorbike that he had built himself (.) and um he he was doing a wheelie and the throttle cable s um stuck it wouldn't go back down so he was still going on this massive wheelie and he didn't have a clutch or anything on it (.) and um he collided with a car and somersaulted over that car and over a police car that was um (.) behind that car landed behind the police car and um well the motorcycle you know was just a scrambler it wasn't a road bike or anything (.) and um his um kneecap came out of his leg.

Cardiff11

there was one time when (.) we were all playing pool on the pool table (.) and I saw you know I saw the latch on the thing so I thought oh I know if I put my hand down this pool table hole you know and I can tief a few games like (.) you know keep the latch up (.) and (.) puts my hand down you know ten minutes later I realise I couldn't get it back out (1.0) (*laughs*) so I thought oh no (.) I got my hand stuck down a pool table (.) you know so had to go and find the caretaker and he was he was like about three hours eventually until they found the caretaker you know I had to stand in this one place and one hand stuck in the pool table you know and one hand trying to eat my tea and my food and stuff (.) and (.) you know come across and he said oh he said how are we gonna get your hand out then (.) and he goes oh (.) well there's only one thing we can do like you know (.) I said what's that he said we'll have to saw the whole pool table in half and I said how you going to do that well he said you know go to the thing goes out to the garden shed like in the back and brings out this massive chainsaw.

RP12

so (.) after that (.) we went (.) ah (.) round to the big wheel (.) and er (.) it was spinning merrily round and then the the bloke decided to stop the wheel and get everyone off (.) and er (*laughs*) a little car fell off it (.) I dunno how high they were (.) God knows how they didn't sort of get squashed I suppose they weren't very high (1.0) um (.) I don't know (.) five metres up in the air or something when it (laughing) fell off (.) and they sort of rolled about the floor a bit stunned (.) stood up (.) looked at this guy and he quickly sort of put this put this little chair back on and they walked off (.) and the bloke pretended as nothing had happened and (.) we were all standing on there (.) totally amazed absolutely flabbergasted I dunno how on it could have happened (.) should have been shut down really I suppose.

SW13

I remember it was about two years ago (.) and ah we were on ((   )) at home (.) and er (2.0) well my father told me and my brother then to take the motorbike (.) and the trailer behind and knock a few posts down to hold to hold the gates open (.) and er (1.0) well after finishing then my brother told me oh let's go up the field to see how the how the contractors are going along (.) and uh we went up the top field as fast as we could on the motorbike a doing about forty forty five miles an hour (.) and we were following the hedge all the way round and the machine was right at the far corner of the field and uh (.) I stopped the bike and asked the boys what's wrong and they said that they had a blockage and so forth (.) an I talked to them for a while and my brother come over and said that we'd lost the trailer (1.0) and we looked around and (.) I saw the motorbike there with only the hitch behind (.) and the trailer was up in the hedge with the wheels (.) well ...

Mid14

I was sleeping in bed and um (.) well I heard this clicking noise cos bats click and (.) we knew there was these bats outside (.) oh and they sometimes fly into the house or there were some in my brother's bedroom and I thought there were some in mine cos I heard them clicking (.) and I shouted my dad and he said (.) oh don't be silly there's no bats in this house cos the windows were shut and um (.) they must have flew in in the day or something like that I don't know but I didn't think they flew in the day (.) and they came in (.) and um (.) I turned on the light and I couldn't see nothing and my dad couldn't see anything a so I went back to sleep heard clicking again (.) and I turned on the light and I could see the the flying round in the (.) in the landing (.) and I shouted my dad and a he came in and knocked it and it must have he must have just chucked it out or something (.) and then I went back to sleep I thought they were all gone and then we heard another clicking noise (.) and I thought nothing of it as cos I thought it was out it must've been they were kind of heard him out from outside.

Appendix B. Table of overall means for Welsh teenagers' evaluations of speakers
           (n=169)

	Do you like	Good at school	Like you	Make friends	How Welsh	Good laugh	Interesting story
Speaker							
Cardiff 1	2.43	2.62	1.88	2.39	2.83	2.34	1.87
Cardiff 11	3.20	2.44	2.53	3.12	2.88	3.75	3.69
NE 2	2.74	3.01	2.22	2.79	1.88	2.97	2.87
NE 9	2.86	2.48	2.26	2.77	1.60	3.24	2.71
NW 7	2.09	2.09	1.53	1.95	3.44	2.27	2.52
NW 10	2.72	2.67	2.22	2.74	3.41	2.97	3.28
SW 4	2.67	2.52	2.01	2.67	4.47	3.17	2.60
SW 13	2.14	2.38	1.65	2.15	3.91	2.16	1.89
Valleys 5	2.23	2.35	1.67	2.14	4.01	2.16	2.58
Valleys 8	2.01	2.40	1.46	2.11	3.76	2.16	1.79
Mid 6	2.13	3.11	1.71	2.19	2.29	1.99	1.89
Mid 14	2.03	3.00	1.66	2.07	2.14	1.98	1.86
RP 3	2.04	3.49	1.73	1.93	1.56	1.70	1.78
RP 12	2.01	3.56	1.70	1.98	1.51	1.88	1.99

Notes

1.   This research was funded by a University of Wales Intercollegiate Research Grant, awarded to Peter Garrett and Nikolas Coupland. We are grateful to Jacqui Guendouzi and Cathryn Williams for their help with data collection.
2.   Some studies employ unidirectional scales that avoid the problem of antonyms, e.g. irritating / not at all irritating. The quality of gradability is still required, however.
3.   Background information on the speaker of each excerpt, referred to by his accent categorisation (Cardiff, NE, NW, SW, Mid., Valleys, RP) and randomly allocated number (1–14). The speakers were all 15 years old. Only the NW and SW speakers spoke Welsh. The Cardiff speakers lived in Cardiff. The NE speakers lived near Mold. The RP speakers were from England – RP3 lived in Cheltenham, and RP12's home was in Devon. The SW speakers lived in Carmarthen. The Valleys speakers lived in Merthyr Tydfil. Mid6 lived near Newtown and Mid14 in Newtown. The NW speakers lived in Blaenau Ffestiniog.

References

Aitchison, John and Howard Carter
  1994   *A Geography of the Welsh Language 1961–1991*. Cardiff: University of Wales Press.
Baker, Colin
  1992   *Attitudes and Language*. Clevedon: Multilingual Matters.
Brown, B. Bradford, Margaret Mory and David Kinney
  1994   Casting adolescent crowds in a relational perspective: Caricature, channel, context. In Montemayor, Raymond, Gerald Adams and Thomas Gullotta (eds.), *Personal Relationships during Adolescence*. Thousand Oaks, California: Sage, 123–167.
Connolly, John
  1990   Port Talbot English. In Coupland, Nikolas (ed.), *English in Wales*. Clevedon: Multilingual Matters, 121–129.
Cooper, Robert and Joshua Fishman
  1974   The study of language attitudes. *International Journal of the Sociology of Language* 3, 5–19.
Coupland, Nikolas
  1988   *Dialect in Use: Sociolinguistic Variation in Cardiff English*. Cardiff: University of Wales Press.
Coupland, Nikolas (ed.)
  1990   *English in Wales*. Clevedon: Multilingual Matters.
Coupland, Nikolas, Angie Williams and Peter Garrett
  1994   The social meanings of Welsh English. *Journal of Multilingual and Multicultural Development* 15, 471–489.
  1999   "Welshness" and "Englishness" as attitudinal dimensions of English language varieties in Wales. In Preston, Dennis R. (ed.), *Handbook of Perceptual Dialectology: Volume 1*. Amsterdam/Philadelphia: John Benjamins, 333–343.
Day, Richard
  1982   Children's attitudes toward language. In Ryan, Ellen B. and Howard Giles (eds.), *Attitudes towards Language Variation*. London: Arnold, 116–131.
de Klerk, Vivien
  1997   The role of expletives in the construction of masculinity. In Johnson, Sally and Ulrike Hanna Meinhof (eds.), *Language and Masculinity*. Oxford: Blackwell, 144–158.
Garrett, Peter, Nikolas Coupland and Angie Williams
  1995   "City harsh" and "the Welsh version of RP": Some ways in which teachers view dialects of Welsh English. *Language Awareness* 4, 99–107.
  1999   Evaluating dialect in discourse: Teachers' and teenagers' responses to young English speakers in Wales. *Language in Society* 28, 321–254.

2003   *Investigating Language Attitudes: Social Meanings of Dialect, Ethnicity and Performance*. Cardiff: University of Wales Press.

Gavin, Leslie and Wyndol Furman
1989   Age differences in adolescents' perceptions of their peer groups. *Developmental Psychology* 25, 827–834.

Giles, Howard
1970   Evaluative reactions to accents. *Educational Review* 22, 211–227.

Giles, Howard, Susan Baker and Guy Fielding
1976   Communication length as a behavioural index of accent prejudice. *International Journal of the Sociology of Language* 6, 73–81.

Heaven, Patrick
1994   *Contemporary Adolescence*. Basingstoke: Macmillan.

Holmes, Janet and Helen Ainsworth
1997   Unpacking the research process: Investigating syllable timing in New Zealand English. *Language Awareness* 6, 32–47.

Hughes, Arthur and Peter Trudgill
1979   *English Accents and Dialects*. London: Arnold.

Lambert, Wallace, R. Hodgson, Robert Gardner and S. Fillenbaum
1960   Evaluational reactions to spoken languages. *Journal of Abnormal and Social Psychology* 60, 44–51.

Marcia, James
1980   Identity in adolescence. In Adelson, Joseph (ed.), *Handbook of Adolescent Psychology*. New York: Wiley, 159–187.

Mees, Inger
1983   The speech of Cardiff schoolchildren: A real time study. Unpublished PhD thesis: University of Leiden.

Nesdale, Drew and Rosanna Rooney
1996   Evaluations and stereotyping of accented speakers by pre-adolescent children. *Journal of Language and Social Psychology* 15, 133–154.

Newman, Philip and Barbara Newman
1988   Early adolescence and its conflict: Group identity vs. alienation. *Adolescence* 11, 261–274.

Paltridge, John and Howard Giles
1984   Attitudes towards speakers of regional accents of French. *Linguistische Berichte* 90, 71–85.

Parry, David
1990   The conservative dialects of north Carmarthenshire. In Coupland, Nikolas (ed.), *English in Wales*. Clevedon: Multilingual Matters, 142–150.

Potter, Jonathan and Margaret Wetherell
1987   *Discourse and Social Psychology*. London: Sage.

Preston, Dennis R
.   1996   Whaddayaknow? The modes of folklinguistic awareness. *Language Awareness* 5, 40–74.

Price, Susan, Michael Fluck and Howard Giles
    1983   The effects of language of testing on bilingual pre-adolescents' attitudes towards Welsh and varieties of English. *Journal of Multilingual and Multicultural Development* 4, 149–161.

Rampton, Ben
    1995   *Crossing: Language and Ethnicity among Adolescents.* London: Longman.

Sharp, Derrick, Beryl Thomas, Eurwen Price, Gareth Francis and Iwan Davies
    1973   *Attitudes to Welsh and English in the Schools of Wales.* Cardiff: University of Wales Press.

Tench, Paul
    1990   The pronunciation of English in Abercrave. In Coupland, Nikolas (ed.), *English in Wales.* Clevedon: Multilingual Matters, 130–141.

Trudgill, Peter
    1990   *The Dialects of England.* Oxford: Blackwell.

Urban, Greg
    1993   The represented functions of speech in Shokleng myths. In Lucy, John A. (ed.), *Reflexive Language: Reported Speech and Metapragmatics.* Cambridge: Cambridge University Press, 241–259.

Waterman, Alan
    1982   Identity development from adolescence to adulthood: An extension of theory and a review of research. *Developmental Psychology* 18, 341–358.

Williams, Angie, Peter Garrett and Nikolas Coupland
    1996   Perceptual dialectology, folklinguistics, and regional stereotypes: Teachers' perceptions of variation in Welsh English. *Multilingua* 15, 171–199.
    1999   Dialect recognition. In Preston, Dennis R. (ed.), *Handbook of Perceptual Dialectology: Volume 1.* Amsterdam/Philadelphia: John Benjamins, 345–358.

Windsor Lewis, J.
    1990   The roots of Cardiff English. In Coupland, Nikolas (ed.), *English in Wales.* Clevedon: Multilingual Matters, 105–108.

Zahn, Christopher and Robert Hopper
    1985   Measuring language attitudes: The speech evaluation instrument. *Journal of Language and Social Psychology* 4, 113–123.

Teachers' beliefs about students' talk and silence: Constructing academic success and failure through metapragmatic comments

Adam Jaworski and Itesh Sachdev

1. Introduction: Communication skills

This chapter focuses on the broad communicative categories of "talk" and "silence" in the context of metapragmatic comments made by teachers about their students' "communication skills". Good communication skills are perceived to be vital for almost anyone entering the job market today. This is explained by Fairclough (1992a) and echoed by Cameron (1985, 2000) as a result of the shift in western economies from the domination of the manufacturing sector to the greater expansion of the service sector. As Cameron (1995: 29) puts it "large numbers of workers who would once have been treated simply as 'hands' are being redefined as linguistic actors needing specific training in 'communication skills'". However, the idea of developing communication skills is not unproblematic.

For example, Fairclough (1992a) observes that the Kingman and Cox Reports advocate teaching standard English (a useful "skill") at school while appreciating the "richness" of other varieties of English and recognizing their place in communication. As Fairclough notes, "learning standard English does give some learners life chances they would not otherwise have" (Fairclough 1991: 14). However, teaching standard English without teaching critical language awareness (about standard English) may open up new opportunities to some as much as it may perpetuate the legitimation of the linguistic and cultural asymmetries in society.

Furthermore, Fairclough (1992b: 33) argues that teaching standard English at schools is part of the "competence-based 'communication skills' view of language education with a new emphasis on 'oracy' and spoken language education", and that this view follows the notion of appropriateness in sociolinguistic variation, which does not take into account the possibility of alternative, competing versions of communication (e.g. multiple ways of performing such speech events as job interviews, medical consultations, etc.). On the contrary, the appropriateness view of sociolinguistic variation, imposes a hegemonic ideology on language use with the effect of delegitimizing "inappropriate" ways of speaking/writing and, ultimately, leading to social, political and economic exclusion of those who do not have the adequate command of the dominant genres.

Likewise, Cameron (1995, 2000) observes that teaching communication skills requires codifying rules of correctness. Such processes take place in specific social, political and economic conditions and raise a host of sociolinguistic problems. For example, with regard to communication skills in business/service settings, Cameron suggests that the fixation of rules of communication (e.g. between sales representatives and customers) is similar to the fixation of accent and grammar in prescriptive grammar. Both types of prescription aim at the minimization of variation and are predominantly based on dominant models of what is perceived as appropriate (cf. Fairclough 1992b). In the case of British businesses, for example, Cameron (2000) cites two such dominant models: the "middle-class" model and the "American" model.

Apart from identifying currently acceptable "models" for developing communication skills, Cameron points to the general inability of those participating in communication skills development programmes to clearly state what the notion of "communication" entails and that most conceptualizations of communication (skills) remain "common sense platitude" in most informants' awareness.

In sum, we approach this study with the following three assumptions:

1. the notion of communication skills is based on strong normative beliefs about what is "right" and "wrong" in language use;
2. these beliefs are frequently anchored in popular, common sense and misleading assumptions about the nature and role of language in communication;
3. the success or failure of a job/university applicant depends, in part, on the evaluation of his/her communication skills; in other words, making metapragmatic comments relating to one's communication skills is an important aspect of "gate-keeping".

2.   This study

Our earlier study of students' beliefs about silence (Jaworski and Sachdev 1998) suggested that, overall, secondary school pupils believed that they were more silent in the classroom than their teachers, which confirmed previous findings of ethnographic and discourse analytic studies of classroom interaction. We suggested that for students silence is the relatively unmarked underlying communicative form in the classroom, while for teachers silence is relatively marked and talk is unmarked. Our study also confirmed students' perception that silence was relatively more important for *learning* than for *teaching*. Specifically, students believed that, other things being equal, they were more silent when learning than their teachers were when teaching.

Of course, we realize that new, "progressive" styles of learning introduced in many schools aim to engage students in verbal classroom activities to a considerable extent, encouraging them to ask questions, express opinions, discuss ideas, voice their doubts, and so on. However, given that our results suggested that silence was perceived to be important for learning, teachers' expectations that students should be verbally active in the classroom may be a potential source of anxiety and conflict for some students (see Jaworski and Sachdev 1998 for discussion).

In this chapter, we report on the data collected from 178 teachers' references written predominantly for secondary school and college students who applied for places on a language/communication related undergraduate degree scheme at a British university through the Universities and Colleges Admissions System (UCAS) for 1997 entry. Our interest in these texts, and the specific mention of "communication skills" in them, came from one of us (AJ) acting as an admissions officer for undergraduate courses in his department. While reading large numbers of the UCAS references, it became apparent that mention of communication skills fell into two general categories: "talk" and "silence", and that overall, talk was referred to positively and silence negatively. Consider two typical examples (more examples are cited later in the chapter):

> He has made a number of excellent oral presentations confidently, and he makes valuable contributions to group discussions. (001, female referee)

> She has a quiet, thoughtful reserve about her but this should not be hastily interpreted. (010, male referee)

The first example above praises a student's loquacity in the classroom and describes it as "excellent" and "valuable". Furthermore, it is positively linked to the student's "confidence" and implies high academic potential/performance of the student. The second example, on the other hand, pertains to another student's "silent" behaviour. In contrast to the enthusiastic references to verbosity as witnessed in the previous example, descriptors such as "quiet" and "thoughtful reserve" paint a rather bleak picture of a *passive* student. This is especially clear when such labels are juxtaposed (by means of a contrastive conjunction "but") with the phrase: "but this should not be hastily interpreted". In other words, being quiet and reserved (however thoughtful they may appear) is, by default, expected to be negatively interpreted by the reader of the reference. In other words, if the first of the above examples had ended with a similar phrase, it would have been awkward because "making oral presentations" and "contributing to group discussions" (apart from being qualified by a number of positive qualifiers) is meant to be ("hastily") interpreted in a positive way. Hence, there is no need, in fact no room, for adding to the first extract anything like the phrase that ends the latter example. Consider how inappropriate it would sound: "... he makes valuable contributions to group discussions *but this should not be hastily interpreted*".

UCAS references (as other types of academic and professional references) are of necessity evaluative texts, although, overall, their content and structure appear to be rather formulaic. This is probably because, in part, current guidelines for referees, which claim not to be very specific, impose a common structure on most references. The guidelines are as follows:

> There is no set format or recommended structure for this [i.e. writing a reference], but selectors find it helpful if the following information about the applicant is included ...:
> – academic achievement and potential including predicted results or performance;
> – suitability for course(s)/subject(s) applied for;
> – factors that may have influenced performance;
> – personal qualities, such as motivation, powers of analysis, communication skills, independence of thought;
> – career aspirations;
> – any health or personal circumstances relevant to the applications;
> – other interests and activities;
> – commitments that will prevent the applicant from attending the interview (UCAS 1997: 14).

In the above list, "communication skills" are grouped under the heading of "personal qualities" and, as can be predicted, they are not in any way defined or specified as to what is understood by that term. Given the rather loose conceptual status of the whole notion, it may well be assumed that the term "communication skills" may mean different things to UCAS officials, the referees, students and the "selectors".

From our experience it appears that UCAS references are predominantly positive in evaluating the students and, in fact, we have not ever encountered any reference which would ultimately *not* recommend a student for the courses of his or her choice (although they are likely to exist). This does not mean, of course, that certain negative evaluations are not present in the references, although they are usually hedged, toned down and softened. One significant area of such negative comments pertains to aspects of "communication skills", and it is this distinction between "good" and "poor" communication skills in the metapragmatic comments by referees that forms the focus of this chapter.

3. Procedure

178 consecutive UCAS references were examined with regard to their explicit mention of the candidates' *talk* and *silence*. By "talk" we mean all the references to students' orality, participation in group discussions, asking/answering questions, and so on, while by "silence" we mean references to students' silence ("silent manner"), reticence, quietness, inability or unwillingness to take part in group discussions, and so on.

Our coding scheme assumed a binary view of "communication skills" for several reasons. First, these categories have been extensively discussed in discourse analytic and ethnographic studies of classroom interaction, especially with regard to teacher talk and student silence (see Jaworski and Sachdev 1998 for review). Second, this dichotomy became strikingly apparent while sifting through numerous UCAS application forms; in other words, we followed our intuition about the salience of "talk" and "silence" as communicative categories in the educational process. Third, our earlier work (e.g. Jaworski 1993, 1997) suggests that in communication in general, other things being equal, silence is construed negatively while talk is construed positively. Therefore, it seemed to make sense to find out whether this same axiological polarity in favour of talk was present in the teachers' references, in which "communication skills" play such an important role (we return to this issue in our Discussion).

The classification of seemingly non-homogeneous types of behaviour into either "silence" or "talk" is only apparently a sign of conceptual sloppiness. As we have argued elsewhere (e.g. Jaworski 1993), talk and silence are not absolute categories with clear boundaries. Any attempt at an empirical study of these two categories involves inclusion of "intermediate" or "fuzzy" forms in either of them. For example, a person who is described as "very silent" or "quiet" may simply speak little. A person's whisper may be, on one occasion, a sign of his or her silencing, while on another a brave attempt at "speaking out". It must also be emphasized that having established the principles of coding, there was little disagreement between 4 independent coders (over 95% concordance) as to the classification of a particular instance of data to the "silence" or "talk" category (see below for more examples).

All the references to talk and silence in the references were noted down and coded for "positive" and "negative" evaluation by the referees, whether they pertained to the academic potential/achievement of the student or to his/her personality characteristics. At this stage it is important to bear in mind two things. First, when we refer to a negative valuation of talk or silence, we do not mean that the reference for the student is necessarily negative. In fact, the opposite is usually the case, e.g. the student may be "good" *despite* displaying certain forms of "negative" silent behaviour (see below). Secondly, although the UCAS guidelines identify communication skills as a useful point to comment on in relation to "personality characteristics" of students, most references to communication skills are made in terms of students' academic success or failure.

Two research students coded the data in the first instance and their coding was subsequently checked and confirmed by both of us in consultation with a secondary school teacher, who was well-experienced in writing UCAS references herself. Where known, we made a record of the students' and referees' gender, location (urban vs. rural) and type (independent vs. comprehensive vs. college) of school, and referee's position/relationship to the student (head vs. principal vs. teacher/tutor vs. other).

In a number of cases talk and silence were mentioned more than once in the reference, which was also noted. This was usually the case when individual A-level subject teachers provided a paragraph each and a principle or head of the school compiled them together into a single reference. (In such cases the gender of individual teachers was not known and the coded gender and position for referee were those of the compiler.)

We have excluded from our analysis all the references (rather numerous in our corpus) to the oral and written skills of students studying foreign languages.

4.   Background information

The majority of the students for whom the references were written were 18 and 19 years of age (65.7% and 21.9%, respectively). There were three 17 years old (1.7%) and 19 students who were between 20 and 44 years old (10.9%). As far as it was possible to establish, only 1.1% of all students where non-white. Forty-eight students were male (27%) and 130 students were female (73%). Eighty-seven referees were male (48.9%) and 56 referees were female (31.5%). In 35 cases the sex of the referee was unknown (19.7%). The position/relationship to student was as follows: 58 Heads (32.6%), 40 Principals (22.5%), 27

Teachers/Tutors (15.2%), 47 Other (26.4%) and in six cases the position of the referee was unknown (3.4%). 112 references were written in urban schools and colleges (62.9%) and 66 in rural ones (37.1%). The breakdown by school type is as follows: 63 comprehensive schools (35.4%), 21 independent (private and grammar) schools (11.8%) and 93 colleges (52.2%). In one case the information was missing.

5.   *Talk* and *silence* in UCAS references

This section provides quantitative and qualitative analyses of our data. It starts with more examples of what we mean by references to "talk" and "silence" with relation to UCAS references. We also give examples of "positive" and "negative" valuation of these concepts, and demonstrate that they are used for commenting on the students' personality characteristics as well as their academic potential and achievement. Preliminary statistics with regard to the frequency of occurrence of these categories in our data are also presented.

5.1. Talk

Overall, a substantial majority (61.8%) of references mention *talk*, demonstrating that it is an important evaluative factor in referees' minds. Talk is mentioned once in 80 references (44.9%), twice in 26 references (14.6%), thrice in three references (1.7%) and four times in one reference (.6%). 68 (38.2%) of the references make no mention of talk.

Talk is related directly to academic behaviour and achievement via communication skills in the vast majority of cases (82.7%), though references to talk being associated with the personal characteristics (17.3% of cases) also relate to communication skills (see examples below).

When the references focus on the notion of communication skills, they centre on the students' ability to express ideas through talk, participation in group discussions, clarity of expression, fluency, and so on. The analyses revealed that *all* (i.e. 100%) of the references to oracy in this context are positive or highly positive (qualified by positive modifiers), e.g. "excellent oral presentations", "her observations are perceptive and sagacious", "fluent *and* interesting", etc. Specifically, the positivity of talk centres on different types of outcomes of talk (making contributions to discussions, expressing ideas, etc.), rather than talk itself, while, as we note later, "silence" does not seem to yield any positive results in the pedagogical process. Consider the following examples:

> Jane is very articulate and willingly contributes to class discussion, her observations are perceptive and sagacious. (003, female referee)

> Rachel makes an intelligent contribution to class discussion where she clearly expresses her ideas. (004, male referee)

One student receives the following set of comments on her communication skills in her reference:

> She is assertive and is willing to speak her mind.
> She expresses herself accurately and fluently, both orally [and in writing].
> She actively participates in class discussions and debates.
> She is a skilled communicator both orally and in writing. (136, female referee)

Positive references to communication skills are also made in relation to the students' personal characteristics, e.g.:

> Keilie is a fluent and interesting communicator, who should perform well at interview. (045, female referee)

> This most pleasant pupil is chatty and gregarious. (118, female referee)

> Marianne is very gregarious, outgoing student with an excellent sense of humour. (075, female referee)

5.2. Silence

Silence is mentioned in our sample far less than talk (20.8% vs. 61.8%). Silence is mentioned once in 22 references (12.4%), twice in 10 references (5.6%), thrice in three references (1.7%), and five times in two references (1.1%). Silence is related directly to academic behaviour and achievement in a majority of cases (65%), with the remainder being associated with the personal characteristics (35% of cases).

Overall, references to different forms of silence (cf. Jaworski 1993) are found to be mainly negative. When silence is associated with academic matters, it is overwhelmingly negative (93% negative; 7% positive). However, when silence is associated with personality traits, it is construed more positively (65% positive), though a significant proportion (35%) of the mentions of silence has negative connotations (see examples below). It is likely that the relative positivity of silence when discussing personality characteristics may be reflective of teachers' general, possibly stereotyped preference for "quiet" students implying submissiveness and obedience over "noisy" students implying insubordination and disobedience.

Qualitative analyses provided a more textured view of the role of silence in referees' reports. The following two are rare examples of positive references to academic silences:

> Betty brings a quietly determined approach to her work. (019, male referee)

> Penny demonstrates a quiet, common sense approach to all areas of study. (150, male referee)

Mention of a positive academic silence is combined, again very rarely, with a positive mention of academic talk. In the following example, positive academic silence is introduced by a reference to the student's contribution as a "good listener":

> She listens intelligently to others and is a sensible and articulate contributor to discussion. (154, female referee)

As mentioned above, the vast majority of references to academic silence, however, are negative. Because all the references in our sample tend to be rather positive, overall evaluations of students being recommended to their chosen universities, the negativity of the mention of silence is toned down by contrasting it (frequently with the use of conjuncts such as *though* and *but*) with some positive aspects of their work or personality, or by placing an overt disclaimer to the negative interpretation of the silence, e.g.:

> Despite the words "quiet" and "reserved" in this reference Emily lacks neither ability or motivation. She is seen as self-contained, mature, thoughtful and interesting girl with genuine, if somewhat latent, talent. She will reach her goals quietly, determinedly and efficiently. (017, male referee)

> Roger works quietly but effectively. (057, ?)

> All of his teachers saw him as fairly quiet but perceptive. (067, male referee)

> Anna is a quiet, conscientious student whose written work and willingness to participate in discussions have improved considerably. (051, male referee)

> Orally she needs to be pressed but can articulate complex ideas when she has the background knowledge. (071, ?)

> ... though quiet she is eloquent and willing to share ideas. (141, male referee)

As the last example above suggests, some of the references to students' reticence are disclaimed in a fashion which borders on contradiction and inconsistency (*quiet but eloquent*). We found other combinations of references which are negative in relation to silence in one type of academic context and positive in relation to talk in another context, e.g.:

> In group discussions she may appear rather reserved but on an individual basis she is highly articulate. (174, female referee)

And in the next example, the student's negative academic silence is contrasted with her seemingly positive social communication skills (i.e. talk):

> Katie relates well to other peers, but is reticent in one to one contact with staff. (045, female referee)

As has been mentioned, silence is relatively frequently linked to personality characteristics. Though negative connotations are present in a fairly significant manner, these references are largely positive. For instance, positive evaluation of social silence is found in the following example:

> She proved to be a quiet, charming and intelligent student. (023, male referee)

The next example, however, displays a different pattern: first, a negative mention of academic silence is made followed by a negative social type of silence, which is then contrasted (or even contradicted) by an overall positive evaluation of the student as a member of his peer group:

> Tim lacks a little confidence when it comes to talking in class ... He is reserved yet enjoys a good relationship with other members of the group. (052, ?)

In the quantitative analyses we do not find any significant overall differences in the frequency of references to talk and silence between the locations of the schools (rural, urban, etc.), their types (state, independent, etc.), and positions of referees. However, analyses with respect to the gender of referees and students indicate some interesting differences. Figure 1 displays mentions of talk and silence of male and female applicants by male and female referees. There appear to be few differences in mentions of the silence of male and female applicants by their female referees (see Fig. 1), though male referees do mention silence more often for female applicants than for male applicants (21.5% vs

11.1%). For talk, female referees did not differentiate between the amount of talk of male and female applicants, though they did mention talk more often for both male and female applicants than male referees (Figure 1). However, male referees mention talk in the applications of male students (62.9%) substantially more often than they do for female students (48.5%). Given that talk is always positively viewed in the references (and silence is generally negatively viewed), such findings may be interpreted as disadvantaging female applicants.

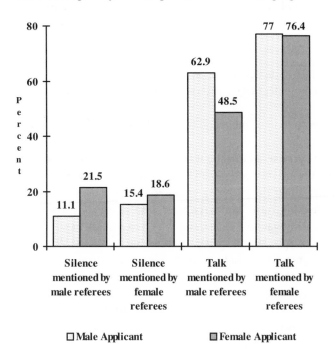

Figure 1. Percentage mentions of silence and talk as a function of the gender of student and referee

6. Discussion

We start this section by recounting some of the points made above. Guidelines on reference writing include "communication skills" under the "personality characteristics". Overall our findings suggest that talk is almost exclusively mentioned in connection with the students' academic abilities and perform-ance, while silence is mentioned in connection with both the students' academic achievement and with personality characteristics. The main difference in the

valuation of talk and silence is that when silence is related to academic achievement, it is viewed negatively much more often than positively, while talk is
never viewed negatively in this context. When silence is mentioned for personal
characterisation of students, it usually invokes positive characteristics but it
also attracts negative valuations. Talk is only positively mentioned in relation
to personality traits of students.

Although this study is based on a rather limited sample of references, we
would like to postulate a number of observations and interpretations in relation
to the following issues, which we discuss briefly in the remaining part of this
chapter:

- general valuation of talk and silence as communicative items;
- talk and silence as major categories with respect to communication skills (in
  education);
- the distribution and valuation of male and female students' talk and silence.

It probably comes as no surprise that in the references examined here talk and
silence tend to be valued positively and negatively, respectively. By now, it is a
well-established fact that, other things being equal, longer pauses, slow tempo
of speech and short speaking turns are associated with communicators who
tend to be stereotyped more negatively than those who make (relatively) shorter
pauses, use faster tempo of speech and longer speaking turns. Perhaps, as Scollon (1985) argues this dichotomous view is predominant among middle-class
Anglo-Americans (see also Philips 1976). Similarly in Britain, a greater tolera-
tion of silence may be encountered outside of the middle-class, white population. For example, Milroy (1981) describes how members of the working class
in Belfast use silence on informal, social occasions with greater ease than what
she would have expected to be comfortable for middle-class British speakers.

In linguistic terms talk has been described as "unmarked" vis-à-vis
("marked") silence (Sobkowiak 1997). This dichotomy represents a kind of
middle-class, Anglo-American and British norm, with mainstream schooling
in the US and in Britain largely subscribing to a white, middle-class ethos (e.g.
Willis 1977; Barton and Walker 1983; Entwistle 1978; Lawton 1975; Walkerdine 1985; Edwards and Redfern 1991; Brantlinger 1993). Evidently, in such
contexts oracy, verbal competence, articulateness and participation in discussions will be prized more highly than silent participation, listenership, and observation.

We started this chapter by referring to Fairclough's and Cameron's work
which advises caution in establishing criteria for the development and assessment of communication skills, which should not be based on simplistic views of

linguistic variation and communication strategies. On the basis of our research, we postulate a further rethink of the link which seems to be customarily made between the broadly defined concepts of talk and silence, their attribution to students and drawing conclusions about their academic success (or failure).

Of course, dominant educational theory favours the approach to talk and silence displayed in the UCAS references discussed above. One study of the "quiet child" in a primary school context is based on "the premise that habitually quiet non-participatory behaviour is detrimental to learning" (Collins 1996: 195, see also Chapter 1). Unfortunately, the author does not give any empirical evidence or references to the work which corroborates such a claim. Although we can agree that the conceptualization of academic silence as a withdrawal from cognitive activity due to the pathology of the child's social environment, for example, is clearly pedagogically undesirable and detrimental to the child's educational success, we would also argue that certain types of silence in the classroom need not be negatively stereotyped. For example, silence may facilitate listening and comprehension. Besides, not all students who talk a lot in class – the "noisy" ones – need necessarily be academically successful.

However, these functions of silence are rarely appreciated due to the perception of silence as unable to perform the ideational function of language, which is central to the education process. This is certainly important, but if we accept communication to be a two-way process, listening and comprehension of ideational meanings is indeed very well served by silence (construed as active listenership), and we know of no empirical studies which demonstrate that students who speak more in class outperform academically those students who do not. (Certainly, classroom talk is not solely content oriented and interaction at the relational/procedural level cannot clearly be ignored, cf. Sarangi 1988.)

Finally, we need to address briefly the issue of a seemingly unequal treatment of male and female students by male referees with respect to the mention of talk in their references. We have shown that references to talk carry more positive value than those to silence. Therefore, giving more weighting to the talk of males in educational settings (by male referees) seems to advantage them over female students. In fact, our finding is consistent with some earlier work on language and gender in education.

It has been argued, for example, that males speak more in the classroom than females (Spender 1982; Jule 2005; see also Kramarae and Treichler 1990), although not all evidence is equally conclusive (Swann 1992, 1988). Overall, boys tend to take more turns but there are also quiet boys and some outspoken girls. Interestingly, much of the talk that boys do in the classroom is not academically related. Swann (1992) quotes French and French (1984), who demonstrate how boys (more so than girls) secure more turns by answering teachers' questions in extraordinary, almost bizarre ways thus eliciting more questions about what they have said and thus drawing teachers' attention to themselves more than girls do. Likewise, Altani (1995) quotes Greek teachers, who seem to agree (and in many cases endorse the status quo) that boys are more disruptive in class than girls.

But then, if boys do talk more in class than girls, even if it is not solely for academic purposes, why do female referees not follow the male referees' pattern of referring to female students' talk less often than to male students' talk?

A possible answer may lie in the subconscious yet discriminatory dismissive view of female students' talk in the classroom. In their study of language and gender in the GCSE oral English examination, Jenkins and Cheshire (1990) and Cheshire and Jenkins (1991) demonstrate that teachers assess the communication skills of boys and girls differently. For example, the cooperative style of girls (allowing others to talk) is negatively assessed as displaying 'not enough content'. Once the female-led cooperative talk leads to a smooth flow of conversation, both male and female students are praised for the supportive nature of talk within their group. Furthermore, boys who receive praise from their teachers for their talk largely depended on being drawn into the discussion by girls, whose role in this respect does not seem to be appreciated.

7.   Conclusion

No study known to us has shown a positive correlation between a student's amount of speaking in class and his/her academic achievement. In fact, if male students do indeed speak more in class than girls, then, in the light of recent press reports, speaking may be detrimental to academic progress as girls in British schools are said to outperform boys in most academic areas (see, e.g. Judd 1998). Therefore, using fairly vague descriptions of students' "communication skills" is not only naive but also potentially discriminatory to some students. Indeed our data suggests that male and female referees tend to provide references that are likely to have differential, and discriminatory effects on male and female applicants. Additionally, there is absolutely no way of knowing for admission tutors or any other addressees of similar references how the references to students' articulateness, clear expression of ideas, reticence, and so on, stand in relation to actual behaviour.

Mehan (1991) examines the discursive and organizational mechanisms of a school committee's decision-making process about the placement of "handicapped" (as opposed to "normal") students in one of many possible "special needs" programmes. Mehan notes that out of the possible twelve possibilities open to the committee only two outcomes prevail, while others are not even actively considered. Most significantly, the legally guaranteed possibility of placing students in the private sector for which the funding must be provided by the local school district is only mentioned to the parents present at these meetings after an alternative decision is made. Thus, Mehan discusses the interplay of the macro structures (or "distal circumstances") and micro structures (or "proximal circumstances") in the process of the school committee constructing the preferred version of "sorting students". He demonstrates how the committee operates under a set of constraints imposed by the policies of governmental agencies, other public organizations, administrative and budgetary limitations on the one hand, and how it organizes its own discursive practice of allocating a student to one or the other programme via a set of recurring, discursive practices, through which a preferred outcome for the committee is achieved. By deconstructing the macro and micro organization of the way in which the committee operates, Mehan attests to this aspect of the educational processes being socially constructed in

> the moment-to-moment, day-by-day work of daily life, including those portions of daily life which are carried out in bureaucratic organizations. Educational sorting practices are a particular form of "social practice" … To "practice" social life is, literally, to work at its production, maintenance and transformation. Practice constitutes social life; it is not an incomplete rendition of some ideal form. Practice encompasses people's application of ideas and norms as well as practical action in concrete situations of choice.

> (Mehan 1991: 82)

Likewise, Adelswärd and Nihom (1998) discuss the practices of teacher–parent conferences in special needs primary schools in Sweden, in which the roles and identities of teachers, parents and pupils are jointly negotiated and constructed in locally produced discourse, following broader educational, political and social ramifications.

Writing (UCAS) references for students appears to be a similar manifestation of the educators' social practice. Constrained by the requirements of evaluating their students for other organizations (here, universities), generally not wanting to jeopardize anyone's chances of success, following the guidelines for what constitutes a "good" or "exhaustive" reference, they rely on a set of educational and common-sense principles realized locally as a set of attributes assigned to individual students. In doing so, they resort to a pool of routines, and we have only looked at a small aspect of the whole refereeing mechanism, in a discourse-based process which constitutes them as gate-keepers, increasing or decreasing their students' chances of getting a place at the university.

In conclusion, the main focus of this chapter is on underscoring the importance of metalinguistic (metapragmatic) comments in the educators' practice of writing references for students. To use Mehan's terminology again, the metalinguistic issues are relevant in terms of both distal and proximal circumstances. On the one hand, the educators subscribe to the system's emphasis on communication skills and general, common sense evaluations of loquacity and reticence, while on the other, they produce texts which imply causal links between the amount of talk produced by individual students and their academic success or failure. For these reasons, we would advocate critical language/communication awareness as part of ongoing teacher training.

Acknowledgement

This chapter has benefited from the comments of numerous participants at the Round Table Meeting on "The Sociolinguistics of Metalanguage" (Gregynog, June 1998). We especially thank Nik Coupland for his useful feedback. We also thank Jamie Ambler, Gareth Burkhill-Howard and Sarah Lawson for their help in coding the data. We are grateful to UCAS for allowing us to quote from the forms. All names in the quotes used in this chapter are fictitious.

References

Adelswärd, Viveka and Claes Nihom
    1998   Discourse about children with mental disablement: An analysis of teacher-parent conferences in special education schools. *Language and Education* 12, 81–98.
Altani, Cleopatra
    1995   Primary school teachers' explanations of boys' disruptiveness in the classroom: A gender specific aspect of the hidden curriculum. In Mills, Sara (ed.), *Language & Gender: Interdisciplinary Perspectives*. London: Longman, 149–159.
Barton, Len and Stephen Walker (eds.)
    1983   *Race, Class and Education*. London: Croom Helm.
Brantlinger, Ellen A.
    1993   *The Politics of Social Class in Secondary School: Views of Affluent and Impoverished Youth*. New York: Teachers College Press.

Cameron, Deborah
  1995   *Verbal Hygiene*. London: Routledge.
  2000   *Good To Talk?* London: Sage.
Cheshire, Jenny and Nancy Jenkins
  1991   Gender issues in the GCSE oral English examination: Part II. *Language and Education* 5, 19–40.
Collins, Janet
  1996   *The Quiet Child*. London: Cassell.
Edwards, Viv and Angela Redfern
  1992   *The World in A Classroom: Language in Education*. Clevedon: Multilingual Matters.
Entwistle, Harold
  1978   *Culture, Class and Education*. London: Methuen.
Fairclough, Norman
  1992a   Introduction. In Fairclough, Norman (ed.), *Critical Discourse Awareness*. London: Longman, 1–29.
  1992b   The appropriacy of "appropriateness". In Fairclough, Norman (ed.), *Critical Discourse Awareness*. London: Longman, 33–56.
Hemmings, Annette
  1996   Conflicting images? Being black and a model high school student. *Anthropology & Education Quarterly* 27, 20–50.
Jaworski, Adam
  1993   *The Power of Silence: Social and Pragmatic Perspectives*. Newbury Park, California: Sage Publications.
Jaworski, Adam (ed.)
  1997   *Silence: Interdisciplinary Perspectives*. Berlin: Mouton de Gruyter.
Jaworski, Adam and Itesh Sachdev
  1998   Beliefs about silence in the classroom. *Language and Education* 12, 273–292.
Jenkins, Nancy and Jenny Cheshire
  1990   Gender issues in the GCSE oral English examination: Part I. *Language and Education* 4, 261–292.
Judd, J.
  1998   Boys still failing to improve at English. *The Independent*, 18 December 1998.
Jule, Allyson
  2005   A fair share: Gender and linguistic space in a language classroom. *Multilingua* 24 (in press).
Kramarae, Cheris and Paula A. Treichler
  1990   Power relationships in the classroom. In. Gabriel, Susan L. and Isaiah Smithson (eds.), *Gender in the Classroom: Power and Pedagogy*. Urbana, IL: University of Illinois Press, 41–59.

Lawton, Denis
    1975   *Class, Culture and the Curriculum.* London: Routledge and Kegan Paul.
Mehan, Hugh
    1991   The school's work of sorting students. In Boden, Deirdre and Don H. Zim-
            merman (eds.), *Talk and Social Structure.* Cambridge: Polity Press, 71–90.
Milroy, Lesley
    1980   *Language and Social Networks.* Oxford: Blackwell.
Philips, Susan U.
    1976   Some sources of cultural variability in the regulation of talk. *Language in
            Society* 5, 81–95.
Sarangi, Srikant
    1998   Beyond language, beyond awareness: Metacommunication in instructional
            settings. *Language Awareness* 7, 63–68.
Scollon, Ron
    1985   The machine stops: Silence in the metaphor of malfunction. In Tannen De-
            borah and Muriel Saville-Troike (eds.), *Perspectives on Silence.* Norwood,
            NJ: Ablex, 21–30.
Sobkowiak, Włodzimierz
    1997   Silence and markedness theory. In Jaworski, Adam (ed.), *Silence: Interdis-
            ciplinary Perspectives.* Berlin: Mouton de Gruyter. 39–61.
Spender, Dale
    1982   *Invisible Women: The Schooling Scandal.* London: Writers and Readers.
Swann, Joan
    1992   *Girls, Boys and Language.* Oxford: Blackwell.
Swann, Joan
    1988   Talk control: An illustration from the classroom of problems in analys-
            ing male dominance of conversation. In Coates, Jennifer and Deborah
            Cameron (eds.), *Women in their Speech Communities.* London: Longman,
            122–140.
UCAS
    1997   *Instructions for Completion of the Application.* Cheltenham: UCAS.
Walkerdine, Valerie
    1985   On the regulation of speaking and silence: Subjectivity, class and gender in
            contemporary schooling. In Walkerdine, Valerie, Cathy Urwin and Carolyn
            Steedman (eds.), *Language, Gender and Childhood.* London: Routledge
            and Kegan Paul, 203–241.
Willis, Paul
    1977   *Learning to Labour.* Farnborough: Saxon House.

Part 4. Metalanguage and stylisation

Introduction to Part 4

Adam Jaworski and Nikolas Coupland

Chapters in Part 4, on "Metalanguage and stylisation", all draw from theories of performance as developed in anthropological linguistics, but also showing important influences from the dramaturgical perspective associated with Erving Goffman. Nikolas Coupland's chapter, "Stylised deception", is followed by two other chapters exploiting notions of performativity and multiple voicing (in the tradition of Mikhail Bakhtin), venturing into the domain of multimodal communication: retail shopping displays in television advertising in Ulrike Hanna Meinhof's "Metadiscourses of culture in British TV commercials', and Kay Richardson's "Retroshopping: Sentiment, sensation and symbolism on the high street".

Coupland's study of strategic uses of stylisation, and particularly stylised deception, adopts a range of analytic approaches: sociolinguistic marking, discourse analysis and inferential pragmatics. Coupland analyses face-to-face communication as represented in the 1950s USA (but by now globalised and timeless) TV comedy, *Sergeant Bilko*. The data are presented as transcripts of the show's dialogues and Coupland analyses the discursive framings, in Goffman's sense, needed to fabricate "transparent deceptions". Discussion of deception is situated relative to other options on the authenticity-falsehood continuum (cf. Wilson's, this volume, discussion of lying). Bilko's deceptions are stylised in that they make use of several of the perceptual indicators of deceptive talk, opening up his strategising to our (the audience's) metacommunicative understandings. Coupland argues that stylisation, especially in the sense of "studiedly performed artificiality", is a comic resource precisely because it can set up dramatic contrasts between different metapragmatic/ inferential states. "Comic rogues" are deceivers who infringe a basic norm for deception – the need to conceal motive.

Meinhof's analysis of metadiscourse is located in a different multimodality – that of British TV commercials. She is primarily concerned with the way metadiscourse (verbal and visual) is used in those ads to foreground certain versions of "foreignness". Not unlike Coupland's stylised deception, the largely humorous ads analysed by Meinhof subvert the dominant genre (the "serious" ad) with their serious representation of the desirable qualities of foreignness (e.g. the unspoilt countryside in Switzerland, or the unspoilt beaches in the Caribbean). The leaked humour of representing foreignness is based on intertextual play, pastiche and parody, which are all terms in the same critical field as stylisation (cf. Hutcheon 1985, 1994). They can only work if they trigger viewers' metasemiotic awareness of how a culture or a foreign country is being symbolically represented, and then transformed via good-natured caricature.

Richardson contextualises the artifacts found in the UK chain of high street shops, *Past Times*. She is not so much interested in the artefacts themselves as in the meta-discourses which contextualise, or in Goffman's term *key*, them as historical performances. The historical metadiscourse around the products is precisely their novelty and their selling point. As Richardson states in her conclusion: "The intrinsic charms of the items as seen, touched, smelled, are not enough ... British history comes to the rescue; it offers a seam of meaning which can protect consumers from the miasma of banality which forever threatens to engulf them' (p. 307).

What the chapters by Meinhof and Richardson usefully illustrate is that the "meta" level performs important strategic, framing functions in non-linguistic, i.e. multimodal and multisensory communicative systems, yet allowing full integration and interplay between different semiotic systems (cf. Kress and Van Leeuwen 2001).

References

Hutcheon, Linda
    1985   *A Theory of Parody*. New York: Methuen.
Hutcheon, Linda
    1994   *Irony's Edge: The Theory and Politics of Irony*. London: Routledge.
Kress, Gunther and Theo van Leeuwen
    2001   *Multimodal Discourse: The Modes and Media of Contemporary Communication*. London: Arnold.

Stylised deception[1]

Nikolas Coupland

1. Style and stylisation

The term stylisation is associated with Bakhtin, who equated it with double-voiced utterance (Wales 1989: 439). But since Bakhtin (e.g. 1981, cf. also Volosinov 1973) argues that multiple voicing is a quality of all language use, he draws us to a position where all language use is stylised, and where to conceive of style monologically is insufficient or naive. Seductive as this may be as a broad-brush claim, I would prefer to maintain a difficult conceptual distinction between style and stylisation, at least until we have a more secure analytical grasp of stylisation as a sociolinguistic process. It is valuable, following Bakhtin, to construe all acts of speaking as the activation or unlocking of social meanings, through utterances being linked to pre-existing social formations, and it is interesting to construe all speakers as ventriloquists. But it may be more profitable, at least as a preliminary, to define stylised utterances as bounded moments when others' voices are, in a somewhat more literal sense, displayed and framed for local, creative, sociolinguistic effect. (As we will see, the most clearly documented instances of stylisation refer to specific utterance events or sequences within specific speech events.)

A simple, constructed, non-linguistic instance of stylised communication might help set the scene. Restaurant-goers and observers of non-verbal restaurant norms will recognise a bodily configuration in the delivery of food which defines "formal serving". Speculating, let's say that postural elements of formal serving include forward lean, straight back, one-handed giving, perhaps a raised head and a benign smile. The most ritualised instances will be proxemically specific (food served over the diner's left shoulder), and have the non-serving arm raised to horizontal and held close to the chest. Is this behaviour styled or stylised? In the context of a formal restaurant, I am assuming it is styled – it is behaviour within the known stylistic repertoire of a formal restaurant, and probably normative in such contexts. This is not to say that real restaurant-goers are not able to appreciate the cultural values recycled non-verbally through formal serving – respect for formal eating as an elitist institution and servers' conventionalised subservience to diners. As in Bell's (1984) provenance hypothesis (his argument that stylistic meanings derive from social meanings, through the association of linguistic varieties with social groups – which is a case I have made too, in Coupland 1988, 2000), participants may recognise the style of the food delivery as being part of "doing formal serving". They will read the social semiosis of formal serving. Non-stylised styles are still definable, meta-communicable semiotic acts, even though their meaning may be non-salient in the routine instance. Especially for acculturated clients at formal restaurants, the server's serving action will be just another seamless element of the social practice.

If, alternatively, I fleetingly replicate the style of formal serving when I hand mundane food to my family around the kitchen table, my action is better de-scribed as stylised. It is marked and metaphorical in its context, drawing from a wider repertoire of culturally valenced behaviours which have social meaning, as I have roughly described above. It is once again semiotically identifiable, and possibly labelable (I am doing "formal serving"), but it is rendered more salient by its out-of-context-ness. It is performance (in the sense of Bauman 1977) rather than just "behaviour". It contrasts my normal style of delivering family food with a self-aware, strategised, staged alternative. It opens up an op-portunity and probably a need for my family to draw inferences, about myself, about my stance and motives, and possibly about their involvement too in the current social context, and about that context's constitution. This inferential work might be quite complex. As for my own identity, stylised serving momen-tarily offers readings of me as both myself and as another – it double-voices me, according to the Bakhtinian line. At least, I lay myself (what we might dare to refer to as "the real me") and the performed persona (the role-played server) open to re-evaluation. There is an inferable contrast between my normal cook-ing and serving practices and those of restaurant chefs and waiters, no doubt identifying me as a lower-grade performer in the kitchen. I might be hoping to benefit, however, from having self-consciously and strategically represented and so acknowledged my incompetence, symbolically. I might be making an implicit case that normal is more us, and perhaps even more authentic.

As for real, formal-serving servers, my performance may have opened them up, fleetingly, for re-evaluation in the eyes of my family. Do we see them as overly formal, affected and indeed "style-conscious", over-dignifying the eve-ryday practice of handing food? That is, my stylised action may be a parody, of myself (behind the performance) and of the social category, social practice and social institution referred to and performed through my actions. My action is marked as potentially parodic by its reframing of current context, and by its inherently hyperbolic enactment (I would probably have exaggerated its salient non-verbal components – *a lot* of forward lean, a particularly haughty smile, a serving hand flourish, and so on). As for the situation, my action offers a contextual alternative to the one we had taken for granted as current (a routine eating event at home). It doesn't blatantly or convincingly recontextualise the event. It reframes it (as a performance moment within a normal mealtime) and again invites reappraisal of it. Do we think this is an OK way to do our eating, in opposition to a more formally designed and executed event? Again, then, my simple action potentially stimulates social comparison and re-evaluation.

These semiotic issues and processes can be applied to the sociolinguistic analysis of style, and some previous studies have shown the value of a focus on stylisation. The most sustained and successful of these is Rampton's (e.g. 1991, 1995) treatment of language crossing among young people of Anglo, Asian and Caribbean descent. Let me collage some of the qualities that Rampton associates with Stylised Asian English (SAE). It is, he writes, an accent "put on" in projecting "a comic persona that was deferential, polite, uncomprehending and incompetent in English"; it was "typically described [by young people themselves] as a subterfuge that Indian and Pakistani youngsters use to undermine white authority figures" (1995: 52–53). Switches into SAE were "often marked out by a change in loudness, pitch, voice quality and/or speed of delivery" (p. 68). Contextually, Rampton notes that "SAE was quite often used where adults were a relevant presence, either as addressees or as butts within earshot" (p. 71). SAE seemed to be located at moments of situational ambiguity and was often implicated in acts of resistance to authority and, more generally, in various sorts of oppositional or confrontational stances. Rampton emphasises the ambiguous, liminal character of moments when SAE occurred, based partly on reports that recipients of SAE felt they were positioned ambiguously: "... in principle the recipient might either flounder, unable to decide on the frame or footing being offered ... or they might take it in their stride, showing deftness and a willingness to play" (p. 80).

The performances enacted through SAE are of course specific to Rampton's ethnographic context. He explores SAE as it is deployed among a culturally specified age-group in a range of liminal settings. SAE is based on a stereotyped persona drawn from racist imagery – the incompetent "babu" speaker. However, Rampton's treatment in many ways transfers to other contexts of stylisation, a few of which have been considered in the sociolinguistic literature. Wolfowitz (1981: 249) talks of "virtuoso performances" in her analysis of stylistic choice in Suriname Javanese, which suggests an in-built self-critiquing function in style-choice. She presents stylistic variation as a dialogic process, with style-choices open to complex negotiation, inferencing and interpretation. In Surinam, Wolfowitz suggests, "The stylization of 'as-if' closeness is itself a kind of distance marker" (1981: 80). Similarly, Eastman and Stein (1993) formalise the notion of "language display", being how, through language (and, in

252   Nikolas Coupland

their research, through lexical choice in particular), "members of one group lay claim to attributes associated with another, conveying messages of social, professional, and ethnic identity" (p. 187). They argue that we should understand the objective of display more in relation to the ingroup than to the outgroup:

> ... the displayer's intention is not to negotiate a definition of self as a member of another speech community but to be seen as an individual with attributes associated with that community of speakers.
>
> (Eastman and Stein 1993: 188)

This reading dislocates "language display" from more established interpretations of related phenomena. For example, accommodation theory (Giles, Coupland and Coupland 1991) specifies socio-psychological effects that linguistic convergence, maintenance or divergence are likely to have on the recipient's perceptions – of the speaker and of the speaker/hearer relationship. These effects depend on perceived degrees of similarity/dissimilarity between the speaker's accommodated style and the listener's own style. Eastman and Stein's perspective is similar, to the extent that the listener's perceptions are still involved, but as perceptions of the speaker in relation to all manner of potential reference groups (cf. Bell's 1984 notion of "referee design").

Language display is also studied by Schilling-Estes (1998), writing about the performance speech of speakers in Ocracoke, North Carolina. These speakers have developed stock phrases that highlight island features – especially raised and backed realisations of "ai" – so-called "hoi toider" for "high tider". Performers like Rex O'Neal, the case studied in detail, "'lay the brogue on thick' for tourists and prying sociolinguists" (p. 56). Schilling-Estes associates this case with a more general phenomenon of rendering dying languages or varieties as "object languages" (p. 53) and performing them for outsiders.

Performance styles in specific cultural rituals are richly documented by cultural anthropologists. (In fact, the stimulus for theorising style as performance comes principally from this source.) A striking instance is Irvine's (1996) analysis of the tradition of insult poems, or *xaxaar*, in Wolof society (in rural Senegal). A poetry session lasting about two hours is performed at weddings, after the bride moves into her husband's household. The poems are "sponsored" and partly composed by the new bride's co-wives and other women who have married into the husband's household. The insults are delivered, however, by lower-ranking women of the bardic class – *griots*. Irvine explains that

> [t]he composition process remains sufficiently secret and collusive that at the actual wedding a particular poem cannot be individually identified with an individual author. The griot woman uttering it can claim to be doing only that – merely acting as a transmitter, with no responsibility for substance, while the

sponsoring women can claim that they sponsored the event only in general, and
have no personal responsibility for the special nastiness of a particular poem.

(Irvine 1996: 136; Hill and Irvine 1993
assemble many key studies in this tradition)

Not all these studies use the term "stylisation". None of them generalises about
the nature of stylised performance itself, although the following list owes a great
deal to Rampton's detailed characterisation of linguistic "crossing". Although
I am not able to develop the theoretical analysis here (but see Coupland 2001a,
2001b), the following characteristics form a reasonable, provisional specifica-
tion of sociolinguistic stylisation:

- Stylised utterances project a persona other than the speaker's presumedly
  current one, through a speaker's own voice – a persona with a well–formed
  socio-cultural profile.
- Stylisation is therefore fundamentally metaphorical; it brings into play stereotyped semiotic and ideological values associated with other groups, situations or times.
- It is reflexive, mannered and knowing; it is a mode which attends and invites
  attention to its own modality, which radically mediates understanding of the
  ideational, identificational and relational meanings of its own utterances.
- It requires an enculturated audience able to read the semiotic value of a
  projected persona; it is therefore especially tightly linked to the normative
  interpretations of speech and non-verbal styles entertained by specific discourse communities.
- It instigates, in and with listeners, processes of social comparison and re-
  evaluation, focused on the real and metaphorical identities of speakers, their
  strategies and goals, but spilling over into re-evaluation of listeners' identities, orientations and values.
- It interrupts a current situational frame, embedding another layer of social
  context within it, introducing new and dissonant identities and values; in doing this, its ambiguity invites re-evaluation of pertaining situational norms.
- It is creative and performed, and therefore requires aptitude and learning;
  some speakers will be more adept at stylisation than others; while style variation (e.g. dialectal style-shifting) is part of a (near-)universal communicative competence, stylisation is more restricted, either by preference or by
  competence; some communities will be more prone than others to stylised
  utterance.
- Since their performer needs to cue frame-shift and dissonant social meanings, stylised utterances will often be emphatic, commonly hyperbolic realisations of their targeted styles.

– Stylisation can be analysed as strategic inauthenticity, with complex implications for personal authenticity in general.

Before moving on, we need to consider the social situations that are conducive to stylisation. The data I consider, below, are from a well-known television comedy show, Sergeant Bilko (licensed to be screened in the UK, over many decades and currently, under the title *The Phil Silvers Show*). Although this may seem a highly specific context of social interaction, for the moment I will discuss context in the broadest possible terms. Stylisation is likely to be most effective when it can play off a mixed audience, and this is where its function in verbal play and humour is often felt. First-level inferential work for recipients is to locate a styliser's social identity. Are we hearing the speaker's own voice (the speaker speaking *in propria persona*, meaning not only the voice we commonly associate with that embodied speaker but the voice that reflects the social identity we expect that speaker to be representing at that moment), or the speaker's voicing of another identity (speaking *in alteris persona*)? If another persona is being voiced, a distance assessment can be made: what sociolinguistic distance is there between the heard and the "normal" voices, and along what dimensions of difference? Also, a search for sociolinguistic provenance is necessary: what are the social attributes and what is the stance of the voiced persona? At a second level, listeners need to determine the pragmatic valency of a stylised voice: is it a "mere" allusion, or a quotation, or an act of ingroup identification, or a parody (emphasising intergroup distinctiveness), or an act of vilification, or an ambivalent fusion of several of these? Different audience members may draw different inferences, or inferences at different levels of complexity. Part of the appeal of stylisation for speakers will be to instigate different inferential chains for co-present ingroup and outgroup listeners (e.g. kids playing off peers against teachers, in Rampton's data) where the different groups are differentially adept at untangling the layers of sociolinguistic coding. It is the element of ambiguity, and indeed that of dissimulation, in stylised performance to mixed audiences that I want to return to below, and this is the link with literatures on deception.

2.   Deception and leakage

Stylisation and deception are surprisingly comparable sociolinguistic processes, most obviously because they both raise issues of speaker authenticity and because both are fundamentally metapragmatic in design. Both processes involve the projection of, in some senses, false personas, and the voicing of non-current realities. In both cases, communicators anticipate and trigger specific sorts of inferencing by recipients about their (deceivers' and stylisers') identities and goals. In particular, I want to suggest that stylisation and deception can be seen in some ways as mirror-image processes.

Definitions of deception can be daunting. The most detailed social psychological theory of truth-telling, falsehood (lying) and evasion is that of Bradac, Friedman and Giles (1986); see Ng and Bradac's (1993) overview. Bradac and his associates present an "intentionality model", based on assumptions about speakers' intentions vis-à-vis their listeners' inferences. They build a complex model around four criteria:

(1)   accuracy – a speaker's intention to produce an accurate belief in a listener regarding the speaker's belief;
(2)   relevance – intention to be relevant;
(3)   utterance – intention to express a proposition; and
(4)   accountability – a speaker's belief that s/he will be held accountable for the utterance through the utterance being heard in one way only by any "reasonable hearer".

By assuming that each criterion can vary between a positive and negative state, Bradac, Friedman and Giles's model then generates a complex array of 16 states, as summarised in Table 1. Not many of the emerging "intentionality conditions" are important for present purposes, but the tabulation does give interesting motivational definitions of different conditions of lying and evasion. For example, in addition to "falsehood" (condition 5) – defined as the intention to produce an utterance that is inaccurate, relevant and unambiguous – we have "devious falsehood" (condition 6), where a speaker intends to lie "unaccountably". These are distinguished from "evasion" (condition 9), defined as a speaker intending to produce a message that is irrelevant but also unambiguously interpretable, and "devious evasion", when the speaker believes s/he will not be accountable.

Table 1. An intentionality model of truth-telling, falsehood and evasion (based on Ng and Bradac 1993)

	Accuracy	Relevance	Utterance	Accountability
Truth-telling	+	+	+	+
Secret	+	+	–	+
Devious truthtelling	+	+	+	–
Devious secretkeeping	+	+	–	–

Table 1. (continued)

	Accuracy	Relevance	Utterance	Accountability
Falsehood	–	+	+	+
Falsehood avoidance	–	+	–	+
Devious falsehood	–	+	+	–
Devious falsehood avoidance	–	+	–	-
Evasion	+/–	–	+	+
Evasion avoidance	+/–	–	–	+
Devious evasion	+/–	–	+	–
Devious evasion avoidance	+/–	–	–	–

I need to side-step many of the more intriguing complexities here, not least because the Table 1 "outcome categories" seem applicable only to single speech acts (including silence) and would prove hard to establish for particular situated instances. I will work with a definition of deception as *the knowing creation of inaccurate beliefs in a listener, which are relevant to that listener, about the speaker's beliefs (knowledge states or intentions)*. This broad definition spans all cases in Table 1 which have a negative in the "accuracy" column, a positive or a negative in the "relevance" column (incorporating evasion strategies), a positive in the "utterance" column (avoiding the issue of deception by avoidance), and a positive or a negative in the "accountability" column (admitting instances where a speaker either does or does not expect to be held accountable).

In certain respects, the category of deceivers we call impersonators (such as thieves self-presenting on the doorstep as gas company representatives) act like stylisers: they voice non-current identities and roles, they perform creatively, skilfully and strategically, they draw metaphorically on stereotyped representations. But they also differ in several crucial dimensions. Deception in general is audience-designed very differently from stylisation. Deceivers assume (or hope for) unsophisticated audiences with low inferential capacity. Deception will work only if normativity reigns – if listeners can be relied on to operate on the basis of social and communicative norms, around which the deceiver plans his or her strategy. Robinson (1996: 99) gives the example of the "foot in the door" sales technique which involves making an initial small request which is inherently difficult to deny, followed up by a much larger one which is then, on coherence grounds, more difficult to refuse/deny.

A deceptive strategy entails the goal of ensuring communication is not seen to be deceptive. (Stylisers intend to be heard or seen as doing stylisation.) As Robinson comments about TV advertising texts:

> …with professional actors using well-rehearsed edited scripts that may have been scrutinized by social psychologists, it is not surprising that the performances recorded in studios do not manifest cues of deceit in the final advertisements. If they did, the recordings would not be used.
>
> (Robinson 1996: 99–100)

As I suggested above, stylisation, on the other hand, invites complex inferencing by listeners to distinguish feigned from intended stances, social identities and sociolinguistic values. Deceivers, and specifically people who deceive through impersonation, attempt deception in the expectation that listeners will be inferential dupes, and that they will fail to recognise the disjunction between feigned and actual identities. Deception *criterially* also includes inauthenticity, but is premissed on the drive to appear authentic. I suggested above that stylisation feigns inauthenticity, although the "complex implications" I mentioned in the stylisation summary may include stylisation actually *strengthening* a speaker's claims to an authentic identity (see Coupland 2003). To this extent, again, we might see deception as a mirror-image of stylisation.

Stylisation and deception also differ crucially with regard to *leakage*. When deception fails, according to the literature, it is either through leakage – "Leakage refers to cues that indicate that deception may be occurring and what the truth may be" (Robinson 1996: 118) – or through available "deception cues" (or "clues") – "Deception cues are indicative that something is being concealed but do not provide information about what or why" (Robinson 1996: 118–119).

The main thrust of deception research in psychology and communication science has been into whether and how deception can be detected, as in the classic series of studies by Ekman (1992). This research has a seductive appeal, offering insiders a potential forensic expertise and therefore a potential relational advantage in face-to-face settings. But, less seductively, it is also, overall, very inconclusive.[2]

But the forensic framing of this sort of research may lead it to miss certain much more obvious "cues" to deception. For example, "implausibility of utterance" is presumably a very general criterion, covering a huge slice of the ideational and pragmatic scope of a lie. The tallness of a tall story is detectable precisely through its hyperbolic nature, purporting that some extraordinary events happened, perhaps in a wildly unpredictable sequence. An attempt at deception or indeed persuasion will be heard as falsely grounded if it draws a listener too far from his or her current field of expectations. This is to say that there are "normal tolerances" on accounts and requests (and all other pragmatic functions) which, once exceeded, begin to perceptually invalidate or render suspect a communicator's motives and his/her otherwise presumed personal authenticity.

Both the main review sources I have quoted on deception, then, are relatively unconvinced by research claiming to identify behavioural predictors of deception. On the other hand, both discuss research on *beliefs* about links between behaviour and deception, and find more promising evidence. That is, there do seem to be regularly-made assumptions (even though they are probably false assumptions) about how deception leaks, and therefore about how we can detect deceivers. Ng and Bradac (following Friedman and Tucker 1990) list the following features as being regularly believed to be indicators of deception: "averted gaze, implausibility of utterance, postural shifting, a slow rate of responding, and a rapid rate of speech" (p. 131).

3.   Stylised deception: The case of Sergeant Bilko

We can turn now to that set of circumstances, and to some data, where key elements of both stylisation and deception are present. In stylised deception, communicators intend to be seen by some recipients as bad or unconvincing deceivers. From a metapragmatic perspective, like all stylised performances, such episodes are multiply embedded. A person knowingly constructs utterances and styles capable of creating inaccurate relevant beliefs in a listener about his/her own beliefs and strategies, and does so through self stylisation. There is sufficient knowing leakage for the listener to infer that the strategy is one of deception. This leakage strips away the contextual basis for the performance to be in fact deceptive, and the speaker is left, in all his[3] manufactured inadequacy, as a risible rogue.

The texts I shall consider are transcripts of scenes from one episode of the 1950s TV comedy series *Sergeant Bilko*. My motive in using fictional, media texts is partly based in the belief (cf. Grimshaw 1996) that fictionalised reality can sometimes reveal social processes more clearly than lived reality, and this seems decidedly true of stylised deception. One apparent drawback is the argument that the televisual representation of interaction removes it to an even more reflexive domain. On the other hand, the mass media play an enormous part in the cultural dissemination of self-aware language and provide richly diverse instances of stylisation. For the moment at least, I am assuming that the participant design of stylisation on TV is not essentially different from that to be found in non-mediated interaction, although of course that case remains to be argued in relation to other sorts of data.

Like most *Bilko* episodes from the long-running American TV comedy series, the one I have chosen here is built around a sequence of scams – deception
episodes where Bilko orchestrates ludicrous solutions to implausible problems,
mainly to his own or his friends' benefit and to the detriment of others. The victims are generally senior officers or other authority figures, and most especially,
as in the present case, Colonel Hall, the officer in charge at Fort Baxter.[4] In the
present episode, Bilko has been absent from Fort Baxter, when he was assumed
to have been on duty visiting Fort Riley, but was in fact in Chicago, consort-
ing with a film star, Lily Laverne. A photograph of the two in a night club has
appeared in *Life* magazine. Colonel Hall is about to see the copy of *Life*, defini-
tively incriminating Bilko.

In Scene 1 (30 seconds), Bilko comes to identify the fact that Colonel Hall is
about to look at the latest and incriminating copy of *Life*. The scene formulates
a possible solution (line 12): =*well what if the Colonel don't see it*, and Bilko's
deceptive goal (lines 14–15): *I gotta stop him from seeing this week's issue.*

Scene 2 (20 seconds), set in the clerk's room outside the Colonel's office, is
a brief sequence in which Bilko's stratagem is refined and particularised: we see
Bilko musing and hitting upon his deceptive course of action – which turns out
to be to rip out the incriminating page from the magazine before Colonel Hall
sees it. He has come to the clerk's room hoping to intercept the copy of *Life*, but
finds that the clerk has just delivered it to the Colonel. Bilko therefore needs to
intervene, to distract the Colonel and retrieve the page.

Scene 3 (55 seconds) is the scam/deception itself; it succeeds, at least in the
short term.

Bilko's *Life* magazine scam

Scene 1: Identifying the problem

Bilko is surrounded by the men at the barracks.

(Across all extracts, B identifies Bilko; 1, 2, 3 and 4 identify different soldiers
in Bilko's platoon; C identifies Colonel Hall; [marks overlapping turns; (.) indicates a slight pause; (1.0) denotes a pause timed in seconds; = denotes immediately contiguous utterances; ? denotes question function, not grammatical question; underlined syllables carry heavier stress than is grammatically predictable;
continuous upper-case denotes shouted speech; (( )) encloses unrecognisable
or only partly recognisable speech; xxxx denotes audience laughter overlapping
the line of text above, with XXXX being louder laughter.)

line
1   B: my p<u>ic</u>ture in <u>Life</u>?=
2   =(general babble of soldiers' voices)
                 [
3   1:   yeah here it is Sarge it just came in
4   2:   see (.) you and Lily Laverne
5   3:   yeah (hee hee hee)
                 [
6   4:   you're <u>fa</u>mous Sarge
7   B: yeah <u>I'm</u> famous my court martial'll make headlines
                 [   ]
8   4:   ha ha   XXXXXXXXXxxxxxxxxxxxxxxxxxxxxxx
9   B: ((don't forget)) I was supposed to be at Fort <u>Ri</u>ley (.)
10   those phoney reports I've been sending in to the COLONEL?
11   (.) if he sees this I'm <u>cooked</u>=
12 2:   =well what if the Colonel <u>don't</u> see it?
13 B: what are you talking about? he gets Life every week he's
14   <u>bound</u> to see it (.) oh I gotta stop him from seeing this week's
15   issue (1.0) I don't mind being a thirty year man (.) but
16   not in Levenworth (music)
                    xxxxxxxxxxxxxxXXXXXXXXxxxxxxxxx

Scene 2: Refining the stratagem

Bilko and 2 in Colonel Hall's clerk's office (the clerk is soldier 5). B and 2 are rummaging through a post sack, looking for the copy of *Life*.

line
1   B: nothing in here (.) keep looking
2   5:   (leaving the Colonel's office; addressing the Colonel) you're wel-
       come sir
3   (to Bilko) <u>hey</u> what do you think you're doing Bilko?
4   B: we're just looking through the mail
                 [
5   5:   you got no right to look for anything
6   in here this is government property (.) I could report you
7   to the <u>post</u>master
                 [
8   B: relax so I was looking through the mail (.) wanna
9   make a whole federal case out of it? I was just gonna bring
10   in the Colonel his mail

11 5: I just de<u>liv</u>ered it (2.0)
12 B: he de<u>liv</u>ered it=
13 2: =so what?=
14 B: mm (.) you stay right here
                       xxxxxxxxxxxxxxxxxxx

Scene 3: The deception

Bilko enters Colonel Hall's office. Colonel Hall is at his desk starting to reading *Life* magazine.

line
1 B: Sergeant Bilko reporting back for duty sir I assume you
2   received the reports? oh here they are sir (.) would you
3   mind looking at the reports sir?
(Bilko moves the pile of reports on top of the copy of *Life*.)
4 C: I knew you were coming back I've had an earache all
5   morning
6 B: (laughing) ooh ho ho ((you always make me amused sir))
                      xxxxxxxxxxxxxxxxxxxxxxxxxxxxxx
7   but we do have to get these reports back would you mind
8   looking at them sir?
9 C: Bilko what's the matter with you (.) you were testing dump
10   trucks not atomic <u>weap</u>ons (.) now go about your business
11   I'd like to read my magazine in peace
                             [
12 B: oh I appreciate
13   that sir but if you would <u>just</u> look at the reports sir then
                                xxxxxXXXXx
14   we can carry on our work knowing that the report's not (.)
    xxxxxxxxxxxxxx
15   sir?
16 C: Bilko I will take these reports home (.) I will read
17   them for the second time very carefully I will analyse them (.)
18   I will forward them to the Pentagon (.) to the Chiefs of
19   Staff (.) what er you looking at?
20 B: at your eyes sir are they always this in<u>flamed</u>?
21 C: in<u>flamed</u>?
22 B: blink them sir (.) that's good now blink them rapidly in
23   succession sir ((7 syllables)) now sir would you mind
24   rolling your eyes? (3.0) rapidly sir (.) that's splendid

```
                    xxxxxxxxxxxxxxxxxxxxxx
```
25   yes I can see when did you have a <u>phys</u>ical last
26   sir?
27   C: <u>three</u> months ago
```
                      [
```
28   B: and your <u>eyes</u> did they <u>pass</u>?
29   C: <u>yes</u> ((Bilko))
```
               [
```
30   B: well we can't be too sure sir (.) my conscience
31   won't be clear if I don't give you this quick eye test sir=
32   C: =but Bilko I haven't got time
33   B: but sir (.) after all it's so important the eyes <u>are</u>
34   the window of the soul sir (.) what is this letter?
```
                         xxxxxxxxxxxxxxx
```
(Bilko holds up an eye-test chart.)
35   C: L?
36   B: that's very good sir (.) now cover the eye (.) now I'll
37   take another letter what is this?
38   C: E
39   B: now will you cover the other eye leaving that eye open?
40   and what do you see there?
41   C: F
42   B: that's splendid but you <u>are</u> familiar with the word we
43   have to jump to another page (.) what is this?
44   C: O
45:   B: now the other eye?
46   C: L
47   B: now BOTH eyes sir (.) splendid
```
                    xxxxxxxxxx
                       [
```
48   C: Bilko I can't see anything
```
                         xxxxxxxxxxxxxxxx
```
49   B: ((now sir)) just press your palms against your
```
            xxxxxxxxxxxxxxxxxxxxxxxxxxxxxxxxxxxxxxxxxx
```
50   eyes sir (.) against the eyeballs sir that's fine now
```
            xxx  xxxxxxxxxxxxxxxxxxxxxxxxxxxxxxxxxxxxxxx
```
51   do you feel any sensation of a swimming swirling noise
52   in your ears?
53   C: NO
54   B: then you're PASSing it SPLENDIDly (.) BOTH eyes OPEN

55		WHAT DOES IT SAY?
56	C:	LIFE
57	B:	THANK HEAVens for that
		xxxxxxxxxxxxxxx
58	C:	<u>thank</u> you Bilko
59	B:	oh no sir (.) in helping the Colonel (.) I believe I've
60		helped myself (.) thank you sir
		xxxxxxxxxxxxxxxxxxxxxxxxxxxxxxxxxxx

In Scene 4 (70 seconds) two different but related goal/scam sequences are played out. After a short sequence (not transcribed) following Scene 3, Bilko's predicament returns when an advertising company has spotted his photograph in *Life* and wants to use the image to promote their products. They have approached Colonel Hall to ask if Bilko can take part in a series of photo-shoots in New York. Bilko's first deceptive attempt here is to deflect what he construes, momentarily, as the stranger having complained to the Colonel about being beaten at poker by Bilko (lines 6–7). Secondly, and back in the main plot, Bilko sees the opportunity to spend more time away from Fort Baxter and earn money from the photo-shoot. He therefore traps the Colonel into letting, even making, him go to New York, through the preposterous threat that Colonel Hall may be seen to be countermanding the Pentagon's authority.

The going to New York scam

Scene 4: Deflecting blame; identifying the opportunity; the deception

Bilko is entering the Colonel's office. The Colonel is there with a stranger (identified as S). Reveille sounds.

line

1	C:	Bilko?
2	B:	hello? did you wish to see me sir?
3	S:	that's him that's the man Colonel
4	B:	I deny it (.) I never saw this man before in my <u>life</u> sir
		[
5	C:	<u>Bilko</u>=
6	B:	=sir I have a rule I never play cards with strangers I
7		don't care <u>what</u> he says sir
		xxxxxxxxxxxxxxx
8	C:	quiet Bilko (.) have you seen this picture in Life
		xxxxxxxx
9		magazine?

10 B: picture oh (.) isn't that Reid Randall? say I do enjoy
11   him in the movies (1.0) is that you? you don't look
12   anything like your ((picture I must say))
                xxxxxxxxxxxxxxxxxxxxx
13 C: not him (.) the soldier at the next table
          xxxxxx
14 B: soldier er <u>what</u> soldier sir?
15 C: yes a soldier in a night club in Chicago when he's
                                              xxx
16   supposed to be ((on duty)) at Fort Riley
          xxxxxxxxxxxxxxxxxxxxxxxxxxxxxxxxxxxx
17 B: oh I see what you're getting at sir there is a <u>start</u>ling
18   resemblance between that soldier and myself but surely sir
19   (.) you don't think that=
20 C: =BUT NOTHing that's you
21 B: sir I never told you this but I had a twin brother when
22   we were infants (.) a roving band of gypsies swept down on
                                              xxxxxxxxxxx
23   our village (2.0) ((are you from the [3 syllables]?))
          xxxxxxxxxxxxxxxxxxxxxxxxxxxxxxxxxxxxxxxxxx
24 C: ((you don't expect me to))
25 B: RODNEY? is that Rodney? my goodness it does look like
                                              [
26 C: QUIET
27   BILKO (.) this is Mister Larken (.) from an advertising
                xxxxxxxx
28   agency in New York (.) that for some strange reason wants
29   to use you as a model (2.0)
30 B: advertise? me? <u>mo</u>del? in New <u>York</u>?
31 C: for<u>get</u> it Bilko (.) you're not going to set foot off
32   this camp for at least a year (.) sorry Larken=
33 B: =oh you're absolutely right sir please Mister Larken
34   convey our regrets to your advertising agency (.) and the
35   Pentagon I'll show you the way out sir if you want to come
                xxxxxxXXXXXXXxxxxxxxxxxxxxxxxxxxxxxxxxxxxxxx
36   with me
37 C: the Pentagon?
38 B: well of course you must have cleared your request
39   through the Pentagon
          xxxxxxxxxxxxxxxxx

40　S:　it's true Colonel we thought it would be better to go
　　　　xxxxxxxxxxxxxxxxxxxxxxxxxxxxxxxxxxxxxxxxx
41　　　through the proper channels
　　　　xxxxxxxxxxxxxxx
42　B:　and they promised you the fullest co-operation right
43　　　down the line?
44　S:　well as a matter of fact <u>yes</u>
45　C:　full co-operation?
46　B:　I know how disappointing this must be for you Mister
47　　　Larken but surely (.) you and your associates must realise
48　　　(.) that the discipline of an army camp (.) comes before
49　　　(.) EVEN THE PENTAGON and their tre<u>men</u>dously important
50　　　<u>pub</u>lic re<u>la</u>tions (.) I'll show you the way out=
51　C:　=<u>wait</u> a minute Bilko
52　B:　no Colonel Hall this is my fault I won't I WON'T HAVE
　　　　xxXXXXXXXXXXXxxxxxxxxxxxxx
53　　　YOU SACRIFICE YOUR INTEGRITY TO PLEASE THE WHIM
54　　　(.) OF SOME FOUR STAR GENERAL IN WASHINGTON
55　C:　<u>I'll</u> be the judge of that (.) ((Bilko))
56　B:　NO SIR YOU GO BACK AND TELL HIM COLONEL HALL
57　　　OVER-RULES THEM SIR
58　C:　BILKO
59　B:　yes SIR
60　C:　YOU'RE GOING TO NEW YORK
61　B:　IS THAT A DIRECT ORDER?
62　C:　IT CERTAINLY IS
63　B:　I'LL BE READY IN AN HOUR (.) (saluting) BYE ((COLONEL))
　　　　　　　　xxxxxxxxxxxXXXXXXXXXXX

4.　The stylising of Bilko's deceptive acts

The scam in Scene 3 and the major one in Scene 4 both feature Bilko's quick-wittedness in outsmarting the vain, insecure, lazy, spineless and often gullible Colonel. But Bilko's deceptions are highly stylised in several respects. First and most obviously, Bilko's deceptive discourse is carefully prefigured. In the plot structure, scenes involving deceptive acts are often set in different physical spaces from problem/goal-formulation and stratagem-development scenes. Scenes 1, 2 and 3 are ordered according to a classical problem-solution format: formulate problem; formulate solution; deliver solution. We are in no doubt about what the risk factors are, what Bilko is seeking to achieve deceptively, who is the target, and when the deception begins and ends. The text is in fact extremely explicit in representing plot elements (see, for example, Scene 1, lines 9–15). We may not always know in advance precisely how the stratagem will be enacted, but this is the only significant aspect of plot development we have to work at interpretively. In Scene 2 we see Bilko conferring sub-vocally (at line 14) with one of his informed confederates, the second soldier; he does think-posture along with his vocalised *mm* and sets a facial expression of discovery (accompanying *you stay right here* in the same line). So it is not only the contextual dimensions of a strategy, but also the cognitive effort of Bilko's strategising that is represented at the surface of the text.

Second, the scams, when they arrive, are marked as scams in their own discourse. Scenes 3 and 4 show Bilko deceiving the Colonel by means that are made highly transparent to us as viewers and to his confederates on screen – in fact transparent to everyone except the Colonel. Bilko makes ironic reference to his own on-going strategies in his aphorisms. In lines 33–34 of Scene 3, Bilko's utterance *but sir (,) after all it's so important the eyes are the window of the soul sir* refers metapragmatically to the fact that Bilko's own face, at that point and from the Colonel's point of view, is anything but a window to his own intentions. Bilko's *THANK HEAVens for that*, at line 57, purports to be relief at the Colonel passing the eye test, but also refers, in the wider context, to the fact that his device for getting the Colonel to close both eyes has succeeded. Bilko's apparently ingratiating utterance *in helping the Colonel (.) I believe I've helped myself* (lines 59–60 of the same Scene) again refers to the fact that his deception has indeed helped Bilko himself – to avoid being found out this far.

Thirdly and most relevant to the earlier discussion of deceptive cueing, Bilko's talk is textually marked as deceptive through various of its paralinguistic and non-verbal stylistic features. Bilko has a facial set that more or less reliably signals when his stance is deceptive. It consists of a held slit-smile, often with raised eyebrows and head-tilt. The slit smile involves tense musculature, and suggests effortful, managed delivery. The facial configuration is in itself a stylised expression – an over-controlled stage smile. Smile might be expected to connote positive facework and co-operativity, but Bilko's smile-mask is a blatantly obvious cover for his strategic moves (though not to the dupe, Colonel Hall). Adopting and releasing the slit smile configuration is a contextualisation cue for switches between deceptive and straight stances. So, in the transition between Scene 1 and Scene 2, as Bilko moves out of the clerk's room into the Colonel's office, still-frame analysis shows him progressively adopting his deceptive facial mask. Conversely, in Scene 3 at line 47, Bilko is retreating backwards out of the Colonel's room, holding the copy of *Life* magazine. Since the

Colonel can't see anything (with hands covering both eyes, as directed by Bilko, as part of the phoney eye-test), Bilko is able to hand the magazine to S5 to tear out the incriminating page (which is what triggers the strong audience laughter accompanying lines 48 and 49). With the Colonel unsighted, Bilko momentarily loses the need for the facial set and we see it lapsing, to be re-established as he says *then you're PASSing it SPLENDIDly* (line 54).

In the early lines of Scene 4 Bilko visually plays out his brief sense of failure, especially after the Colonel's implicit accusation in lines 8–9, and again in lines 15–16. These are the text-lines where Colonel Hall confronts Bilko with his knowledge of Bilko's unauthorised absence. But in each of these two cases, Bilko's facial expression shifts from fear/dejection, through symbolised silent strategising (marked by frowning and lip licking), to the slit smile as his fabrications are voiced (lines 1–12, and line 17ff). The overt facial marking is accompanied by vocal tenseness and generally quick-fire prosody in many of the utterances which build Bilko's deceptive efforts with the Colonel. Part of Bilko's deception strategy is ideational, in the claims he makes, and partly stylistic/textual, in that he "overtalks" or drowns out the slow-witted and hesitant Colonel, hurrying him into confusion and compliance, while appearing sycophantic. There is therefore also a striking vocal style switch at the major transition point mentioned above (between Scenes 2 and 3, and in Scene 4 at the beginning of line 4, after the pause in line 10, in line 17, and at the onset of line 33).

But Bilko performs a wider range of vocal styles and personas than implied so far. Lines 21–23 of Scene 4 are where Bilko makes a brief and preposterous claim that the person pictured in *Life* is his lost twin brother, Rodney. Bilko delivers the phrase *a roving band of gypsies* in an over-articulated, quavering, mock-tragic voice, plus tragic face and hand on heart. Multiple tonic syllables within an utterance and extended, flattened tones convey stagily "intoned" delivery and project an actor persona. That is, in this short sequence Bilko's projected persona is that of an actor acting being bereaved, more than that of a bereaved brother. Even Colonel Hall refuses to acquiesce, which is why Bilko changes deceptive tack at line 33. Another of Bilko's stylised personas is the hyper-efficient and vigilant military man, and much of his feigned sycophancy to Colonel Hall is constructed through this style – see for example the truncated, barked utterances at the end of Scene 4.

Earlier, we reviewed contextual and behavioural features which may betray deceptive communication and others (a longer list) which are reliably but wrongly believed to indicate deception. Not surprisingly, several of these are features of Bilko's stylised deceptions. Bilko's raised pitch, louder and faster speech leaks his goal-oriented "arousal". His over-talking of Colonel Hall of course includes lexical repetition and "distancing from message content" as he deflects the Colonel with wild irrelevancies. "Implausibility of utterance" is Bilko's hallmark during deceptive sequences – e.g. the roving band of gypsies. Postural shifting similarly. In short, familiar stereotypes of deceptive communication constitute a repertoire of creative possibilities for Bilko's projections to fail as deceptions (except for Colonel Hall) and succeed as stylisations.

5.   Social motivations for stylisation

The Bilko character – the likeable, inventive, self-serving, implausible, transparent deceiver – is a familiar one in literature, theatre and television. The tradition includes Groucho Marx in international cinema, Eric Morcombe in UK television, and several of Molière's creations in French theatre (such as the cunning Dorante's manipulation of Monsieur Jourdain in *Le Bourgeois Gentilhomme*, or Maître Jacques's dealings with the miser Harpagon in *L'Avare*). Like Bilko, these 'comic rogues' have generally targeted their deceptions against gullible and inept authority figures. They have drawn us, as audience, into their confidence by exposing us (but also their fictional confederates) to their schemes, then played out scams which leak massively. The extent of leakage is so great – and none greater than Bilko's – that their stylised deceptions are far more stylisations than deceptions, except in that they often succeed in deceiving arrogant and naïve superiors. Rogues who are transparently inauthentic in the story frame – performing feigned personas to achieve their ends – earn themselves authenticity in another frame, the performance frame in which we, as audience, are implicated.

Their person play is primarily designed to be entertaining, but can be more than that. It can conjure ideological values – such as Bilko's undermining of establishment values, and even of militarism itself in the post-War decades when the series was first made. Molière's ironic critique of courtly manners, and Eric Morcombe's of film and TV stardom, from the perspective of a 'simple northerner', are not dissimilar. In Bilko's case, it seems to matter that his personifications are *in*expert. That is, not only are we carefully led to know that his personas are concocted to meet particular strategic ends; the impersonations (e.g. of the hyper-efficient and loyal military man, and of the bereaved brother) are caricatures of these identities. More exact representations would perhaps be more effective in the story frame where deception is being attempted, but in the performance frame, where deception is known *ab initio* to be being stylised, less exact representations are more effective. They are more conducive to showing the ridiculousness, or the inappropriateness to the situational realities, of the social roles being voiced. As Bauman and Briggs (1996) argue, studying the details of entextualisation in performance can help us understand the dialectic between authoritative and anti-authoritative discourse.

Goffman's line (e.g. 1981) is that theatrical dynamics also characterise everyday social interaction, and other studies will need to determine what reflexes of stylised deception may appear outside the domain of theatre. It is precisely the vividness and analysability of stylisation that is attractive in the Bilko case. It is able to fill out and exemplify several of the key contextual dimensions that I took, in the early part of this chapter, to constitute stylisation in general. Bilko's deceptions are stylised, for example, through being performed to a very richly enculturated audience. TV comedy shows build familiar plot lines and characters, allowing audiences to anticipate how "new" plots will develop and how characters will address "new" social situations. Would-be deception involves particularly clear instances of non-current-persona construction and deployment. The multiplicities of persona ownership in its stylisation are vividly portrayed in Bilko's case, where we (as audience) know him to be quite other than the figures he offers to Colonel Hall, from moment to moment. Certainly, in everyday social interaction, contextual parameters will be less clearly defined. Motives will not be represented at the surface of discourse. Ownership of voices will be less clearly demarcated. More inferential work will be necessary. Audiences will not be segregated so clearly (or so physically) from addressees; in fact, much stylisation will require addressees to cast themselves as audiences, to build hypotheses about what stances a speaker is adopting, and why. Stylisation will itself be a cue that a frame is being shifted, rather than stylised and non-stylised utterances being apportioned to different dramatic scenes.

One line of analysis worth following in future studies will be to model stylisation as a potential strategy for own positive face enhancement, building personal authenticity through apparent inauthenticity. As Bauman (1992: 41) comments, "performance usually suggests an aesthetically marked and heightened mode of communication, framed in a special way and put on display for an audience". As a specific mode of communicative performance, stylisation will generally focus its audience's attention on the performer her or himself. It will, in Bauman's terms, "intensify" the communicative experience; it will make the speaker "communicatively accountable" (p. 44). If, during an intensified moment of social practice, when a speaker is more-than-normally accountable, the speaker plays with self-identification, offering a range of identity configurations for interpretation, that speaker must expect to have his or her own real identity, behind the performance, evaluated. Because performers are metacommunicatively sensitive (cf. Hymes 1972), they will be at least partly aware of the chain of evaluative events their performances are setting in train. It follows that stylisers are likely to be motivated by self-presentational goals, and that stylisation will often be a strategy for esteem enhancement.

Despite this, stylisation implicates a wide range of social motivations and sociolinguistic effects, many of which are yet to be worked through analytically. Rampton, as we saw earlier, demonstrates how the use of stylised Asian English by UK school students can express ideological resistance to authority. But stylised performance may more generally function in humour, and then in a wide range of styles and keys, from "innocent" play to parody and ridicule. Style-shifting in speech is popularly thought to indicate personal insecurity and attracts judgements of inauthenticity. But a stylising speaker can escape this sort of censure precisely by presenting his or her constructions as inauthentic. S/he can gain status, either simply as an entertaining mimic,[5] or for having the apparent security in his or her authentic group membership to be willing to parade alternative identities for evaluation as if they were his or her own.

For the sociolinguistic analysis of style, theorising stylisation has, I believe, particular importance. Sociolinguistics has been too ready to invest in the cultural authenticity of speakers, and to treat them as honest souls. The concept of stylisation qualifies this "straight" reading of speech, speakers and speech communities. It problematises the perspective on style shift which sees speakers neutrally "adjusting" their styles from person to person, or from situation to situation, as part of a regimen of appropriateness. It may well be that speech communities exist which deserve to be, and regularly are, considered culturally authentic, and that some speakers do instantiate values through their speech which earn them a meaningful quality of personal authenticity. Speech accommodation processes are demonstrably real and pervasive. But releasing speakers from the necessary ownership of the speech styles they deploy, and reconstruing behaviour more in terms of performance, allows us to conceive of far wider and probably far more interesting social negotiations. By studying stylisation we can move beyond acknowledging the possibility of people having "multiple sociolinguistic identities" to analysing how speakers put their communicative styles to work, metalinguistically.

Notes

1.   I am grateful to Adam Jaworski, Justine Coupland, Peter Robinson and Ben Rampton for valuable critical comments on a much earlier version of this text, although I have not been able to take up all of their constructive suggestions in this chapter, or do full justice to the ones I have taken up.

2. Ekman's research does suggest there are certain recurrent features of failed deception (summarised in Robinson 1996). These include contextual parameters. Deception is more likely to fail if, for example, a listener is suspicious, or if the deceiver is unpracticed, with "a biography of failed lies", or if the stakes are high. Ekman also claims that certain "behavioral clues" are associated with specific "types of information concealed". For example, slips of the tongue and what he calls "tirades" and "emblems" indicate the concealing of "nonemotional information" such as "facts, plans and fantasies". Raised pitch, louder and faster speech indicates concealed excitement, fear or anger. Increased eye-blinking, pupil dilation, lowered pitch, slower speech, rapid or shallow breathing, sweating and frequent swallowing (Robinson 1996: 126–7) are other potential indicators, although only weakly predictive. This research tradition incorporates studies of the effectiveness and reliability of physiological indicators used in various forms of polygraph test, which Robinson describes as "infuriatingly variable and unpredictable" (p.129). Ng and Bradac (1986) are also sceptical about the likelihood that deceptive intent will be apparent in verbal features, because verbal messages are relatively controllable. They do suggest that "deceivers will tend to use a high level of lexical repetition in their utterances" (p.129) and that they will show low verbal immediacy (low involvement with message content). They also suggest that "nonverbal leakage may occur".

3. Rogues and scoundrels are generally male, in fiction if not in fact.

4. Another recurrent misogynist theme is the deception of women. One memorable episode, echoing *The Taming of the Shrew*, included Bilko duping a fellow soldier's wife to believe her husband had not been out gambling all night with Bilko, by changing clocks and making out that the sunrise is particularly bright moonlight – the time when the soldier had agreed to get home.

5. It is useful to connect notions of stylised performance with previous studies of imitated and mimicked speech, where similar insights have emerged. Speidel and Nelson (1989), for example, argue against the assumption "that imitation is a rather primitive, simple behavior requiring minimal skill and no thought or understanding" (p. 4). They propose instead that "Verbal imitation ... entails many complex [cognitive] transformations". They further suggest that individuals differ widely in their ability to imitate speech sounds accurately, but again stress that copying produces change, and links this point to views from art history. Similarly, Snow (1981, and cf. 1983) distinguishes "exact" from "reduced" and "expanded" imitations in child language learning, and introduces a criterion of salience – what is the "focus of attention ... which in turn determines what becomes stored as a deferred imitation" (p. 8). Bell (1992) and Preston (1992, 1996) comment in detail on the inaccuracy and incompleteness of forms used in dialect imitation.

References

Bakhtin, Mikhail M.
   1981   *The Dialogic Imagination* Edited by Michael Holquist, translated by Caryl
          Emerson and Michael Holquist. Austin: University of Texas Press.
Bauman, Richard
   1977   *Verbal Art as Performance*. Prospect Heights, IL: Waveland Press.
   1992   Performance. In Bauman, Richard (ed.), *Folklore, Cultural Performances,
          and Popular Entertainments: A Communications-centered Handbook*. Ox-
          ford: Oxford University Press, 41–49.
Bauman, Richard and Charles Briggs
   1990   Poetics and performance as critical perspectives on language and social
          life. *Annual Review of Anthropology* 19, 59–88.
Bell, Allan
   1984   Language style as audience design. *Language in Society* 13, 145–204.
   1992   Hit and miss: Referee design in the dialects of New Zealand television
          advertising. *Language and Communication* 12, 327–340.
   1999   Styling the other to define the self: A study in New Zealand identity mak-
          ing. *Journal of Sociolinguistics* 3, 523–541.
Bradac, James. J., Erich Friedman and Howard Giles
   1986   A social approach to propositional communication: Speakers lie to hear-
          ers. In McGregor, Graham (ed.), *Language for Hearers*. Oxford: Pergamon
          Press, 127–151.
Coupland, Nikolas
   1988   *Dialect in Use: Sociolinguistic Variation in Cardiff English*. Cardiff: Uni-
          versity of Wales Press.
   2001a Dialect stylization in radio talk. *Language in Society* 30, 345–375.
   2001b Stylisation, authenticity and TV news review. *Discourse Studies* 3, 413–
          442.
   2001c Language, situation and the relational self: Theorising dialect style in so-
          ciolinguistics. In Eckert, Penelope and John Rickford (eds.), *Style and So-
          ciolinguisticVariation*. Cambridge: Cambridge University Press, 185–210.
   2003   Sociolinguistic authenticities. *Journal of Sociolinguistics* 7, 417–431.
Eastman, Carol M. and Roberta F. Stein
   1993   Language display: Authenticating claims to social identity. *Journal of Mul-
          tilingual and Multicultural Development* 14, 187–202.
Ekman, Paul
   1992   *Telling Lies: Clues to Deceit in the Marketplace, Marriage, and Politics*.
          New York: WW Norton.
Friedman, Howard S. and Joan S. Tucker
   1990   Language and deception. In Giles, Howard. and W. Peter Robinson (eds.),
          Handbook of Social Psychology and Language. Chichester: Wiley, 257–
          270.

Giles, Howard, Justine Coupland and Nikolas Coupland (eds.)

1991   *Contexts of Accommodation: Developments in Applied Sociolinguistics.*
        Cambridge: Cambridge University Press.

Goffman, Erving

1981   *Forms of Talk.* Oxford: Blackwell.

Grimshaw, Alan (ed.)

1996   *Conflict Talk.* Cambridge: Cambridge University Press.

Hill, Jane and Judith T. Irvine (eds.)

1993   *Responsibility and Evidence in Oral Discourse.* Cambridge: Cambridge
        University Press.

Hodge, Robert and Gunther Kress

1988   *Social Semiotics.* Cambridge: Polity Press.

Hymes, Dell

1972   Models of the interaction of language and social life. In Gumperz, John
        J. and Dell Hymes (eds.), *Directions in Sociolinguistics.* New York: Holt,
        Rinehart and Winston, 35–71.

Irvine, Judith T.

1996   Shadow conversations: The indeterminacy of participant roles. In Silver-
        stein, Michael and Greg Urban (eds.), *Natural Histories of Discourse.* Chi-
        cago: University of Chicago Press, 131–159.

Ng, Sik Hung and James J. Bradac

1986   *Power in Language: Verbal Communication and Social Influence.* New-
        bury Park, CA: Sage.

Preston, Dennis R

.   1992   Talking black and talking white: A study in variety imitation. In Hall, Joan,
        N. Doane and D. Ringler (eds.), *Old English and New: Studies in Lan-
        guage and Linguistics. Papers in Honor of Frederic G. Cassidy.* New York:
        Garland, 326–355.

1996   Whaddayaknow? The modes of folk linguistic awareness. *Language
        Awareness* 5, 40–77.

Rampton, Ben

1991   Interracial Panjabi in a British adolescent peer group. *Language in Society*
        20, 391–422.

1995   *Crossing: Language and Ethnicity among Adolescents.* London: Long-
        man.

Robinson, W. Peter

1996   *Deceit, Delusion and Deception.* Thousand Oaks, CA: Sage.

Schilling-Estes, Natalie

1998   Investigating "self-conscious" speech: The performance register in Ocra-
        coke English. *Language in Society* 27, 53–83.

Snow, Catherine E.

1981   The uses of imitation. *Journal of Child Language* 8, 205–212.

1983   Saying it again: The role of expanded and deferred imitations in language acquisition. In Nelson, Katherine E. (ed.), *Children's Language*, vol. 4. Hillsdale, NJ: Erlbaum, 187–230.

Speidel, Gisela E. and Katherine E. Nelson
1989   A fresh look at imitation in language learning. In Speidel, Gisela E. and Katherine E. Nelson (eds.), *The Many Faces of Imitation in Language Learning*. New York: Springer Verlag, 1–19.

Volosinov, Valentin Nikolaevic
1973   *Marxism and the Philosophy of Language*. Translated by Ladislav Matejka and I. R. Titunik. New York: Seminar Press. [First published 1929 and 1930.]

Wales, Katie
1989   *A Dictionary of Stylistics*. London: Longman.

Wolfowitz, Clare
1991   *Language Style and Social Space: Stylistic Choice in Suriname Javanese*. Urbana: University of Illinois Press.

Metadiscourses of culture in British TV commercials

Ulrike Hanna Meinhof

1. Introduction

In this chapter I will concentrate on one particular set of metadiscourses found in particular in British TV commercials or, to be more precise, in a sub-genre of these – the humorous ads – for which British advertising is so renowned (Pitcher 1989). Ads, and TV ads even more than any other form, can be seen as a type of discourse (Cook 1992), which is essentially multimodal (Kress and Van Leeuwen 1996, 2001). Whereas printed ads, from magazines to posters combine different visual codes (shape and size of print, colour, lay-out, etc.) with linguistic, imagistic content, and radio commercials combine different acoustic codes, TV commercials can draw on all of these simultaneously and can exploit interrelations between these in complementary or contradictory ways. This multiple encoding includes the possibility of one set of codes providing metacommentary on the other. In the world of moving images and sounds, and simultaneous complex textual interrelations, it is no longer sufficient to think of the verbal as simply a form of anchorage for the visual as Barthes suggested (Barthes 1977: 38–41). Instead the possibilities of combining conflictual or complementary discourses – from whichever source they may arise and for any number of interactions between image and sound – are regularly employed in all kinds of televisual genres. This is nowhere more pronounced than in the hyper-sophisticated semiotic world of television commercials. Reducing a discourse analysis of TV ads to an interpretation of the spoken or written language alone would thus make little sense as analysing a pop video clip by exclusive reference to the wording of the song. This is widely recognised by most recent writing on TV advertising (Fowles 1996; Tolson 1996; Myers 1999), even where titles suggest a more narrow concentration on language. For example, a book entitled *Words in Ads* (Myers 1994), whilst focusing on many linguistic features also provides wider semiotic readings.

My interest in this chapter lies not with TV advertising discourse in general, but more specifically in two areas: first in the discourses, and especially the metadiscourses about other cultures feature in British ads, and secondly how in doing so they exploit the different possibilities of sound and vision.

2. Discourses and metadiscourses of foreignness

Let me begin with an attempt to differentiate between discourses and metadiscourses of foreign culture as they appear in TV commercials. TV commercials traditionally deploy references to other cultures as a means of evoking
desire about "the Other", to sell their products through connotations aroused
by the evocation of, for example, a particularly desirable landscape or exciting cityscape. Stock images of palm-fringed beaches in the Caribbean (exotic
drinks), the golden undulating landscapes of Tuscany (healthy Italian food),
green mountain-fringed meadows with grazing cows in the Alps (pure Swiss
chocolate) are easily available and transnationally recognised signs suggesting
the exotic, the healthy, the pure, the natural, and inviting potential buyers to
transfer such qualities to the product in question. Where advertising discourses
are constructed for a more specific national target culture, they may employ
cultural stereotypes more specifically held by the target culture about the other
(see Kelly-Holmes 2000 for multiple connotations of "Irishness", and Meinhof
1998, 2002 for those of "Germanness" and "Italianness" in TV ads addressing
the British market). Such discourses of foreignness do not connect with any
originating social reality – present or past – of that culture, but are free-float-
ing images which only metonymically stand in for meanings associated with
them – as symbolic material which has acquired cultural currency. They are
what Barthes has described as "myth": naturalised, dehistoricised second order
representations (Barthes 1972). All myth depends on having acquired cultural
salience by prior form of symbolisation: the palm-fringed beach is instantly
recognisable irrespective of our ever having seen one in real life because of
endless discourses from travel brochures, films, and a myriad of other similar
representations. Their success depends on the transfer of desirable associations
from the image to the product itself. In this analysis myth works through cover-
up of its actual source, a form of manipulation which (intellectual/academic)
deconstruction can help to undo and thus render ineffective.

By contrast, a form of TV commercials which employ what I would like to
call metadiscourses of foreignness, make a witty form of "deconstruction" itself
their selling point. They, too, reproduce discourses of foreignness, but instead
of using them merely for pleasant connotations, they entertain and sell by consciously, deliberately and ludically drawing attention to the fact that they are
merely constructions. Such commercials answer to our post-modern appetite
for knowledgeable allusion, and are particularly frequent on British TV within
the sub-genre of the humorous TV ad. They are re-representations, which invite
us to detect and cherish the different chains of signification they have under-
gone. Such metadiscourses therefore do not naturalise signs but play with their

very constructedness by employing strategies such as intertextual play, pastiche, even parody. All make use of the elements which Coupland (this volume) refers to as forms of "stylisation" in contra-distinction to "style", a distinction which can equally be applied to what I want to differentiate here and which I will discuss further below. To give just one set of examples at the beginning: the friendly, sociable, happy community which sells us *Olivio* margarine via an amusing story of a tug-of-war between the young and the old men at a village outing invites us to share in the myth of that kind of happy existence in an imaginary Italian culture. By contrast, commercials such as the Heineken ad discussed further below, which shows a successful boxer return through the Calabrian landscape to his home village remind us of the particular symbolic contexts in which we have seen that Italy on our cinema or television screens. Its reference is not a stereotypical pre-packaged image of Italian culture, but a particular intertextual version of Italy which can be placed, celebrated, and made fun of precisely for its prior appearance in (popular culture) media genres. The pleasure offered to us viewers by this kind of metadiscourse is to unpick the multiple chains of meanings, share the joke, rejoice in our own semiotic competence, rather than fall for the second order representation of the myth.

I would now like to discuss this in more detail by concentrating on some of the key elements which can be identified in many metadiscourses of foreignness in British TV commercials and which are all closely related to one another: one, intertextual play, two, parody and three, stylisation.

3. Intertextual play

This is not the place to introduce a discussion about the complex and often confusing definition and application of the term of intertextuality in the theoretical literature (but see Frow 1990; Fairclough 1995, Meinhof and Smith 2000 for an extensive discussion of its multiple range of meanings). For the purpose of this analysis of cultural metadiscourses in commercials, a relatively restricted textual version of the term is implied, in that the humour of the commercial directly depends on the viewers being prompted to imagine certain sets of meanings as a result of intertextual references. By alluding to a set of recognisable other texts or textual genres, the viewers' expectations are directed to one set of cultural meanings which the commercial then goes on to subvert by an unexpected twist to the ending. Obviously intertextual references instigated as part of a textual structure do not guarantee that viewers will make the required inferences, but my argument is that if they do not, they will miss the humour to a large extent, and the commercial may fail in its purpose. The form of intertextuality which interests me in this context is therefore one which is more tightly controlled by the producers' construction of the text: after all, TV commercials undergo many forms of testing before appearing on the screen to make sure of their success with the target buyers. If such an intertextual reference remains entirely unnoticed by the target group, the ad itself may misfire. However, a sophisticated play with intertextuality can sometimes cause the ad to fail in its commercial function for the obverse reason, in that we may remember the intertextual wit, but fail to remember the name of the product. Presumably we all know instances of that kind from our own incidental viewing. My own anecdotal example for one such ad was for a car, whose brand name neither I nor any of my colleagues that I asked about it can remember, though we all remember the ad and its intertextual references in great detail. This stylish car commercial featured the actor made popular in the UK by having played the character of Titmus in a televised dramatisation of John Mortimer's novel *Paradise Postponed*. The ad intertextually played on the haunting images of an achingly beautiful but also sinister Venice echoing those strange carnivalesque figures in gondolas from the feature film *Don't Look Now*, based on a Daphne du Maurier novel. Even now I remember the ad in sharp detail, without having ever ascertained the name of the car which the character drives away with such pleasure, once he had escaped from the beautiful but morbid (and car-deprived) beauty of the Venetian canals. No producer of TV ads can risk failure of that kind, and it is for that reason that sometimes the most celebrated and sophisticated TV ads attract prizes for their originality but are quickly withdrawn because they fail to promote the product. The form of intertextuality in ads considered here is thus conceived as a deliberately strategic move, which invites viewers to entertain chosen layers of meaning for functional purposes, rather than a more general and open-ended property of any form of semiosis where meanings are constantly made and remade in the processes of communication (see Kress 2000).

An interesting disjuncture can occur between product and cultural narrative in these intertextual commercials in the sense that there needs to be no transfer of cultural connotations from the symbolic representations to the product. Whereas 'mythical' discourses of foreignness in commercials lend a particular quality associated with that culture to the product, no such relation is necessary when metadiscourses of the other are intertextually invoked. The connection between the cultural origin of the product – a car, an insurance firm, a beer – and the intertextually associated cultural images of a particular form of – say – Italianness, Germanness, Frenchness may be completely incidental. Let us briefly recall a particularly witty ad for the Dutch lager beer Heineken. The scene opens with a boxing champion and his manager on what they imagine to be a triumphant home-coming. As the train pulls into the station of a small Calabrian town, there is indeed an expectant crowd on the platform. However, to the dismay and scorn of the boxer, it is not him that they are so eagerly waiting and cheering for, but a little old man who turns out to be the owner of the key to the bar with the fridge full of Heineken beer. The punch-line, delivered by one of the happy beer drinkers is spoken in Italian with English sub-titles: "Why are Alfredo's holidays always so very long?". This ad thus uses a Calabrian land-scape and medieval village square even though none of these images of Italy suggests any kind of connotation for the beer as such. The justification given by the commercial's final surtitle, that Heineken Export was first introduced into Italy in 1933, forms part of the commercial's humorous narrative, rather than providing any direct selling point for a British audience. The Italian im-ages themselves are already part of prior symbolic encodings from (Hollywood) feature films, here in particular *Raging Bull* – also the story of a boxer – whose sound track also provides the music to this particular ad, as well as some echoes from other films popular with UK audiences such as *Cinema Paradiso*. (An im-age from the latter was also used in a very brief double advert for the new Brit-ish TV channel Channel 5 and Stella Artois beer.) Their point lies in allowing the ad to tell a story through the intertextual replay, thus arousing a set of expec-tations in the viewer connected with the earlier narrative, and then subverting these through the unexpected witty twist. The intertextual sequences, leading up to that moment of revelation, provide the foil for one type of story – the poor boy from Southern Italy returning as a celebrity – allowing the final sequences of the TV commercial to subvert this by its humorous ending. All of this hap-pens in the highly condensed form typical for prime-time TV commercials.

Similarly, the wit of a commercial for the Royal Insurance draws on images of a seedy Italo-American pub in some sinister back-street of New York which are recognisable by their prior appearance in films such as *Godfather* and *God-father 2*. Here the viewers' understanding from these films, namely that insults to Mafia bosses will have fatal consequences, needs to be imported in order to supply the subtext for the witty punch-line, reminding us that an insurance firm not only deals with car, but also with life insurance policies:

> Don Franko (in the famously broken voice recalling Marlon Brando's ren-dering of Godfather): You better ring the Royal.
> Gangster (referring to the car): It's only a scratch.
> Don Franko: I'm not talking about the car.

In the two instances I have just discussed, the otherness of the foreign culture – Italy, Italo-America is not employed in order to invest the product – the beer, the insurance firm – with any cultural connotations imported through the inter-textual play. There are other types of similarly constructed ads which do retain an element of transfer by linking a particular characteristic of foreignness in the product with the intertextual narratives, but again the emphasis is on the humorous, tongue-in-cheek allusion directed at a knowledgeable viewer rather than on the creation of a myth. A good example of this latter type is the commercial for a product already perceived as quintessentially Russian – Vodka – which takes the film about the storming of the Winter Palace during the Russian Revolution as its intertextual foil. The twist here is that successive revolutionary leaders are seduced by the Smirnoff bottle left behind on a table in the Palace, thus becoming themselves mistaken for a member of the aristocracy and arrested one after the other. A car commercial for the Ford Cougar uses cultural imagery of the Southern landscape of the Untied States, showing two men racing each other – one in a car, the other on a motorcycle. Again some link between the American landscape and its straight empty open roads and the superior speed of the car could be suggested, but any direct import of these connotations would miss the key reference of the ad. Obvious to anyone who has seen the film, the commercial quotes what is perhaps the most famous and regularly re-screened road movie, *Easy Rider* (1969), through its images, the music – the song "Born to be wild" by Steppenwolf, and a direct allusion to the final scene of the film which ends by the motorcyclists' getting killed by the passenger in a passing truck. In the car commercial the tension of that final fatal encounter is humorously subverted. Here the motorcyclist is a direct visual quote from the film in the form of the youthful figure of one of *Easy Riders'* leading characters "Billie", played by Dennis Hopper. In this ad he is racing against and losing out to the man in the car, played by Dennis Hopper's own older self. In all these cases the references to foreignness are intertextual quotations not of a particular cultural imagery with generalised stereotypical associations, but of other symbolic forms which are already in the domain of popular culture. By such quotation the commercials create metadiscourses which playfully comment on, and comically subvert the narratives of the source material.

4.   Parody

Intertextual play can be a source of humour irrespective of whether the narrative is enlisted for its positive or negative connotations. Where its function is linked with parody this implies some critical perspective, however mild. In TV commercials any strongly parodic cultural reference runs the risk of creating unflattering connotations, either directly for the product itself, or indirectly via the culture with which it is associated. An enjoyment of such a parodic style is itself culture-specific – or at least advertisers seem to think so. Negative advertising, where the ad makes fun of the product itself is, for example, virtually unknown in Germany. A well-known British commercial for the German car Volkswagen Polo shows a young exotic-looking lady becoming infuriated by the present of the car, which her equally exotic-looking lover supposedly has given her. This ad with its punch-line full of sexual innuendo – "The car is not the surprise" – was never shown in Germany itself. In the UK, such "subversive" advertising does exist, again as a sub-genre of the humorous ad. It seems to be particularly popular in relation to products where the associated cultural origin is linked with pre-existing negative stereotypes. The art of such commercials is to turn such negative stereotyping to their own advantage: the car – the VW Polo – is, of course, not "the surprise" being as "dully" reliable as VWs tend to be. (Though earlier when driven blind-folded through the town, the lady in the ad does mistake it for a sports car: a double take, which unmasks her later dislike of the car as unjustifiable prejudice.) Many British TV commercials for German technological products, from Continental Tyres to VW cars use parody in this way, by enlisting the stereotype of the humourless, obsessive, desperately reliable German. In the same vein, some British TV commercials for Australian beer draw on those of the loud-mouthed, vulgar Australians who do nothing but drink beer. A good example for this is the ecological parody of the Foster lager ad, which begins like a broadcast on behalf of an environmental lobby with catastrophic predictions about the damage caused to the environment. It ends by inviting us to forget about it all, and instead – quite irresponsibly – enjoy life by drinking Australian lager. Even the sound of the language itself can be employed for such purposes. Since VW Audi's memorable slogan "Vorsprung durch Technik" made the sound of the German language itself into a self-referential sign in UK advertising (see also Myers 1994), there have been several other ads which heighten their parodic appeal by using German voice-overs or quotes from (supposedly) German characters. "Vorsprung durch Technik" itself – an innocent enough phrase translating roughly as "advantage through technology" – has been undergoing parodic adaptations by various follow-up ads with different foreign pronunciations, depending on the context in which the Audi is being featured. One such ad which first appeared on the screens during the year when Hong Kong was repatriated into China was cast in the form of a spoof spy story and added "Vorsprung durch Technik – as they whisper in China". An ad for Continental Tyres subtitles the English translation of a female German voice-over to a car speeding crazily on the open roof-top of a high-rise building: "Deutsche Ingenieure machen prima Reifen aber miese Dachterassen" 'German engineers produce brilliant tyres but awful roof terraces'. One can just imagine, by contrast, what a roof terrace would look like in a commercial for a French or Italian food product. A commercial for VW Passat – slogan: "A car born out of obsession" – has a German lady show us through her house as if the viewers were prospective buyers. But her real enthusiasm about the house only shows through at the point when she enters the huge garage with curtained windows, which is "the home" of the car. All of these ads parodically play with negative stereotypes of Germans as humourless and obsessive. The parody does not undercut the stereotype itself – it enlists it in a witty way precisely to suggest the brilliance of the craftsmanship of German engineering. Obsessive concern and devotion to work are after all rather welcome qualities where the construction of a car is concerned. Compare this parodic use of the German language with the use of French or of French accentuated speech in perfume and chocolate ads, or ads such as the one for Boursin cheese (slogan: "Du vin, du pain, du Boursin") – where the sounds of French simply set out to enhance the sensuous appeal of the products.

5.   Stylisation

I would now like to return to the distinction between style and stylisation, by looking at one form of commercials which has emerged in particular in the post-modern era with its appetite for multi-modal complex structures. These ads specifically exploit the possibility of the two channels – the visual as against the sound-track – to create double-edged narratives. Some of these simply tell parallel stories, such as a generic ad for "British Meat" which shows in the visual sequences a father not coping very well with the bike-ride his son makes him endure, whilst the voice-over hears him give a false more boastful account to his wife. Another such example is the ad for the cognac Courvoisier, where French actor Gerard Depardieu is heard telling a tall story about his success with fishing, whilst the images show him failing abysmally, purchasing the fish from a market stall instead. But here the sound track is simply producing a witty alternative, which undercuts the authority of the main character in the spot. More intriguing and more interesting for sociolinguists are those ads where the sound track offers alternative readings of the visuals not by what the characters say but by how they are saying it.

   In this section, I discuss three instances of well-known ad campaigns in the UK which epitomise this particular sub-genre of TV advertising: first, (British) Homepride Sauces, second, (Manchester) Boddington bitter beer, and third (Italian) Ranieri ice-cream. All three play on the social meanings of linguistic variation in English in order to subvert what are easily acceptable cultural stereotypes within the British ad-worlds: from the closely knit Asian-descent British family in the kitchen to the romantic and sexy Italians in a glamorous setting.

It is for the discussion of these more subtle ads that I would like to return to Coupland's helpful definitions set out in this volume, and differentiate between discourses of style and of stylisation. Drawing in particular on Rampton's description of how adolescents perform different personas by putting on different accents in their conversations (Rampton 1995), Coupland produces a useful set of criteria which together help define the nature of stylised speech, of which the following are most relevant for my purposes. According to Coupland, the elements of stylised speech which differentiate them from mere "styled" speech lie in their "fundamentally metaphorical" as well as "reflexive, mannered and knowing" nature (p. 253). Coupland wants to retain a distinction between style and stylisation which he sees as being overlooked by Bakhtin's account of all language use as inherently "double-voiced" (Bakhtin 1981, 1986). The "double-voicedness" of stylised speech thus depends on the conscious performance of a particular form of linguistic or paralinguistic behaviour which needs to be consciously recognised for its metaphoric value. In other words, it needs to be recognised as a performance of something other than itself. It is these properties of stylised utterances, which in Coupland's words, make them into an "elitist mode". They address a particular "in-group" community within a potentially much larger speech-community who may not be able to recognise the speech as performance, or even if they do, may not know how to decode the semiotic value of the performance. I have argued here, that all metadiscourses of culture in TV commercials have elements of such stylisation, in that the references to the cultures they invoke are precisely of that metaphoric, intertextual, or parodic kind. What makes this last group of ads into particularly good instances of stylisation is that they are specifically exploiting the socio-cultural values associated with forms of speech. Specific to these ads is their double-encoding: the narratives which are carried predominately by the visual channel are much more accessible and in tune with generalised notions of the cultural styles of certain groups. The sound track, by contrast, draws on connotations of particular ways of speaking, which invite an alternative metadiscursive commentary. The less obvious connotations of such performed speech depend on a recognition of the social meaning of various non-standard ways of speaking, be it a foreign or a socially-regionally determined accent. The inferential work expected from viewers of such ads is that they not only need to be able to process conflictual information from two channels, but at the same time need to be able to identify and pragmatically place the quality of the stylised voice. Such is their cultural specificity that fluent English-speakers in other countries – (I informally tested this with audiences in Germany, Spain, Italy, the Philippines and Japan) – who are perfectly able to follow a lecture in English, cannot understand the point of the sound track, nor understand why it could or should be read as humorous.

In this sense the ads in question are perfect examples for the kinds of in-group competence which stylised utterances require.

Let us begin with the discourses of style carried by the visuals. In the case of the series of commercials for Homepride Sauces, we are offered images of families and groups of friends from distinctly ethnic background within contemporary British settings. In the Korma Sauce ad, the wife and mother is presented as a woman wearing traditional Indian dress, preparing and serving food for her family – husband and son. In the Boddington beer ads, we are offered highly glamorous images of exotic settings and exotic men and women – there is a gondola with a beautiful relaxed sexy woman counter – cut to another gondola with a glamorous sexy male coming towards her. The Ranieri ice-cream ad again shows a glamorous woman draped in long silky floating gowns twirling in what looks like a Renaissance palace – interspersed with equally sensuous images of the ice-cream itself as it is spooned out and slowly consumed by the same woman. In all three cases expectations are aroused which perfectly match the cultural clichés associated with their setting. Let us now look at this in more detail.

5.1. Performance through surprise: Homepride Sauces and Boddingtons Bitter

In the Korma Sauce ad of the Homepride series, the visual narrative shows an Indian family with the wife preparing and serving a curry dish to her husband and her son:

Wife:	Homepride's new Korma sauce makes a deliciously creamy curry. They've improved the balance of spices, so that's even more mouth-watering, and you get that full rich flavour in just 20 minutes. It's the best taste of Korma this side of Watford.
Husband:	Cracking Ruby
Voice-over:	Homepride Sauces. Authentic sauces from all around the world. Also available in London.

Although the setting of the kitchen, stove, furniture, etc. is positioning the family in an average British home, the characters ethnic Indian descent, made obvious by their looks, their style of clothing and the dish itself – an Indian curry – creates an expectation that these people will be speaking in an Indian-accentuated English, just as the parallel ad with a Chinese family in Glasgow makes us expect a Chinese-accentuated variety. Although the population of British multicultural society speaks many different varieties of English which may well correspond to their ethnic origin, but may equally echo their contemporary social and regional position in the UK, the ad's humour depends on the expectation of an ethnic variation, only to subvert it by the characters' East-London speech, which bears no trace of an Indian intonation or accent. There are also other witty culture specific references in the wording which require cultural knowledge, such as the mentioning of Watford – a town north of London and itself some kind of symbolic divide between the North/Midland regions of England, and its South – and the reference that this (British produced) sauce is available "also in London". But it is the accents which are the main source of humour. Spoken in an urban working-class accent, this sound track is metadiscourse *par excellence*. The expectation of a particular form of culturally-determined speech aroused by the visual representation is challenged in a comical way in the sound track by the presentation of another socially-determined form, which transfers the family away from its Indian context into a working class British one. For such a reading to be established, a viewer needs not only to be able to process the cultural reference points aroused by the visual, but also and simultaneously understand the social value of the spoken variety of English.

The Boddingtons ad, set in what seems to be a Venetian canal, but which turns out to be the Manchester shipping canal with Strangeways Prison looming large in the final shot, uses a similar strategy. The woman (named "Gladys", in the gondola seems to fit perfectly into the first exotic setting until her unladylike behaviour and non-standard speech reveal her to belong to a very different social background. As she gulps down the beer, snatched from the man gliding past in his gondola, she exclaims in working-class accented Northern English:

> *Gladys:*   Oh, by 'eck, it's gorgeous.

Both the Homepride series and the Boddington series of commercials of which the two just mentioned form a part make use of accents associated with inner-city working class communities, and import these as meta-commentaries on another set of more exotic cultural expectations aroused by the visual. They are highly culture-specific, since their reading depends on an understanding of complex cultural connotations of forms of British English and their values within the UK. Outside the UK, their humour is incomprehensible.

5.2. Performance through exaggeration: Ranieri ice-cream

The final ad I would like to discuss, a commercial for Ranieri ice-cream, has a visual sequence which was also shown in other European countries. It intersects images of a beautiful woman dressed in creamy-coloured, flowing silk drapes in a Renaissance Palace with shots of her eating ice-cream. The creamy colour of the ice-cream with a dark centre (vanilla and chocolate), its soft texture underlined by the way it melts onto the spoon and into the woman's mouth, blends with the sensuality of her dress and movements, and with the sensuous images of the Palace itself and its long drawn curtains blowing in the breeze. The mythical evocation of Italian sensuality for an Italian food product in these visuals is further strengthened by the music, which accompanies them. The difference between this ad as shown in other countries and its UK version lies in the voice-over, not because it is in English since the other language versions also used the respective national languages. But there is an extra twist in the sound-track of the British commercial which is missing from those in the other languages.

This is what the text says:

> Ranieri
> nothing looks like it
> nothing tastes like it
> nothing feels like it
> its smooth creaminess embraces a velvety centre.
> Ranieri – so intensely ice-cream

Most of the wording of this ad is perfectly straight-forward commercial speech in its parallel structuring, its alliteration and its rhythm. However, the final ungrammatical collocation of "intensely" with ice-cream gives an indication for the possibility of a camp reading for the heavily eroticised sequences of the visuals. But it is only in conjunction with the exaggerated accent and the quality of the male voice that the sound track evokes comic rather than erotic connotations of Latin accents. Such humorous readings are particularly available for those "in-group" viewers who pick up on what seems to me to be the parodic intertextual reference here. Intertextually, the exaggerated lengthening of the vowel in [lu:ks laik it], the quality of the [a:] vowel in nothing, and the whole intonational pattern in general will for many British viewers recall the voice of Manuel, the unfortunate (Spanish) waiter in John Cleese's classic TV comedy *Faulty Towers*. Any such reminder will entirely and comically subvert the erotic appeal and provide a self-ironic commentary for the very qualities suggested and aroused by its own visual track. This commercial can be seen as a classical instance for discourses and metadiscourses of culture living side by side in the same text, with one channel bringing us the mythical quality of Italy through its visual connotations, whilst the other performs an ironic deconstruction of it by a form of stylised speech. The sign system of Italian sexuality is thus both used and playfully undercut.

6. Conclusion

I have argued in this chapter that contemporary British TV commercials often make use of metadiscourses as a means of commenting on, playing with and ironising the more cliched representations of other cultures which offer stock images of otherness for more stereotypical ads. The strategies of intertextual play, parody and stylisation provide the means for a humorous appeal to the viewers' in-group semiotic competence. All metadiscourses employ a form of stylisation, since they work by consciously drawing attention to other forms of symbolic representation, for those "enculturated" viewers who are able to decode the references. But a particular category of humorous TV commercial exploits the potential of "double-voicing" by drawing on discourses of culture in the visual sequences, and on metadiscourses about these, arising from the accompanying spoken text. In these commercials the difference between "style" and "stylisation" can be located in a discrepancy between the two channels. Whereas the visual track in these ads often represents the stylistic (and stylish) forms of another culture true to its global, or sometimes culture-specific stereotypical attractiveness, the sound track ironises the very same images by deliberate stylisation. In thus providing a self-reflexive and double-voiced metacommentary about the imagistic narratives of desire, these TV commercials can be seen as rooted in a distinctly British context playing to the assumed preferences of British audiences for irony, parody and subversive humour.

References

Bakhtin, Mikhail M.
   1981   *The Dialogic Imagination* Edited by Michael Holquist, translated by Caryl Emerson and Michael Holquist. Austin, TX: University of Texas Press.
   1986   *Speech Genres and Other Late Essays*. Edited by Caryl Emerson and Michael Holquist, translated by Vern W. McGee. Austin, TX: University of Texas Press.
Barthes, Roland.
   1972   *Mythologies*. London: Jonathan Cape.
   1977   *Image – Music – Text*. London: Fontana.
Cook, Guy
   1992   *The Discourse of Advertising*. London: Routledge.
Fairclough, Norman
   1995   *Media Discourse*. London: Arnold.

Fowles, Jib
  1996   *Advertising and Popular Culture*. London: Sage.
Frow, John
  1990   Intertextuality and ontology. In Worton, Michael and Judith Stills (eds.),
          Intertextuality: Theory and Practices. Manchester: Manchester University
          Press, 45–55.
Kelly-Holmes, H.
  2000   Intertextuality and identity: A study of three Irish advertising texts. In
          Meinhof, Ulrike Hanna and Jonathan Smith (eds.), *Intertextuality and the
          Media: From Genre to Everyday Life*. Manchester: Manchester University
          Press.
Kress, Gunther
  2000   Text as the punctuation of semiosis: Pulling at some of the threads. In
          Meinhof, Ulrike Hanna and Jonathan Smith (eds.), *Intertextuality and the
          Media: From Genre to Everyday Life*. Manchester: Manchester University
          Press.
Kress, Gunther and Theo Van Leeuwen
  1996   *Reading Images: The Grammar of Visual Design*. London: Routledge.
  2001   *Multimodal Discourse*. London: Arnold.
Meinhof, Ulrike Hanna
  1998   *Language Learning in the Age of Satellite Television*. Oxford: Oxford Uni-
          versity Press.
  2002   Italian longings: British TV commercials and the myth of the South. In
          Bachmair, B., Gunther Kress and C. Scalamonti (eds.), *Media, Culture and
          the Social World*. Napoli: Liguori,
Meinhof, Ulrike Hanna and Jonathan Smith (eds.)
  2000   *Intertextuality and the Media: From Genre to Everyday Life*. Manchester:
          Manchester University Press.
Myers, Greg
  1994   *Words in Ads*. London: Arnold.
  1999   *Ad Worlds: Brands, Media, Audiences*. London: Arnold.
Pitcher, F.
  1989   Searching for European cultural identity: Vivent les Différences. *Interme-
          dia* 17, 20–25.
Rampton, Ben
  1995   *Crossing: Language and Ethnicity amongst Adolescents*. London: Long-
          man.
Tolson, Andrew
  1996   *Mediations. Text and Discourse in Media Studies*. London: Arnold.

Retroshopping: Sentiment, sensation and symbolism on the high street

Kay Richardson

1. Introduction

In this chapter I want to use the concept of metalanguage as a tool for exploring the nature of contemporary consumer culture, in its late 20th/early 21st century form in Britain. I will do this by means of a case study of a particular high street chain store operating mainly in the UK for the sale of gifts. This particular store goes by the name of *Past Times* and I will elaborate below the character of its particular enterprise.

The term "metalanguage" is, however, unsatisfactory for the purposes of this case study in one important respect: it is not sufficiently inclusive. *Past Times* does sell its products by using "language about language", but it also sells them by using language about images, about sounds, about textures and about smells. The modes of meaning-construction in the store are not restricted to linguistic ones but include visual, tactile and olfactory ones too. The multimodal meanings in play are all subject to "meta" formulation, notably in the catalogue with which the store advertises its products for mail order. For example:

> Made in Ireland for *Past Times*, our beautifully soft chenille serape and beret are inspired by Queen Victoria's love of the tartan, and combine warmth with elegance.
> (*Past Times* catalogue 1997).

I will have more to say about this example later: notice how the language of the catalogue draws attention to the salient semiotic properties of the products ("beautifully soft") as well as proposing to its readers why we should value those properties ("warmth", "elegance").

Past Times is relevant to the topic of metalanguage because:

(a) It is a store which is also a discourse: a substantive set of representations.
(b) Its mode of representation is metasemiotic because it depends not merely on language but also upon visual, auditory and even olfactory symbolism.[1]
(c) The "meta" aspect of its mode of representation is present in its conscious appropriation of a particular tradition – British national culture – as a set of signs.

2.   The social meaning of things

There is a popular situation comedy on British television called *Keeping Up Appearances* which features a principal character called Hyacinth Bucket (she prefers to pronounce it *Bouquet*). In one episode of the programme, Hyacinth takes a consumer's revenge on a brother-in-law who has caused her to lose face in front of her middle class neighbours. Since he has done her a good turn, by delivering to her house a new three piece suite, she concedes his right to have a cup of tea before he leaves. But, she declares, he won't be drinking out of her Royal Doulton china with the hand-painted periwinkles. That will be his punishment for his lack of gentility and her revenge for the loss of face. Onslow, the brother-in-law, of course won't care about this "insult"; but Hyacinth will have expressed her feelings in the kind of terms which make most sense to her, and honour will have been restored. And the detail is important. Hyacinth gives us not just a brand name but a detail of design which acts as a sign of distinction (Bourdieu 1986), reinforced by reference to the mode of production, which asserts the superiority of the crafted over the mass-produced.

Not all of us are quite as obvious as the redoubtable Hyacinth Bucket in showing the extent that our things define us and give meaning as well as pleasure to our lives. But the characterisation works because of its recognisability as a type, and also because of the echoes and resonances it offers with our own motivations as members of that same consumer society – in which Royal Doulton china is not the only kind of artefact with an established place in the landscapes of taste. There is considerable metalinguistic and metasemiotic work to be done in allocating artefacts to their rightful place in these landscapes: advertising and marketing is about nothing if it is not about this work.

This is one way of thinking about what it means to live in a consumer culture. Objects are invested with meanings over and above their functions. Appadurai (1986) talks about "the social life of things" and the kinds of meaning which they can carry at different moments in their own histories. One of the most important functions of things is as possessions. People relate to things as possessions, extensions of the self, and they use their possessions to achieve their own self-fashioning, in a world where identity is a matter of display, carried on the body and its proximate accoutrements, and in the home, as the body's most significant spatial context.

At the same time, those who manufacture consumer goods do so in order to provide the resources with which to undertake this self-fashioning. *Past Times* is a gift shop. Gifts are a particular subcategory of consumer goods, one in which style is as important as substance – often more so. Gifts are items bought by one person and given to another, to express the value of the relationship, at particular moments conventionally recognised as appropriate for the purpose, such as birthdays, anniversaries, Christmas. In our culture the gift-giving enterprise has developed in such a way that gifts invoke *taste* – the taste of the purchaser, the taste of the recipient, the alignment between these. In this context it is not surprising that the function of the item is of secondary concern.

3. The re-enchantment of the life world

Subjectively speaking, one of the reasons we attach value to things is that they speak to our need for enchantment – for pleasurable affective meaning which allows escape from the banality of the everyday. Children understand the potential of things, in their excitement to unwrap the Christmas presents and see what Santa has come up with. Adults are more cynical, since they have a more realistic sense of what money can buy. They also have more reflexivity concerning their own interests in gifts and in relationships. But there is always room for sincerity and hope – and hence always scope for the stores to fashion and refashion their offerings, to raise them above the banality of their functions. Secular societies like our own do not give much official encouragement to the types of value framework formerly offered by religion. Alternative sources of meaning such as science or social progress either refuse an affective content, or have come to seem altogether hollow at the end of the 20th century. In this context, it has been suggested, we do continue to seek out meaning in our daily lives, but we do so in ways which have become highly individualised – our entertainments, our beliefs, our personal attachments are treated as matters of personal choice which have little or nothing to do with the communities into which we are born and to which we belong. Community membership itself is widely seen as elective rather than ascriptive, and tastes become defining of identity.

But in the face of this weakening of value, there is some resistance. *Past Times* is an enterprise of compromise between individuality and community: its own contribution to the re-enchantment of the lifeworld is as modern as the consumer culture itself, whilst the particular taste culture it promotes is one which stakes a claim upon tradition. It is a particular tradition. In *Past Times*, Imperial Britain is close to the surface; minority groups marginalised or excluded. It is much closer to Peregrine Worsthorne than to Benjamin Zephanaia. Here are a couple of quotations from the company's own literature: a one-page document from 1997:

> *Past Times* is one of the retail success stories of the 80's and 90's in Great Britain. Our Company sells high quality historical gifts and decorative accessories, imaginatively themed by historical period. ...
>
> The merchandise range is of high quality and good value, with accessible price points. An increasing proportion of the lines are exclusive *Past Times* designs. Selected to have a broad appeal to women buying both gifts and for themselves, the range includes fashion garments and accessories, leisure items such as books, music, crafts and games, decorative accessories for the home and garden as well as toiletries.
>
> The chronological historical theming is reinforced by detailed and historically correct item descriptions. *Past Times* shops are designed to have more than a hint of museum shops, with extensive labelling, display cases, and period music playing.[2]

One of the first writers to see that citizens of modernity attached value to the past, often to the national past, as a way of reintroducing significance into daily life was Patrick Wright (1986). The consolations of the late 20th century in Wright's analysis are few, and often individualised rather than shared and social. Hence the attraction of the national: ideological or not, there are consolations to be had from belonging to a national community. And the consolation is the greater if the nation has produced, and is still capable of producing, phenomena of value. In *Past Times* the privileged values are aesthetic ones, though truth and goodness also get a look in. What cultural critics call the art-culture system (see Lury 1996) is important to the product range, which carry their "historic" aura in their surface design characteristics, just like Hyacinth Bucket's hand-painted periwinkles.

4.   Classification and pedagogy

In the gift market there is nothing new about retro design (and museums have become rather good at this, as *Past Times* acknowledges in its own literature – see above): what was new in the 1990s was the idea of a store devoted entirely to products of this kind, and one making historical reference, rather than the function of the items themselves, its principle of classification, for the purpose of presentation and shelving. Similarity of purpose is fragmented (there are "notelets" in every section of the store) and similarity of design is foregrounded ("Celtic" notelets are shelved alongside Celtic jewellery, books about Celtic symbolism and mugs with Celtic designs drawn from the domain of manuscript illumination). Elsewhere on the high street – in the stationers' WH Smith, for example – the complementary principle has traditionally prevailed. In such stores, it has been similarity of purpose which provided the basis of store organisation, and this is by far the more familiar kind of layout. The *Past Times* project hovers on the edge of a pedagogic discourse, instructing its consumers in the phases of British history, or, rather, attempting to flatter them in their prior knowledge of and affection for that history. It is instructive that *Past Times* understands its appeal in terms of an international, as well as a national market:

> We currently supply mail order customers in over 180 countries. A number of overseas versions are now available – US, French, German and Japanese – with all copy in the native language and prices given in the local currency.

> Any overseas customers who visit Great Britain will find *Past Times* retail shops sited in many of our most prestigious shopping areas, including Regent Street and Knightsbridge in London, Oxford, Cambridge and Edinburgh etc. as well as at Heathrow and Gatwick airports.

> *(Past Times* cataloge 1997)

This of course fits in with the more general use the use of "heritage" principle to sell the culture both to its residents and to sympathetic visitors.

The heritage principle as interpreted by *Past Times* can only function if the primary semiotic forms (the ornate Celtic crosses, the Victorian decoupage) are given metasemiotic assistance. We have to be *told* that the crosses are Celtic, that the decoupage is Victorian. The primary metasemiotic mechanism for providing this assistance is that of classification of the artefacts into sections, each section being allocated to its own distinct space within the store. In the Autumn of 1998 the store was thus divided into 12 sections, 9 of which mapped on to the chronology of British history, with an Anglo-centric focus. The remaining 3 represent a principle of division by "space" within the domestic environment, with a nostalgic and upper-class flavour.

1. Roman
2. Celtic
3. Medieval
4. Medieval Christmas
5. Tudor and Stuart
6. Eighteenth century
7. Victorian
8. Victorian Christmas
9. 20th century

10. The Study
11. Period Garden
12. The Nursery

The number of items displayed and the total space occupied by any section varies from town to town, depending upon the total floor space available. In years previous to 1997 there have been other sections besides the ones listed here: since 1997 there have been further innovations and adjustments. During 1997 there was a section, "Arts and Crafts", referring to the Arts and Crafts movement of the late 19th century. The artefacts in this section were later included within the larger category of the Victorian period, where previously their distinctiveness had been recognised through the processes of classification and display.

The pedagogy of this organisational system is, however, not insisted upon, for although the sections are separated physically, and labelled like the rooms in a museum, there is no attempt (or very little) to organise the sections within the store into their correct chronological sequence. Nor are dates provided. The knowledgeable will provide sequence for themselves, and the ignorant won't care. It is not easy to impose sequence in the physical context of a store – not if the idea is to have people move through the store in the right order. *Past Times* in Liverpool is a small store and customers have to avoid columns as well as one another in moving through it.

Furthermore, like all systems of classification, that of *Past Times* is a "leaky" one, and it is not always obvious where particular items belong. It is instructive, for example, to see what items have been seen as pertaining to "The Study" – the following account is based upon the catalogue rather than any of the actual shops, since shops in different towns stock variable ranges. As a spatial rather than a chronological category, The Study can accommodate artefacts of different "period" associations. For example, the Ex Libris silk tie is "Inspired by Edwardian library bookcases" and sits alongside the Oscar Wilde t-shirt, bearing the inscription "I have nothing to declare except my genius" – a Wilde epigram which we are told dates from 1882 – the Victorian era. In the study we find, of course, books: *The 100 Greatest Military Leaders*; *Dad's Army: A Celebration*, *The 100 Greatest Women of All Time*; *The Book of Meditations* – and many others. As well, there are videos and CDs – presumably on the principle that these are shelved in the study in the same way as books. Books are present too as a design element: the design on the Ex Libris silk tie is "decorated with rows of leather bound volumes" – as is the Library Cushion, the Ex Libris Tote Bag, the cover on the front of the Literary Crossword – a book of crossword puzzles "each with a distinct literary theme" – and the Ex Libris Clock, "Inspired by novels in the Bodleian Library, Oxford". Having pictures of books on a tie is a primary, visual sign: that this is a tie which signifies "The Study" takes us into metasemiotics.

It will be seen from the list above that the advantage of the non-chronological categories in the store (i.e. "The Study" as opposed to "Victorian") is that it allows the inclusion of items whose associations (like the Bodleian) are "old", or "traditional" without being specific to any particular period. Studies are spaces where writing takes place; spaces with organisational requirements which would justify the inclusion of The Millenium Calendar 1999 – since writers need to know about dates; the Abacus Paperweight – since writers need to ensure that their writing paper remains where they left it. Similar reasoning applies to the Medieval Manuscript Pen Set, the Revolving Compact Disc Stand and the Edwardian Letter Rack.

A "Study", by tradition, is the preserve of the male, not the female, and thus in this domain of the house we find a considerable number of artefacts whose associations are with sport (the Golfing Hip Flask); with the military (Dad's Army videos; the World War I Storm Lighter); with drinking (Whisky marmalades), with male dress (Cuff links inspired by Charles Rennie Mackintosh designs) and with the male love of the "gadget" (Pocket weather forecaster).

Women, however, are not overlooked: this section of the catalogue lists a "cloisonné egg from China" and the photograph shows this to be a decorative item with very little of the masculine in its design. The same could be said for the Dark Chocolate Orange Slices and Cherry Truffles, in the same part of the catalogue. Perhaps the Study is being signified here as a place of secluded indulgence where it is permitted to enjoy solitary, gendered pleasures – whether that be a game of Table Snooker or a dip into the Cherry Truffle box. Or even reading.

As for the chronological classification system itself, there are certainly reasons why the periodisation of the artefacts is not insisted upon too strenuously. For one thing, a heavy-handed pedagogic discourse would begin to undermine the pleasure of consumption, as well as risking the encouragement of a critical reception for their artefacts. As it is, the pleasure derives not principally from knowledgeability, or even the promise of knowledgeability (though the number of instructional books on sale is interesting in this connection), but from something like a sentiment of solidarity with national forebears of taste and talent – at least for consumers who belong to the same story as the one on show in the store. It is a national story, though not one xenophobically closed to extra-national themes and influences provided they are labelled as such.

5.   Stylised consumption

For *Past Times*, as elsewhere in contemporary cultural life, the use of semiotic associations for consumption purposes has become all-pervasive, and it is appropriate to view not just the artefacts but the store itself as a semiotic environment, conceived and planned for an overall look and feel which is distinctive on the High Street and in keeping with its particular ethos of consumption – *good* taste and historical associations, via a mixture of (primary) semiotic and metasemiotic forms and strategies. To visit the store is to walk into a space which has been designed for a consistent overall "look". The desire to evoke museum shop displays is very apparent, beginning from the use of the shop's own walls. Walls are vertical surfaces which can readily be "sectioned" to facilitate the classification process. Each section is provided with its own background: panelling made of dark wood yet fashioned in a "brick" design, as if to look like a wall. Against this background, supports are provided so that artefacts can be displayed up to and even a little above eye level, in a balanced visual composition but so that items put their best face forward towards the consumer, and also so that they can be easily lifted off their supports for examination by the shopper who is exercising careful choice before settling upon the preferred goods. Away from the walls there are columns which provide further vertical surfaces to be used in this way. In addition, there are cabinets, also in dark wood, allowing for the display in a horizontal plane of small, precious objects, under glass and locked away. This is where the jewellery can be found; this is the stuff that must be carefully protected from shoplifters because of its size and its value. (In electrical shops it is small goods such as electric shavers which are protected in locked cabinets.)

6.   Meaning as mystery

When history becomes too familiar it can also become as banal as the present, and as free from deep affect. What *Past Times* needs is the *mystery* of the past: the cachet of its artefacts depends upon that mystery, and this is a further reason for eschewing the language of education, whether of the classroom or of the museum, in the presentation of those artefacts. But as with all mystery there must be a hint at answers and solutions. The purchasers of artefacts from *Past Times* are not only buying their way into a valued national culture: they are also buying the privilege of access to meanings not shared by the generality of citizens. It is as if the national culture is suffused with *opaque* symbols. *Past Times* consumers are invited to lift the veil, and to see what lies behind. Nowhere is this theme of demystification more apparent than in the range of books on offer in the store. Some of the titles:

> *Nota Bene*: A guide to familiar Latin quotes and phrases
> *Forgotten English*: A 365 day calendar of vanishing vocabulary for 1998
> *The Scoundrel's Dictionary*: A copious and complete compendium of 18th century slang
> *The secret language of symbols*: A visual key to symbols and their meanings
> *How household names began*: Maurice Baren tells the stories behind our favourite brands

Notice how these titles bring together the ordinary and the mysterious: 18th century slang is decidedly exotic now. Conversely with household names: they are anything but exotic, but they have interesting stories behind them which are worth telling.

By comparison with other artefacts, books have the most scope for familiarising people with the histories of words and other symbolic forms. But the use of symbols, words and letters as design items is also part of the *Past Times* discourse, whether opaque or transparent in meaning, and this is by no means restricted to books, nor even to the packaging on non-book items. Opaque symbolic designs would include for example the runic patterns on bracelets and other jewellery items from the Anglo-Saxon and Viking section, as well as the t-shirt with the Latin slogan "Emptrix nata sum" translated on the packaging as "Born to shop". *Past Times* is nothing if not reflexive about its purposes. Transparent designs are popular too. These range from artefacts using display initials such as trinket boxes and bookmarks through to the Oscar Wilde t-shirt displaying the quotation "I have nothing to declare except my genius".

7.   The language of desire: Text in the *Past Times* catalogue

To examine the most overtly metasemiotic levels of signification in the discourse of *Past Times* it is necessary to move from the shop itself to the catalogue, where the multimodal combinations of texts and photographs operate to deliver appropriate "readings" of the items on offer. In a sense, any object with "retro" design features comes into the category of opaque semiosis – semiosis which is motivated by association with the past but only opaquely so – its historical associations require explanation to the potential consumer. In most cases the "explanation" positions the semiosis as indexical in type, so far as its period character is concerned. There is no meaning to explicate, beyond that of co-occurrence: flower designs occurred in the 18th century, bobble night-caps in the 19th century, art nouveau in the 20th century. Because so much of the semi-osis is opaque and indexical, metadiscourses are required to translate. It is in the *Past Times* catalogue that this function is most fully developed: where every featured item is "explained". The first example, which I cited in shortened form earlier in this chapter, is by way of preliminary illustration of what is required:

CHENILLE TARTAN SERAPE AND BERET

Made in Ireland for *Past Times*, our beautifully soft chenille serape and beret are inspired by Queen Victoria's love of the tartan, and combine warmth with elegance. The self-fringed serape has generous circular cut to give the garment movement and drape. 100% acrylic. Serape 54" x 70", elasticated beret will fit most heads. 8690 serape £65.00, 8688 Beret £1 9.99. 8759 Serape and Beret £82.50.

The task in this case is to take a design feature (tartan cloth) which has an exist-ing signification in contemporary culture (Scottish) and to establish its claims to an additional signification (Victorian). There is nothing incompatible between these two meanings, since the existing one is space-bound and the new one is time-bound (provided that the time-bound meaning is not taken restrictively). But the interesting thing is the logic of association here – another species of in-dexical meaning and a more attenuated kind than previously discussed. The ex-plicit account focuses not upon production, but upon consumption: specifically, upon the tastes of one particular "Victorian", albeit the most important Victorian of them all. By implication there may be more than this: perhaps the serape and beret are also the kinds of garments she would have worn. Perhaps we have seen "her" or her surrogate in movies, paintings, plays, wearing just such garments. The catalogue does not supply these connections but the readers may well do.

Each entry in the catalogue is of about this length, and with this combina-tion of elements. Schematically, the text is composed thus: description, code number, code name, price in pounds sterling: the function of the description is to excite interest in the product and anchor the accompanying illustration. The function of the other elements is to call readers back to the world of commercial exchange, via the mechanisms of mail-order: the code elements are to be en-tered by the consumer on the order form, and the price upon an accompanying cheque (though credit card payments are also acceptable).

Thus it is within the description that we must look for semiotic enhancement, product "stylisation" which is provided because a name alone is not enough, not even with an accompanying photographic image. I will say more about the images below: for now I want to offer some more analysis of the "recipe" by which *Past Times* artefact descriptions are generated.

There is little redundancy in these short descriptive texts and a functional project with three main elements:

1. To provide objective characterisation of the object and its physical properties including size, material of composition, type of visual detail, etc.
2. To provide aesthetic evaluation of the object; to point to the value-scheme appropriate for its evaluation.
3. To associate the object with its uses.

Other textual elements serve to establish a relationship of *ownership* between *Past Times* as a producer and/or retail outlet with its products. This is based principally upon the use of the exclusive first person plural pronoun in the possessive form: the store is selling *our* chest, *our* mirror, *our* cardigan. The descriptive discourse, contextualised within this relationship, creates a kind of "aristocratic", country-house effect – the proprietor shows the visitors the treasures of the estate. Even though in the real country estate, it is the uniqueness of the artefacts which gives them their cachet, whilst *Past Times* can produce as many copies as the market will bear, this does not in itself undermine the metaphorical force of the underlying image.

It is possible to develop a more refined analysis of the *Past Times* description recipe, though only by including a range of options not all of which are included within any particular description. Thus, for example, the first element within a description I have identified as being the element concerned with material properties. The range of choices available here is as follows:

1.	NOMINATION
1.1.	Of item(s)
1.2.	Of part(s) of item(s)
1.3.	Of supplementary item(s)
1.4.	Of design forms used
1.4.1.	Visual
1.4.2.	Verbal
1.4.3.	Other
2.	SIZE
2.1.	Of item(s)
2.2.	Of part(s) of item(s)
2.3.	Of supplementary item(s)
3.	MATERIAL
3.1.	Of item(s)

3.2.	Of part(s) of item(s)
3.3.	Of supplementary item(s)
4.	QUANTITY
4.1.	Of item(s)
4.2.	Of part(s) of item(s)
4.3.	Of supplementary item(s)
5.	TECHNIQUE
5.1.	To produce item(s)
5.2.	To produce part(s) of item(s)
5.3.	To produce supplementary item(s)
6.	DESIGN FORM
6.1.	Verbal
6.2.	Sensual
6.2.1.	Aural
6.2.2.	Visual (excluding verbal)
6.2.3.	Olfactory
6.2.4.	Tactile
6.2.5.	Taste-related
7.	PERIOD PROVENANCE
7.0.1.	Structural
7.0.1.1.	Of item(s)
7.0.1.2.	Of part(s) of item(s)
7.0.1.3.	Of supplementary item(s)
7.0.2.	Of design forms
7.0.2.1.	Verbal
7.0.2.2.	Sensual
7.0.2.2.0.1.	Aural (excluding verbal)
7.0.2.2.0.2.	Visual (excluding verbal)
7.0.2.2.0.3.	Olfactory
7.0.2.2.0.4.	Tactile
7.0.2.2.0.5.	Taste-related

This apparatus may, even yet, be incomplete – and it has not been possible to do as full an analysis of the possibilities under the other two headings (the aesthetic evaluation of the artefact; the use of the artefact). However, it is important to say more about the evaluative discourse, and I shall do so by way of two further examples:

JACOBEAN CHEST
Our handsome wood chest is hand-carved with an original Jacobean leaf
motif. Ideal for storing candles, it comes with 15 standard 8" candles with
3/4" base. Chest in hardwood from replenished forests with brass hinges.
10'/4" x 5'/2" x 6'/4".

Reorganised by function, this can be displayed in table form:

Table 1.

Possessive relation	Detail	Evaluation	Use
our	wood	handsome	
	Chest		
	hand-carved		
	Jacobean	original	
	Leaf		
	motif		
		ideal	for storing candles
	comes with 15 standard candles		
	with 3/4" base		
	chest		
	in hardwood		
		from replenished forests	
	with brass hinges		
	10'/4" x 5'/2" x 6'/4		

Detail. The detail column clearly shows the different elements of the item which
merit inclusion:

Wood: chest: hand-carved: jacobean: leaf: motif: comes with 15 standard
candles: with 3/4" base: chest: in hardwood: with brass hinges:10'/4" x 5'/2" x
6'/4

Material of construction is mentioned (wood, hardwood); the object is
nominated (chest) and so are any special parts (hinges) and accompanying objects (candles). These in their turn have their material of construction specified

(brass). I take it that in the case of the candles, material of construction remains unspecified because a default assumption that candles are made of candlewax applies. Size information is given in respect of the chest itself and also in respect of the candles; quantity information is given in respect of the candle comple-ment. Surface design characteristics are mentioned (leaf motif) drawing upon a vocabulary (typology?) of design forms.

The description of the chest as "hand-carved" deserves further comment, because it takes us beyond the directly observable. An "observable" provides a point of departure: the fact that the item is "carved" has a descriptive mean-ing in respect of its texture: the catalogue (unlike the store itself) can't gratify tactile senses by reproducing texture directly upon its glossy pages but the lines, shapes and shadows which appear in a photographic image represent that tex-ture to visual perception. It is also a reference to the process by which that tex-ture came about, and attention is drawn to that meaning by making it explicit that this item is hand-carved: it is the work of a craftsperson not of an imper-sonal industrial process. Also taking us beyond the directly observable is the adjective "Jacobean": this belongs to the typology of period which constitutes PT's distinctive contribution to the semiotic enrichments of gift goods.

Evaluation. I have classified four elements of the text within the "evaluation" column: "handsome", "ideal" (for storing candles) "from replenished forests", and "original". These various elements point towards different schemas of eval-uation. The first of these, "handsome", is the most straightforward, pointing as it does towards aesthetic judgement (is there still an element of masculinity in the adjective itself?). "Original" is different: the item itself is not original but the design element is claimed as such. It is not aesthetics which is at stake here but authenticity – the association between the design motif and its proper period. The "ideal" of "ideal for storing candles" is also evaluative, here in the domain of uses (see below). Finally, "from replenished forests" is by way of a nod to environmental discourse: an apology or justification for the use of desirable but vulnerable hardwood timber, and thus a construction of the item's desirability which is, at least in part, a moral one.

Uses. A specific function (candle-storage) is specified; the text evaluates the item as "ideal" for this purpose (see above) and even undertakes to provide some candles for an extra charge, whilst at the same time ensuring that other uses are not precluded (though neither are they specified). The phrasing "Ideal for storing candles" may seem somewhat redundant, since the item in question is listed as a "Jacobean candle chest with 15 candles". However it is possible to purchase the chest without the candles, and thus to contemplate other uses for this small carved box with its rounded lid section – the shape of the lid is apparent from the illustration though is not mentioned in the text.

Another example:

SHAKESPEARE T-SHIRT
Our exclusive pure cotton T-shirt carries the line spoken by the old servant, Adam, in Shakespeare's "As You Like It". It will make a perfect present for any ageing would-be Romeo you know! One size fits up to 48" chest. 8962 T-shirt £9.99

Table 2.

Possessive relation	Detail	Evaluation	Use
Our		Exclusive	
		Pure	
	Cotton		
	t-shirt		
	Carries the line spoken by the old servant, Adam, in Shakespeare's As You Like It	perfect	It will make a ... present for any ageing would-be Romeo you know!
	One size fits up to 48" chest.		

The elements in this table bear considerable similarity to those discussed in relation to the Jacobean chest. The possessive relation is there, as is the detail, the evaluation and the use. Within the descriptive section the item is nominated ("t-shirt"), its material of construction is identified ("cotton"), size is specified ("One size ... chest") design detail is mentioned ("Carries the line ... 'As You Like It'" – note that here it is necessary to refer to the photograph to read the actual text, which it reads: "Though I look old, yet I am strong and lusty". More than this, the photograph shows other semiotic properties of the item besides the words themselves, to wit the font, which is elegantly calligraphic, and the ornate rectangular border, reminiscent of illuminated manuscripts although in monochrome, and a source reference for the quote). A line of verse differs from a leaf, as a design element, though both are treated equivalently in the way that their provenance is specified: "Jacobean" in one case and Shakespearean in the other. In the case of the leaf it is the visual form of the element which is the crucial property that supplies "distinction". The new leaf has to look like the old one. In the case of the Shakespearean line, the visual form is at the discretion of the modern designers. It is word choice and word order which is fixed; altogether a different formal level of construction.

In the evaluation column there are elements comparable to those for the Jacobean chest ("perfect" here compares with "ideal" in the case of the chest: both are judgements in respect of the use of the item – though the use of the t-shirt is related to the personality of the user and recipient of the gift, and this was not the case with the chest). "Pure" of course modifies "cotton": at one level this is a matter of detail (no other material of construction is involved) but the associations of the word with cleanliness, virtue, etc. are also in play. In this context our understanding of cotton as a "natural" material is relevant; the more pure the cotton, the more natural the item. Within discourses of nature there are real contradictions: the preservation of "nature" (environmentalism) is at odds with the use of "natural" goods. It is important that these contradictions are suppressed within the consumer discourses of the catalogue and the store.

Then, too, there is the reference to the exclusivity of the item. What exactly does this mean? Not uniqueness: *Past Times* will produce as many Shakespearean t-shirts as they can sell. Of course, it has to do with the unavailability of this item from other stores. It would seem that *Past Times* is so confident of its own worth that it is willing to use the store's imprimatur as a mark of distinction in its own right.

The evaluative value schemes already identified from the Jacobean chest are those of aesthetics, use, morality and authenticity. In the light of the analysis of the t-shirt we can add to these. The reference to the purity of the cotton evokes a schema which is hard to give a name to. There is a moral dimension but this is in the background rather than the foreground. Constructional integrity, wholeness, plays a part, and the fact that this is pure cotton (and not pure polyester!) is crucial – cotton is natural, and what is natural is good for you. It is question-begging to specify "purity" as a value-scheme in its own right, and so I have come to the conclusion that we should view this element as evoking a health schema. The additional schema which is of relevance here is that of rarity, via the use of the adjective "exclusive".

In the use column the reader is instructed to think of a particular personality as the potential wearer/owner of this garment, and thus of the item as a potential gift for such persons. The exclamation mark is an attempt to specify that use in a marked "tone of voice", one which is tinged with humour. This is different from the case of the chest: the chest's suitablity for its function is constrained within the terms of the practicalities of storing candles – within which perspective the semiotic characteristics become irrelevant. The "wearability" of the t-shirt is the equivalent to this. Aspects of wearability are certainly hinted at – the comfort of the fabric, the capacity of the 48" size – but the explicit aspect of use is inflected towards the surface design elements of the item rather than towards practical considerations, via the sentiment corresponding to the line of Shakespearean verse. Use is a matter of semiotics primarily and utility secondarily.

It is possible to make some generalisations about the modes of evaluation for *Past Times* artefacts. The following categories seem to account for most examples, though in what proportions I have not determined.

(a)   *Aesthetics*
      This is usually about visual aesthetics, though other sense-perceptions may sometimes be involved.

(b)   *Authenticity*
      The products themselves would only be authentic if they were antiques, and this is not the point of the enterprise. So authenticity is displaced. It is expected that there will be some point of association between the new item and a precursor in a specified period from the English/British past.

(c)   *Utility*
      If a function is specified, an evaluative adjective or adverb may underline the item's suitability for that function. There is some circularity in all of this. I would include durability in this category.

(d)   *Morality*
      Product evaluation may gesture towards ethical considerations even if only to forestall ethical criticism

(e)   *Health and well-being*
      Product evaluation may indicate, directly or otherwise, that the product has a contriubtion to make to the owner's physical or mental well-being. I would include comfort in this category.

(f)   *Assets*
      The basic classification of PT texts separates evaluation from description. But description can have evaluative implications. This is particularly true where the description is able to point to the "extra" features that an item does not need to have in order to function, or to satisfy the provenance requirement, enhancing beauty, comfort or durability

(g)   *Maximisation of assets*
      Under this heading I include all those elements of evaluative language which function to convince the reader that the qualities and attributes possessed by the product are possessed to the fullest degree.

(h)   *Rarity*

Curious as it may be for a store producing multiple copies of its stock range, enough to satisfy every desiring consumer, PT uses a discourse of rarity, coded mainly in the adjective "exclusive", to give value to its products. The store's imprimatur acts as a sign of distinction in its own right (even if this is just wishful thinking!).

(i)   *Preciousness*

If the materials of construction include any such as gold, diamond, etc., which are considered valuable and marketable even in a "raw" state, this will be mentioned (though N.B., goldness can be just a colour).

8.   The visual image

It is important, in talking about the *Past Times* catalogue, to consider how the items are visually displayed and the effects which are sought for in such displays. At first glance the distribution and framing of the pictures (photographic images of the gifts) are consistent with a simple "illustration" function, alongside accompanying text which names and describes those gifts as well as giving ordering information. There are between 8 and 12 such illustrations on each double page spread. Most illustrations are "boxed" within rectangular frames, just as text is kept within column restrictions; occasionally, for variation, an "overlay" effect is achieved (as for example with a bead necklace, looped to allow the text to sit within the loop. Such unframed illustrations go along with a slight shading of the background paper colour – not enough to undermine the legibility of the text, but enough to hint at a context for the illustrated artefact beyond that of the catalogue pages. The distribution of items on the page is not too regular – excessive regimentation of display would undermine the pleasure principle – yet across each double page spread the composition is balanced according to design principles which are conventional in the industry for this type of publication.

The photographic modality of illustration is the normal one for catalogues; it is the strongest pictorial modality in its evocation of the reality of what it depicts. There are exceptions to this rule in the world of catalogues: the well-known J. Peterman catalogue of women's clothing is a case in point. In the Peterman catalogue the illustrations are in the form of watercoloured line drawings, more like the initial sketches of dress designers than like the finished results fully realised in their coloured and textured fabrics. It is the "illustration" principle which results in photographs which can be seen as literal in their iconic function. And yet there is something beyond this literal reference. There is often an evocation of context, of use – yet this is kept very much in the background. No people are seen – not even a hand, or a mouth. And yet the "Small Carved Chest of Drawers" is illustrated with one drawer slightly open, and items spilling out, "naturalistically" – an handkerchief, a necklace. The symbolism is very delicate, very feminine (a small sprig of flowers lies on top). Too much context would detract from the potency of the object in and of itself: a totally decontextualised object might seem cold and lacking in nuanced meaning. But the naturalism (if that is what it is) of these contextualising touches must be set alongside the intensifcation of focus. Consider how rarely objects, rather than people, are focal in movies and TV shows. The objects have to be salient in the drama (the smoking gun) to deserve the camera's attention. In the *Past Times* catalogue it is the objects which are the constant, unvarying object of attention. And the fascination of the objects is enhanced through the use of colour in the publication, for the colour is both dense and bright throughout – like the Christmas card display in a shop.

9. Conclusion

The question I want to ask about this material is whether or not it amounts to a new form of consumerism, and if so, upon what terms. I can think of several ways in which it is not new at all. There is nothing new in the specialisation of objects as gifts, and of particular stores as gift stores. There is nothing new in branding practices which appeal to the past and to tradition. There is nothing new in the emphasis upon surface decoration. Could the novelty reside in the post-modern sensibility which says: don't worry that this item combines a modern purpose with a "traditional" design which may or may not be "authentic"? Probably not. We have lived with postmodernism long enough to be familiar with its preference for bricolage: themes and motifs from different times and places combined with no respect for consistency or authenticity. In fact the pedagogic, museum-like elements of the *Past Times* discourse run very much counter to the full blooded versions of postmodernism.

If there is anything that's new about consumerism in this form, it is the contribution of the metadiscourse. The intrinsic charms of the items as seen, touched, smelled, are not enough. The enchantment, such as it is, is not forthcoming without the support of a semiotically enriched shaping context. The resonance of the individual artefacts is attenuated when they are removed from that context: the notelets become mere notelets, the scarf just a scarf; the chocolates just chocolates. British history comes to the rescue; it offers a seam of meaning which can protect consumers from the miasma of banality which forever threatens to engulf them.

Notes

1.   Like other high street shops, *Past Times* sells smells. *Past Times* sells the usual
      kinds of good smells, for personal use – soaps, perfumes, bath oils. It also sells
      smells in book form, such as the book for children with scratch and sniff pages
      illustrating Victorian smells. Some of these are not so good.
2.   *Past Times* has changed in a number of ways since this chapter was originally
      prepared. It is now possible, as it was not in 1998, to shop on-line and so an elec-
      tronic classification system adapted to hypertext form now coexists with a print
      catalogue and with the actual shops in high streets, airport concourses, etc. The
      predominant online classification system is functional and not section-based, i.e.
      the screen customer is invited to browse by "department" rather than by catalogue
      section: the departments include "Jewellery" "Games", "Clothing and acessories"
      amongst others. However, the print catalogue still uses a modified version of the
      earlier merchandising approach, and it is possible to search online by catalogue
      section as well as browse by department. Hypertext here delivers on its promise of
      making "reading" (read: browsing and searching) more flexible. At the same time,
      the catalogue sections are different from those used in 1997/8; more specific in
      some cases ("Edwardian Picnic" rather than just "Edwardian") but also somewhat
      less national overall with more exotic sections ("Roman Vill", "Moorish Garden")
      as well more trans-national ones "Art Deco"). The full semiotic and metasemiotic
      significance of all these changes would require another study: the primary expla-
      nation for all of these changes is ultimately economic.

References

Appadurai, Arjun
      1986   *The Social Life of Things: Commodities in Cultural Perspective*. Cam-
              bridge: Cambridge University Press.
Bourdieu, Pierre
      1986   *Distinction: A Social Critique of the Inducement of Taste*. London:
              Routledge.
Lury, Celia
      1996   *Consumer Culture*. Cambridge: Polity.
Wright, Patrick
      1985   *On Living in an Old Country: The National Past in Contemporary Britain*.
              London: Verso.

Commentary

Out of the bottle: The social life of metalanguage

Deborah Cameron

No contributor to this volume mounts a sustained argument against the notion of "metalanguage" as something worth distinguishing for analytic purposes from "language-in-general", even though some contributors express scepticism about any account which assumes that the "meta" can ultimately be separated from what it is supposedly "about". As Theo van Leeuwen (this volume) says: "meta-communication is part and parcel of everyday communication. ... Metalanguage, the resource needed for meta-communication, therefore permeates the language as a whole and should not be conceived of as a specialised register used only by linguists". In fact it is hard to think who Van Leeuwen is arguing against here, for the idea of metalanguage as "part and parcel" of language is a longstanding orthodoxy among linguists (see Coupland and Jaworski, this volume). It is routinely affirmed, for instance, in those staples of introductory textbook discourse on the question "what is language?", the "design features" account associated with Charles Hockett and the list of "functions" associated with Roman Jakobson. In both of these accounts, which have been endlessly recycled, natural languages are defined in part by their metalinguistic potential. A language that lacks resources for reflexive comment on its own characteristics is incomplete, perhaps not really a "proper" language at all (like the imaginary Ur-language of the builders in Wittgenstein's *Philosophical Investigations* (1953), or the communication systems used by various non-human animals).

Even if we accept that metacommunication is "part and parcel" of communication in general, though, it may still be asked whether metalanguage should be treated analytically as one kind of language practice among many – a different question from whether it is a "specialised register" – or whether it is in some sense a precondition for any kind of language practice. Jef Verschueren (this volume) appears more inclined than Van Leeuwen to take something like the second view, but his phrasing is cautious: "singling the metalinguistic dimension of language out for separate scientific attention is ... a valuable heuristic strategy in order not to forget its fundamental contribution to all pragmatic functioning".

Elsewhere (Cameron 1995) I have argued for a dual view of metalanguage. Rather than saying it is either foundational for all language use or else that it is

one specific practice in a whole constellation of them, I want to say that these
are two indivisible aspects of the same phenomenon. (I am reminded of Saussure's image of the signifier and signified which make up the linguistic sign as
two sides of a single piece of paper, which cannot be cut apart.) Metalinguistic
resources are necessary to allow language to function as the extremely flex-
ible means of communication we know it to be. Without such resources we
would be reduced to the level of Wittgenstein's builders, able only to exchange
a limited set of predetermined messages (and with no recourse if the communication happened to fail). In that sense metalanguage is, if not a precondition
for all language then a necessary resource for the successful use of language in
communicative acts. At the same time, metalanguage is rather like one of those
supernatural wish-fulfilling creatures that so often appear in myths and fairy
tales – a genie, for example. Freed from the bottle, the genie agrees to grant the
liberator's every wish; at first the requests are for necessary, useful things, but
as the story progresses they become more and more excessive. No one can stop
a person who has secured a Genie's services from using them for unnecessary
and even ridiculous ends. The Genie's promise is unconditional, and it cannot
be taken back ("you can't put the Genie back in the bottle"). Thus also with
our capacity to comment on and evaluate as well as merely use our languages.
We deploy it for what might be considered communicative necessities – like
retrieving meaning when communication misfires – but we also use it for more
"frivolous" purposes – like arguing about how best to translate the Bible into the
invented "alien" language Klingon (I discuss this example in Cameron 1995).
We do not "need" a Klingon Bible, let alone a full-scale debate about the merits
of competing translations, but the possibility of producing these things arises
from a capacity that we *do* need.

It might well be objected here that the distinction I have just made between
"necessary" and non-necessary or "frivolous" uses of metalanguage is deeply
suspect, derived from a view of language in which the fundamental reason for
using it is to exchange information, while anything else is treated as a kind of
optional extra. I agree. It is part of the mission of sociolinguistics (and socially-
oriented pragmatics[1]) to question that view. Contributors to this volume make
clear that understanding metalanguage is central to the project of understanding
the full range of things we can do with words. Not only with words, either; Kay
Richardson's analysis of the "metasemiotics" of the retail chain Past Times
makes a point endorsed by a number of other contributors (e.g. Van Leeuwen,
Meinhof) that metacommunication is not exclusively a linguistic phenomenon.
In addition to the term "metalanguage", therefore, below I will use terms such
as "metacommunication", "metapragmatics" and "metasemiotics" as seems appropriate for the particular example under discussion.

It has long been evident to sociolinguists that one purpose for which language users deploy their "meta" communicative competence is to make sense of – and participate in – the process of social differentiation through linguistic variation. This is the subject of chapters in the present volume by Tore Kristiansen and by Peter Garrett, Nikolas Coupland and Angie Williams, who investigate the metalinguistic apparatus that underpins speakers' judgements on their own and others' speech. One interesting feature of the method used by Garrett and his associates is that it elicits characterisations of speakers (such as "sheepshagger" or "prat") which are obviously not just descriptive identity labels but quite overtly evaluations of the relevant group. Here metalinguistic vocabulary is deployed (quite typically, I would suggest), not merely to categorise others, but to signal approval or disapproval of them. This points to an important general theme in the study of metalanguage: *morality*. Metalinguistic resources seem very often to be deployed to connect various aspects of linguistic behaviour to a larger moral order.

Sociolinguistic variation is not, of course, the only object of moral metadiscourse. John Wilson's chapter deals with a social domain (politics) and a kind of linguistic behaviour (deceptive speech) in which moral judgements on language-use are highly salient for obvious reasons. Dariusz Galasiński's chapter is located in another domain (media reporting) where moral considerations to do with the "correct" or "fair" representation of events, actions and – as in this case – words occasion systematic concern. Adam Jaworski and Itesh Sachdev's chapter, on the other hand, shows how the less obviously loaded issue of whether/how much pupils speak in the classroom becomes moralised through a metadiscourse on the meaning of silence.

In the chapters written by Ulrike Meinhof and Kay Richardson, attention is focused on what might be dubbed the "ludic" dimension of metalanguage, where archaic, foreign and otherwise "exotic" languages acquire value through their very inaccessibility and uselessness for practical purposes of communication. A t-shirt emblazoned with a slogan in Latin is unlikely to be purchased and displayed because of the message communicated by the words, which most observers will be unable to decode. What they will "get" will be a meta-message: the juxtaposition of ancient and modern, high and low culture in a Latin t-shirt slogan is incongruous and therefore amusing regardless of what the slogan actually means – the joke need not depend on knowing that its English translation is "born to shop" (though it acquires an extra dimension if you do know). Here the metalinguistic function seems closely allied to what Jakobson (1960) called the poetic function, where attention is drawn to formal qualities of language in order to produce special (generally, aesthetic) effects through an "excess" of meaning. Though Jakobson himself was very clear about the difference between metalingual and poetic functions, it seems evident that poetic effects would not be possible in a semiotic system with no "meta" dimension, nor could they be recognised by a language-user unable to function at a "meta" level of interpretation. Any notion of "form" and "content" as distinct dimensions of a message is intrinsically metalinguistic.

Richardson and Meinhof follow many other commentators in finding that the poetic (and therefore arguably also the metalinguistic) function is highly salient in the products of consumer culture, such as retailing and advertising (cf. Cook 1992). Many of those products also have the characteristic of being mediated, directed to a mass audience using technologies of mass communication, and it is of interest to consider whether mediated communication makes particular demands on people's metacommunicative competence. This is one of the issues explored in Nikolas Coupland's discussion of an episode of *Sergeant Bilko*, where once again the production of pleasure (in this case, humour) through an excess of meaning appears to be an important motivation for the intensive deployment of metacommunicative resources.

Though applied here to a "classic" piece of television, arguably something like Coupland's notion of "stylisation" is increasingly useful for researchers seeking to analyse the workings of all kinds of media texts. Contemporary television, for instance, is strikingly inclined to a sort of reflexive irony that both assumes and requires an equally reflexive, knowing and sophisticated viewer. There is, for instance, a TV commercial running in Britain as I write which might deserve the label "meta-advertising". It plays with the generic convention in which a product (in this case, a credit card) is promoted using a series of short vignettes in which a "man with a clipboard", representing the producer, elicits laudatory comments from a series of different product users. In this commercial, the first vignette initially appears conventional,[2] but by the second there is clearly something "wrong", for after explaining how useful she finds the product when shopping, the female consumer adds: "because that's what women do, isn't it, shop?" Then we cut to a Black man who looks up at the camera and says: "and of course, no commercial would be complete without the token Black man". Finally, clipboard man steps out of role and begins to make comments based on the assumption that "everyone knows I'm not really a spokesperson for company X, but someone employed to deliver an ad agency's script in a commercial for company X". His parting shot is a sniffy: "I'm a classically trained actor, I'll have you know".

Virtually throughout, this commercial calls attention to its own status as *not* the slice of consumerist life advertisements generally purport to be, but a highly crafted, conventionalised representation. And of course there is a further layer of pragmatic meaning in addition to the self-parodic text. Viewers can be expected to realise that the sequences which set out to explode the realist pretensions of the typical commercial are themselves also scripted. The actors are not just playing (as they themselves admit) the roles of "clipboard man" and "cheerful product user", but also (as they do not admit) the roles of "classically trained actor forced to slum it in a commercial" and "token woman/Black man". The conventions of advertising are exposed as a sham, but the exposure nevertheless takes place within the frame of advertising. This is still a commercial promoting a particular product, and the underlying intention, as we know perfectly well, is still to get us to consume. Experienced viewers (or veterans of media studies courses) will have little difficulty constructing a rationale for the agency's strategy of self-parody. "They want to flatter us with our own knowingness", perhaps, or "by admitting so openly that 'normal' adverts are manipulative they think they'll come across as *not* trying to manipulate us".

Discussing linguistic and other representations with students, I have regularly been struck by the ubiquity in their discourse about discourse of formulations like "they want us to…", "they think we…". Everyday metalinguistic, or metacommunicative, discourse is very often *not* about the text itself (its formal characteristics: the words that have been chosen, the grammatical "packaging" of particular eventualities, etc.) but about the likely intentions of the producer of the text and the responses the text is designed to evoke in its recipients. When one teaches certain kinds of textual analysis to students – Critical Discourse Analysis (CDA), for instance – the difficulty is not to get them to notice that texts are ideological or to talk about the ideological effects of a given text, but to get them to focus on the formal means whereby certain intentions are *evidenced* in texts. What is hard for students (what they need to be instructed in if they are to master something like CDA) is to *know how they know* the things they say they know about the meaning of a text.

Teaching students how to do CDA is not a matter of putting some metalinguistic apparatus where before there was none, but of trying to put a certain kind of expert metalinguistic apparatus in place of an everyday or "folk" one. The relation between folk and expert metalanguages is an issue of considerable interest, and one which crops up recurrently in the foregoing chapters. As I noted at the beginning of this discussion, contributors to this volume in general reject the approach to metalanguage that would reserve the term for the descriptive vocabulary or "specialised register" used in scientific enterprises, including linguistic science. But the question remains of how (whether?) folk and expert metalanguages are different from one another. Dennis Preston gives various reasons why it is important for sociolinguists systematically to investigate the lay metalinguistic beliefs and practices which prevail in the communities they study, citing the need for scientific completeness, the danger of falsely exoticising other cultures by naturalising the beliefs of one's own, and the desirability of establishing firm foundations for contrastive analysis. I would unhesitatingly endorse all these points. But do sociolinguists not also need to interrogate the origins, implications and status of our own metalanguages (cf. Van Leeuwen, this volume)?

One field of inquiry in which this question has been aired is the study of "language ideologies" (e.g. Schieffelin, Woolard and Kroskrity 1998), many of whose adherents would define themselves as linguistic anthropologists rather than sociolinguists. Language ideologies are meta-level phenomena – in the words of Kathryn Woolard (1998: 3), "representations … that construe the intersection of language and human beings in a social world". And typically they are investigated not just by looking at what people do with their languages (e.g. the language socialisation practices of a given community) but at how people *talk about* their languages.

The way my students tend to talk about the meaning of texts, for instance (see above), suggests they belong to a community that subscribes to a language ideology in which what is said is, ideally, both what is meant by the speaker and what is true about the world. Moral disapproval of the text-producers who "want us to think" what they are unwilling to say "in so many words" is common in this community's folk metadiscourse, and it is hardly surprising that students should reproduce it in the classroom. (I once taught a student who actually began to cry when she became convinced that even the BBC did not report events in the world in a completely transparent and neutral fashion.) Of course, from the expert pragmaticist's perspective, the attitude of the students rests on a considerable idealisation of the "facts" about how people in their own communities use language. One of the things they will be expected to learn is that successful communication does not in practice depend on "saying what you mean in so many words". But comparative work across cultures shows that even the *ideal* of "saying what you mean" is not embraced by all language-using communities. Just as communicative practices themselves vary, so does the metadiscourse in which people represent and reflect on those practices. To give only one (fairly recent) example from a copious ethnographic literature, Don Kulick reports on a New Guinea village where verbal exchanges often manifest a high degree of obscurity, and villagers explicitly hold that the purpose of using language is to "hide" meaning, not reveal it (Kulick 1992).

The New Guinea village example is suggestive in this context because it involves not only the villagers' talk itself but also their explicit talk *about* talk. But even where this meta dimension is not foregrounded in an ethnographic study, the existence of variation raises questions about the expert metalanguage used in western pragmatics (especially the tradition stemming from Grice 1975 which specifies informativeness, truthfulness, relevance and perspicuousness as default conditions for communication). Some commentators, notably Elinor Ochs [Keenan], have asked whether the Gricean framework is based more or less unreflectively on a folk metapragmatics which is culturally specific rather than universally applicable (Keenan 1976). The study of folk metalanguages, then, may have implications for researchers' own expert ones; at the very least, we need to be aware that the latter are no less "ideological" than the former.

Understanding what the ideological presuppositions of expert metadiscourse on language might be is particularly important if we decide to try to intervene critically in particular folk metadiscourses where we believe this serves some wider public interest. In this volume Jaworski and Sachdev, for instance, raise the possibility that teachers might make fairer evaluations of their students if they had opportunities for critical reflection on the meanings and functions of speech and silence in education. This recommendation for what might be dubbed "critical metalanguage awareness" extends to the pragmatic or discoursal level an approach already familiar in relation to grammar and pronunciation. The critical interrogation of lay judgements on speech couched in folk terms like "sloppy", "illogical", "nasal", "slang", has long figured in sociolinguists' attempts to displace discriminatory attitudes to nonstandard varieties. I would agree with Jaworski and Sachdev that in current conditions it may well be desirable to offer similarly critical analyses of common-sense judgements on people's "communication skills" (see Cameron 2000). But we should not suppose that an expert metadiscourse will always and necessarily be more valuable than a "folk" one in constructing an effective critique of some particular social practice.

A case in point: in 1997 I was contacted for professional advice by the clinical director of a National Health Service (NHS) psychiatric hospital.[3] He and his colleagues were troubled by a set of changes that had occurred – indeed they had been imposed by *fiat* – in the official discourse of the NHS. For example, the people whom doctors had been accustomed to refer to as "patients" had been renamed "users" or "service users", or even in some contexts as "customers". These changes were seen by the medical professionals as emanating from a cadre of health service managers who had become both more numerous and more powerful following a radical reform of the NHS by the then Conservative government. The purpose and effect of reform, according to many official documents, was to "empower" NHS "users" and to guarantee the "quality" of the service provided to them. The word "quality", which the doctors understood to mean something like "a high standard", was used in this discourse to mean "a consistent and measurable standard". The word "empowerment", they claimed, was an empty slogan that had no clear meaning at all.

What the psychiatrists wanted me to do was to help them think through their very negative feelings about this new language. They wanted to understand why they disliked it, and they wanted an expert explanation of what was "wrong" with it. To put it another way, the doctors wished for a metalanguage in which they might more clearly and convincingly articulate their opposition to certain ways of using language in and about the NHS. Convinced of the value of expert discourse in their own domain, psychiatric medicine, they found it natural to assume that expert discourse would have a similar value in the domain of linguistic analysis. Hence they consulted an expert, me. Linguistics was their "genie"; but could it grant their wishes?

To begin with I conceptualised my task as giving the psychiatrists access to a metalanguage in the sense of a specialised register – in this context, essentially that of CDA. The much-mistrusted term *empowerment*, for example, is an instance of something discussed extensively by critical discourse analysts, namely nominalisation. The rather weasely quality which the psychiatrists were responding to at a "gut" level can be related to the erasure, in nominalisations, of the argument positions required in a full sentence by the verb (in this case, who is giving power to whom?). But although my audience responded very positively to this and other items from my linguist's bag of tricks, I quickly realised that this was rather beside the point, for they and I were operating with fundamentally different language ideologies. Their response to the language of the new NHS was framed in terms of a powerful folk theory about how language works and how it ought therefore to be used; ultimately I came to feel that even if it were possible to undermine that, it might well be undesirable to do so.

One of the things the psychiatrists considered most objectionable about the introduction of new linguistic representations was that *only* the language had changed: there was, to their minds, nothing in the reality of the reformed NHS that corresponded to the terms in which it was now described. They noted for instance that it is misleading to use the term *customer* in a context where most people are obliged to use local health services and cannot choose to take their "custom" elsewhere. Some also pointed to the gap between the managerial rhetoric of NHS user "empowerment" and the reality, routinely reported by the media and debated in Parliament, of long waiting lists, decrepit hospital buildings and *de facto* rationing of expensive treatments such as new generation anti-psychotic drugs. This line of argument bears a superficial resemblance to the arguments made within critical linguistics about discourse and social change (see, e.g. Fairclough 1992), but at a deeper level it is quite different, for it assumes that the normal and desirable state of affairs is for linguistic representations to correspond directly and exactly to the real-world phenomena of which they are representations. The real-world phenomena are taken to precede the language used to describe them, and where that hierarchy is overturned, the resulting discourse is assessed as ideologically-motivated deception. Critical linguists by contrast are more likely to view discourse as constitutive of what we take to be the real world, and have long since abandoned as crude the idea of ideology as a wilful misrepresentation of reality, whose opposite is simply "the truth".

As I have already noted, the psychiatrists were more inclined than most non-linguists I had previously dealt with to believe that an expert on language and discourse must necessarily have a better, more correct, more effective and more powerful analysis of a linguistic problem than they could come up with themselves. Yet I soon reached the conclusion that their faith in me was misplaced. Expert discourse about language is not "better" for every purpose than the folk kind. If one is engaged in a conscious, political struggle over language, it may actually be *less* effective, rhetorically speaking, to marshal a theoretically so-phisticated argument about meaning than to stick to what the community at large considers obvious common sense (e.g. words should correspond to what is "out there" in the world, and if they do not, it means someone is trying to pull the wool over your eyes). The general principle is illustrated over and over again in the history of language planning and verbal hygiene. The reforms that "stick" are not the most "natural", "efficient" or "rational" in linguistic terms, but those which are found to be congruent with widely and deeply held beliefs about "the way things ought to be" (for example, in the domain of feminist language planning, see Cameron 1995; Pauwels 1998).

The literary and cultural theorist Raymond Williams argued that "a defini-tion of language is always, implicitly or explicitly, a definition of human beings in the world" (Williams 1977: 21). A definition of language is also, of course, an instance of metalanguage, using language to talk about language. The study of metalanguage encompasses both the implicit and the explicit ways in which people define what language is, what it is for, and what it is worth. And as Wil-liams's observation implies, much of the interest and value of the enterprise of studying metalinguistic phenomena arises from the fact that the definitions are always, on inspection, about far more than just language. As the foregoing chapters illustrate, there is no use in sociolinguists trying to confine the meta-language genie in a hermetically sealed bottle.

Notes

1. "Socially-oriented pragmatics" is implicitly contrasted here with the kind of pragmatics that is allied to cognitive science. I would place, for instance, most work in the paradigm of Relevance Theory in this category (Sperber and Wilson 1986).

2.   In fact, there are clues from the beginning that the commercial is a parody. The action takes place in the kind of suburban setting (tidy houses, well-kept gardens) that conventionally if vaguely signifies domestic contentment and a certain level of affluence, but here the scene is constructed and lit to produce an effect of "hyperreality" – the colours are unnaturally bright, the objects and people unnaturally clean and tidy. While this supports the point made by Van Leeuwen and other contributors to this volume that metacommunication is not just linguistic but multimodal, I do find it interesting that I, at least, only noticed the visual clues retrospectively, *after* linguistic evidence had been provided for a parodic reading.

3.   Here I would like to thank Dr Angus MacKay and his colleagues for a number of interesting and stimulating discussions; I also acknowledge the support of the Royal College of Psychiatrists in Scotland, and of pharmaceutical companies SmithKline Beecham and Zeneca.

References

Cameron, Deborah
    1995   *Verbal Hygiene*. London: Routledge.
    2000   *Good To Talk?* London: Sage.
Cook, Guy
    1992   *The Discourse of Advertising*. London: Routledge.
Fairclough, Norman
    1992   *Discourse and Social Change*. Cambridge: Polity Press.
Grice, H. P.
    1975   Logic and conversation. In Cole, Peter and Jerry L. Morgan (eds.), *Syntax and Semantics. Volume 3: Speech Acts*. New York: Academic Press, 41–58.
Jakobson, Roman
    1960   Closing statement: Linguistics and poetics. In Sebeok Thomas A. (ed.), *Style in Language*. Cambridge, MA: MIT Press, 350–377.
Keenan, Elinor Ochs
    1976   The universality of conversational implicature. *Language in Society* 5, 67–80.
Kulick, Don
    1992   *Language Shift and Cultural Reproduction: Self, Socialization and Syncretism in a New Guinea Village*. Cambridge: Cambridge University Press.
Pauwels, Anne
    1998   *Women Changing Language*. London: Longman.
Schieffelin, Bambi B., Kathryn Woolard and Paul V. Kroskrity (eds.)
    1998   *Language Ideologies: Practice and Theory*. New York: Oxford University Press.

Sperber, Dan and Deirdre Wilson
    1986   *Relevance: Communication and Cognition.* Oxford: Blackwell.
Williams, Raymond
    1977   *Marxism and Literature.* New York: Oxford University Press.
Wittgenstein, Ludwig
    1953   *Philosophical Investigations.* Translated by G. E. M. Anscombe. Oxford:
            Blackwell.
Woolard, Kathryn
    1998   Language ideology as a field of inquiry. In Schieffelin, Bambi, B., Kathryn
            Woolard and Paul V. Kroskrity (eds.), *Language Ideologies: Practice and*
            Theory. New York: Oxford University Press, 3–47.

Index

ALONG VIRGINIA'S
ROUTE 58

ALONG VIRGINIA'S
ROUTE 58

TRUE TALES FROM BEACH TO BLUEGRASS

JOE TENNIS

THE
History
PRESS

Published by The History Press
Charleston, SC
www.historypress.net

Front cover, top left: Wilburn Ridge, along the Appalachian Trail. *Author photo*; *top right*: Mabry Mill in Floyd County, just off the Blue Ridge Parkway. *Author photo*; *center left*: A 1940s-era postcard depicts the Virginia Beach Boardwalk. *Author's collection*; *center right*: A 1972 photograph shows traffic on U.S. 58/Virginia Beach Boulevard, with Pembroke Mall, at left, in Virginia Beach. *Courtesy Virginia Department of Transportation*; *lower left*: U.S. 58 overlaps I-81 in Washington County, between Bristol and Abingdon. *Author photo*; *lower right*: U.S. 58 curves just below the peak of Whitetop Mountain. *Author photo*.

Back cover: Virginia ends on a mountain at the Tri-State Peak, just north of where U.S. 58 terminates after entering Tennessee for about a half mile. *Author photo*.

All color photographs by Joe Tennis.

First published 2015, Second printing 2016

Manufactured in the United States

ISBN 978.1.46711.884.2

Library of Congress Control Number: 2015945704

A previous edition of this book was published as *Beach to Bluegrass: Places to Brake on Virginia's Longest Road* in 2007.

For my son, John Patrick

U.S. 58 spans more than five hundred miles from
Virginia Beach to Cumberland Gap National
Historical Park, making it the longest road in
Virginia. *Courtesy Virginia Tourism Corporation.*

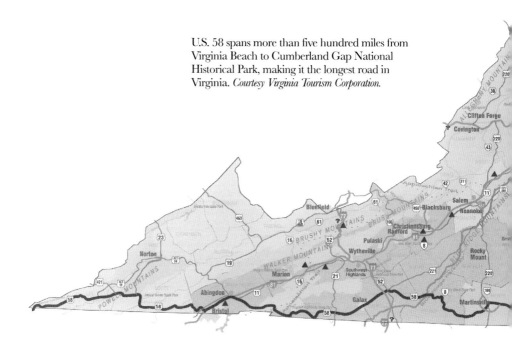

CONTENTS

Contents

ACKNOWLEDGEMENTS

Special thanks for help in this project to J. Banks Smither, Darcy Mahan, Daniel Rodgers, Lois Stickles, Jennifer Hurst-Wender, Carlos Wilson, Harold Barkley, Mike West, Colonel William J. Davis, Liona Bourgeault, Albert Joynes, Deloras Freeman, Robin K. Rountree, Lee King, Connie Henderson, Dave Sadowski, Frank Malone, Jack Hite, Elaine Bowers, Scott Shanklin, Justin Kerns, Mary Page Richardson, Robert Benning, Ed and Carol Brown, J.C. Eldreth, James Sheppard, Wyatt Barczak, Julie Allen, John Reynolds, Beth Ford, Ellen Brown, David Sheley, Tim Cable, Tom Perry, John Grooms, Henry Ayers, Ella Sue Joyce, Sharoll Shumate, Felecia Shelor, Coy Lee Yeatts, Ann Vaughn, Ronald W. Hall, Joe Wilson, Nancy Riggins, Paul Dellinger, Shirley Gordon, Bob McKinney, Emily Spencer, David and Nerine Thomas, Jaye and Joan Baldwin, Jack and Rubinette Niemann, Hendrika Schuster, Eleanor Grasselli, Charlie Moore, Skip Blackburn, Lawrence Dye, Bob McCracken, Pete Sheffey, Bill McKee, Donnamarie Emmert, Raven Marin, Melissa Watson, Carol Hawthorne-Taylor, Kimberly Roberts, Howard Fergus, Ben Jennings, Mary Dudley Porterfield, Richard Rose, Debbie Addison, Kathleen Bundy, Eleanor Walker Jones, Robert Weisfeld, William Booker, Anne West, Tim Buchanan, Steve and Kim Rhodes, Darlene Cole, Rita Forrester, Fern Carter Salyer, Tim White, Rex and Lisa McCarty, Kenny Fannon, June Presley, Bob and Suzy Harrison, Frank Kilgore, Jean Kilgore, Lucille Cowden Necessary, Jerry Ivey, Craig Seaver, Tony Scales, Jerry Cox, Judy Davidson, Rebecca Jones, Robert Estes, Robert Monroe, Rhonda Robertson, Billy Heck, Michael

Brindle, Carol Borneman, Martha Wiley, Scott Teodorski, Steve Galyean, Marc Brodsky, Jennifer McDaid, Jennifer Wampler, Jennifer Bauer, the staff of the Washington County Public Library in Abingdon, the Peanut Patch at Courtland, Lisa Johnson and Food City, the Crooked Road and all fans of "Beach to Bluegrass."

More help, advice, encouragement and support came from fellow authors, writers, editors and historians: V.N. "Bud" Phillips, David McGee, Linda Hoagland, Carol Jackson, Keith Bartlett, Jim Campbell, Cara Ellen Modisett, Kurt Rheinheimer, Theresa Lewis, Sherry Lewis, Jan Patrick, George Stone, Erin Parkhurst, Melissa M. Stewart, Angela Blue, Betsy DiJulio, Phyllis Speidell, Tracy Agnew, Gloria Oster, Tom Netherland, Stephanie Porter-Nichols, Lisa Clary, Mark Sage and May-Lily Lee.

Sincere appreciation also to family members: Maggie Caudill; James and Melissa Caudill; Rob and Michelle Tennis; Ben Tennis; Pat and Angie Wolfe; Thomas Wolfe; Amber Wolfe; Ralph Boswell; Steve and Stephanie Talbert; Dr. Walter Wolfe; John Wolfe; Homer Wolfe; my parents, Richard and Jeanette Tennis; my wife, Mary; and most especially my daughter, Abigail, for traveling the highways and constantly cheering "58!" and "Beach to Bluegrass!"

Introduction

TRAIL OF TALES

In the early days of the American colonies, going beyond the Appalachian Mountains to the bluegrass of Kentucky would mirror how the Jamestown settlers sailed the Atlantic Ocean to reach the beach of Virginia. The journey to either destination was filled with mystery and confrontation.

Along Virginia's Route 58: True Tales from Beach to Bluegrass links these journeys with its own. From Cape Henry to the Cumberland Gap, tales of triumph and tragedy lie sandwiched between Cape Henry's "Gateway to the New World" and Cumberland Gap's "Gateway to the West."

The fifty-eight-chapter story lies largely along U.S. 58, Virginia's longest road. This east-to-west highway spans more than five hundred miles and passes through every type of town and terrain imaginable in the Old Dominion, from the traffic-tied Tidewater to the pastoral piedmont, the lofty Blue Ridge to the once-perilous Powell Valley, lying as far west as Detroit.

Varied in its journey, U.S. 58 ranges from ten lanes in urban Virginia Beach to two-lane sprints that are as serpentine as streams near Creek Junction. Connecting communities just above the borders of North Carolina and Tennessee, U.S. 58 once held the distinction of being the longest U.S. highway to be contained within one state. But in 1996, a tunnel opened near Cumberland Gap on U.S. 25E, and that shifted the westernmost stretch of U.S. 58 southward, for about a half mile, into Tennessee.

Still, Virginians like to think of this as *their* road. It is, after all, the longest numbered highway in the Old Dominion.

During the Great Depression of the 1930s, U.S. 58 was established on the former paths of state highways 10 and 12. It connected the main streets of textiles towns in southern Virginia. Since 1989, much of this route has changed considerably. Some scary sections—like "Suicide Strip," a two-lane portion between Suffolk and Emporia—are now just bad memories. Yet some portions remain as two lanes and still await improvement while many miles are upgraded to become a four-lane superhighway as part of the Virginia Department of Transportation's U.S. Route 58 Corridor Development Program.

What may not be a memory: Emporia's speed trap. Infamously, this section of U.S. 58 has been known among motorists as a place where tickets are frequently given.

On the east, U.S. 58 cuts through the downtown districts of Coastal Virginia, also called "Tidewater" or "Hampton Roads," while reaching ever westward across a series of swamps. Water and war define this region, rich in military landmarks, legends and lore.

In the piedmont, grassy hills frame farms on the outskirts of Lawrenceville as the road rises to the west. Though called either "Southside" or "Southern Virginia," this land remains revved up with racetracks and hooked on hosting fishing tournaments at Lake Gaston and Buggs Island Lake. Highway 58 rolls through this pastoral region like a runway, connecting Emporia and Edgerton to South Hill and South Boston.

Climbing into the Blue Ridge Highlands, Virginia's longest road becomes the Crooked Road: Virginia's Heritage Music Trail. The route truly climbs,

Construction crews work on widening U.S. 58 in Brunswick County, about four miles west of Lawrenceville, during the summer of 1966. *Courtesy Virginia Department of Transportation.*

A 1959 scene shows the U.S. 58 bridge on what is now the highway's business route near the Martinsville Power House and Dam on the Smith River. *Courtesy Virginia Department of Transportation.*

Actor Mel Gibson once walked part of U.S. 58 on Jackson Street in Scott County's courthouse town, Gate City, to film a 1984 movie called *The River*. *Courtesy George Stone.*

A landslide on Powell Mountain caused a cave-in on U.S. 58 in June 1971 along the Scott-Lee county line. *Courtesy Virginia Department of Transportation.*

curls and becomes quite crooked, indeed, as trout streams tumble into tiny waterfalls and Christmas trees grow at ear-popping elevations.

To the west, scenic valleys boast vibrant villages—from artsy Abingdon to the state line–straddling city of Bristol. Crossing Lee County, much of U.S. 58 follows the path used by frontiersman Daniel Boone to move west to reach Kentucky's bluegrass through the Cumberland Gap.

My father, Richard Tennis, coined the phrase "Beach to Bluegrass" when I told him I wanted to write about U.S. 58's ramble. All along, this road snakes just above Virginia's southern border, linking the sandy shores of the Atlantic Ocean to Cumberland Gap National Historical Park, located partially in the Bluegrass State of Kentucky.

Yet that title has also grown beyond this book's first edition, published in 2007. State officials have since borrowed "Beach to Bluegrass" for Virginia's "Beaches to Bluegrass Trail," a pedestrian path that, largely, links abandoned railroad grades turned into trails paralleling the U.S. 58 corridor—including the Tobacco Heritage Trail, Virginia Creeper Trail and Wilderness Road Trail.

With a mix of history and legend, the path from beach to bluegrass connects man-made and natural landmarks, meeting famous generals and musicians, a witch, a waterfall, a schoolhouse in a cyclone and a lake that never was. The chapters of this trail of tales relate and intertwine with one another, revealing many great stories of Virginia, all tied by that long and winding road.

1

BEACH

Cape Henry

For five days and nights, storms raged over the ocean. Waves crashed, lightning flashed, rain pounded. And there! In the middle of all that mess stood Virginia, just as morning broke on April 26, 1607.

A tired band of more than one hundred Englishmen feasted hungry eyes. And, probably, they dreamed of gold. Their three ships—*Discovery*, *Susan Constant* and *Godspeed*—had traveled across the Atlantic Ocean for more than four months, first casting off in England before Christmas 1606. Their plan to land in Virginia, for the Virginia Company of London, must have seemed like a modern-day mission to the moon.

These men had orders to launch the first permanent, English-speaking colony in the New World. But they must have been wary, knowing that equally ambitious Spanish explorers could be waiting to attack. And less than a generation earlier, other Englishmen had tried the same idea on nearby Roanoke Island, North Carolina, and had simply vanished.

These men of 1607 had fights. Captain John Smith, a war veteran, got shackled in one of the ship's prisons for an alleged mutiny.

These men had superstitions. Master George Percy kept a journal of the expedition and noted "a blazing Starre" on February 12. That comet was seen as a sign of impending doom.

These men also had greed. Many believed Virginia held a wealth of gold, and they were willing to brave the Atlantic Ocean to find it, even though people thought sea serpents might wander out of the waves, or beasts could be lurking in the jungles of this mysterious, virgin land.

The English settlers of Jamestown may have landed in 1607 at these "faire meddowes" of the Chesapeake Bay at Virginia Beach's First Landing State Park. *Author photo.*

Making landfall, the crew explored what are now the sandy shores of Cape Henry in Virginia Beach, Virginia, at the mouth of the Chesapeake Bay. They discovered a paradise Percy described in his journal as "faire meddowes and goodly tall Trees, with such Fresh-waters running through the woods." But that same day, the English were ambushed. Percy wrote, "The Savages creeping on all foure, from the Hills like Beares, with their Bowes in their mouthes, charged us very desperately in the faces."

These "Savages" of the sand "Hills" wounded two men, Captain Gabriel Archer and Mathew Morton, a sailor. Obviously, these Chesapeake Indians viewed the foreigners as a threat. For years, the Indians had lived in this coastal area. And now here comes these overdressed, odd-speaking, fanciful strangers who acted like they owned the place.

The English fired a musket, and the Indians, according to Percy, "retired into the Woods with a great noise and so left us."

The following day, the English walked a few miles inland and found a fire where the natives had been roasting oysters. The Indians were gone, having "fled away to the Mountaines," Percy noted, so the explorers "ate some of the Oysters, which were very large and delicate in taste."

The English later explored the Chesapeake Bay in a small boat called a "shallop." They also marched on land, finding more fires, more oysters and

Piles of boulders called "breakwaters" stand at the Atlantic Ocean to prevent erosion near the Cape Henry lighthouses. *Author photo.*

what Percy called a "good store of Mussels." Finally, giving thanks to God for their safe journey, the men spent April 29 erecting a wooden cross at Cape Henry, a place they named for the Prince of Wales and son of King James I.

Then they left. Captain Christopher Newport, in following orders of the Virginia Company, rejected settling at Cape Henry, fearing the cape was too exposed in case of attack. So the men sailed up the James River. On May 13, they reached a swampy isle they called Jamestown. There, the English established the long-suffering village that grew into the foundation of America.

No one knows exactly where the English landed at Cape Henry. Some say the first landing occurred south of the cape at what is now Virginia Beach's Forty-ninth Street, the site of a sealed-up inlet once leading to Crystal Lake. Others guess the landing might have been westward, just inside the Chesapeake Bay toward the Lynnhaven River.

Geographically, Cape Henry juts out of Virginia Beach with the odd shape of a duck head. The bill points west to the mouth of the Lynnhaven, and the head curves along the Chesapeake Bay until it reaches the Atlantic Ocean. At the center lies the Desert, a barren area marked by a maritime forest, tall pines and one-hundred-foot-high sand dunes, possibly what Percy called "the Mountaines." For more than two centuries after the English arrived,

This 1905 scene shows the new Cape Henry Lighthouse, left, standing just 357 feet from the old Cape Henry Lighthouse, which was built in 1791–92. *Courtesy Library of Congress.*

the Desert remained in the public domain at Cape Henry's "Gateway to the New World."

Cape Henry, though, could be dark and dangerous. At times, it was illuminated with big bonfires. But pirates would play games with the flames by moving those fires, confusing sailors and then plundering ships.

In 1789, the newly formed United States Congress approved lighting up the sky. Two years later, New York's John McComb Jr. began building an octagonal lighthouse at Cape Henry atop a forty-foot-high sand dune. Fish oil was used to fuel the lighthouse lamps, but that oil soaked into the wooden staircase and continually posed a fire hazard.

The sandstone lighthouse never succumbed to fire. Instead, cracks on the stone structure put the landmark out of commission. In 1881, the lighthouse was left standing as a second Cape Henry Lighthouse was built just 357 feet away. This new beacon, rising 163 feet, or about twice the height of the first, was made of black-and-white cast iron.

Around the two lighthouses, a collection of cottages grew at Cape Henry. And those oysters! Those same juicy Lynnhaven oysters that Percy's group had stolen from the Indians—and relished with such delight—would make history again.

President William Howard Taft ate so many Lynnhaven oysters at Cape Henry in 1909 that he said he felt "like an oyster." The fat and happy president then proposed building a fortress at Cape Henry— what became Fort Story, a military base named for General John P. Story. This base grew into one of the most heavily fortified areas on the Atlantic coast by World War II, taking on such nicknames as "Gibraltar of the East."

Much of Cape Henry's nearby Desert became Virginia Beach's Seashore State Park in 1936, later renamed First Landing State Park. The preserve includes sand "Hills" and "Mountaines," plus cypress pools of "Fresh-waters," marshy "faire meddowes" and "goodly tall Trees."

Nearby, a stone cross was planted inside Fort Story in 1935 to replicate the wooden cross the English had erected centuries earlier. The landmark was dedicated on April 26, commemorating that stormy day in 1607 when the English set foot on that mysterious, virgin land.

The stone replica of the "First Landing" cross at Cape Henry was constructed in 1935. *Author photo.*

CAPE HENRY:
FORT STORY AND FIRST LANDING STATE PARK

Cape Henry lies inside Joint Expeditionary Base East (formerly the Fort Story Military Reservation) in Virginia Beach. To get there, start at the crossroads of U.S. 58 (Laskin Road) and U.S. 60 (Atlantic Avenue). Follow U.S. 60 (Atlantic Avenue) for four miles north of Laskin Road (U.S. 58/Thirty-first Street) to the junction of Eighty-ninth Street and Atlantic Avenue. Stop at the checkpoint of the entrance gate (showing proper ID, proof of insurance

A circa 1940 aerial view of Virginia Beach shows Atlantic Avenue, where the two routes of U.S. 58 begin at Seventeenth Street (U.S. 58 Business/Virginia Beach Boulevard) and Thirty-first Street (U.S. 58/Laskin Road). *Courtesy Virginia Tech.*

and car registration.) Then continue north for one mile to the Cape Henry lighthouses (583 Atlantic Avenue) and the First Landing Cross. Preservation Virginia acquired the Old Cape Henry Lighthouse in 1930 and maintains the structure, which is open for tours. To reach First Landing State Park from the military base's entrance gate, continue west on U.S. 60 (Shore Drive) for 3.5 miles. The 2,888-acre state park (2500 Shore Drive) includes a campground, hiking trails, a playground and a visitor center. From here, retrace the route to U.S. 58 at Laskin Road.

2

MONOPOLY ON THE OCEANFRONT

Virginia Beach

Talk about a "Monopoly" on the oceanfront. Streets in the resort area of Virginia Beach share names not only with Atlantic City, New Jersey, but these same avenues—Atlantic, Pacific, Mediterranean and Baltic—show up on the board game Monopoly. In Virginia Beach, you can even sleep in a hotel on Boardwalk.

Originally, the Virginia Beach Boardwalk was made of actual boards in 1888, not cast in concrete like it is today. It also flanked the fabulous Princess Anne Hotel, a landmark that faced the Atlantic Ocean and catered to famous folks like President Grover Cleveland and Alexander Graham Bell.

The Princess Anne Hotel featured a ballroom, a post office and enough space for four hundred people. But just before daybreak on June 10, 1907, the hotel caught fire, forcing guests to escape in their pajamas. Tragically, a maid who had helped wake up the guests lost her life in the flames as she stood on a rooftop. Later, when the smoke cleared, the finest hotel on the Virginia Beach shoreline was gone. That same fire also consumed much of the original five-block boardwalk.

Virginia Beach stayed little more than a colony of cottages dotting the dunes for the next few years. But then, in the 1920s, the private Laskin Road became a public highway leading to the three-block-long Seaside Park Casino, and a new Virginia Beach Boardwalk was paved along the sand.

Still, this little Atlantic City needed more, something grand for dignitaries, something like the old Princess Anne Hotel. In April 1927, the town of

The original Virginia Beach Boardwalk was built of actual boards in the vicinity of Sixteenth Street near the old Princess Anne Hotel, which stood to the left of this scene, circa 1905. *Courtesy Library of Congress.*

Virginia Beach got all that with the celebrated opening of a real-life castle called the Cavalier.

Talk about a monopoly on the oceanfront. The Cavalier had it. There wasn't anything in Virginia Beach like it. The looming landmark stood seven stories, composed of more than 500,000 bricks and surrounded by sixty acres of manicured grounds. It was the town's tallest building and designed like a Y-shaped pillar of colonial architecture. The Cavalier could fill the void left by the destruction of the Princess Anne Hotel. But unlike the Princess Anne, the Cavalier did not sit down at the Boardwalk—it stood far above, perched on a sand dune.

When the $2 million hotel opened as part of "a scheme for the building up of Virginia Beach as a health and recreational resort," Norfolk's *Virginian-Pilot* called the enterprise a "Great Resort Development at [the] Gateway of New World."

Inside, the Cavalier lobby offered a barbershop, a beauty parlor, a dress shop, a drugstore and a stockbroker's office. Also, in bedrooms, guests could lap up luxury with taps running four kinds of water—hot, cold, ice-cold and salt water for bathing.

The Cavalier Hotel, depicted in this circa 1940 postcard, was constructed on a sand dune in Virginia Beach. *Author's collection.*

The hotel, nicknamed the "Aristocrat of the Virginia Seashore," hosted the likes of writer F. Scott Fitzgerald, actress Judy Garland and artist Hank Ketchum, who showed up in 1953 and featured the Cavalier in his "Dennis the Menace" cartoon sketches.

Several presidents booked accommodations. And the leader who resigned, President Richard Nixon, stayed overnight and had fireside chats with fellow guests in the Hunt Room, a private men's club for hunters, horsemen and fishermen.

Another guest was Adolph Coors, the man whose name is on canned and bottled beer. At age eighty-two, Coors fell from a window on the sixth story of the Cavalier on June 5, 1929. But the circumstances of his death, which occurred during Prohibition, remain a mystery.

Many presume Coors was profoundly unhappy. Yet stories cannot say whether the founder of the Adolph Coors Company was pushed or fell on his own. Either way, a legend whispered among the walls of the Cavalier says that the ghost of Adolph Coors can now be seen as an unexplained image of a man that shows up in photographs, wearing 1920s-era clothing.

Longtime doorman Carlos Wilson could not say much about Coors. That event took place before his time, even though Wilson began working at the Cavalier in 1938 at age fifteen. Still, while on the job at age eighty-four, the late Wilson recalled his own ghostly encounter in a kitchen near the Hunt Room of the Cavalier.

He said, "I heard some pans rattling on my way upstairs, and I was checking out that night. I saw a shadow behind the cooking range. I got on close to it. And it just vanished and went away."

Wilson started to leave, but he heard the pans rattling again. He turned. "I went back to make sure that I wasn't seeing things," he said. "And as soon as I got close to it, it just vanished and went away."

At first, Wilson told no one about seeing the shadow or hearing the rattles, until a fellow employee volunteered a corroborating story. After that, Wilson said, "I knew it was a ghost."

The Cavalier, itself, looked ghostly during the blackouts of World War II. The navy used the hotel for three years as a radar training school. Sailors moved into the horse stables, and classes were sometimes moved to the dark bottom of the indoor swimming pool.

At the end of the war, lights shone all night as people celebrated at the Cavalier Beach Club, a ritzy room that once hosted big bands led by the likes of Benny Goodman and Guy Lombardo.

In 1973, it looked like the party was over for the Cavalier. The then-outdated hotel was shuttered, as a more modern hotel—the Cavalier

The Coastguard Station depicted in this circa 1940 scene of the Virginia Beach Boardwalk is now the Old Coast Guard Station Museum in Virginia Beach. *Author's collection.*

Oceanfront—opened a bit closer to the beach. The original hotel reopened in 1976 and was later renovated. But in 2014, it had been shuttered again, and much of its contents were sold at a huge sale. Still, the grand dame miraculously escaped the wrecking ball. With financial help from the city, the Cavalier was slated for a multi-million-dollar renovation: an honor for a historic landmark still standing as a symbol of pre-Depression prosperity.

VIRGINIA BEACH: THE CAVALIER HOTEL AND THE BOARDWALK

Start at the junction of Atlantic Avenue and Laskin Road (U.S. 58/Thirty-first Street). At the terminus of Laskin Road, a twenty-six-foot-tall King Neptune statue stands along the Virginia Beach Boardwalk, close to the junction of Laskin Road and Atlantic Avenue; the Seaside Park Casino formerly stood nearby. To find the Cavalier Hotel from here,

Travel tip: Virginia Beach's Old Coast Guard Station Museum, 2401 Atlantic Avenue, stands midway between the two paths of U.S. 58 at Twenty-fourth Street and the Boardwalk. The station features exhibits of maritime history.

go one block west on Laskin Road to Pacific Avenue and then go north for a half mile. The 1927 hotel is on the left at Forty-second Street and Pacific. From Laskin Road (Thirty-first Street), Atlantic Avenue stretches fourteen blocks south to meet the terminus of U.S. 58 Business (Seventeenth Street/Virginia Beach Boulevard). Here, a statue of muscleman John Wareing overlooks the ocean at the Boardwalk. (The late Wareing owned a Virginia Beach gym; he became famous for televised stunts, like holding back a motorcycle with his teeth.) The Wareing statue rises about a block north of the site of the Princess Anne Hotel, which stood in the vicinity of Sixteenth Street.

3
FRANCIS LAND HOUSE

Virginia Beach

Virginia Beach grew from a tiny town into the "World's Largest Resort City" after merging with Princess Anne County in 1963. Land values also skyrocketed, especially along Virginia Beach Boulevard, where almost every block seems blitzed with commercial development—*almost* every block, spare the seven acres that surround the Francis Land House.

Curiously, this brick landmark stands like an island in the city's asphalt sea, and no one knows when it was built. But "1732" is mysteriously etched into a brick in the cellar, and that was once used to date the structure.

The Francis Land House originally belonged to a prosperous family who just could not get enough of using the same name for each successive generation. It's believed that five or maybe six men named Francis Land lived here, as early as the 1650s, on what was once a 1,020-acre plantation in now-extinct Princess Anne County. Possibly, the Land family built this house around 1805 or 1810, according to a scientific analysis of the brickwork, hand-hewn timbers and the floor's pine planks. Behind the house, small boats could once navigate the narrow Pine Tree Branch, a silted-in stem of the Lynnhaven River.

In 1853, the Georgian-style house passed out of the Land family. One century and one year later, it passed into the hands of Colin Studds, who extensively remodeled the house for Rose Hall Dress Shop for the Ladies and Their Daughters. But then Rose Hall was sold, and the upscale dress shop was fitted for a wrecking ball. In fact, it was so sure to be destroyed that a photo caption in a pictorial book lists the landmark as "scheduled to be torn down in 1974 to make way for a new shopping center."

The Francis Land House along U.S. 58 (Virginia Beach Boulevard) was formerly a dress shop called Rose Hall. *Author photo.*

Still, there would be rejoicing for Rose Hall. In 1975, the house remained intact, and the Virginia Beach City Council voted on buying it. Half the council said yes. The opposing half said paying $735,000 for the house and the surrounding thirty-five acres was "extremely expensive" and a case of "excessive spending." Stepping into the fight, Mayor J. Curtis Payne cast the deciding vote, and eleven years later, the Francis Land House opened as a city-owned museum, interpreting the long-lost lifestyle of old Princess Anne County.

VIRGINIA BEACH: FRANCIS LAND HOUSE

From Atlantic Avenue, both U.S. 58 Business (Seventeenth Street/Virginia Beach Boulevard) and Laskin Road (U.S. 58/Thirty-first Street) span about four miles, going west, until joining near Great Neck Road (VA-279). The U.S. 58 Business route slips through the residential community of Seatack (named for its proximity to a "sea attack" on Cape Henry during the War of 1812), while the parallel path of Laskin Road climbs over Hilltop (named for a twenty-seven-foot-high hill on the crest of Pungo Ridge). West of Great Neck Road, the combined U.S. 58 runs 1.5 miles to the Francis Land House, on the left, 3131 Virginia Beach Boulevard. The house is listed on historic landmark registers. The grounds include a large garden. Nearby, a wooden boardwalk—with interpretive markers—overlooks the Pine Tree Branch of the Lynnhaven River.

4

MOUNT TRASHMORE

Virginia Beach

W hen Virginia Beach built a grassy mountain, it got as trashy as it could get. The city piled up old motors, tires, refrigerators, food scraps and newspapers, all before the days of recycling. All through the early 1970s, it stacked up 640,000 tons of trash.

The idea came from Roland E. Dorer, the director of the state's Bureau of Solid Waste and Vector Control. Dorer figured it was better to pile trash rather than dig down and disturb the city's shallow groundwater supply.

So, with layer after layer of garbage and dirt, the city covered all of its rotting debris. It would make a mountain out of a landfill. Then, comically dubbing the hill "Mount Trashmore," a funny nod to Mount Rushmore, the old garbage dump became a major city park.

At an original height of sixty-eight feet, Mount Trashmore registered as barely a blip on a topographic map. But still, this gently sloping peak could compete with Cape Henry's sand dunes for being the tallest elevation on the Virginia Beach flatlands.

At the side of the mountain lies the city seal, a round emblem displaying symbols of Virginia Beach history, like the first Cape Henry lighthouse. One legend said the huge seal could be opened and that trash could still be put inside the mountain. That's not true. Then, neither was the story about Mount Trashmore's impending explosion of "low-flying dirt clods" in 1992.

That year, on April Fool's Day, morning deejays on rock radio station WNOR-FM broadcast that Mount Trashmore was in big trouble. They said a seismologist had inspected this old landfill and that a high amount of methane gas was building up, and—oh, golly—Mount Trashmore was just about to blow!

Morning commuters must have laughed. The stunt was, after all, an April Fool's Day joke. It was all just rubbish. But something went awry as deejays Henry Del Toro and Tommy Griffiths announced evacuation routes. Their broadcast sounded too real. Many people panicked, calling the city's parks and recreation office. Others clogged the emergency phone lines.

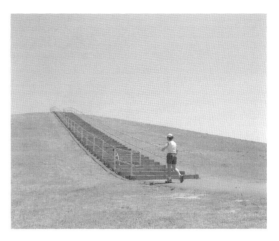

Stairs help hikers reach the peak of Mount Trashmore, which has been recapped and now stands little more than sixty feet high in Virginia Beach. *Author photo.*

The Federal Communications Commission later investigated the incident and sent the station's owners a letter of admonition. The joke about the former landfill also turned into a stinky situation for the station's staff, with some members tied up on suspension without pay for as long as two weeks.

VIRGINIA BEACH: MOUNT TRASHMORE PARK

From the Francis Land House, follow U.S. 58 (Virginia Beach Boulevard) for three miles west, passing through a commercial district that once included German prisoner-of-war camps during World War II, including a prison at the location of the Wayside Village Shoppes at the corner of Thalia Road. Enter Virginia Beach's downtown district at Pembroke (named for a nearby brick home called "Pembroke," built in 1764) in an area where skyscrapers rise near Independence Boulevard. To reach Mount Trashmore, turn left on Independence Boulevard and go 1.4 miles. Then turn left on Edwin Drive to enter Mount Trashmore Park. The mountain can be climbed using concrete steps. The park (310 Edwin Drive) includes a playground, fishing lakes and picnic areas. From here, retrace the route to U.S. 58.

5

WITCH IN AN EGGSHELL

Virginia Beach

Grace Sherwood got whopped with charges of being a witch and was literally tied up: a true case of sink or swim. Later, the legends of her life grew like the rosemary that she had allegedly smuggled home from England in an eggshell.

Consider the time, not long after the witch-hunt scares of Salem, Massachusetts, in 1692. What's now called Virginia Beach was then called Princess Anne County, named for Anne, the daughter of King James II of England. Folks in this close-knit and proper society knew of the witchery that had spellbound Massachusetts, and they must have feared that some of that madness was spreading to their seaside farms, especially where Grace Sherwood lived in the Pungo area along Muddy Creek.

Either that, or Grace Sherwood just couldn't get along with others.

In the late 1690s, neighbors accused Sherwood of blighting their cotton crops, bewitching the weather and causing cows to give sour milk. The uproar caused Sherwood and her husband, James, to boil over like cauldrons, and they slammed back with a series of slander suits.

In particular, Grace Sherwood went hex-to-head with Elizabeth Barnes, a woman who had accused her of coming into her room late one night and riding her. Barnes also said that Sherwood turned herself into a black cat and slipped out of her room through either a keyhole or a crack in the door.

More gossip grew around an odd story saying Sherwood was a witch in an eggshell. Folks said that Sherwood could make herself so small that she could fit inside an eggshell and that she used it to scramble across the

The true-life story of Grace Sherwood has lent its name to the Witch Duck Point neighborhood in Virginia Beach. *Author photo.*

Atlantic Ocean to England. Returning in a single night, Sherwood brought back a batch of rosemary that, according to legend, has been growing wild ever since.

Unfortunately for the Sherwoods, all the slander suits did little but cast a spell on them. They couldn't win their cases. And when James Sherwood died in 1701, Grace was left a widow with three sons and even more vulnerable for attack.

The feisty widow did win a case against Mr. and Mrs. Luke Hill after Mrs. Hill had physically beaten Sherwood. But that trial's outcome seemed to antagonize the Hills, who fought back by formally accusing Sherwood of witchcraft in court. Sherwood, subsequently, was strip-searched by an all-female jury, which declared that she had weird-as-witch markings on her body.

Next, the court of Princess Anne County ordered a trial by water, and Sherwood consented to an odd but simple test. Her right big toe was tied to her left thumb, and her left big toe was tied to her right thumb. Sherwood would be tossed into water, a substance that was believed to deem people good or evil. If she sank, she would be innocent but, obviously, dead. If she didn't sink, she was clearly a witch.

The day of the trial arrived. On July 10, 1706, folks flocked to the ducking by the hundreds. They cried, "Duck the witch!" along the shore of the Lynnhaven River and treated the event as a circus.

Sherwood proved that she had the trappings of a circus-quality performer. In an act that even Harry Houdini would have admired, she managed to untie herself and float to the surface of the river. But, of course, look at what that proved—she was allegedly capable of witchcraft. Fished out of the water, she was cast into the county jail.

A statue of Grace Sherwood by sculptor Robert Cunningham stands on the corner of North Witchduck Road and Independence Boulevard. *Author photo.*

Little is known about Sherwood beyond her jail time or exactly how long she stayed locked up. Royal Governor Alexander Spotswood granted Sherwood several acres of land in 1714. She died in 1740.

Even with death, her legend persists. It's said that in her last breaths, Sherwood asked one of her sons to put her feet at her fireplace's warm ashes. The next day, Sherwood was not only dead, but also her body was gone, and all that remained in the ashes was a hoof-print.

Sherwood's story never died. Today, it's told, a ghostly light shines on Witch Duck Bay each July at the site of her ducking. The celebrated tale of Sherwood's "witch duck," in turn, has lent its name in Virginia Beach to a point of land, a road, a housing subdivision, a shopping center and a bingo parlor.

The ducking was reenacted in 2003, with actors playfully gathering along the Lynnhaven River. Kayakers cried, "Duck the witch!" as twin sisters Gale Johnson and Molly McDermott took turns playing Sherwood. Three years later, on the 300th anniversary of the trial, Governor Tim Kaine formally exonerated Sherwood, declaring her no longer a witch.

VIRGINIA BEACH: WITCH DUCK POINT

From Independence Boulevard, follow U.S. 58 west for 1.1 miles to Witchduck Road at an intersection called "Chinese Corner" (named for a Chinese man who farmed here circa 1900). Turn right on Witchduck Road and follow north for 1.7 miles. Turn left on Sullivan Boulevard and go about two hundred yards. Then turn right on North Witchduck Road and proceed for 1.5 miles (crossing Independence Boulevard). Pass into the Witch Duck Point neighborhood. This area marks the vicinity where the 1706 ducking of Grace Sherwood took place. The Witch Duck Bay, part of the Lynnhaven River, is not publicly accessible here by land, but some of the river can be seen between houses along the road, which intersects the appropriately named Sherwood Lane and Witch Duck Bay Court. A life-size statue of Sherwood stands in a grass median, near a historic marker, at the intersection of North Witchduck Road and Independence Boulevard. From this point, retrace the route to U.S. 58.

6

CHIMNEYTOWN

Norfolk

In the middle of World War I, a rash of random fires broke apart businesses in downtown Norfolk. Firemen fought flames alongside the city's soldiers, sailors and marines on January 1, 1918. But water froze on clothing, icicles hung on hair and one fireman was killed when he was caught beneath burning timbers at the old Monticello Hotel. Estimated property loss: $2 million.

During another war, after another fiery New Year's Day, you would have had a hard time even finding Norfolk.

Lord Dunmore sparked that story. This last royal governor of Virginia fled the colonial capital at Williamsburg in 1775. Dunmore sent men to Norfolk to destroy a newspaper known for criticizing him. Then he took control of the press and printed his own paper, declaring martial law and offering freedom for slaves who took up arms. That same year, Dunmore's troops skirmished with Patriot soldiers at Kempsville in what is now Virginia Beach and Great Bridge in present-day Chesapeake.

But Dunmore really took aim at Norfolk, a port town with about six thousand residents. His small squadron of ships sat at Norfolk's harbor on the Elizabeth River while Patriot soldiers teased British sailors from shore, even sticking their hats on bayonets and waving, like a dare. Finally, in gridlock, Dunmore's fleet opened fire and blasted cannons on January 1, 1776.

Homes and businesses flew into flames. And Dunmore's men landed on shore, torching Norfolk's warehouse row. Colonial rebels, meanwhile, ran in gangs and burned buildings that belonged to Dunmore's loyalists.

Contrary to popular belief, this cannonball in Norfolk has not remained amazingly in place since it bombed a wall at St. Paul's Episcopal Church in 1776. *Author photo.*

Truth be told, colonists burned most of Norfolk. But Dunmore got the blame in newspapers. The following February, colonial troops burned whatever was left to deprive Dunmore of shelter. Then, with hardly more than chimneys popping out of rubble, "Norfolk Towne" became "Chimneytown" for the rest of the Revolutionary War.

Today, little more than the brick walls of St. Paul's Episcopal Church predate Norfolk's fires of 1776. It took a decade to rebuild the church. But something was missing; a cannonball, long lodged in the church's south wall, had fallen from its perch. In 1848, a servant digging with a spade discovered the ball about two feet below the earth. Symbolically, the weapon—now a famous reminder of the "Chimneytown" era—was patched in place above an immortal inscription: "FIRED BY LORD DUNMORE / JAN. 1, 1776."

NORFOLK: ST. PAUL'S EPISCOPAL CHURCH

From the Witchduck Road intersection, follow U.S. 58 west into Norfolk for seven miles, passing Military Circle Mall and Broad Creek, in a commercial district. On the right, at 1010 Church Street, stands the 1919 Attucks Theatre, the oldest theater in the nation that was designed, developed, financed and operated entirely by African Americans. Three blocks west of the theater, turn left on Monticello Avenue and veer left as the road immediately turns into St. Paul's Boulevard. The UFO-shaped building standing on the right is Norfolk Scope, a civic center. A half mile beyond Norfolk Scope, St. Paul's Episcopal Church stands at the corner of St. Paul's Boulevard and City Hall Avenue. Dating to 1739, the church is listed on historic landmark registers and is open to visitors.

7

YOUNG DOUGLAS

Norfolk

G eneral Douglas MacArthur talked about going to war with "Red" China. But as a thirteen-year-old newspaper boy in Norfolk, he had trouble hawking what's black, white and read all over.

Young Douglas was afraid to make newspaper sales, facing competitors his age. Once, even, he returned to his mother's family home with an unsold stack of newspapers. There, his mother simply told him to be a good salesman, no matter what.

The next day, MacArthur sold every newspaper. But this time he returned with ripped clothes, a black eye, a bloody face and torn-up knuckles.

MacArthur remained a fighter—a Romanesque warrior, you might say. He became a five-star general and spent a fifty-two-year career in the army, serving in several wars. Then, at the end of his eighty-four years, it looked like the old soldier sailed away—with his final resting spot in a navy town, Norfolk, where his body lies encased in marble beneath a two-story rotunda.

The general's parents had married at Norfolk in 1875. But his mother's family, the Hardys, hardly warmed to MacArthur's father, a Union army officer. Some of the Hardy men, after all, had fought for the Confederacy during the Civil War.

In 1880, Douglas MacArthur was born at Little Rock Barracks, Arkansas, four years after the birth of his eldest brother, Arthur MacArthur III. Another MacArthur boy—Malcolm, in the middle—died in childhood and was buried in 1883 at Norfolk.

A statue of General Douglas MacArthur stands outside the MacArthur Memorial in Norfolk. *Author photo.*

In 1951, the general visited the site of his mother's Norfolk home, the now-demolished Riveredge, standing along the Elizabeth River. By then, his beloved mother had long been laid to rest at Arlington National Cemetery. A decade later, MacArthur would make plans for his own memorial in Norfolk.

As an officer in the army and the son of an officer, MacArthur really had no home. He had lived all over the world. Still, Norfolk held a connection to the Hardys. Long-lost brother Malcolm was buried there. And besides, Norfolk had offered its 1850 city hall to be the MacArthur Memorial, with a museum and repository plus a gift shop selling replicas of the general's famous corncob pipe.

MacArthur's body arrived in 1964, after three thousand people turned out for his funeral in Norfolk at St. Paul's Episcopal Church. By the turn of the next century, the boy who had scuffled on Norfolk's streets would also have his name on another landmark: a three-level urban shopping center called the MacArthur Center.

NORFOLK: MACARTHUR MEMORIAL

From St. Paul's Episcopal Church, continue one block west on City Hall Avenue to the MacArthur Memorial, on the left, at the corner of Bank Street. MacArthur Center stands between the church and the memorial. The memorial building is listed on historic landmark registers and features a library of MacArthur's papers plus exhibits on his life. A theater shows a film documenting the general's career. The museum is open for tours and contains the tombs of Douglas MacArthur and his second wife, Jean.

8

ELIZABETH RIVER

Norfolk

She slips in and out by the tug of the moon. And she curls around cities with floating tugboats, battleships and barges. Her branches—Eastern, Western and Southern—spread into the heart of Hampton Roads, a region's name that actually refers to the "roads" of shipping lanes on waterways like the Elizabeth River.

Captain John Smith sailed between this river's sandy shores in 1608. Going about six or seven miles inland with a crew, Smith observed tall pines, cultivated fields and Native American lodges.

Oh, how Smith would be lost today. The Elizabeth River has since been dredged to twice its original depth. It has lost up to two-thirds of its original width.

Naïve planners once filled in creeks and marshes with old boards from shipwrecks—only to see those boards rot and become a place where mosquitoes flourished. Birds, boats and the crab-pot buoys of working watermen still dot this urban river. But since World War II, about half of its wetlands have been filled or drained, destroying the habitats of oysters, crabs, birds and fish.

First called Chesapeake for the local Indians, the Elizabeth River was renamed for Princess Elizabeth Stuart, daughter of King James I of England. Really, though, it's not a river; the Elizabeth is actually a tidal arm of the lower Chesapeake Bay.

President George Washington authorized the construction of Fort Norfolk along the Elizabeth in 1794. Later, the fort was rebuilt in about 1810 with officers' quarters, soldiers' barracks, a guardhouse and a carpenter's shop.

Rebuilt in about 1810, Fort Norfolk overlooks the Elizabeth River with cannons pointing to giant navy vessels. *Author photo.*

Fort Norfolk stayed busy through the War of 1812 when it was used to defend Norfolk's inner harbor. But by 1848, the fort fell into disuse and had become the home of a squatter, Lemuel Fentress, who not only moved in but also billed the War Department $1,500, saying he had taken care of the place.

Confederates used Fort Norfolk during the Civil War to supply ammunition to the CSS *Virginia*, one of the world's first iron ships. The hulking ironclad was built in Portsmouth on top of an old wooden boat called the *Merrimack*.

In 1862, the *Virginia* stormed down the Elizabeth, shooting apart the Union's wooden ships and instantly making obsolete the wooden navies of the world. That March, the *Virginia* confronted a Union ironclad, the USS *Monitor*, where the Elizabeth meets the James River. This meeting marked the world's first battle of iron ships. But the confrontation was a draw; neither ship could really damage the other. In the next few weeks, however, the Union took over both Norfolk and Portsmouth. Fearing then that the *Virginia* would be captured, the Confederates blew up their iron ship at Craney Island, near the mouth of the Elizabeth River.

NORFOLK: ELIZABETH RIVER

From the MacArthur Memorial, follow City Hall Avenue west for one block. Turn left on Atlantic Street and go three blocks to the Waterside, a shopping

The Midtown Tunnel on U.S. 58 slips beneath the Elizabeth River. This scene was captured on July 11, 1962, soon after the tube's completion. *Courtesy Virginia Department of Transportation.*

center overlooking the Elizabeth River with a dock for passenger ferries connecting Norfolk's Town Point Park to Portsmouth's Olde Towne. To the right, on One Waterside Drive, stands Nauticus, the National Maritime Center, which features extensive nautical exhibits and tours of the USS *Wisconsin*.

From the Waterside, go two blocks east on Waterside Drive. Turn left on St. Paul's Boulevard, and go one mile to rejoin U.S. 58. Turn left and pass the Chrysler Museum of Art, on the right, within 0.3 miles. (The Chrysler features more than fifty galleries and takes its name from art collector Walter P. Chrysler Jr., the namesake son of the founder of the Chrysler Corporation.)

U.S. 58 becomes Duke Street, and the route turns right on Brambleton Avenue (named for nineteenth-century landowner George Bramble). Immediately cross Smith's Creek at Ghent (a 1890s-era neighborhood named for the Treaty of Ghent, which ended the War of 1812). The Y-shaped water at Smith's Creek is known as the "Hague" (named by Ghent's Dutch developers for the capital city of the province of South Holland in the Netherlands).

To find Fort Norfolk, continue 0.5 miles beyond the Smith's Creek bridge, turn left at Colley Avenue, go 0.3 miles and turn right on Front Street. The fort is operated by the U.S. Army Corps of Engineers and is not always open to the public. From here, retrace the route from Fort Norfolk to the Colley Avenue intersection at Brambleton Avenue. Continue west on U.S. 58 for 0.7 miles to enter the mile-long Midtown Tunnel to Portsmouth beneath the Elizabeth River.

9

THE COMMODORE

Portsmouth

It should have been smooth sailing for James Barron. The navy man had been promoted to the rank of commodore. And, at thirty-nine, he commanded his own ship, the *Chesapeake*.

But soon after setting sail for the Mediterranean on June 22, 1807, the British frigate *Leopard* stopped Barron's ship off the coast of Virginia, and a messenger said four deserters were aboard the *Chesapeake*. Barron refused to allow the British to search the *Chesapeake*. In return, the *Leopard* opened fire, blasting Barron's boat at a distance of fewer than two hundred feet.

The *Chesapeake* was helpless. It wasn't properly fitted for battle, and much of the crew was inexperienced or sick. Finally, for the sake of honor, Barron fired one shot and then ordered his flag lowered. By then, three men had been killed and at least eighteen were wounded.

The British boarded Barron's surrendered ship and carted off the alleged deserters. The badly wounded Barron sailed the *Chesapeake* back to Norfolk.

Americans were outraged. Why, it all sounded incredible. To be fired on in peacetime!

Within days, President Thomas Jefferson ordered all armed vessels of Great Britain to leave the territorial waters of the United States. And then? The public, and especially officers of the navy, hunted a scapegoat. Their scorn fell on Barron.

In 1808, Commodore Barron was put on court-martial. He tried to explain that the *Chesapeake* had been under repair, that the cannons were un-mounted and that the ship was defenseless. His arguments were to no avail. Barron was

A mural by artist Sam Welty depicts Commodore James Barron and the ships involved in an 1807 incident at Hampton Roads. This painting at Olde Towne Portsmouth was completed in 2015. *Author photo.*

kicked out of the navy for five years without pay and found guilty of "neglecting, on the probability of an engagement, to clear his ship for action."

Ultimately, tensions between the United States and Great Britain flared into the War of 1812. Separately, too, Barron and the *Chesapeake* sailed into even more doom. The British captured the *Chesapeake* off the coast of Massachusetts. Barron's job on a merchant ship, meanwhile, left him marooned in Denmark and unable to safely cross the Atlantic Ocean until the end of the war.

All the while, Commodore Stephen Decatur publicly criticized Barron, especially for the *Chesapeake-Leopard* affair. Again, Barron tried to explain the particulars of the encounter, still to no avail. Finally, for the sake of honor, Barron challenged Decatur to a duel.

On March 22, 1820, the two commodores met on a field at Bladensburg, Maryland, just outside Washington, D.C. Each man fired one shot at eight paces. Barron was struck near the groin and fell to the ground, crying, "Decatur, I forgive you from the bottom of my heart." Almost as soon, Decatur exclaimed, "Oh, Lord, I am a dead man!"

Decatur dropped on the ground and simply lay there. He made peace with Barron but died later that night.

A wrought-iron gate surrounds Commodore James Barron's grave at Trinity Episcopal Church in Portsmouth. *Author photo.*

The Commodore Theatre was built in 1945 at Portsmouth and took its name from Commodore James Barron. *Author photo.*

It took more than a year for Barron to heal from his gunshot wound and even more time for the public to forgive him for killing Decatur, a popular prince among navy officers. Once again, Barron would try to explain himself, this time at a trial of his navy peers in 1821. But not every mark was cleared against him, and it was still a few more years before Barron was assigned a new post in the navy.

In some circles, Barron's name was never cleared. As an old man, he was recognized as a leading citizen of Norfolk and a senior officer in the navy. He oversaw Portsmouth's Gosport Navy Yard for six years. And he was still called the "Commodore" when he died in 1851. Yet some could not resist adding, "He was the one who killed Decatur."

A century later, Barron was honored. His title showed up in lights when William "Bunkie" Wilder opened a Portsmouth movie theater named the Commodore in 1945. The original one-thousand-seat theater remained open through 1975. Fred Schoenfeld later renovated and reopened the Commodore in the 1980s. Curiously, the theater marquee nearly illuminates Barron's grave, nearby, on the lawn of the Trinity Episcopal Church.

PORTSMOUTH: COMMODORE THEATRE

Coming out of the Midtown Tunnel on the Portsmouth side, continue west on U.S. 58 for 1.7 miles. Turn left on High Street and go 1.4 miles to the Commodore Theatre (421 High Street). Commodore James Barron's grave lies inside a wrought-iron fence at the lawn of Trinity Episcopal Church, next to the Commodore Theatre, at the corner of Court and High Streets. Both the church and the theater are listed on historic landmark registers. At the church, turn right on Court Street and walk (or drive) two blocks to see a mural of Commodore James Barron at 612 Court Street and the County Street intersection. Then retrace the route to the church.

10

IRON FIST AND STICKY FINGERS

Portsmouth

Hardly anyone admired the style of Union major general Benjamin Butler, especially the people of Portsmouth and Norfolk during the Civil War. This cross-eyed, middle-aged lawyer from Massachusetts ruled these occupied cities with an iron fist and sticky fingers.

Particularly, Butler had a fetish for knives, forks and spoons. He inspected houses and earned his nickname "Spoons" for pocketing people's silverware. Butler won another tag—"the Beast"—for doing much worse. He seized funds set aside for children in Norfolk orphaned by the yellow fever plague of 1855. He charged oystermen a monthly fee to tong the rivers and bays. He levied a tax on all goods shipped into his military district. Butler also made a rule that every fourth dog would be killed unless the owner paid a two-dollar ransom.

At Portsmouth's Olde Towne neighborhood, Butler made his headquarters at the William Peters House, a Colonial Revival structure built in 1859. Butler's soldiers moved into other private homes, and they became infamous for stealing or destroying property while conducting inspections.

Beginning on May 10, 1862, Union troops occupied Portsmouth for three years. During that time, a home at the corner of Crawford and London Streets became known as the "Pass House" because citizens would have to obtain a pass there in order to leave town. Federal soldiers might also make Portsmouth's people take an oath of allegiance to the Union.

One old woman said no. Then, when faced with not obtaining a pass or even going to jail, the woman finally agreed. Without hesitation, she exclaimed, "Damn every Yankee soldier to hell!"

Union major general Benjamin "Spoons" Butler made his headquarters at the William Peters House, built in 1859 at Portsmouth's Olde Towne. *Author photo.*

After that, the woman asked God's forgiveness for swearing and said, "While I was taking an oath, I thought I might as well make it strong."

PORTSMOUTH: OLDE TOWNE

From High Street at Trinity Episcopal Church, turn left on Court Street at Four Corners (site of the large Confederate War Memorial). Go 0.4 miles through Olde Towne to the privately owned William Peters House, 315 Court Street, on the right. The Olde Towne Historic District spans about twenty blocks and includes Colonial, Federal, Greek Revival, Georgian and Victorian architectural styles. Continue straight for two blocks past the Peters House to Crawford Parkway and an overlook of Crawford Bay on the Elizabeth River. Turn right and follow for 0.5 miles as the road becomes Crawford Street. Turn right on High Street and return two blocks to Four Corners, where the 1846 Courthouse, 420 High Street, houses a museum with local history exhibits. From here, continue following High Street for 2.0 miles to U.S. 58 (Airline Boulevard).

11

GLORIOUS PARADISE

Great Dismal Swamp

William Drummond escaped the quicksand, the briars and the bobcats. He had journeyed to the center of the Great Dismal Swamp in 1665 and found a mysterious pool with waters the color of whiskey. That lake was later named for Drummond. Yet no one knew why Drummond was the only hunter in his group to survive that trip through these weird wetlands.

Maybe that's not surprising. The Great Dismal Swamp can be deadly. The forest teems with rattlesnakes, and it's a given you'll get religion if you get lost beneath its thick summertime canopy. You may never find your way out of the endless log ferns, inky puddles and prickly thorn bushes.

Certainly, the name "Dismal Swamp" sounds gloomy. But it's actually quite repetitive. The words dismal and swamp were once interchangeable. Over time, this place became both.

Still, this is not half the swamp it used to be. The Dismal once spread across 500,000 acres. But it was logged from the late 1700s to as late as 1976 and has lost up to half its size. What remains on the Virginia–North Carolina border covers about 110,000 acres in the Great Dismal Swamp National Wildlife Refuge.

The swamp smells both sweet and pungent. It looks both rich and desolate. It sounds both lonely and crowded with the calls of warblers, hawks and heron.

William Byrd II hated it. In 1728, this aristocratic Englishman sloshed through the swamp—and nearly got killed—while surveying the boundary between Virginia and North Carolina. Byrd called the Dismal a "vast body of mire and nastiness" and a place where "foul damps ascend without ceasing, corrupt the air, and render it unfit for respiration."

However, Byrd saw opportunity. He suggested the Dismal be drained and used for farms. George Washington would later agree. In 1763, a young Washington rode his horse around the entire swamp, surveying the ground. Washington also dropped his surveying equipment, according to legend, and hopped on a juniper tree to escape a bear.

By George, the swamp began to change. The Father of Our Country called the Dismal a "glorious paradise" and figured it would be a good spot to grow rice—only, it really wasn't. The peat soil hardened like cement.

Still, Washington remained adventurous. He rounded up a group of influential partners, including Dr. Thomas Walker, an explorer famous for finding the Cumberland Gap in search of Kentucky's bluegrass. By the late 1760s, Washington's partners owned forty thousand acres of swampland. They called their operations "Dismal Swamp Land Company" and "Adventurers for Draining the Great Dismal Swamp." These men slashed up the swamp with artificial waterways, such as the nearly five-mile-long Washington Ditch, used to transport timber. Each partner contributed money plus five slaves to the effort.

A few slaves lived in shacks at a place called "Dismal Town." But in years to come, some slaves became so familiar with the area that they ran away and used the swamp as a refuge from their dismal lives.

Both Washington and Virginia governor Patrick Henry proposed plans to build a canal through the swamp. Construction began in 1793, and the shallow Dismal Swamp Canal was completed in 1805, tying the Southern Branch of the Elizabeth River to the Pasquotank River at Elizabeth City, North Carolina. Boats used the canal to reach the long-gone

The Dismal Town Boardwalk leads through the Great Dismal Swamp, where George Washington oversaw a farming expedition and lumber camp in the late 1700s. *Author photo.*

Lake Drummond Hotel, which straddled the state line. Some came here for quick weddings, since North Carolina allowed marriages at a young age. Others came to fight duels, since you could simply run to the next state to avoid punishment.

Many, too, drank the whiskey-colored water of Lake Drummond. The roots and bark of juniper and cypress trees have turned this lake water brown. Even so, sailors once favored this "juniper water" on long voyages, since it can stay fresh for up to a year.

Lake Drummond is one of only two natural freshwater lakes in Virginia. The other, Mountain Lake, lies near a fault line in Giles County and is known for draining and refilling itself through rock crevices that shift during earthquakes. One tremor in 1959 caused crystal-clear Mountain Lake to rise by 20 feet. A drought in 2008 nearly made the 100-foot-deep Mountain Lake disappear, as it drained down to become a pond of only 225 square feet.

Controlled by a dam operated by the U.S. Army Corps of Engineers, much larger Lake Drummond's levels don't fluctuate like those at Mountain Lake. The sandy-bottom lake lies on an elevation higher than most of the

Lake Drummond is a natural lake in the Great Dismal Swamp, with waters that have been compared to the colors of whiskey, tea, coffee or blood. *Author photo.*

surrounding swampland. And it's no small pond. At 3,100 acres, Lake Drummond spans more than fifty-five times the size of the 55-acre Mountain Lake. However, it reaches depths of only about six feet.

How was Lake Drummond formed? Possibly it's a collapsed sinkhole, or maybe a slow fire burned a hole in the swampy peat, and that filled with water. Maybe there's some truth to the Native American legend about a giant "fire bird" above the swamp; perhaps this oval-shaped lake was formed by a meteor crash.

Hosts of other legends surround the swamp, from sightings of a "swamp creature" that looks like Bigfoot to the famous Lady of the Lake paddling her white canoe on Lake Drummond. People have seen this lady, her lover and her lamp, which is reputedly powered by fireflies—or at least they think they have. Mysterious lights that hover above the lake surface have also been attributed to fox fire, an illumination produced by certain fungi as wood decays.

Still, science hasn't stopped the story. As it goes, the Lady of the Lake travels back and forth, crossing the dark lake with her lover. But, unlike Drummond, for her there is no escape.

CHESAPEAKE/SUFFOLK: GREAT DISMAL SWAMP NATIONAL WILDLIFE REFUGE

From High Street at Portsmouth, continue west on U.S. 58 (Airline Boulevard) for 11.7 miles, briefly cutting through a small portion of Chesapeake (a city named for the Chesapeake Indians). Bear right at Suffolk's U.S. 58 Business route exit and go 1.4 miles. Turn left on VA-337 (Washington Street) and go 0.7 miles east. Make a sharp left turn at VA-642 (White Marsh Road) and continue south, passing the Jericho Ditch entrance at 0.7 miles and the Washington Ditch/Dismal Town Boardwalk entrance after another 4.5 miles. The Dismal Town Boardwalk, near Washington Ditch, stretches about a mile through the swamp.

From here, continue south on VA-642 for one mile. Turn left on VA-604 (Hosier Road) and go 1.7 miles to the Great Dismal Swamp National Wildlife Refuge office, on the left. Trails follow roads through the swamp to Lake Drummond; maps are available at the refuge office, 3100 Desert Road. The lake lies in both Suffolk and Chesapeake. From the refuge headquarters, retrace the route to U.S. 58 Business at VA-337.

12

RIDDICK'S FOLLY

Suffolk

After a fire destroyed buildings across Suffolk in 1837, Mills Riddick insisted on using bricks to build his new home. Rising nearly four stories, with sixteen fireplaces and twenty-one rooms, Riddick's mansion became a gargantuan sight. Neighbors jokingly called it "Riddick's Folly," saying that it was a folly to build such a massive Greek Revival structure.

But it proved perfect for Union major general John James Peck, who took over Riddick's Folly as a hospital and a headquarters for his staff of army officers during the Civil War.

Peck arrived in Suffolk just a few months after Union troops of the First New York Mounted Rifles marched into town on May 12, 1862. The Union sent twenty-nine thousand troops to hold Suffolk, hoping their might would provide a buffer between the already-captured port cities of Norfolk and Portsmouth and the railroads leading west.

Then came trouble. Confederate forces under General James Longstreet flanked the area in April 1863, laying siege to Suffolk. For nearly a month, Longstreet's forces kept the Union unable to move, until Longstreet withdrew on May 4, 1863, without an actual battle. By the end of the summer, Peck had left Suffolk, too.

When the Union occupation was over, Riddick's son, Nathaniel, returned to the family home at Riddick's Folly. The younger Riddick found the mansion looted and stripped of its furnishings. Only a single chair remained. Riddick also found penciled messages all over the walls. Henry Van Weech, a cavalryman from New York, wrote "E Pluribus Union [sic]." There was also

Mills Riddick insisted on using bricks to build his new home, Riddick's Folly, after losing his former house to a fire in 1837. *Courtesy Riddick's Folly House Museum.*

Confederate graffiti, saying, "Yanks you ought to be here / Know that we would give you a good time / Go home and stay there."

In his law office, Nathaniel Riddick discovered a mysterious message from Lieutenant Amos Madden Thayer, a signal officer in the Union army. Thayer had used the office during the occupation and noted to Riddick his "great respect for the taste displayed in ornamenting your grounds." But, Thayer added, "I must confess that I believe the cause in which you are engaged decidedly wrong—We shall see however—I hope to meet you on friendly terms in more peaceful times and enjoy you socially."

SUFFOLK: RIDDICK'S FOLLY

From VA-337 (East Washington Street), head west on U.S. 58 Business for 2.5 miles and proceed into downtown Suffolk. Just beyond the Suffolk Conference Center, turn left on Main Street. The Riddick's Folly House Museum, 510 North Main Street, stands immediately on the left. The house is listed on historic landmark registers and is open for tours.

13

PEANUT CAPITAL OF THE WORLD

Suffolk

Mr. Peanut came out of his shell wearing a chef's hat. In another sketch, the cartoon goober carried a lunch box that said "Planters." Suffolk schoolboy Antonio Gentile created this hand-drawn character in 1916 and won five dollars when Mr. Peanut became the symbol of the Planters Nut & Chocolate Company.

Established in Pennsylvania, Planters moved its headquarters to Suffolk in 1913. At the time, similar peanut factories had been in operation among Suffolk's sprawling peanut farms.

Peanuts had been grown commercially in Virginia since the 1840s, when Dr. Matthew Harris harvested a crop near Waverly. Large crops are now concentrated in the southeastern corner of Virginia in counties called Southampton, Sussex, Surry, Isle of Wight, Dinwiddie, Prince George and Greensville. Still, it took the vision of Planters founder Amedeo Obici—as a community leader, businessman and philanthropist—to truly transform sleepy Suffolk into the "Peanut Capital of the World."

Much of Obici's success can be boiled down to his relentless marketing of Mr. Peanut in the early 1900s. One of Gentile's original sketches called the character "Mr. P. Nut Planter from Virginia." A commercial artist later dressed the nut-shaped fellow with a top hat and monocle. Soon, Mr. Peanut showed up on product labels, in magazines and on the backs of nut-shaped cars, called "Peanutmobiles," driven by Planters sales representatives.

A statue of Mr. Peanut stands at Suffolk's Character Corner. *Author photo.*

Today, the character remains a fixture of Suffolk's parades and festivals, long after the deaths of Obici and Gentile. Likenesses of the debonair icon can also be seen all over the "Peanut Capital" and the world.

SUFFOLK: CHARACTER CORNER

From Riddick's Folly, follow Suffolk's Main Street into the downtown district for 0.6 miles. A three-foot-tall cast-iron statue of Mr. Peanut stands atop a granite monument at the Character Corner, where Main Street meets Washington Street. Turn left at the Character Corner, follow Washington Street for 0.2 miles, turn right on Hall Street and then turn immediately left on Culloden Street to reach the Planters Peanut Factory, on the right. From Character Corner, retrace Main Street to rejoin U.S. 58 Business near Riddick's Folly.

14

THE FLOOD

Franklin

Forecasts looked treacherous. Heavy winds and relentless rain clobbered the Carolina coast. And then? This storm took aim at a Virginia city that some say was named for Benjamin Franklin. The local newspaper issued a warning—"Region Braces for Floyd"—on September 16, 1999. But by then, Hurricane Floyd had found Franklin and flooded it.

Water cascaded over concrete median walls dividing Franklin's U.S. 58 Bypass while more than 180 downtown businesses stood in at least three feet of water. Some Franklin stores were lost in liquid deeper than an Olympic-size swimming pool. Coffins and concrete vaults floated out of the ground at cemeteries in nearby Southampton County. And the city park at Barrett's Landing simply slipped into submersion.

Franklin didn't exactly start on high ground. Surrounded by swamps, Franklin was settled in the 1830s at the head of navigation on the Blackwater River. Steamboats once connected passengers to railroads.

By the late 1800s, Franklin had become the home of a paper mill, headed by Paul D. Camp and his brothers Robert and James. The business grew into Camp Manufacturing Company, later Union Camp Corporation, and ultimately became a parcel of International Paper Company.

The flood paralyzed operations, and soon rumors swirled like all that unwelcome water flowing out of the Blackwater River. Some surmised that Franklin's largest employer would be shuttered.

It took a week for both the floodwaters and rumors to recede. The paper plant reopened. In a few days, boats could no longer float over Franklin's soggy streets.

Barrett's Landing provides access to the sometimes-overflowing Blackwater River at Franklin. *Author photo.*

And like a phoenix, the city rose again, surviving the greatest flood in the city's history—but unfortunately, not its last.

In 2006, history nearly repeated itself with another overflow in Franklin. This time, however, the waters did not rise as high, nor was the damage as devastating, as the event in 1999. Still, not all news remained rosy. What was known simply as "The Mill" shut down in 2010, putting more than one thousand out of work. Thankfully, though, the plant remained dormant only until 2012, when a portion of the mill reopened to make fluff pulp.

FRANKLIN: BLACKWATER RIVER

From Suffolk's Main Street at Riddick's Folly, turn left on U.S. 58 Business and go three miles to rejoin U.S. 58. Continue west for 8.5 miles to the Holland/Franklin exit. Proceed for 0.6 miles into Holland (named for early merchant Z.T. Holland), passing a monument noting the first Ruritan Club formed at Holland. (The civic organization began here in 1928. It took its name from a newspaper reporter, Daisey Nurney, who invented the word *Ruritan*, using Latin terms to reflect the club's rural setting.)

Continue west on U.S. 58 Business, passing through Carrsville (named for early settler Jonas Johnston Carr). At 10.5 miles beyond the Ruritan monument, reach the downtown district of Franklin. Turn left on Main Street and go through town to Barrett's Landing on the Blackwater River. From here, retrace Main Street for a half-mile to U.S. 58 Business (Fourth Avenue). Turn left and go 5.0 miles to rejoin U.S. 58.

15

GO INTO JERUSALEM

Courtland

N at Turner had visions. The slave saw figures of white spirits and black spirits engaged in battle, and he found drops of blood on corn, as though it were dew. Turner also saw an eclipse in February 1831 and figured that was a sign from God—and a time to revolt.

By the end of the year, Turner and a band of fellow slaves turned Southampton County's cotton fields into killing fields. They beheaded men, women and children. They axed every white body they found.

All told, Nat Turner's insurrection was the greatest slave uprising in the history of the United States. It inspired paranoia among slave owners and debates over the future of slavery. It also came as a great surprise. Previously, there had been no sign of revolt among the slaves of Southampton County.

The insurrection leader, "Preacher" Nat Turner, was well liked and well treated. Born in 1800, Turner had convinced his followers that he had divine guidance. He had a plan to "go into Jerusalem," the courthouse town of Southampton County. There, Turner would gather more recruits, and the slaves would fight their way to freedom.

But first, Turner took another cue from the sun. It appeared like a circular plane of polished silver on August 13, 1831. The atmosphere turned hazy, gloomy and green. Turner saw this strange day as God's final message: his insurrection must begin.

About a week later, Turner and his recruits marched into darkness, swinging swords and hatchets. On August 22, at 2:00 a.m., the slaves crept into the house of Joseph Travis, Turner's master and a white man

A historic marker at Cross Keys remembers Nat Turner's bloody slave rebellion in 1831.
Author photo.

whom Turner actually liked. Travis slept. Turner stabbed him, drawing the rebellion's first blood. Other slaves then slaughtered everybody else in the Travis house, even bashing out an infant's brains against a brick fireplace.

The killing continued. Plundering houses and littering lawns with bloody corpses, Turner's army enlisted other slaves to join the rampage. The runaways massacred at least ten students at a school for girls, and the force grew about tenfold with up to sixty slaves, many on horseback.

At the home of Nathaniel Francis, a three-year-old white boy stood in a lane, watching the slaves' horses. The little boy asked for a ride. He was picked up, beheaded and tossed back to the ground. The boy's eight-year-old brother screamed, and he, too, was slashed to death.

Brandy turned the tide. At the home of James W. Parker, some of Turner's recruits rolled barrels of apple brandy into the yard and drank so much that they stopped to slumber in the shade. The slaves then encountered the county militia, armed with guns.

Many slaves fled. Some even went home and said they had been forced to join the raid. Turner's diminished force regrouped the next day. But at the home of Dr. Simon Blunt, some slaves turned on Turner's gang and defended their master. Troops moved in, and then the insurrection was over. By then, Turner's army had killed as many as sixty whites.

Turner somehow escaped. He eluded hundreds looking for him across Virginia, Maryland and North Carolina. For weeks, reports arrived of his capture or whereabouts on the nearby Nottoway River; in the mountains near Fincastle, Virginia; or as far as the West Indies.

Several slaves were executed for participating in the rebellion. Vengeful white mobs, meanwhile, murdered as many as two hundred free and enslaved blacks. The head of one black man was cut off and stuck on the "Blackhead Sign-Post" on the road to Jerusalem, a warning against any future insurrections.

All the while, Turner hid himself in dugouts. He had scratched one hole, what he called a "cave," under a pile of fence rails in a field, not far from where his rebellion began. Finally, at gunpoint, Turner was caught on October 30. Dragged into Jerusalem, he was put on trial and sentenced to die. Standing on a scaffold in his last moments, Turner made a haunting prediction. He promised it would grow dark and rain for the last time. After that, it did rain, and then came a drought.

Turner was hanged on November 11. His body was slashed and skinned. Oil was made from his flesh, and his skeleton was cast off for souvenirs.

The Southampton County Courthouse where Turner's trial was held is now gone. A new one was constructed at the same site in 1834. After 1888, also, the road taken by Turner no longer went into Jerusalem. The town was renamed "Courtland." Postmistress Fannie Barrett had suggested a new name was needed, saying residents were tired of people making annoying references to "Those Arabs from Jerusalem."

COURTLAND: SOUTHAMPTON COUNTY COURTHOUSE

From the westernmost entrance to Franklin, continue west on U.S. 58 for two miles. Veer right on U.S. 58 Business at Courtland and pass the Southampton Agriculture and Forestry Museum (with exhibits related to local history, including the relocated Rebecca Vaughan House, which was one of the homes visited during the killing rampage of Nat Turner's Rebellion), on the right at 26315 Heritage Lane. After two miles, reach the Southampton County Courthouse on the left. Mahone's Tavern, a historic landmark constructed in about 1796, stands on the right. (This landmark was known as Vaughan's Tavern in 1831 when the owner, Henry Vaughan, was accused of overcharging the state of Virginia for food and drink consumed—a bill of $800—while the state militia used the tavern for its headquarters during Nat Turner's Rebellion.)

Continue through town for another 2.5 miles. At Courtland's westernmost junction of U.S. 58 Business and U.S. 58 Bypass, go south on VA-35 for 7.7 miles to the "Nat Turner's Insurrection" historic marker. From the marker, return north on VA-35 for 0.2 miles. Turn left on Cross Keys Road and go 1.4 miles. Turn right on Clarksberry Road (VA-668) and go 2.0 miles to the Cabin Pond Lane (VA-702) intersection. Nat Turner's Insurrection began in this vicinity. Retrace the route from Cabin Pond Lane: return 2.0 miles on Clarksberry Road (VA-668), turn left on Cross Keys Road and go 1.4 miles, then turn left on VA-35 and go 7.5 miles north to U.S. 58.

16

THE APPLEJACK RAID

Emporia

It was just before Christmas, and a fresh batch of brandy waited in homes across Virginia. Farmers like Benjamin Bailey called this "applejack," and Bailey had about twenty-five barrels of it hidden under haystacks on his farm a few miles north of Hicksford.

Then came the march of the Civil War. In the snow and sleet of 1864, Union major general Gouverneur K. Warren headed south from Petersburg to Hicksford with more than twenty-six thousand men. Warren wanted to destroy the section of the Petersburg and Weldon Railroad that ran between Stony Creek and Hicksford's Meherrin River bridge, a vital supply line to the Confederacy.

On December 7, Warren's troops followed the Jerusalem Plank Road but were spotted by Confederate scouts. Word reached Confederate leaders major general Wade Hampton, major general W.H. Fitzhugh Lee and Captain William H. Briggs, and they quickly devised a defense while meeting at the finest home in Hicksford, a circa-1795 mansion called "Village View."

Along the route, several Union soldiers stopped marching after finding some of the applejack hidden under Bailey's haystacks. Casually, these men from Maine threw a big party instead of heading south with the invasion. Scores got drunk, laughing and singing, and forty-three wandered off, later to be listed as missing.

Then came gunfire on December 9. Bullets blasted Belfield, the small town that adjoined Hicksford along the Meherrin River. Confederate troops fired back, and five local boys voluntarily scuttled into the crossfire. The boys

Confederate leaders met in 1864 at Village View—in what is now Emporia—to stop what became known as the "Applejack Raid." *Author photo.*

followed the Confederate plan to torch a wagon-road bridge. When that burned, the Union troops were cut off from moving farther south.

Warren withdrew on December 10 after his troops had destroyed more than fifteen miles of the railroad and severed the Confederate supply line. While in retreat, Warren's troops ransacked homes across Sussex County, drinking more confiscated applejack and later prompting the Hicksford Raid (or Belfield Skirmish) to be comically called the "Applejack Raid."

The name "Belfield" came from developer Belfield Starke, who laid out the town in the 1790s. The original name of "Hicks Ford" came from an Indian trader, Captain Robert Hicks, who had settled around 1709 along the Meherrin River, a watercourse named for a local Indian tribe. In 1887, the tiny towns of Belfield and Hicksford combined to form the singular city of Emporia, borrowing the new name from Emporia, Kansas.

EMPORIA: VILLAGE VIEW

From the VA-35 junction at Courtland, go 23.5 miles west on U.S. 58, passing through Capron (named for a railroad official) and Drewryville (named for a local Drewry family). Use the Emporia exit at U.S. 58 Business and follow for 1.5 miles. Turn left on Main Street (VA-301) and go south for 1.0 mile. Turn left at Briggs Street and go one hundred yards. Village View stands immediately on the left, beyond the railroad tracks at the Clay Street corner. Listed on historic landmark registers, the Federal-style house, 221 Briggs Street, is sometimes open for tours. From Village View, retrace Main Street to U.S. 58 Business and turn left. Go through Emporia for 0.5 miles and then bear right on Market Drive to rejoin U.S. 58 West.

17

BRUNSWICK STEW

Lawrenceville

Stewmasters of Brunswick County would cook squirrel, but they just can't find many. Over the past century or so, the natural squirrel population has been largely depleted. So they'll likely chop chicken, instead, when they stir early in the morning.

It's all for the Battle of the Brunswicks. Both Brunswick County, Virginia, and Brunswick, Georgia, claim to be the birthplace of Brunswick stew. The debate has even simmered into a "stew war," with contests pitting "stewmasters" of the Old Dominion against chefs from the Peachtree State. One skirmish actually ended in interstate controversy when the mayor of Brunswick, Georgia, walked away with a contest trophy after stealing it from the winning Virginians.

In the ladle of history, Georgia points to a statue of a stewpot and says the first Brunswick stew was made in it in 1898 on St. Simon's Island.

Virginia's claim dates much earlier. In 1828, Dr. Creed Haskins went hunting with friends a few miles north of the Brunswick County Courthouse in Lawrenceville. A slave cook named Uncle Jimmy Matthews stayed in camp, shooting a few squirrels and skinning them. Matthews tossed the squirrels in a pot with some stale bread, butter and onions. The returning hunting party liked eating his concoction so much that they tried making "Squirrel Stew" again.

Over the years, the thick stock has been renamed "Matthews Stew" (for Uncle Jimmy) and "Haskins Stew" (for the family that preserved the recipe). Cooks added tomatoes, corn and butter beans, plus one slice of bacon and

Brunswick County welcomes travelers on U.S. 58 with the claim of being "The Original Home of Brunswick Stew." *Author photo.*

The Brunswick County Museum in Lawrenceville pays tribute to the town and county's heritage. *Author photo.*

one small onion for each squirrel. Some cooks substitute rabbit for squirrel. Some say only lamb will do, instead of chicken, if enough squirrels cannot be found.

In 1988, the county's cooks brewed a big batch in Richmond, Virginia, and the Virginia General Assembly declared Brunswick County "the original home of Brunswick Stew."

The "Brunswick" name, by one theory, comes from the German duchy of Brunswick-Luneburg, one of the possessions of King George I. As for the "Lawrence" of Lawrenceville, one account says he was the favorite horse of Colonel James Rice, who gave land for the site of the courthouse town. Another says the name honors Captain James Lawrence, the naval hero who cried, "Don't give up the ship" while aboard the *Chesapeake* during the War of 1812.

LAWRENCEVILLE: BRUNSWICK COUNTY COURTHOUSE AND BRUNSWICK COUNTY MUSEUM

From the westernmost U.S. 58 Business exit at Emporia, follow U.S. 58 west for 17.0 miles, passing through Pleasant Shade (named for a large grove of trees). Turn right at the Lawrenceville exit on U.S. 58 Business and go 1.6 miles to Lawrenceville's courthouse square. The Brunswick County Museum, 221 North Main Street, stands on the left, next to the circa-1853 courthouse. From here, continue for 1.0 mile west on U.S. 58 Business to U.S. 58.

18

FORT CHRISTANNA

Brunswick County

C annons boomed. It was 1716, and Royal Governor Alexander Spotswood ceremoniously inspected Fort Christanna, a five-sided outpost built to improve trade relations between Indians and white settlers. Prior to 1714, when Fort Christanna was established, some white settlers had grown infamous for getting local Indians drunk on rum and cheating them in business deals. But Spotswood's Virginia Indian Company tried to change that by regulating and restricting trading to the confines of the fort.

Spotswood had coined the name "Christanna" by combining the names of Jesus Christ and Anne, the Queen of England. Under the command of Captain Robert Hicks of nearby Hicks Ford, Virginia, Fort Christanna could protect both settlers and local tribes against raids by the northern Iroquois and the Tuscaroras of North Carolina. The fort also included a school to teach Indian children the three R's, plus Bible verses. Strategically, these same Indian children could double as hostages in case the fort was attacked.

Still, some Virginia leaders had argued against the company's monopoly on trade. Others simply suspected that Spotswood personally profited from the enterprise. Ironically, the peace that the fort provided triggered its doom, starting with the dissolution of the Virginia Indian Company in 1717. Within months, Fort Christanna's organization became unclear, and rangers turned mutinous, refusing to stand guard.

Local Saponi Indians continued to live at Fort Christanna as late as 1729. But nearly all traces of the fort were gone in 1924, when a small cannon was erected as a monument to mark the site. Decades later, archaeological

A cannon monument remembers Fort Christanna, near Lawrenceville, in Brunswick County. *Author photo.*

excavations uncovered the outline of the fort, shaped like a pentagon with sides spanning about one hundred yards long.

According to legend, three of Fort Christanna's original cannons were dumped at the bottom of the fort's well. A fourth was eventually moved to the Williamsburg campus of the College of William & Mary. A fifth was overstuffed with gunpowder in 1887 and exploded during an inauguration celebration for President Grover Cleveland at nearby Lawrenceville.

Brunswick County: Fort Christanna

From U.S. 58 at Lawrenceville, continue straight on VA-46, going south, for 2.6 miles. Turn right on VA-686 (Fort Hill Road) and go 1.1 miles to the cannon monument, on the right, and several markers noting the site of the fort. From here, retrace the route to U.S. 58 West.

19

SOUTH OF THE HILL

South Hill

There is no "South Hill"—much less a mountain—in Mecklenburg County. But a big hill standing northwest of town was once dubbed a "mountain." It even inspired the name "Mountain Creek" for a stream at its base. A community near that "mountain" was called "South of the Hill" in the early 1800s. That moniker was soon shortened to "South Hill." Then that same name traveled to the post office of the present South Hill, which was previously called "Ridgefork."

Incorporated in 1901, South Hill was once literally a round town. Like Troutdale, Virginia, the municipality's boundaries formed a perfect circle, with a center spike pounded in the ground near the railroad depot.

In 1924, South Hill's original train station burned to the ground. The next station, made of bricks, literally went to the birds as a home for pigeons after being abandoned for several years. Renovated in the late 1980s, the South Hill Depot became a repository for two unlikely collections: model railroads and dolls.

Retired schoolteacher Virginia S. Evans donated the dolls, a five-hundred-head collection ranging from Kewpie dolls of the 1920s to a likeness of Mr. Peanut. Ralph Schneider, a German shipbuilder, used old postcards for reference when he designed the depot's detailed model of the Atlantic and Danville Railway. Volunteers used green fiber, toothpicks and hair spray to make a landscape of ten thousand little trees for the model.

The model railroad shows miniature versions of Clarksville, LaCrosse and South Hill, all before 1967, the year South Hill's boundaries expanded beyond its original circle.

The South Hill Depot was built in 1924 along the Atlantic and Danville Railway. *Courtesy Frank Malone.*

Possibly, the circle of South Hill meant more than anyone knew. It was just a line on the map. But maybe it could have been viewed from outer space, like a crop circle. At the least, it did seem strange when South Hill's C.N. Crowder reported seeing a UFO in the vicinity of the town's East Ferrell Street on April 21, 1967, just a few weeks after the town's new boundary was drawn.

Crowder said the UFO—with a twenty-foot metal storage tank and legs about three and a half feet high—blasted off with white fire and left a burned spot on the road. Representatives of NASA investigated the incident. So did media representatives and curious sightseers, to little conclusion.

SOUTH HILL: SOUTH HILL DEPOT

From the VA-46 junction, continue west on U.S. 58 for 15.6 miles, passing through Brodnax (named

Travel tip: Open since the 1930s, the Horseshoe Restaurant of South Hill, 311 West Danville Street, naturally took its name from its horseshoe-shaped lunch counter. Yet it is also known for being the site of the 1938 arrest of Roy Kelly, a small-town gangster who called himself "Machine Gun Kelly"—the same name as a more famous gangster.

for a local family that operated a large cotton market) and LaCrosse (named either for the crossing of two railroads, or the game lacrosse). These two towns are connected by the Tobacco Heritage Trail, a recreation route built on the former path of the Atlantic and Danville Railway. Spanning 17.0 miles from Lawrenceville to South Hill, this trail runs parallel to U.S. 58 and is part of Virginia's Beaches to Bluegrass Trail.

Turn right at South Hill on U.S. 58 Business and go 1.1 miles. Turn left on Mecklenburg Avenue and go 0.2 miles to South Hill Depot, 201 South Mecklenburg Avenue. From South Hill Depot, follow west through South Hill for 3.0 miles, on U.S. 58 Business, passing the Horseshoe Restaurant, on the left, before rejoining U.S. 58 West.

20

BOYD TOWN

Boydton

Alexander Boyd collapsed. Maybe it was a heart attack or maybe a stroke. But on August 11, 1801, Boyd suddenly fell over his judge's bench in a Mecklenburg County courtroom and died at age fifty-four.

The well-liked leader left behind a namesake son, but this Alexander Boyd soon found foes. People said the younger Boyd held a monopoly in Mecklenburg County for owning the site of the county courthouse, part of the property inherited from his father.

To appease opponents, Boyd sold two acres to the county for one dollar in 1811 and then conveyed fifty acres to create "Boyd Town," later called "Boydton." Still, Boyd grumbled, saying any attempt by others to remove the courthouse from his property would be "wanton confiscation."

Boyd's property included Boyd Tavern, a sprawling structure that once belonged to his father. Boyd spent big bucks enlarging this inn, built around 1790, and he served his guests liquor imported from Europe. But his finances collapsed, just like his father had. In 1824, he sold the tavern to William Townes, operator of Boydton's short-lived racetrack.

The tavern stayed a hospitality hot spot, especially for horseracing participants. All gathered, winner or loser, for the hotel's lavish balls. But then, after 1832, all bets were off. Townes's racetrack became the site of Randolph-Macon College, and the tavern became a meeting place for students and professors.

During the Civil War, Confederate troops mustered outside Boyd Tavern. Randolph-Macon College, meanwhile, lost both students and professors to

In the 1850s, the Boyd Tavern was a stop on a seventy-three-mile-long wooden plank road that connected Boydton to Petersburg by stagecoach shuttles. *Author photo.*

battlefields plus most of the school's endowment to worthless Confederate bonds. In 1868, the Boydton campus closed, and Randolph-Macon relocated to Ashland, Virginia, to be closer to a railroad.

Boyd Tavern remained. It survived a downtown fire in 1907 and a dynamite explosion used to stop its own fire in 1916. It also inspired vague legends of ghosts to explain its creaky floorboards and the mysterious voices heard in its basement. Restored as a meeting place, the tavern's dollhouse quality detail has been delicately preserved, especially on its fanciful front porch, which faces the grave of the elder Alexander Boyd.

BOYDTON: BOYD TAVERN

From South Hill, continue west on U.S. 58 for 12.7 miles. Turn left on U.S. 58 Business, which runs through Boydton for 1.3 miles to another junction with U.S. 58. The original campus of Randolph-Macon College stood near the corner of Jefferson and School Streets. Boyd Tavern stands at the corner of Madison and Washington Streets. Alexander Boyd's tombstone, on the lawn next to the Mecklenburg County Health Center, includes a poem explaining his death:

> *Twas on the bench 'pon a court day*
> *No doubt you'll read with sorrow*
> *For I was dead before the night*
> *Prepare my friends to follow.*

21

REBELLION ON THE ROANOKE

Clarksville

Nathaniel Bacon cooked up a plan. The young lawyer had grown tired of the Susquehannock Indians who raided outposts on the Virginia frontier. And he was equally upset about Royal Governor William Berkeley's failure to do much about it.

So Bacon went west with about two hundred men in May 1676 and approached the Occaneechi Indians living at a four-mile-long island on the Roanoke River. The Occaneechi had a monopoly on furs, and they had a business association with Berkeley, trading animal skins.

Bacon convinced the Occaneechi to expel a band of marauding Susquehannocks. After that, something happened. No one knows exactly what, but stories say the Occaneechi refused to turn over their prisoners and plunder to Bacon. One of Bacon's men was shot. A two-day battle ensued, with Bacon slicing apart the Occaneechi village and killing an unknown number of the tribe. Bacon then took off with the Occaneechis' beaver pelts.

Virginians at the colonial capital of Jamestown hailed Bacon as a hero for fighting Indians. But an enraged Berkeley acted like he wanted to throw Bacon into a frying pan for waging war with the Occaneechi, his business partners. Berkeley deemed Bacon's action a rebellion on the Roanoke and said Bacon had no official commission to fight Indians.

Bacon, on the other hand, proved to be just as pigheaded as Berkeley. Backed by hundreds of followers, Bacon marched on Jamestown, protesting Virginia's high taxes and low prices paid for tobacco. He also demanded a

A wigwam replica at Occoneechee State Park shows how the Occaneechi Indians might have lived nearby in the 1600s on an island now beneath the waters of Buggs Island Lake. *Author photo.*

commission to fight Indians. For safety, Berkeley fled Jamestown and sailed to Virginia's Eastern Shore.

With Berkeley gone, Bacon essentially took over the government. He issued a declaration citing Berkeley as a corrupt official who played favorites and protected the Indians for his own benefit. Then Bacon turned destructive. He burned the major buildings at Jamestown in September. About a month later, Bacon found himself fried with fatigue. He met a not-so-noble death, succumbing to dysentery in October 1676.

"Bacon's Rebellion" crumbled. More than two hundred of Bacon's supporters were later tried and hanged, including William Carver, an early settler at Portsmouth, and William Drummond, the lone hunter whose name remains on the lake at the center of the Great Dismal Swamp.

The Occaneechi Indians who remained fled Virginia. Some returned in the early 1700s and lived at Fort Christanna, near Lawrenceville.

A century later, the nearby Occoneechee Plantation borrowed the tribe's name, but only until 1898, when candles on a Christmas tree sparked a fire that burned the plantation's twenty-room mansion. The day after the fire, an article in the *Boydton Gazette* theorized: "The Plantation was destined to tragedy, being named for the famous Occoneechee Indians who were massacred on one of the nearby islands in 1676."

CLARKSVILLE: OCCONEECHEE STATE PARK

At Boydton, follow U.S. 58 west for 7.8 miles, passing the Rudds Creek Recreation Area (with a boat ramp, picnic area and swimming beach) on the right. Turn left at Occoneechee State Park. The 2,698-acre park on Buggs Island Lake includes a playground, picnic shelters, a campground, a boat ramp, fishing areas, hiking trails, a visitor center, cabins and the historic site of the Occoneechee Plantation. A wigwam replica at the park shows what the Occaneechi Indians might have used when they lived on Occaneechi Island (now under the waters of Buggs Island Lake).

22

SIR PEYTON'S PLACE

Clarksville

S ir Peyton Skipwith kept his love in the family. He married his late wife's
sister and caused alarm among members of the clergy.

But wait—Sir Peyton loved his sister-in-law. Jean Miller was a liberated
and progressive woman. She was born at Blandford, near what is now
Petersburg, and spent her formative years as a teenager in Scotland. She
learned business, literature, music and gardening.

After marrying Sir Peyton in 1788, Jean became a "lady" to match his
"sir," a title for being an English baronet, a rank just above a knight. The
Skipwiths had four children, adding to the four that Sir Peyton already had
with Lady Ann Miller, Lady Jean's older sister.

Near the banks of the Roanoke River, Sir Peyton built a magnificent
mansion with stones quarried on site. Largely completed in the 1790s, Sir
Peyton's place was named Prestwould, a word meaning "near the trees."
The ten-thousand-acre plantation once employed hundreds of slaves for
large-scale crop farming.

According to an oft-repeated legend, Skipwith had gambled in cards with
William Byrd III to win the land to build the house. But members of the
Prestwould Foundation—the caretakers of the landmark—have soundly
dismissed that story as unfounded, insisting that the wealthy Skipwith paid
for this tract of land.

The Skipwiths operated a ferry, shuttling passengers across the Roanoke
River near Occaneechi Island. The ferry continued after Sir Peyton's death
in 1805. But the widowed Lady Jean gained a reputation for watching her

Prestwould was built in the 1790s in Mecklenburg County. *Courtesy Library of Congress.*

ferryboat operators like a hawk. She calculated exactly what a fare would bring and how many ferries should run each day.

Lady Jean's astute business sense kept Prestwould prosperous. The plantation was also glamorous, with the home's interior draped in custom wallpaper, fitted with Georgian woodwork and lined with hundreds of books. Outside, rows of boxwoods, flowers and fruit trees dotted Lady Jean's garden.

Fittingly, Lady Jean was laid to rest near that beloved garden, beside Sir Peyton. But in death Lady Jean created a mystery: her tombstone lists the year she died as 1826, but it fails to say what year she was born.

CLARKSVILLE: PRESTWOULD PLANTATION

From the Occoneechee State Park entrance, go west on U.S. 58 for a half mile. Turn north on U.S. 15/VA-49 and follow for two miles. Turn left on Route 1601 and go a half mile to the entrance of Prestwould Plantation. Listed on historic landmark registers, the mansion features many original furnishings and outbuildings, including a loom house, a smokehouse, an octagonal summerhouse and a rare, eighteenth-century slave house. Prestwould is open for tours. From here, retrace the route to U.S. 58 West.

23

LAKE COUNTRY

Clarksville

Clarksville sat on the riverbanks awaiting the final flood. The little town had survived a fire in 1893 and decades of drunken, lazy ferryboat captains. Now, with a concrete dam built many miles downstream, Clarksville would watch its shoreline submerge into the ever-rising waters of the Roanoke River.

Far upstream from Clarksville, the Roanoke River tumbles out of the Allegheny Mountains near Christiansburg, Virginia. The river breaks through the Blue Ridge and rolls across Virginia in a rocky streak.

Then somewhere, between a dam at Smith Mountain Lake and the shores of Clarksville, the watercourse loses its identity. The name changes from Roanoke, an Indian term meaning "shell money," to Staunton, for Henry Staunton, who fought Indians on Virginia's Piedmont frontier.

No one has a clear answer for the name change. Perhaps early settlers didn't know the Staunton and the Roanoke was the same river, and that's how it got two names. But beyond Clarksville, it becomes only "Roanoke" again and makes its way south to the Albemarle Sound, emptying near Roanoke Island, North Carolina.

Settlers and politicians talked in the late 1700s about taming this river. They wanted to clear its obstacles and create a navigable waterway. The Roanoke Navigation Company won a charter to do business in Virginia, and by 1816, much of the clearing work had been accomplished.

Anticipating traffic, places called Haskinton, Abbyville and Springfield became ports for the tobacco trade in Mecklenburg County. Around the same time, a tavern owner named Clark Royster petitioned the Virginia General Assembly to form his own little village overlooking the river's Occaneechi Island.

Only Royster didn't have a name for his town. Briefly, it was listed on a legislative bill as "Roanoke." In 1818, the settlement officially became Clarksville, for Royster's first name.

Like his father, Royster operated a ferryboat, linking Clarksville to Mecklenburg's mainland. The Royster operation was one of several ferries crossing the river, but by the mid-1800s, James Sommervill had gained a monopoly on river traffic.

Sommervill's boats were notoriously messy. They leaked. Service was shoddy. One man, Eaton G. Field, had to pole a boat for a drunken ferryboat captain. Another time, an inebriated captain fell out but was saved when a woman pulled him back in by his hair.

By 1905, a toll bridge connected Clarksville to the mainland. The ferry era ended, but the floods did not. In 1940, a rainy overflow killed three people, caused property damage amounting to millions of dollars and drowned farm animals in their pastures. The river also flooded Occaneechi Island.

Immediately, talk turned beyond taming the river. The U.S. Army Corps of Engineers then began to study ways to turn thirty-nine miles of the river into a reservoir.

During 1952, the old, low-lying bridge, at right, on U.S. 58 at Clarksville remained open to traffic as construction continued to build a new bridge, left, over what is now Buggs Island Lake. *Courtesy Virginia Department of Transportation.*

The town dock at Clarksville, at right, provides access to Buggs Island Lake, next to the U.S. 58 crossing. *Author photo.*

The task would not prove easy. Cemeteries, schools and houses had to be relocated. Hundreds of residents were told to move. According to legend, at least one survey crew was told to do the same when a woman brandished a shotgun, determined to keep her farm from the waters deep.

Congressman John Hosea Kerr of North Carolina fought to create this reservoir along the Virginia–North Carolina border. The new lake was named for him. But the dam's construction in the late 1940s was most commonly called the Buggs Island Project for its proximity to a wooded isle near Boydton once owned by Samuel Bugg.

Virginians loved Bugg. They loved the early settler's name better than Kerr's, at least. In 1952, when the dam was completed, Virginians rejected the official name, John H. Kerr Reservoir. Instead, they insisted on Buggs Island.

Today, the reservoir spreads across nearly fifty thousand acres, making it Virginia's largest lake. Clarksville, in turn, became a gateway to Virginia's "Lake Country." But its shoreline changed dramatically: Clarksville's streets now start at Second, since First Street slipped underwater in the final flood.

CLARKSVILLE: BUGGS ISLAND LAKE

From U.S. 15/VA-49, head west on U.S. 58 Business for 1.0 mile across the Philip St. Julien Wilson Memorial Bridge (named for Virginia's first highway commissioner) to enter Clarksville. (In crossing, look to the right, near the railroad trestle, to view the site of the flooded Occaneechi Island, several feet

Travel tip: For local history displays, visit the Clarksville Regional Museum on Eighth Street, just north of U.S. 58.

below the surface of the lake. At this point, both the east and west sides of the highway bridge are in Mecklenburg County, but the center actually rests in Halifax County, where the county border remains at the confluence of the Roanoke and Dan Rivers.) Reaching Clarksville, immediately cross Second Street, with a public access to the lake, on the left. From here, U.S. 58 Business runs 2.5 miles through town until it rejoins U.S. 58.

24

FOUNTAIN OF LIQUID GOLD

Buffalo Springs

Thomas F. Goode turned on the faucet. But first, he had to find it: the old spring that the locals had once loved the most at Buffalo Springs—the one with waters containing the mineral lithia—had become hidden in an overgrowth of brush. For a while, that lost spring flowed underground, emptying into a small tributary of Buffalo Creek in Mecklenburg County.

But Goode befriended an old woman, and, by using her memory, he learned the location of that nearly forgotten fount. Then he hooked that water into his bottling plant in Mecklenburg County, calling the source "Spring No. 2." The new spring joined the three that Goode had begun operating when he took over the Buffalo Springs Resort in 1874.

Goode made Spring No. 2 a fountain of liquid gold. The entrepreneur marketed it as "Buffalo Lithia Water" and claimed it to be "Nature's Nerve Tonic" as he sold it across the United States and Europe during the late 1800s in as many as twenty thousand outlets.

People once thought drinking mineral spring water—or even bathing in it—would cure diseases of the throat, skin and blood. That's why bottles of Goode's water boasted: "PHYSICIANS OF NATIONAL REPUTATION, both in the UNITED STATES and in Europe have used this water, they have RENOWNED it as of GREAT VALUE and have RECOMMENDED it to their PATIENTS."

In 1811, John Speed acquired Buffalo Springs and eventually operated a tavern at the site—a place that had been named for the buffalo that once roamed the nearby hills. By the 1850s, a resort had grown with a hotel, a

Above: The refurbished springhouse at Buffalo Springs is open to visitors. A water-bottling plant once stood behind the structure. *Author photo.*

Right: A 1930 bottle label advises consumers to "drink six to eight glasses daily" of Buffalo Mineral Water, a product bottled at Buffalo Springs, Virginia, just off U.S. 58. *Author photo.*

bowling alley and a large dining hall. The resort was later advertised as a safe haven from Civil War battlefields.

Under Goode's leadership, alcohol was not allowed, leaving guests to rely solely on the springs to quench their thirst. Still, it's rumored that a long row of buildings on "Bachelors' Row"—for single men—became more commonly called "Rowdy Row" because its occupants liked to use Buffalo Spring Water to make moonshine in the nearby woods.

The bottling company and resort continued to operate through the 1930s, long after Goode's death in 1905. But by then, the popularity of Buffalo Springs had dried up, like that of other spring resorts across Virginia. Doctors no longer prescribed mineral water, and the Great Depression soaked up people's vacation money.

During the late 1940s, the Buffalo Springs hotel building was dismantled when part of the resort was set to flood with the construction of Buggs Island Lake. The building was moved to a site on nearby U.S. 58 and reopened as a nightclub, using names like Club 58 and the Greek Goddess. About thirty years later, the old hotel building mysteriously burned.

MECKLENBURG COUNTY: BUFFALO SPRINGS WAYSIDE

From the westernmost junction of U.S. 58 and U.S. 58 Business in Clarksville, follow U.S. 58 west for 4.7 miles. Turn right on VA-732 (Buffalo Springs Road) and go 0.2 miles to the Buffalo Springs Wayside, on the left. A gazebo-style picnic shelter (a refurbished springhouse) stands near the once-famous Spring No. 2. Visitors can bottle the Buffalo Mineral Water for free. From the wayside, return along VA-732 to U.S. 58.

25

THRILL OF BERRY HILL

South Boston

In the antebellum South, James Coles Bruce had just about all the wealth in the world, with more than $1 million, hundreds of slaves and a mansion that looked like a piece of Greece. But what he did not have, after 1850, was his beloved wife, Eliza. And Bruce grieved to the point of lying on Eliza's grave and crying for her to come back to him.

For years, Bruce's emptiness prevailed, until he found himself exasperated by the downturns of the Civil War, and he died on March 28, 1865. Lying on his deathbed just two weeks before the war ended, Bruce said he knew that the lifestyles of wealthy plantation owners and slaveholders like him would come to ruin at the end of the Civil War.

Bruce was born rich. His father, James Bruce, had struck gold with agricultural interests plus a chain of general stores across North Carolina and Virginia. In 1841, with his father gone, the younger Bruce acquired land to build a dream house for Eliza.

The couple's plantation, Berry Hill, once stretched across Halifax County as far east as present-day South Boston, a town named for Boston, Massachusetts, but dubbed "South" to distinguish it from Virginia's other Boston in Culpeper County.

James Coles Bruce made a great living on the outskirts of this tobacco town, overseeing crops at Berry Hill whenever he was not overseeing legislation as a member of the Virginia General Assembly. From 1842 to 1844, Bruce spent $100,000 building his seventeen-room Berry Hill mansion, which features stuccoed and whitewashed brick walls three feet

Berry Hill's spookiness may come from its former caretaker, Richard Cecil Rogers, whose 1960s poem, "The Ghost of Berry Hill," claimed, "Something tip-toes up the double stairs / Like a Persian cat in her high-toned airs." *Courtesy Library of Congress.*

thick, and eight Doric columns rising on the front porch, similar to the Parthenon of ancient Athens.

Bruce imported marble fireplaces from Italy, and he added false doors to the interior of the house simply for symmetry. He had silver-plated doorknobs and silver washstands in bedrooms. And in the great hall, Berry Hill boasted its greatest architectural oddity—a horseshoe-shaped staircase built like it's floating, seemingly unsupported.

It all looks surreal and, some say, spooky. The mansion eventually became the Inn at Berry Hill, a hotel offering luxurious accommodations. Still, the real thrill of Berry Hill must be tracking down its legendary apparitions, like the ghostly young boy wandering the great hall or spirits dancing atop graves on the plantation lawn. Some people say they feel touched by something unseen as they walk the hotel's creaky floors or climb the steps of the floating staircase.

In 2005, bell captain Wyatt Barczak even reported seeing somebody walk "through" a door. "But I didn't hear any footsteps or anything," he said. "I just kind of caught it out of the corner of my eye."

South Boston's Berry Hill includes a horseshoe-shaped staircase, built to look like it's floating. *Courtesy Library of Congress.*

Even more intrigue lies in the whereabouts of Berry Hill's silver. According to tradition, James Coles Bruce ordered his butler to bury a silver table service and washstands in case Union troops tried occupying the house. Some believe the silver fortune lies there still, buried somewhere on the plantation grounds.

SOUTH BOSTON: BERRY HILL

From VA-732 near Buffalo Springs, follow U.S. 58 west for 13.6 miles to U.S. 501 at South Boston. Turn right on U.S. 501 (not the truck route) and go north for four miles. Turn left on VA-654 and go 0.7 miles. Bear left on VA-659 when the road forks and go 1.3 miles. Turn right but remain on VA-659 for another mile to Berry Hill, 3105 River Road, on the left. From here, retrace the route to rejoin U.S. 58 West at U.S. 501.

Travel tip: Visit the South Boston-Halifax County Museum, 1540 Wilborn Avenue, or the Prizery, 700 Bruce Street, in South Boston to see local history displays.

26

LAST CAPITOL OF THE CONFEDERACY

Danville

Confederate president Jefferson Davis dashed off to Danville as Confederate general Robert E. Lee went on the run. The year was 1865. Union forces had finally triggered the fall of the Confederate capital at Richmond, and Danville was as far south as Davis could go and still stay in Virginia.

Danville had been spared from Civil War battles but was plagued with wartime gloom. Six of Danville's tobacco warehouses had been converted into prisons, with thousands held captive, susceptible to starvation, dysentery and disease. About 1,300 prisoners died in Danville in 1864 during a smallpox epidemic. Many prisoners had been shipped to town from overloaded confines in Richmond.

Now, on April 3, 1865, the Confederate government headed down to Danville, too.

Davis and members of his cabinet endured a journey of 140 miles. Taking fifteen hours by rail, it would prove as terrifying as tiresome: the government train passed over busted-up tracks, and the floorboard of one railcar gave way near South Boston, sending at least five men to gruesome deaths, slaughtered by the crunch of the train's rolling wheels.

Finally, in Danville, Davis met Major William T. Sutherlin. A well-respected businessman, Sutherlin became Danville's mayor in 1855 and served as its chief wartime quartermaster, in charge of medicine, arms and food supplies. With Davis's arrival, Sutherlin's stately mansion on Main Street became the last capitol of the Confederacy.

The Sutherlin Mansion stands along a line of homes known as Danville's "Millionaires Row." Confederate president Jefferson Davis spent a week here in 1865. *Author photo.*

Davis stayed in a rear bedroom that had an escape route. He also held meetings with cabinet members and discussed options for carrying on the Confederacy. But Davis, really, could only wait and worry. He needed the protection of Lee's Army of Northern Virginia.

Just before leaving Richmond, plans had been made for the Confederate general to reach Danville, regroup and keep fighting. Unfortunately, with communication lines cut, Davis had no way of knowing Lee's location.

On April 4, at the Sutherlin mansion, Davis wrote what became his last official proclamation as president of the Confederacy. He acknowledged "the occupation of Richmond by the enemy," but to his citizens he promised, "It is my purpose to maintain your cause with my whole heart and soul; that I will never consent to abandon to the enemy one foot of the soil of any one of the States of the Confederacy."

The proclamation was grandiose and optimistic. Yet it was hardly reflective of the reality of both Davis and Lee in retreat.

Almost immediately, Davis turned to military matters and inspected earthwork fortifications surrounding Danville. He had once thought the town was defensible, in that the Union troops could be held back against the

Dan River and nearby Staunton River. But he would conclude Danville's earthworks were "as faulty in location as construction."

Confederate troops built bigger fortresses. But Danville approached mild chaos—refugees overcrowded streets, hoping to be safe in the shadow of Davis's government.

On April 8, Davis finally received a direct word from Lee through a young messenger. Lee's army had suffered disastrously near Farmville at the Battle of Sailor's Creek. That news, unfortunately, was two days old. The next day, Lee surrendered his army to Union general Ulysses S. Grant at Appomattox Court House.

The war was over. But it took a full day before Davis found out. At first, he sat in silence. Then he prepared to move again, still hoping to maintain the Confederate cause.

He thanked the Sutherlins for their hospitality. He bade farewell to the people of Danville. Then, in the darkness of April 10, 1865, Davis boarded a railcar. At little more than an hour before midnight, his train pulled out of sight.

DANVILLE:
DANVILLE MUSEUM OF FINE ARTS AND HISTORY

From U.S. 501 at South Boston, head west on U.S. 58 for thirty miles, passing through Turbeville (named for its first postmistress, Mrs. Eugene C. Turbeville). Turn left on Danville's Main Street (VA-293) and cross the Dan River on the Martin Luther King Jr. Bridge. Follow Main Street for one mile to the Sutherlin mansion, on the left. Built in 1857, this Italian villa–style house briefly served as a hospital during the flu epidemic of 1918 and, for years, was a public library. The mansion is now the Danville Museum of Fine Arts and History and includes Civil War exhibits and art collections.

27

WRECK OF THE OLD 97

Danville

Country music is all about love, heartbreak and train wrecks. The latter actually helped the genre get started—a Danville disaster was turned into a million-selling hit by singer Vernon Dalhart. The song also stirred a fierce debate over its copyright.

Had it not been for that song, the 1903 crash of the "Old 97" would have gone down as just another train wreck. Instead, the song elevated—to mythic proportions—the story of engineer Joseph Andrew "Steve" Broady's attempt to make up for lost time. It captured the imagination of train enthusiasts. It even inspired the names of some Danville businesses.

On September 27, 1903, the express mail train No. 97 ran nearly an hour behind, with the delay possibly beginning with a wait for other cars at Washington, D.C. But it didn't matter where or when. The train would still be fined for not delivering mail on time.

So, quickly, Broady climbed aboard engine No. 1102 at Monroe, Virginia, and headed train No. 97 south toward Spencer, North Carolina. Broady was a substitute driver, but he had steered trains on this line before. Briefly, he stopped at the train station in Lynchburg. Then, in a rush, he took off again with seventeen-year-old Wentworth Armistead still on board. Armistead, a station employee, had jumped on the train only to lock the safe.

After making another stop for water at what is now Gretna, Virginia, the train continued rolling through Pittsylvania County. Its speed grew to about fifty-five miles per hour, maybe more. At any rate, it was too fast for

A mural by Wes Hardin shows scenes of the famous wreck of the "Old 97" at Danville. *Author's collection.*

Broady to safely approach the curved Stillhouse Trestle, standing forty-five feet above a ravine north of Danville's downtown.

The locomotive whistle moaned long and loud. And No. 97 derailed, taking a nosedive at 2:42 p.m. The runaway train flew for more than seventy-five feet, and the locomotive landed on its top. Dust clouds rose out of the ravine, and canaries fluttered out of cracked cages in a wrecked cargo car, all on an otherwise quiet Sunday afternoon.

Hundreds raced down the hillside to the horrible scene of the dead and injured, scalded by steam. Broady died as skin peeled from his body. Armistead died too, but his remains were not immediately found. All told, eleven people were killed and six were injured.

Before long, writers began penning songs and poems about the eerie disaster. In 1924, the mangled mess of the wreck rose out of the ravine and onto store shelves with records by Henry Whitter and Vernon Dalhart. Both singers borrowed the tune of a folk standard, "The Ship That Never Returned." Some say Dalhart borrowed, or just plain copied, the words from Whitter's earlier recording. Still, it was Dalhart's version of "Wreck of the Old 97" that sold more than 6 million copies. It was also Dalhart's success that spurred a series of complicated copyright claims over who actually wrote the song.

Legends about the wreck also grew, largely because various versions of the song changed facts, like elevating the speed of the train to "makin' ninety miles an hour." A state highway historic marker also listed the wrong number of casualties, based on premature reports. Broady's body, meanwhile, was taken from the wreck and buried on a hill, more than 150 miles away, at Blackwell, Virginia, between Abingdon and Saltville.

Today, in Danville, the ravine lies overgrown with brush. Still, mysteries remain about the engineer's last moments and his tragic attempt to, as the old song goes, "put her in Spencer on time."

DANVILLE: OLD 97 MURAL AND WRECK SITE

From the Danville Museum of Fine Arts and History, retrace the route on Main Street for 0.7 miles to the Memorial Drive intersection. To the left, a mural by Wes Hardin depicts the "Old 97" story on a building at the corner of Main Street and Memorial Drive. From here, continue for 0.3 miles on Main Street to U.S. 58 Business (Riverside Drive). Turn left and go 0.4 miles to a historic marker on the left, next to a convenience store, immediately west of the intersection of Highland Court and Riverside Drive. The train derailed immediately south of U.S. 58 and crashed in the ravine. The Stillhouse Trestle and the train tracks are no longer in place.

28

GIVE ME LEATHERWOOD!

Henry County

Just four years after shouting, "Give me liberty or give me death!" at St. John's Church in Richmond in 1775, Patrick Henry stood at the edge of the frontier, overlooking the Blue Ridge. Who knows—Henry might have then shouted, "Give me Leatherwood!"

For five years, Henry's Leatherwood Plantation provided liberty with its remote location. It might have also saved him from death as he suffered bouts with malaria.

Starting in 1776, Henry served three consecutive one-year terms in Williamsburg as Virginia's first non-royal governor. But by 1779, with the American colonies embroiled in war against England, he simply wanted peace in the woods.

He had been west before. In the late 1760s, Henry tromped through the unsettled Holston Valley of Virginia and into present-day Kingsport, Tennessee. He roamed mountains while speculating on land with his brother William and his brother-in-law William Christian. The trip excited Henry's imagination.

So it might have seemed only natural that Henry would have gone to such a sparsely settled spot as Leatherwood in newly formed Henry County, which was named in his honor. He sold off Scotchtown, his house near Ashland, Virginia, and bought his ten-thousand-acre Leatherwood Plantation along the twisted course of Leatherwood Creek.

Back then, it was quite a summer's journey to what Henry called his "retirement," traveling with about fifty people, including his wife,

Above: Undeveloped sand dunes at Virginia Beach's False Cape State Park likely appear the same as they did in 1607, the year the Jamestown settlers landed in Virginia.

Left: King Neptune stands over the Virginia Beach Boardwalk at the terminus of U.S. 58 (Laskin Road/Thirty-first Street).

Left: The "new" Cape Henry Lighthouse was constructed in 1881 at a cost of $125,000.

Below: Green letters shout out the name of the Cavalier Hotel, a legendary landmark built in 1927 at Virginia Beach.

Anna Hyatt Huntington's statue *The Torchbearers* was installed in 1957 outside the Norfolk Museum of Arts and Sciences, which later became the Chrysler Museum of Art.

The Elizabeth River provides a dividing line between Norfolk and Portsmouth at the heart of Hampton Roads.

Legend says that you once could walk from Norfolk to Portsmouth on the bows of boats in the busy harbor of the Elizabeth River.

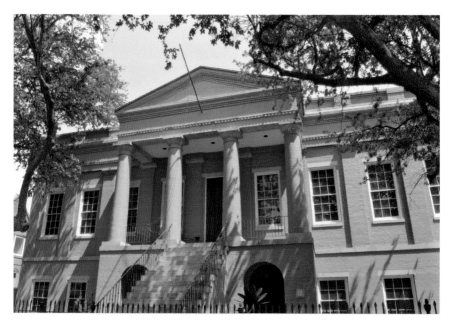

Built with brick in 1846, the Portsmouth Courthouse in Olde Towne now houses the Portsmouth Art & Cultural Center.

Mahone's Tavern in Courtland was the boyhood home of William Mahone, a Confederate general and railroad builder. The tavern served as a Confederate hospital during the Civil War.

Sunset falls over Buggs Island Lake at the site of the submerged Occaneechi Island near Clarksville.

Stretching more than a mile, the multi-million-dollar bypass bridge on U.S. 58 at Buggs Island Lake opened in 2005, providing a postcard view of Clarksville.

Lovers Leap in Patrick County affords a priceless view of mountains and valleys north of U.S. 58.

Meadows of Dan's gift shops attract visitors along U.S. 58, near the Blue Ridge Parkway, at Patrick County.

Dogwood bloom in magnificence at Mabry Mill, just off the Blue Ridge Parkway, about 1.5 miles north of U.S. 58.

The New River near Bridle Creek is part of a popular canoe path along U.S. 58. This stretch of the river was slated to become part of a lake in the 1970s.

Fields Dam is a thirteen-foot-high barrier constructed on the New River in the late 1920s by Fields Electric in Grayson County. It stands alongside U.S. 58 near Mouth of Wilson.

Natural overlooks afford long-range views at Grayson Highlands State Park and the adjacent Mount Rogers National Recreation Area.

Split-rail fences line U.S. 58 outside Grayson Highlands State Park near Rugby in Grayson County.

Wild ponies roam the Mount Rogers National Recreation Area and Grayson Highlands State Park in Grayson County.

The Appalachian Trail winds along the base of Wilburn Ridge in the Mount Rogers National Recreation Area.

Above: Odd outcrops stand
in the prairie of Whitetop
Mountain along the
Appalachian Trail.

Right: Snow falls often
at Whitetop in Grayson
County, a place famous for its
Christmas tree farms, along
U.S. 58.

Straight Branch Falls tumbles fourteen feet at the edge of U.S. 58, about 6.3 miles east of the Damascus Town Park in Washington County.

Whitetop Laurel Falls splashes below the Virginia Creeper Trail near Damascus in Washington County, about one mile west of the trail's Straight Branch parking lot.

Bryan Blevins constructed the Appalachian Trail sign at Damascus Town Park as an Eagle Scout in 1990. The Appalachian Trail's relocated Deep Gap Shelter stands behind the sign, at right.

The Virginia Creeper Trail includes a long trestle over Fifteen Mile Creek at Watauga, between Damascus and Abingdon, along U.S. 58.

The Copper Creek Trestle stands near the Clinch River at Clinchport.

Natural Tunnel in Scott County stands inside a state park, just off the combined routes of U.S 23/58/421.

Cumberland Mountain rises behind the replica of Martin's Station at Wilderness Road State Park in Lee County, near Ewing.

Cumberland Gap dips majestically on Cumberland Mountain at Virginia's borders with both Kentucky and Tennessee.

newborn baby, older children and a son-in-law, plus several slaves. Leatherwood stood 180 miles, or about a week away, from Richmond, where the state capital had recently moved from Williamsburg.

The Henrys had to initially clear their Leatherwood land of several squatters who had planted cabins in the plantation's hollows. Next, they built a two-room brick home and planted tobacco. They also grew enough corn to help feed American troops needing supplies after crossing the Dan River near present-day South Boston in 1781.

Only Henry wasn't always around. He kept getting appointed or elected or simply suggested for political office. He turned down a chance to serve in Congress, but he accepted a bid in 1780 to join Virginia's House of Delegates. Still, plagued by poor health, he served only a few days.

By the end of 1780, Henry found himself among other politicians, serving in the Virginia General Assembly. His "retirement" at Leatherwood languished. He championed the cause of defending America's frontier. He also successfully sponsored a bill to clear the Roanoke River and make it a navigable waterway.

Elected Virginia's governor again in 1784, Henry left

Patrick Henry made his home in Henry County in the 1780s. *Courtesy Library of Congress.*

A monument pays tribute to Patrick Henry's Leatherwood Plantation in Henry County. *Author photo.*

Leatherwood and moved to Chesterfield County, near Richmond. About a dozen years later, he finally found his retirement at Red Hill in Brookneal, Virginia, his last home and where he was buried in 1799.

Henry's Leatherwood home no longer stands, but his name remains on places across his namesake county, including a community college, a bank, a real estate development, an insurance agency and the Patrick Henry Mall. In 1790, his name was also used when forming Patrick County, giving Henry the honor of being the only person to have two of Virginia's counties named for him.

HENRY COUNTY: PATRICK HENRY MONUMENT

From the Wreck of the Old 97 historic marker at the center of Danville (0.4 miles west of the Dan River bridge on Main St.), follow U.S. 58 west for 21.6 miles, passing through Brosville to reach Axton (named for a local congressman's home, the Axton Lodge). Turn left on VA-620 (Old Liberty Drive) and follow for 2.2 miles to the ten-foot-high Patrick Henry monument, on the right, marking the site of Patrick Henry's Leatherwood Plantation. (A plaque on the boulder, erected in 1922, lists Henry's time in Henry County as "1778 to 1784.") From here, retrace VA-620 to U.S. 58. Turn west and go 1.7 miles to a historic marker, located at the entrance to Patrick Henry Farms at Route 1095 (St. Johns Circle). This marker stands 0.2 miles east of U.S. 58's easternmost junction with U.S. 58 Business at Martinsville.

29

CANNONS TO THE COURTHOUSE

Martinsville

When John Fogerty sang, "They point the cannon at you" in Creedence Clearwater Revival's "Fortunate Son," he wasn't singing about Martinsville, Virginia. But he could have been, looking at the imposing cannons fronting the old Henry County Courthouse.

The cannons—a pair of nineteenth-century naval guns—arrived on a train from Fort McHenry, Maryland, a gift to Martinsville by the federal government. But they proved too heavy to be moved by conventional horsepower. So those cannons simply lay beside the train station, in the mud.

Later, a circus stopped in town, according to one tale, and the cannons were finally dragged from the train depot to the courthouse square with elephant power. Still, another tale says it was not elephants but a pair of mules that had taken the task of dragging those cannons to the courthouse—through mud, over the course of a month. The weapons have, either way, proven an intimidating sight on the lawn of the old courthouse, even though their barrels are full of cement.

Since the 1920s, these ten-foot-long iron cannons have pointed at the uptown portion of Martinsville, a city known since 1947 for all the horsepower under the hoods at Martinsville Speedway, its NASCAR track. That speedway lies on the south side of the city, just off U.S. 58 Bypass. At 0.556 miles, the paperclip-shaped track is the smallest on the NASCAR circuit. It is also the oldest. Just as much as for racing, though, the track is known for the popularity of its concession stand's hot dogs, made with a secret recipe and served on waxed paper.

Cannons at the old Henry County Courthouse point to uptown Martinsville. *Author photo.*

Dating to 1824, the old Henry County Courthouse was rebuilt in 1929 at the center of Martinsville, a city named for General Joseph Martin. Like his contemporary Patrick Henry, Martin settled along Leatherwood Creek in Henry County. Martin also served in the Virginia General Assembly in the 1790s, representing the Henry County region.

MARTINSVILLE:
OLD HENRY COUNTY COURTHOUSE

Immediately west of Route 1095 (St. Johns Circle), continue west into Martinsville on U.S. 58 Business for 5.0 miles. Bear right on Church Street at the Starling Avenue intersection and go 0.3 miles. Turn right on Clay Street, then immediately turn left on Main Street and go 0.3 miles to the Old Henry County Courthouse, on the right.

From the courthouse square, continue straight for 0.1 miles. Turn left on Moss Street and go one block. Turn left on Church Street and go 0.7 miles. Turn right on U.S. 58 Business (Starling Avenue) and follow for 2.3 miles to rejoin U.S. 58 Bypass on the west side of Martinsville, on the right. Along the route of U.S. 58 Business, Martinsville's Virginia Museum of Natural History, featuring multifaceted exhibits, stands at 21 Starling Avenue.

30

TRAGEDY ON TOBACCO ROAD

Critz

Abram Reynolds must have thought he was in high cotton. Why, he had gone down to North Carolina and had done just what his father, Hardin Reynolds, told him. He traded beans, flour and apples. Then the fifteen-year-old boy returned to Virginia, ready to restock his family's country store. Trouble was, Abram's newly gotten cotton had come from mills on the Deep River that had been quarantined for smallpox.

Hardin went haywire. Having heard of North Carolina's deadly smallpox outbreak and fearing for his family, he hastily vaccinated his children—at a risk. In 1862, vaccinations were not always considered safe. And, in less than a week, three of the Reynolds children died—two boys and a girl, all under the age of seven, all suffering the aftereffects of the vaccine.

Abram, still upset by the tragedy, enrolled at Virginia Military Institute. He then joined the Confederate army, became a major in the Civil War and accompanied Confederate president Jefferson Davis from Richmond to Danville in 1865. Abram considered going farther south with Davis as the war ended. But first he rode his horse to the Reynolds Homestead—the "Rock Spring Plantation"—of Patrick County.

Hardin enthusiastically embraced his wayward son. "The Yankees have been here and torn up everything, and my Negro men have all gone with them," Hardin told Abram. "But, since you have come back alive and well, it is all right. We can rebuild our lost fortune."

The Reynolds family had amassed its fortune by manufacturing raw tobacco. That success was due to Hardin's thrift and industriousness, along with the help of the young Reynolds boys, including Abram and his younger brother Richard Joshua Reynolds, the one they called "Dick."

Abram joined his father as a business partner in 1867. Three years later, Dick showed up as a salesman, carrying tobacco products on a wagon.

Trouble was, Abram didn't always like how his little brother did business along the Tobacco Road.

Once, Dick had such bad luck making cash sales in the postwar economy that he simply bartered off a load of tobacco worth $2,000. He came home with a wagon piled with animal skins, beeswax, ginseng, furniture and a gold watch. Abram was not pleased. Then Dick held an auction. As it turned out, he earned about 25 percent more cash from the auction's proceeds than he would have by selling the tobacco.

Abram—known as Major A.D. Reynolds—went west in 1872 to Bristol, Tennessee, and started a tobacco company that eventually employed about five hundred people. He sold it in 1897 and died in 1925.

Dick—known as R.J. Reynolds—left home in 1874 for what is now Winston-Salem, North Carolina. He, too, started his own tobacco company, and it grew into nothing short of an empire, selling such products as Camel cigarettes, and employing as many as ten thousand people by the time of his death in 1918.

A younger brother, Hardin Harbour Reynolds, also took up business along the Tobacco Road. Born in 1854, Harbour became a business partner

Reynolds Homestead is the birthplace of cigarette king R.J. Reynolds. *Author photo.*

with his father in 1876. Later, Harbour promoted his own brand of chewing tobacco, Red Elephant, as having one thousand spits to the chew.

Harbour worked in Bristol for Abram. He also had his own tobacco factory. But when that factory at South Boston went up in flames, Harbour returned to Patrick County to live with his wife and children at the Reynolds Homestead.

Unfortunately, there would be more tragedy on Tobacco Road. Harbour's young daughter, Nancy Ruth, died at age six in 1912. Where or even how she died, however, has since inspired debate.

For years, it was told, little Nancy died at the Reynolds Homestead, the place where her body is buried in the family cemetery. As the story goes, Nancy awoke early and reached for her Christmas stocking on a fireplace mantel, but her nightgown caught fire, and she died after deeply inhaling the flames.

All this, however, possibly conflicts with a loftily worded obituary printed about six weeks after Nancy's death.

"She begged her parents to allow her to go to Danville with her teacher to spend a few days at Christmas," says the obituary, published in the February 13, 1913 edition of the *Enterprise* at Stuart, Virginia. "At first, they tried to dissuade her and her father seemed to have a foreboding of danger."

Still, Harbour and his wife, Annie, made all necessary preparations—and, according to the newspaper, the six-year-old girl traveled by train to spend the holiday away from her parents at Danville. There, the obituary says, she met her final fate: "On Christmas morning, as she was standing in front of an open grate looking at her presents her clothing caught fire and she was fatally injured. In ten minutes she was in bed in a Danville hospital with three physicians and a trained nurse in attendance…At four o'clock in the afternoon, she fell into a peaceful sleep to wake in that 'better land.'"

CRITZ: REYNOLDS HOMESTEAD

From the westernmost junction of U.S. 58 and U.S. 58 Business at Martinsville, follow U.S. 58 west for 17.0 miles, passing through Spencer (named for the family of first postmaster Peter D. Spencer) and Penns Store (named for a local Penn family that operated a store and tobacco factory). Turn right on VA-626 and follow for 3.3 miles, passing Critz (named for early settler Haman Critz Sr.). Turn left at VA-798 (Homestead Lane) to enter the Reynolds Homestead. Built in the 1840s, the brick home is listed on historic landmark registers and is open for tours as a museum operated by Virginia Tech.

31

A BOY NAMED JAMES

Stuart

Even as a nine-year-old boy, James Stuart wouldn't let a sting knock him out of action. As his brother William Alexander ran for cover in a swarm of hornets, James simply stood on a tree branch, taking swats until a huge hornet nest lay on the ground below him.

It was a sweeping skirmish, maybe even foreshadowing the battles that James would later lead as a great Confederate cavalryman, a time when he was known as "Jeb" Stuart. However, James wasn't called "Jeb" on Laurel Hill in Patrick County. Born on February 6, 1833, he was simply a boy named James, the seventh child and youngest son of Archibald and Elizabeth Stuart.

The "Jeb" nickname, formed from the initials of his name, James Ewell Brown, would come much later, in the 1850s, when red-haired Jeb became known for his jokes and singing. Stuart, also, was quite cavalier, wearing a red cape, knee-high boots, a bushy beard and an ostrich plume in his hat.

Stuart learned to ride a horse while on the family farm at Laurel Hill, several miles south of the Patrick County Courthouse. The Stuarts lived so close to North Carolina that their mail came from Mount Airy. But their neighborhood, called the "Hollow," was really part of Ararat, Virginia, named possibly for a Tarratt family, maybe the Indian word *tarraratt*, or perhaps Mount Ararat, the peak where Noah's Ark landed after the Great Flood.

For the Stuarts, a defining moment would be the great fire. It ripped down the family's wooden farmhouse during the winter of 1847–48, and they were left to live in a detached kitchen.

Laurel Hill is the birthplace of Confederate major general J.E.B. Stuart. *Author photo.*

Before the fire, Stuart attended school in Wytheville, Virginia, living with his namesake uncle. He later enrolled at Emory & Henry College, graduated from the United States Military Academy at West Point and served in the army.

Just after the outbreak of the Civil War, he joined the Confederate army and became the eyes of General Robert E. Lee, serving as cavalry commander in the Army of Northern Virginia. In 1862, Stuart and his 1,200 men rode around Union general George McClellan's entire 100,000-man Army of the Potomac. Stuart lost only one man in the action and supplied Lee with valuable information.

Still, with bodies piling up on battlefields, it was only natural that Major General J.E.B. Stuart questioned his mortality. He told his wife, Flora, to prepare for the worst. He also longed for his "dear old hills" of home in Patrick County. In 1863, he wrote, "I would give anything to make a pilgrimage to the old place, and when this war is over quietly spend the rest of my days there."

He never got the chance. Laurel Hill was sold out of the family in 1859. Then, on May 11, 1864, Stuart was mortally wounded near Ashland, Virginia. A Union soldier from Michigan buzzed out of a nest of Federal troops and took a swat at him. Stung by a shot in his side, Stuart had to be pulled off his horse by his men.

Confederate president Jefferson Davis showed up in Richmond at Stuart's deathbed. Flora Stuart arrived on May 12, but it was too late. Stuart was gone, dead at age thirty-one.

Patrick County's courthouse town gave up its name for the general. Once called Taylorsville for eighteenth-century settler George Taylor, the name changed to Stuart in 1884.

STUART/ARARAT:
PATRICK COUNTY COURTHOUSE AND LAUREL HILL

From the U.S. 58 junction at VA-626, follow U.S. 58 west for 7.4 miles, passing through Patrick Springs (the site of a spring water resort in the early 1900s). Turn left at the Stuart exit on U.S. 58 Business (East Blue Ridge Street) and go west for 0.7 miles to the Patrick County Courthouse, with a monument on the lawn dedicated to J.E.B. Stuart. To reach Laurel Hill, turn left at the courthouse on North Main Street (Route T-1009) and go through town, veering left as the road turns to South Main Street and joins VA-8 (Salem Highway) After 4.0 miles, turn right onto VA-103 (Dry Pond Highway) and go 8.7 miles, passing through Claudville (named for a congressman, Claude Augustus Swanson). Turn right on VA-753 and go 10.6 miles to Laurel Hill, on the right.

The seventy-five-acre Laurel Hill tract is unique because it is listed on historic landmark registers even though no historical structures exist on the site. The property features trails, including a short trek to a six-foot-high waterfall.

From Laurel Hill, retrace the route to the Patrick County Courthouse at Stuart. Then turn left on U.S. 58 Business to immediately reach the Patrick County Historical Museum, 116 West Blue Ridge Street, with displays related to J.E.B. Stuart. From the museum, U.S. 58 Business runs one mile west to rejoin U.S. 58.

32

CROSS ROCKS

Fairy Stone State Park

Long ago, fairies frolicked, dancing beside a spring. Then came news from an elfin messenger: Jesus Christ, the Son of the Great Creator, had been crucified. The fairies cried, shedding tears that turned into "fairy stones" shaped like St. Andrew's, Roman and Maltese crosses.

This story is, quite literally, a fairy tale. And scientists dismiss it, saying fairy stones are actually brown staurolite, a combination of iron, silica and aluminum. When subjected to great heat and pressure, these minerals crystallize to form a cross. Possibly, the inch-long oddities called "cross rocks," "fairy stones" or "fairy crosses" were formed when the earth's plates shifted and pushed up the Blue Ridge Mountains.

Fairy stones are found in only a few places, like Fairy Stone State Park in Patrick County or along parts of the New River in North Carolina. One tale, aside from the fairies, says the Cherokee formed these cross rocks as they were pushed from their ancestral homes on the Trail of Tears.

In Virginia, Patrick County's fairy stone fields once belonged to Julius B. Fishburn, a Roanoke newspaper publisher. Fishburn was a partner at Fayerdale, an iron-mining town in the early 1900s located at the present site of Fairy Stone State Park. Fayerdale is now the name used by the state park's conference center; the word was coined by combining geologist Frank Ayer Hill's first initial and middle name with the middle name of another business partner, H. Dale Lafferty.

Fishburn donated 4,868 acres to create the park. It opened in 1936 as one of the first six state parks in Virginia. Contrary to popular belief, however,

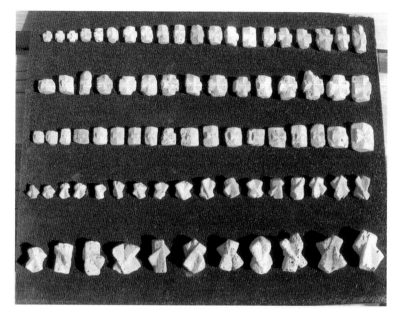

Fairy stones or "cross rocks" are said to be the teardrops of fairies who cried after the death of Jesus Christ. *Author photo.*

Fairy Stone State Park opened in 1936 as one of the first six state parks in Virginia. *Author photo.*

fairy stones cannot be found all over the park; only a small vein runs through a corner of the grounds.

President Teddy Roosevelt and inventor Thomas A. Edison both carried fairy stones. Legend says wearing such stones wards off witchcraft, sickness, accidents and disaster. Fairy stones have also crossed into literature; they are portrayed as a symbol of luck and love in John Fox Jr.'s 1908 novel *The Trail of the Lonesome Pine*.

PATRICK COUNTY: FAIRY STONE STATE PARK

From the westernmost entrance of U.S. 58 Business at Stuart, follow U.S. 58 west for 2.0 miles. Turn right at VA-8 (Woolwine Highway) and go 3.9 miles north. Bear right on VA-57 and continue north for 7.7 miles. Turn left on VA-346 and go 1.0 mile to Fairy Stone State Park, 967 Fairy Stone Lake Drive. The park features a campground, a beach, a fishing lake, a playground, hiking trails, a visitor center and cabins. To reach the park's Fairy Stone Hunt Site, retrace VA-346 to VA-57, then turn left and follow VA-57 north for 2.7 miles. The hunt site is on the left, next to a small store.

33

KISSING BRIDGES

Woolwine

Walter G. Weaver concentrated on caskets. That's what he made, mainly. But Weaver also designed a couple of covered bridges. He even built the Bob White Bridge, which once spanned the Smith River.

Lovers loved it. Courting couples would stop a buggy in the bridge and carve their initials on the wooden walls. Some smooched. Naturally, covered bridges became "kissing bridges" and also "wishing bridges," since it was tradition to make a wish as you passed through.

Some believe bridges were covered so that horses would not get spooked as they crossed water. Actually, covered bridges had roofs simply to protect floorboards from rot.

Covered bridges are rare. About one hundred once stood in Virginia. Fewer than ten now remain, and more than half, ironically, are located close to one another, with three in Giles County, all near Newport, and two once standing in Patrick County, both near Woolwine. Virginia's oldest covered bridge, the 1857 Humpback Bridge near Covington, arches one hundred feet over Dunlap Creek on the headwaters of the James River.

When Weaver constructed the eighty-foot-long Bob White Bridge in 1921, he made it into a family affair. One of Weaver's sons helped with carpentry. Another son poured cement. A daughter brought lunches to the work site.

The Weavers built the bridge to reach the Smith River Church of the Brethren. No one really knows for sure, but the Bob White Bridge and the long-gone Bob White Post Office were both possibly named for the traditional "bob white" song of the area's quail.

Jack's Creek Covered Bridge stands beside a modern replacement bridge near Woolwine in Patrick County. *Author photo.*

Bob White Covered Bridge was a landmark at Woolwine in Patrick County, a few miles north of U.S. 58, until destroyed by a flood on September 29, 2015. *Author photo.*

The Bob White Covered Bridge stood until September 29, 2015. Floodwaters destroyed the structure during an overflow on the Smith River and washed it downstream.

Nearby, Weaver also designed the Jack's Creek Bridge at Woolwine, a Patrick County community named for its first postmaster, Thomas B. Woolwine. Still, that landmark's name is misleading, since the Jack's Creek Bridge spans forty-eight feet across the Smith River. Constructed in 1914–16 by Charles Vaughan, the bridge was named because it leads to Jack's Creek Primitive Baptist Church.

Who was Jack? Perhaps he was the same boy who went up the hill to fetch a pail of water. Consider this: the rippling waters of Jill Creek join Jack's Creek about a mile north of the Jack's Creek Bridge.

WOOLWINE:
BOB WHITE BRIDGE AND JACK'S CREEK BRIDGE

From the entrance road at Fairy Stone State Park at the VA-346 intersection, return south on VA-57 by driving 7.7 miles. Turn right on VA-8 and go 3.7 miles north. Turn left at VA-615 and go 0.1 miles to Jack's Creek Bridge, on the right. Then retrace VA-615 to VA-8, turn left and go 0.8 miles north. Turn right on VA-618 and go 1.0 mile to a right turn on VA-869, which leads about 200 yards to the site of the Bob White Bridge. The Jack's Creek Bridge is closed to vehicular traffic but open to pedestrians. From the site of the Bob White Bridge, return to U.S. 58 by retracing the 1.0 mile on VA-618. Turn left and follow VA-8 South for 8.4 miles to U.S. 58.

34

VIRGINIA IS FOR LEAPING LOVERS

Patrick County

All over the Old Dominion, so many cliffs are called Lovers Leap, you might figure the state's motto should be "Virginia Is for Leaping Lovers."

Lovers Leaps are perched at Whitetop Mountain, Natural Tunnel State Park, Jump Mountain near Lexington and along Johns Creek near New Castle. One hugs the Shenandoah River in Clarke County, not far from Berryville. Another pierces the lip of the Breaks Canyon in Dickenson County.

Like all the others, the Lovers Leap of Patrick County boasts a long-standing legend of a boy and a girl, each from warring Indian tribes. These lovers, forbidden to be together, play a fatal game of jumping into the afterlife, probably hoping to wake up on a star somewhere in each other's arms. For sure, if you jumped into the jungle below Patrick County's Lovers Leap, at an elevation of more than three thousand feet, you would see stars—from toppling into treetops and bouncing off outcrops while flying fast into the Smith River Valley.

Patrick County's original Lovers Leap lies on private property. What is now called Lovers Leap is a nearby public wayside. But it also boasts a grand overlook. And it also stands between some suggestively named geography, with Spoon Mountain on the east and Naked Ridge on the west.

A sign at the Lovers Leap wayside says it's unlawful to vandalize or deface public property. But love is blind. So have a heart for all those blind-eyed scribes, spray-painting and scratching this wayside's wall with proclamations: "Tammy + Bill," "Carol Loves Larry" or "Fay Hartless and Ben Fields

Patrick County's Lovers Leap Overlook provides great views—if fog is not around. *Author photo.*

2gether 4-Ever." At least the graffiti seems patriotically applied in red, white and blue. The colors even contrast, beautifully, when sunset's orange creams into crimson.

Travel Tip: DeHart Botanical Gardens stands on the right, 3.5 miles beyond VA-8 (or two miles before reaching Lovers Leap). This 172-acre nature preserve includes a 3.2-mile-long strenuous loop trail that leads past a fourteen-foot-high waterfall.

PATRICK COUNTY: LOVERS LEAP

From the VA-8 junction west of Stuart, head west on U.S. 58 for 5.4 miles as the road makes a steady ascension to Lovers Leap wayside, on the right. Immediately west of the Lovers Leap wayside, the Fred Clifton Park features picnic tables, grills and short trails leading to scenic overlooks in a garden of rhododendron.

35

DAN RIVER QUEEN

Meadows of Dan

Virginia lighthouse lists never mention the stone sentinel at the headwaters of the Dan River, roughly three hundred miles from the sea. Just twelve feet high, this little lighthouse once stood guard over the watercourse of the *Dan River Queen*, a side-wheeler paddleboat that Shirley Mitchell operated during the 1960s on the ten-acre Cockram Millpond.

Tourists loved to cruise on the fifty-two-foot-long boat. One poor couple with very little money came here on their honeymoon and pretended to be on a fancy cruise ship. Others waved at the pond's birds and animals living near the lighthouse on a little island. The one-dollar boat ride was advertised as a "cruise on a quiet, peaceful lake 3,600 feet up in the Blue Ridge Mountains."

Mitchell spent a fortune constructing places along the perimeter of the pond. He also restored the 1884 Cockram Mill. Mitchell, in turn, lost a fortune. Nearby, along U.S. 58, he also operated the Circle M Zoo with 100 exotic birds and 110 unusual animals—elephants, hyenas, buffalo and monkeys—all shown to visitors on bus safari tours.

Over time, the lighthouse remained, but the boat and the zoo disappeared. The Cockram Milldam broke in 1989, and the pond turned into wetlands. The *Dan River Queen* was sold for salvage.

Then along came Sharoll Shumate. In 1999, this world-traveling motivational speaker bought the property near the Blue Ridge Parkway and used part of the Cockram Mill to open a pizza parlor. Shumate also built an ice cream shop for "swingers"—a place where patrons sit on swings hanging from the ceiling.

Above: The *Dan River Queen* was a popular attraction in the late 1960s at Meadows of Dan, where visitors could embark on a riverboat ride along U.S. 58. *Courtesy Patrick County Historical Society.*

Left: The stone "lighthouse" on the Dan River once guided boat tours on the Cockram Millpond, just off U.S. 58. At right of the lighthouse, in the background, sits the wooden hull of the *Dan River Queen*, resting on the millpond's grassy banks near the Cockram Mill, which stands at rear right. *Author photo.*

Shumate's plans to establish a resort with cabins and turn a rock quarry into a concert hall sounded ambitious for tiny Meadows of Dan, maybe even reminiscent of the late Shirley Mitchell. But Shumate disproved doubters by 2001. He discovered the whereabouts of the long-lost *Dan River Queen* and hauled the hull home, allowing Dan River's little lighthouse to shine within sight of the *Dan River Queen* again.

MEADOWS OF DAN: COCKRAM MILL

From the Lovers Leap wayside and Fred Clifton Park, continue west on U.S. 58 for 4.5 miles, passing through Vesta (named for the Greek goddess of the hearth). The Cockram Mill, named for former owner Walter A. "Babe" Cockram, stands on the right and is listed on historic landmark registers. The lighthouse stands a few yards from the mill, near the *Dan River Queen*.

Cockram Mill marks the eastern gateway to Meadows of Dan, a scenic area with gift shops near the Blue Ridge Parkway. The community lies along meadows at the head of the Dan River, a watercourse that took its name either from a Saura Indian chief called "Danaho" or as a reference to the ancient tribe of the Danites, as told in the Bible's Joshua 19:47.

Travel tip: About 1.5 miles west of Lovers Leap, turn left on Busted Rock Road (VA-610) and go 8.0 miles to Primland Resort. The upscale retreat includes hiking on a former section of the Appalachian Trail. Spanning twelve thousand acres, Primland takes it name from its founder, Didier Primat.

36

THE REAL MAYBERRY

Blue Ridge Parkway

Lizzie DeHart Mabry worked for years alongside her husband, Edwin Boston Mabry, a stout man known to all as "Uncle Ed." He was a chair maker, a miner, a blacksmith and a farmer. The man could fix whatever you broke. But as a claim to fame, Uncle Ed built what may be the most photographed mill in America.

Mabry Mill shows up on road maps and brochures. With more than 1 million visitors a year, it is possibly the most popular spot on the entire 469-mile Blue Ridge Parkway. Yet maybe Mabry should have been "Mayberry" for the same "Mayberry" where Andy and Opie went whistling down to the old fishing hole.

The Mayberry name comes from Isaac Mayberry, who secured a land grant in 1787 and gave his name to the Mayberry hamlet where Virginia's Patrick, Carroll and Floyd Counties meet. Uncle Ed is one of Isaac's descendants. So is Charles Mayberry, a son of Isaac, who shortened the family name from Mayberry to Mabry.

Mabry Mill stands about four miles north of Mayberry, Virginia, where one of actor Andy Griffith's grandfathers once regularly sold ginseng roots at the Mayberry Trading Post. As it came time to name the TV town on *The Andy Griffith Show*, the store's longtime proprietor, Coy Lee Yeatts, figured, "There was no other Mayberry around to come up with that name."

Who knows? Everyone has already figured North Carolina's Pilot Mountain morphed into TV's "Mount Pilot." Virginia's Fancy Gap made its way into *Griffith* scripts. Story lines also referenced the real-life Snappy Lunch, Wiener Burger and Grand Theatre.

So, why not Mayberry? It's just twenty-eight miles from Andy Griffith's hometown of Mount Airy, a lively city in North Carolina where Mayberry names are fixed on places offering haircuts, squad-car tours, Barney Fife T-shirts, pork-chop sandwiches and all kinds of trinkets.

Unincorporated Mayberry appears much more modest. Locals pay little mind to TV connections, and there are only a handful of landmarks noting the name, like the Mayberry Trading Post, which stands in sight of the Blue Ridge Parkway. This folksy, old store served as the now-closed Mayberry Post Office until 1922.

Locals believe the name "Mayberry" on *The Andy Griffith Show* comes from the Mayberry Trading Post, just off the Blue Ridge Parkway. *Author photo.*

Just a few whistles away, the Mabrys' mom-and-pop mill survived a quarter century but then looked as tired as the Mabrys do in old photographs. Uncle Ed built the mill around 1910, pulling water from every creek, stream and branch he could acquire. But Uncle Ed often had to wait for a wet spell, even a flood, to get his wheel turning.

Around 1930, the operation nearly ground to a halt. Ed suffered some kind of illness, losing the use of his legs. Lizzie took over. Then Ed died. Brokenhearted, Lizzie sold the mill to the National Park Service. She died in 1940.

Today, Mabry Mill looks dressed for tourists with a little log cabin designed to be the Mabrys' make-believe home. Fact is, Blue Ridge Parkway planners did not think the Mabrys' real home, a two-story frame house, looked rustic enough, so they tore it down in 1942 and moved in the log one.

The mill has since become legendary for its loveliness, even if its landscape is not historically accurate. The grounds burst with blooming flowers, and the millpond attracts ducks and dogs and is the muse of many a painter. So

Mabry Mill is one of the most photographed landmarks along the Blue Ridge Parkway. *Author photo.*

beautiful, so romantic—if there was ever a place to steal a kiss, surely, Mabry Mill would be it.

BLUE RIDGE PARKWAY:
MABRY MILL AND MAYBERRY TRADING POST

From the Blue Ridge Passage Resort at Cockram Mill, follow U.S. 58 west for 0.5 miles, then turn left on U.S. 58 Business at Meadows of Dan. Continue for 1.0 mile to the Blue Ridge Parkway entrances. Turn north on the Parkway and go 1.6 miles to Mabry Mill, on the right, at mile 176.1. A short trail leads past farm implements, a moonshine still, millstones and outbuildings. Also on site is a gift shop and short-order restaurant, open spring to fall, with a screen-porch dining room. On Sundays, musicians often play bluegrass music on the grounds.

To reach Mayberry, turn south at the Parkway entrance and go 2.6 miles to the Mayberry Trading Post, 883 Mayberry Church Road, on the left, between mileposts 180 and 181.

37

SHOOTOUT STORY

Hillsville

It started with a kiss and ended with a killing. Five people lay dead after the trial of Floyd Allen turned into a bullet-flying bloodbath in the Carroll County Courthouse. When the smoke cleared, the dusty-street town called Hillsville would be locked in legend and loaded with lore.

Talk about a morning after. On March 15, 1912, sleepy Hillsville found its way onto the front pages of newspapers across the nation, with screaming headlines like "Awful Tragedy Enacted in Virginia Courthouse." Newspapers remained entrenched with the story of Floyd Allen and his gun-toting clan for a solid month. Journalists filed lengthy dispatches about the "outlaw" Allen family on the run—until, ultimately, America's attention turned to the icy Atlantic and the sinking of a ship called the *Titanic*.

Talk about sensationalism. News accounts flew almost as madly as the bullets in the Carroll County Courthouse, whipping up stories in all directions. One tale said that store owner Floyd Allen later tried to kill himself with a pocketknife. Another reported that his runaway brother, J. Sidna Allen, had been surrounded at a stop called Squirrel Spur. Yet one more account said that J. Sidna's wife was killed in a subsequent shootout.

Maybe half of the reports were accurate. The story of the post-trial gunfight at J. Sidna's house—the one in which his wife was "killed"—never happened at all.

Talk about ironies. Unpretentious Hillsville has not blatantly tried to capitalize on the infamy of this incident. But, courthouse tours are offered. Also, in 2005, the Historical Society of Carroll County moved its library into the shooting site, where a bullet hole can still be seen on a front step of the 1872 courthouse.

On Labor Day weekends, you can also see guns carried all over Hillsville as part of the local VFW's gun show and flea market, an all-enveloping event that attracts thousands and ties up the town with turtle-speed traffic.

Back around 1910, traffic wasn't a problem. Why, there wasn't even a car in Hillsville when, as best as anyone can tell, the shootout story started at a corn shucking at nearby Fancy Gap. Nineteen-year-old Wesley Edwards found a red ear of corn, and that entitled him to kiss a girl of his choice. But, as fate would have it, the girl he kissed was already dating another young man, William Thomas.

To trace it now, that smooch would be like a kiss of death. It would lead to a fistfight outside a church and then assault charges for Wesley Edwards and his brother, Sidna Edwards. Their uncle, Floyd Allen, stepped in, but he soon found himself under arrest for interfering with the law as deputies tried to lock up his nephews.

About a year later, Allen's long-delayed trial arrived in March 1912. And it promised to be a spectacle of intense local drama. Allen, for one, swore that he would never go to jail. People all over Carroll County also knew that Allen—a fifty-five-year-old former law officer—was quite a tough guy. But they also knew there brewed a political war between the staunch Democrats of the Allen family and the Republicans who ran the county.

As many as three hundred people crowded into the courtroom. Many carried guns. Coming from nearby Pulaski County, Judge Thornton L. Massie didn't see much wrong with that—lots of people carried sidearms in those days.

Talk about a deadly mistake. Just seconds after Massie sentenced Allen to a year in jail, Allen replied, "I ain't a-goin'," and the shooting began. Who knows who fired first, but fifty-seven shots blasted in ninety seconds as the flying lead spread to the courthouse lawn. Both county officers and members of the Allen family fired weapons. Massie was killed. So were Sheriff Lewis Webb, Commonwealth's Attorney William Foster, juror Augustus Fowler and spectator Betty Ayers.

Now, talk about a great escape. Floyd Allen's gun-toting brother, J. Sidna, wound up as far away as Des Moines, Iowa, with the Allen brothers' nephew Wesley Edwards, the young man who stole the kiss and, seemingly, started it all. Finally, about six months after the shooting, detectives caught the runaways, and they were sentenced to lengthy jail terms. Floyd Allen and his son Claude were executed in 1913 for their roles in the shooting.

The old Carroll County Courthouse in Hillsville was the site of a shooting on March 14, 1912. *Author photo.*

The tragedy of the day never really went away. It inspired books, songs and even a rock opera. A famous ballad, "Sidney Allen," tells a slightly fictionalized story of J. Sidna Allen and was recorded in 1924 by Henry Whitter, a guitarist and fiddler known for recording the songs "The Wreck of the Southern Old 97" as well as "New River Train."

HILLSVILLE: OLD CARROLL COUNTY COURTHOUSE

From the Blue Ridge Parkway at Meadows of Dan, follow U.S. 58 Business west for one mile. Turn left and continue west on U.S. 58 for 16.5 miles, passing Tory Creek (a refuge for Tories during the American Revolution), Laurel Fork (a stream named for wild laurel) and Crooked Oak (named for a bent and twisted oak tree). Take the exit to Hillsville/Dublin, and turn right on Danville Pike (U.S. 58-Business) and go 2.6 miles, as the road becomes East Stuart Drive. Turn north on U.S. 52 (Main Street) at Hillsville and go 0.2 miles to the Old Carroll County Courthouse, 515 North Main Street, on the right.

38

CAPITAL ON THE CROOKED ROAD

Galax

C orwin Matthews took his guitar for a ride on the "New River Train" on a Friday night at the old Galax High School. Matthews performed that folk song as part of the first Old Fiddlers Convention, organized by the Galax Moose Lodge #733 in 1935.

The competition proved so popular, selling three hundred advance tickets, that another was held later that same year. And then came another, summer after summer, until the Old Fiddlers Convention grew into one of the world's largest gatherings of traditional string artists.

Onstage, fiddlers play for prizes during the second week of August at Galax's Felts Park. Night after night, practically all ages arrive, like a parade of pickers, carrying banjos, mandolins, dobros and guitars.

Offstage, musicians informally jam in campgrounds and parking lots. It's a friendly scene. But for a while, the frolics of the Old Fiddlers Convention seemed more like that fiddlin' sound the devil made when he went down to Georgia: rough and marred by moonshine, fights and routine arrests. "At one time, they didn't have the police here," said banjo player Roger Sprung of Newtown, Connecticut. "And it was a little rough. It was wonderful. But it was rough—drinking and everything. Finally, for some reason…the police came in and cleaned the place up."

The now-cleansed convention has since become an exit on the Crooked Road, a 253-mile driving tour through Virginia. This snake-shaped path follows U.S. 58 and several secondary highways, linking the mountain music sites of Galax with the Blue Ridge Institute and Museum in Ferrum, Floyd

Musical roots runs deep along the Crooked Road: Virginia's Heritage Music Trail at Galax, the "World's Capital of Old-Time Mountain Music." *Author photo.*

Country Store in Floyd, Heartwood in Abingdon, the Birthplace of Country Music Museum in Bristol, Carter Fold in Hiltons, Country Cabin in Norton and the Ralph Stanley Museum in Clintwood.

The Crooked Road originated in 2002. The late Joe Wilson, a music historian, coined the phrase. Wilson also suggested his words may have had several origins. "The Crooked Road" captured what Wilson called "the mighty sweet sound of the little, country, two-lane, twisty road." That could specifically reference U.S. 58, Wilson once said, noting that the route was often called the "Crooked Road" on the stretch between Damascus and Volney. This term is also sometimes used for fiddle tunes with a non-recurring part. "Those are called 'crooked tunes,'" Wilson said. "And sometimes people say, 'I'm going to take *the crooked road* on the fiddle tune.'"

Consider Galax the capital on the Crooked Road. It claims to be the "World's Capital of Old-Time Mountain Music." The city hosts Friday night old-time and bluegrass music shows at the Rex Theater, a renovated 1939 movie house on Grayson Street. More music can be heard during the summer at Galax's Blue Ridge Music Center, just off the Blue Ridge Parkway.

Some say, even, that there are more old-time fiddlers, banjo pickers, guitarists, mandolin players and dulcimer strummers surrounding Galax than any other place in the world. On August 4, 2015, attendees of the Old Fiddlers Convention sought to prove such a statement by having more than 490 mandolin players perform at the same time in an attempt to set a new world record.

Galax took its name from the heart-shaped galax leaf, among the first cargo shipped by rail on what became known to musicians as the "New River Train." The local railroad inspired that song, but the actual tune dates as early as 1895, years before the tracks reached Galax. That abandoned Norfolk Southern line has since evolved into the New River Trail State Park, a recreation path that borders the New River for thirty-nine of the trail's fifty-seven miles.

Galax: The Crooked Road and New River Trail State Park

From the U.S. 52 junction at Hillsville, follow West Stuart Drive (old U.S. 58) west for 1.2 miles to rejoin U.S. 58. Then continue following U.S. 58 west for 11.3 miles, passing the Harmon Museum, featuring local history displays, at Woodlawn (named for an early settler, Colonel James Wood). The New River Trail State Park in Galax lies on the right at Chestnut Creek (about 10.0 miles west of I-77) at a red caboose. From here, the rail trail runs 2.2 miles north to reach the park's Cliffview Ranger Station, located along VA-721. The New River Trail is open to hiking and biking. You can also ride horses—north of Cliffview (but not between Galax and Cliffview)—to the trail's terminus near Pulaski. The trail includes another access near Galax at Chestnut Yard, off VA-607, in Carroll County. Follow the trail south from this point for about one mile to see an overlook at the ten-foot-high Chestnut Creek Falls.

Near the trailhead parking in Galax, turn south on VA-89 to reach sites along the Crooked Road. Look for Felts Park along Main Street and the Rex Theater, 113 Grayson Street, both in the downtown district. From here, continue south on VA-89 for 7.0 miles to the Blue Ridge Parkway. Then turn north and go 2.0 miles to the Blue Ridge Music Center entrance, near mile 213. The center features a large amphitheater, museum exhibits and live performances of traditional mountain music.

39

THE DAM PLAN

New River

If you liked the idea of building a couple dams in Grayson County, people called you a "beaver." If you wanted to keep the "New River Like It Is," you might have been labeled an "elitist."

Such was the scene of the New River controversy, a struggle of poor farmers, politicians and a power company. The dam plan attracted national attention, endless editorials, artistic statements and even a radio message from Earl Hamner Jr., creator of the television show *The Waltons*. The controversy also flooded into a series of appeals and arguments that meandered through time like the river itself.

The New River had already been dammed in Virginia long before the New River controversy began in 1962. By 1903, Colonel Francis Henry Fries had washed Bartlett's Falls off the maps of Grayson County when he built a thirty-nine-foot-high dam to power his textile mill.

The colonel's factory town of Fries—called "freeze" (the correct pronunciation) in the winter and jokingly pronounced "frys" in summer—employed thousands over eight decades. But the Fries Dam also encouraged further ideas on how to harness the river.

Just downstream from Fries, the newly formed Appalachian Power Company constructed dams on the New River at Byllesby and Buck in 1912–13 and, in so doing, put the site of a prosperous resort, Grayson Sulphur Springs, underwater. In 1939, the company built the much bigger Claytor Dam in Pulaski County and submerged twenty-one miles of riverbed, this time flooding the oldest settlement west of the New River, the circa 1744 Dunkard's Bottom.

Next came plans for the biggest dam yet: Appalachian Power's Blue Ridge Project. It would squeeze more power from the New River to generate electricity. And it would form two lakes, flooding about twenty thousand acres, making the flat water above the Fries Dam look like a backyard pond.

The New River gets its start in North Carolina's High Country. It waddles across the Virginia–North Carolina border, zigzagging for a few miles before finally setting its backward course, uniquely running south to north and then west. Downstream of Claytor Dam, the river wraps around Radford University, fumbles over the falls of McCoy and finally joins the Gauley River to form the Kanawha River in West Virginia.

Appalachian Power planned to cage the river right above that Virginia-Carolina zigzag by building two dams in southern Grayson County. By 1968, however, the initial plan doubled, taking a suggestion by the Department of the Interior, which wanted the waters of the New to flush out the industrial wastes of West Virginia that lay downstream.

This bigger plan would flood about twenty-six thousand acres in Grayson County and about fourteen thousand acres in North Carolina, mostly in Ashe County. The sheer size of the two lakes would nearly rival the twin-lake scene of Lake Gaston and Buggs Island Lake, also on the Virginia–North Carolina border. The New River lakes also promised the same big-time recreation and development, with marinas, beaches, dozens of islands, a state park in Virginia and another in North Carolina.

Some politicians liked the idea of opening the sparsely populated Appalachian Mountains to this opportunity. A few "beavers" saw riches in building the dams and later collecting the big bucks tourists would leave behind.

Still others opposed the great walls of water. These lakes would destroy two-hundred-year-old farms and displace nearly three thousand people. In Grayson County, the water would completely swallow Mouth of Wilson and bury a big part of Baywood. It would flood forever about forty-four miles of the main river channel, more than twice the length of Claytor Lake.

There were court cases. There were debates. More than one hundred newspapers turned in editorials against the project, and Hamner was heard on radio stations saying, "Please think twice before you destroy the New River."

In Ashe County, about three thousand people against the project gathered at the Festival for the New River on July 26, 1975. This event celebrated the river's beauty and history, with singers and artists performing for the attendants. But it might have also seemed like a funeral. By then, the Federal Power Commission had already issued a license to build the dams, and much land had been acquired for the flood zone.

A giant lake was once slated to flood this section of the New River at Baywood, just off U.S. 58. *Author photo.*

Some landowners refused to sell. They vowed to fight forever; they wore their anti-dam slogan, "New River Like It Is," on T-shirts and displayed it on their cars with bumper stickers. In turn, the power company launched a national advertising campaign to promote the dam, calling its opponents "elitists." But many of these opponents simply were farming families who had lived along the river for generations, and not knowing when the lake would be built, they had put their lives on hold.

As it turned out, the lake was never built. In 1976, Congress passed a bill that designated a twenty-six-and-a-half-mile section of the New River in North Carolina a National Wild and Scenic River. This action essentially revoked the company's license to build the dams in Grayson County. President Gerald Ford signed the bill into law on September 11, 1976, and one of the strongest opponents of the dams, North Carolina governor James E. Holshouser, presented a certificate naming Ford an "Admiral of the New River Navy."

An old-age claim helped persuade politicians to save the New River. Scientists had said the New River was actually the "Old River," predating the surrounding Appalachian Mountains, and that's why it flows backward. The "New" moniker likely came from the way mapmakers once called Virginia the "New World," and what lay beyond the Blue Ridge Mountains, including this river, was called "New Virginia."

Today, the New River retains its curvy figure along its Carolina-Virginia zigzag. Still wild and scenic, its waters slide and fall, meandering through time.

BAYWOOD: NEW RIVER

From the New River Trail State Park at VA-89 in Galax, continue west on U.S. 58 for 8.0 miles to the New River bridge and public river access at Baywood, on the right. This area would have been flooded under plans of the Blue Ridge Project. (A float downstream from Baywood leads 8.0 miles to a public landing at Riverside, with a journey through Class I–II rapids. The Riverside takeout lies off VA-274, about 7.5 miles north of U.S. 58.)

The Baywood area was once called Hampton Cross Roads or Hampton Valley for circa 1830s settlers Griggs and Phyllis Sutherland Hampton. It took its present name, tradition says, when it was named for the bay tree by late 1800s resident Arch Moore.

40

PEACH BOTTOM FALLS

Independence

E ven when it was privately owned, folks still made treks to Peach Bottom Falls at Independence. Maybe that was trespassing. But the landowner simply let people go swim and slide anyway. As with any good waterfall, property owners couldn't keep the curious away. So, in 2004, it seemed to make sense when the Grayson County Board of Supervisors bought the beautiful collection of cascades for $90,000 and established a public park.

Size-wise, with a total drop of one hundred feet, Peach Bottom ranks somewhere among the tallest of Virginia's hundreds of waterfalls. In the 1780s, Matthew Dickey operated Point Hope Furnace at this natural landmark. Dickey harnessed the waterfall's power, forged tools from locally mined iron ore and shipped his wares west on the Holston River, far beyond Independence.

Peach Bottom Falls briefly became "Powerhouse Falls" in the early 1900s. Garnett Davis used the waterfall to turn a mill at his wooden powerhouse. That mill, in turn, supplied electrical power for a few hours a day to the people of Independence.

This town's name remembers an independent group of citizens who refused to take sides during a fight to move the county courthouse. Ultimately, the courthouse moved to this group's neighborhood in 1850. More than a century later, the townsfolk rallied to save the old courthouse of Independence—a brick landmark built in 1908, with conical towers pointing to the sky. This majestic structure faced destruction in 1981 following the construction of the modern Grayson County courthouse. Residents opposed

The Grayson County Board of Supervisors paid $90,000 for the Peach Bottom Falls and surrounding land near Independence. *Author photo.*

The Grayson County Board of Supervisors auctioned off the old county courthouse for $110,000 at the center of Independence. *Author photo.*

tearing down the old building, so the county government simply put it up for auction. Local businessman Dan Baldwin bought it for $110,000 in 1985 and later donated the courthouse to a nonprofit foundation. The old courthouse became a community center while an old courtroom was turned into a two-hundred-seat auditorium bearing Baldwin's name.

Truly, the town of Independence is a patriotic place. Thomas Jefferson, for one, would love it—the local newspaper is called the *Declaration* (of Independence). And one of the town's biggest parties of the year happens on the Fourth of July.

INDEPENDENCE: PEACH BOTTOM FALLS AND 1908 GRAYSON COUNTY COURTHOUSE

From the New River bridge at Baywood, continue west on U.S. 58 for 5.5 miles to Route 1124 at Independence. Turn right and go 0.5 miles, then turn right on VA-685 (Powerhouse Road) and go 0.9 miles to Peach Bottom Falls, on the left, at Peach Bottom Creek (named for the peach orchards of early settlers). A short trail leads to the waterfall. The powerhouse no longer stands, but stone foundations of the mill remain attached to the creek's rocky slopes. From here, retrace the route to U.S. 58. Turn right and go 0.9 miles to the 1908 Grayson County Courthouse, 107 East Main Street, at U.S. 21. This brick landmark contains a museum with exhibits of local history, a gift shop and an auditorium that often features live bluegrass music.

The courthouse also serves as a backdrop for the town's Mountain Foliage Festival, held on the second Saturday of each October. This annual event includes the comical Grand Privy Race, in which townsfolk put outhouses on wheels and roll them down public streets.

41

WILD PONIES

Grayson Highlands State Park

In 1976, the president of the Wilburn Ridge Pony Association made a prediction to a local newspaper, saying sales of a small herd of feral ponies living near Mount Rogers would one day "put Chincoteague Island and its pony auction off the map."

Whoa! Talk about an aspiration—Chincoteague Island's famous pony auction dates back to 1925. Each year, thousands show up to bid and also watch about 150 wild ponies swim from the marshy forest of Assateague Island to suburban Chincoteague Island on Virginia's Eastern Shore.

The rock-hopping horses of Virginia's High Country, however, live in an inverse environment. At elevations reaching five thousand feet, about 125 ponies tromp among the topsy-turvy terrain of Wilburn Ridge, where rocks form stairways to heavenly views.

It snows often in this windblown portion of Grayson County. But the Grayson Highlands ponies possess thick and beautiful manes—woolly like a bear's, flopping over their faces—practically perfect for withstanding winters of subfreezing temperatures. Still, these playful ponies look for warmth where they can find it, sometimes turning the area's Appalachian Trail shelters into stables.

About twenty-five Shetland ponies arrived in the Mount Rogers National Recreation Area in 1974 to clear brush from the area's balds. Prior to the ponies, Forest Service officials had trotted out similar experiments with other animals. But the winters turned too harsh for cattle, too cold for goats and too barren for sheep—they munched on mountain laurel instead of spring grass and dropped dead.

Wild ponies roam among the rocks at Grayson Highlands State Park and the adjacent Mount Rogers National Recreation Area. *Author photo.*

The wild ponies have thrived near Mount Rogers. They have done so well that excess numbers, like those of the Chincoteague ponies, are auctioned annually to keep herd numbers low. Park officials round up wild-running mares and stallions from behind rocks and brush for an annual health inspection. Then, though the event is not as famous as the Chincoteague auction, a few yearlings are sold each September during the fall festival at Grayson Highlands State Park. The ponies fetch about $100 to $500 each, and the proceeds help pay for the veterinary care of the remaining herd.

Some environmentalists, meanwhile, have complained about the presence of the ponies, saying the animals might be invasive to the Mount Rogers area's fragile subalpine environment. The ponies, in turn, are locked out of certain places, including the Lewis Fork Wilderness Area, home of the actual summit of mile-high Mount Rogers.

GRAYSON COUNTY:
GRAYSON HIGHLANDS STATE PARK

From U.S. 21 at the 1908 Grayson County Courthouse, continue west for 24.5 miles, as U.S. 58 threads its way through a curvy collection of inclines. Along the way, the route passes through Bridle Creek (named for an early settler who found the bridle of his horse on this creek after it had been stolen by a horse thief); Fox (named for an early hunter who lost track of a fox on what became Fox Creek); Mouth of Wilson (named for the mouth of Wilson Creek, which took its name from a state-line surveyor named Wilson who died from a stomach disorder); and Volney (named for Volney Hash, whose father, Elijah Hash, helped establish the local post office).

Turn right at the Grayson Highlands State Park entrance on VA-362 and follow the park road for about 4.0 miles to the Massie Gap parking area. From here, you can see Grayson Highlands ponies by following the Rhododendron Trail for about 2.0 miles to Wilburn Ridge. You can also follow the park road to the campground, where ponies sometimes stand in fields along the road. The 4,935-acre state park features a playground, a picnic area and a visitor center with trail maps and mountain heritage displays. Park trails lead to overlooks on outcrops as well as waterfalls on Cabin Creek and Wilson Creek.

42

VIRGINIA'S ROOFTOP

Mount Rogers

Curtains of moss hang heavy on nearly everything atop Mount Rogers, except for one well-known rock planted at the top, a God-given point for picnics. Looking up, the clouds are so close that it feels like only a short hop to Heaven.

Elevation: 5,729 feet above sea level.

This is Virginia's rooftop, an isolated island in the sky where fog rolls in on a whim and five feet of rain falls each year. Mount Rogers holds the claim of the tallest spot in Virginia, with Canadian-style woods supporting a sanctuary of ferns, firs and wood sorrel. An intricate plant, the wood sorrel appears similar to a shamrock and makes mystical Mount Rogers look like a land where leprechauns live.

How appropriate. Often, early settlers compared high, lonesome lands like this to their ancestral homes of Ireland, Scotland and Germany. These transplanted Europeans brought time-honored traditions of religion, food and song to the Virginia Highlands, and their fiddle tunes blended beautifully with the shrill of songbirds and babbling brooks, the natural music of the mountains.

Such mountain music inspired Albert Hash for fifty-five years. And, through his legacy, that inspiration continues. A grandson of a medicine-show fiddler and a descendant of early settlers, Hash was born near the foot of Mount Rogers in 1917. He played fiddle and made fiddles. He also taught his craft to many Mount Rogers musicians, including world-renowned guitarist and guitar-maker Wayne Henderson. Just a year before he died, the

Snow falls outside the arched entrance to Mount Rogers School, a longtime landmark used for pancake suppers during the Whitetop Maple Festival, held each spring. *Author photo.*

affable Hash expanded his music lessons in 1982 to his alma mater, the tiny Mount Rogers School in Grayson County along U.S. 58.

Both handsome and charming and built from stones in the 1930s, the Mount Rogers School welcomed kindergartners to high school seniors from the Great Depression to the Great Recession. Children here would also enthusiastically strum banjos, dulcimers and guitars, while faraway suburban students blew into saxophones, trombones and trumpets. A violin at Mount Rogers School was always called a fiddle. The school band repertoire, like picking "Wildwood Flower," would overlap with family tradition. Students at Mount Rogers School said they had no interest in a horn-blowing band; mountain music suited them just fine.

Yet then came consolidation—even in the island-like isolation of mountainous Grayson County. Mount Rogers School closed in 2010 and was left standing, but that meant displacing the Albert Hash Memorial Band to other locations as students moved to schools at Troutdale and Independence.

Mount Rogers School and the summit of Mount Rogers are both named for William Barton Rogers, the state's first geologist. In 1835, Rogers began

Moss hangs on nearly everything along the trail to Mount Rogers, the highest peak in Virginia. *Author photo.*

an exhaustive geologic survey of Virginia. His crew's ambition, however, went unfulfilled—the Virginia General Assembly cut funding for the study in 1842. Rogers later founded the Massachusetts Institute of Technology. In 1882, he collapsed in mid-speech while delivering that school's commencement address. He said his final words—"bituminous coal"—and died at the podium.

Earlier, Mount Rogers was called "Balsam Mountain" for its native balsams, trees now referred to as Fraser firs. The peak marks the northernmost natural range of the Southern Appalachian spruce-fir.

The Appalachian Trail rings the mountain, but thru-hikers often bypass the half-mile spur leading atop, saying they've heard there is no view. Truly, there is none, at least in the way of seeing far into a valley. But in the early 1970s, thru-hikers had no choice. The AT ran right across the top of the peak. Then, in 1975, longtime trail volunteers David and Nerine Thomas rerouted the hiking path following a Forest Service request to protect the mountain's rare plants from being trampled.

Later, in 1991, David Thomas became a Mount Rogers legend for trucking logs by bulldozer along the Lewis Fork, four miles from any road. His volunteer crew built an Appalachian Trail shelter—and quick. Thomas said, "The day we finished that shelter, they were lined up there to spend the night—a group of boy scouts. There were twenty-five waiting for us to nail down the floor."

To Thomas's surprise, Mount Rogers National Recreation Area officials later named the hut "Thomas Knob Shelter." It sits about one mile above sea level, less than one mile down the trail from the summit of Mount Rogers.

GRAYSON COUNTY:
MOUNT ROGERS AND MOUNT ROGERS SCHOOL

A moderate hike reaches the actual summit of Mount Rogers from Massie Gap at Grayson Highlands State Park. Follow the park's Rhododendron Trail to the Appalachian Trail, reaching Wilburn Ridge in about two miles, and go another two miles (passing through a rock passage called the "Fat-Man Squeeze Tunnel") to a sign marking the half-mile Mount Rogers spur, just beyond the Thomas Knob Shelter.

Wilburn Ridge takes its name from Wilburn Waters, a legendary local hunter in the 1800s. One story says Waters once captured an enormous wolf, tied it up and attempted to take it home alive.

You can also reach Mount Rogers from Elk Garden (an area named for once being inhabited by wild elk). To get there from Grayson Highlands State Park, follow U.S. 58 west for 3.7 miles to Mount Rogers School, on the left, and then continue on U.S. 58 for another 3.9 miles (7.6 miles west of Grayson Highlands State Park). Turn right on VA-600 at the Whitetop Post Office. Go 2.7 miles north to Elk Garden at the Appalachian Trail parking lot. From here, follow the Appalachian Trail north for four miles to the Mount Rogers spur. (The Appalachian Trail is marked by vertical, two-by-six-inch white paint blazes. A double blaze—one above the other—is placed before turns or junctions.)

43

ELEANOR ROOSEVELT WAS HERE

Whitetop Mountain

When Eleanor Roosevelt walked atop Whitetop Mountain on August 12, 1933, as many as twenty thousand people turned out to see her. Some stood by roadsides, waving, while others stood beside overheated vehicles, stranded on the side of the road. It was the most celebrated moment during all of the Whitetop Folk Festivals in the 1930s. And, as a way to roll out the red carpet, the road ascending the 5,520-foot-high peak was widened so the first lady could arrive in a luxury sedan.

The Whitetop Folk Festival had been going on for a couple years as a contest of old-time mountain musicians, overseen by Abingdon attorney John Blakemore, Annabel Morris Buchanan of nearby Marion and John Powell, a classical composer. Each August, players vied for ten-dollar prizes, a precious reward during the Great Depression.

Their stage could not have been more grand: a dance hall and big rows of tents stood on the grassy carpet of Whitetop's prairie, a field that looks white at a distance. Some guess this mountaintop bald could have been caused by Cherokees burning off trees to attract deer to an open area. A legend says the Cherokee once used this space for signal fires.

Eleanor Roosevelt considered Whitetop Mountain and the nearby community of Abingdon part of the puzzle of her youth. This is where her father, Elliott Roosevelt, spent two years of his life and communicated with his long-distance daughter through a series of letters, calling her "Little Nell."

A handsome hunter and sportsman, Elliott Roosevelt had shown up in Abingdon in 1892. Warm, inviting and everywhere the life of the party, Roosevelt said he came to the Virginia Highlands to look after the Whitetop Mountain timber interests owned by his sister Corinne and her husband, Douglas Robinson. Roosevelt also sought renewed health from shattered nerves.

First Lady Eleanor Roosevelt visited Whitetop Mountain's music festival on August 12, 1933. *Courtesy the National Archives.*

The truth was, the other well-heeled Roosevelts of New York had exiled Elliott for his drinking. Often, he had turned violent and mortified his wife and Eleanor's mother, Anna, who said she didn't want him back until he had proven his sobriety. So off he went to Virginia, away from his wife, away from Little Nell and away from the political spotlight that shined ever so brightly on his brother—and future president—Teddy Roosevelt.

On the hunt, Elliott Roosevelt rounded the Virginia hills with his dogs and horses; sometimes he stopped at farms, asking for pitchers of buttermilk. Roosevelt rewarded five-dollar pieces to whoever quenched his thirst. He also rewarded hungry families at Christmas, distributing hundreds of turkeys that he had bought from local farmers.

Roosevelt, too, enjoyed horseplay. During one particularly snowy winter, he rallied in the streets of

Abingdon for everyone young and old to come out and go sledding. He even ripped down fences for people to use sleds.

But Roosevelt's life took a real slide. His wife, Anna, died of diptheria at age twenty-nine. His namesake son, Elliott Jr., died a few months later. By the summer of 1894, Roosevelt had returned to New York. He was drinking again. Then, in August, he was dead at age thirty-four after falling down a flight of stairs. Little Nell was only ten.

Growing up an orphan, Eleanor Roosevelt always wondered about the years she missed with her father. In 1915, she married a distant cousin, Franklin Delano Roosevelt, and in 1932, she found herself on the way to the White House. The following spring, Eleanor contacted Buchanan and made arrangements to attend the Whitetop Folk Festival.

Little Nell wanted to see her father's old stomping grounds and meet some of his old friends.

Her train from Washington, D.C., arrived in Abingdon at 10:00 a.m., greeting a large crowd. Mayor Ray B. Hagy delivered a speech and was probably nervous, using notes he had placed inside his straw hat. Washington County sheriff Keys Boardwine then led the long charge uphill to Whitetop, driving Eleanor in a borrowed Lincoln for more than thirty-five miles.

A 1930s-era postcard displays rock outcrops providing sweeping views of Virginia, Tennessee and North Carolina from atop Whitetop Mountain. *Courtesy George Stone.*

143

Cars travel atop Whitetop Mountain, circa 1930, on a meadow of grass. This peak was earlier known as "Meadow Mountain." *Courtesy Virginia Tech.*

Musicians atop the mountain met the first lady with mutual admiration. They sang "Happy Days Are Here Again," and she smiled. "To the people who live here," Eleanor told the crowd, "I want to say a special word of gratitude. They have given me the feeling that they remember affectionately my father, whom I adore."

Eleanor ate fried chicken and Virginia ham. And she was framed by a swarm of cameramen, including one newspaper photographer from Washington, D.C., who ventured too far on an overhanging ledge to get a better shot. "He slipped and fell," John Blakemore told a newspaper reporter years later, "but by grabbing a tree limb saved himself from crashing into a 200-foot abutment."

By the afternoon, the first lady left the mountain with flowers and gifts. Just before nightfall, she boarded the train at Abingdon and was whisked away to Washington. The original Whitetop Folk Festival continued for a few more years after Eleanor was here but never past 1940, when heavy rains temporarily washed out the road ascending the peak.

Now Whitetop Mountain slumbers in silence, draped in winter with blankets of ice and snow. The old Whitetop Dance Hall used during the festivals has since been torn down; parts were salvaged to build the nearby Mount Rogers Fire Hall. But, in August, you can walk Whitetop's ageless bald, find wildflowers and soak up its vast and gorgeous view—warm and inviting, just like that day when Eleanor Roosevelt was here.

WHITETOP: WHITETOP MOUNTAIN

From Mount Rogers School at VA-751, follow U.S. 58 for 3.9 miles to the Whitetop Post Office. Turn right on VA-600 and go north for 1.5 miles. Turn left on USFS-89 and go 3.0 miles to reach the top of the mountain. Whitetop's gravel forest road makes wide-swinging switchbacks in the meadow atop the mountain. Here, the Appalachian Trail crosses the road. Following the trail south from this point leads 1.0 mile downhill to Buzzard Rock, an outcrop that overlooks North Carolina, Virginia and Tennessee.

The road on Whitetop Mountain provides wide-ranging views of seemingly endless peaks and valleys. One spur leads to a circular drive; another ends at a set of radio towers. Car radios, by the way, are able to receive an amazing number of stations up here, with a voice or tune heard at nearly every dot on the dial from distant cities.

44

CREEPER COUNTRY

Green Cove

O. Winston Link loved steamy sights, especially a puffy plume curling into clouds above a steam locomotive. But in the late 1950s, the New York photographer had to race against time to lasso such snorting iron horses. Steam trains were slated for extinction on the Norfolk and Western Railway; they would soon be replaced by diesel engines.

So Link packed cameras in his convertible and captured all he could. He wandered beside an old logging line, the Abingdon Branch of the Norfolk and Western Railway, and shot one of his most famous frames, "Old Maud Bows to the Virginia Creeper," at the Green Cove Depot, using one camera loaded with color film and another with black and white.

Standing since 1914, the Green Cove Depot was built when the Abingdon Branch was still called the Virginia-Carolina Railway. Thousands of men once cut wood along its attached arms of narrow gauge lines, reaching far into ancient Appalachian forests of poplar and chestnut. In the early 1900s, this mountain scene was like a gold rush, and a few prospectors raped the ridges for any virgin timber an axe could find. Some left entire mountainsides barren, studded by stumps and worth no more than practically acorns on the acre.

After more than twenty years, operations in the lumber town of Konnarock sawed out on Christmas Eve 1928. Large-scale logging was over, and much of the surrounding land later became part of a national forest, with hopes that, someday, riches would return.

With or without a load of logs, trains slowly kept chugging on the steep grades of the railroad, rumbling over trestles and rambling past campsites

Creek Junction boasts two long trestles on the Virginia Creeper Trail, between Green Cove and Taylors Valley. *Author photo.*

used by Daniel Boone in the 1700s. At its height, the line spanned seventy-six miles, linking Abingdon, Virginia, to Elkland, North Carolina.

In between stood Green Cove, the place where Link shot "Old Maud Bows to the Virginia Creeper" in 1956. This photo artistically states the passing of two endangered eras with a scene of a big white horse bowing to the snort of a steam locomotive. Recalling in 1995 that he "had this horse set up," Link said that his railroad photographs worked well, generally, because he carefully placed props with the cooperation of train officials. In this case, the horse named "Old Maud" belonged to a local family and probably acted naturally; it's been said that she had a habit of holding her head down in a bowing position.

The Green Cove Depot belonged to William M. Buchanan, a schoolteacher turned station manager known best as "Mr. Buck." Buchanan bought the wooden one-story and used it for a general store, thereby saving it from destruction when all trains—even the diesel engines—stopped running on the Abingdon Branch on March 31, 1977.

Even without the lure of steam and steel, Link returned to Green Cove. In 1984, he stood behind the weighing scales of the old depot and married

A stone marker outside Green Cove Depot depicts a likeness of O. Winston Link's famous 1956 photograph "Old Maud Bows to the Virginia Creeper." *Author photo.*

his second wife, Conchita, a dark-haired woman who was more than twenty years his junior. Not a decade later, this marriage derailed. The couple divorced, and Conchita was later sent to prison when she was convicted of stealing 1,400 of Link's photographs and attempting to sell them.

Along the way, a thirty-four-mile section of the old railroad became the Virginia Creeper Trail by the late 1980s with major stops at Abingdon, Watauga, Alvarado, Damascus, Green Cove and Whitetop. In 2008, it was named a major component of Virginia's Beaches to Bluegrass Trail. The multipurpose path uses the nickname for the Virginia-Carolina Railway. Some say "Virginia Creeper" comes from the steam train's slow creep uphill. Others swear it stems from the Virginia creeper vines lining lush jungles, sprawling over once-naked slopes in the national forest.

Casual cyclists coast through the rich woods of the Creeper country, following downhill from a life-size replica of the original Whitetop Station to the Green Cove Depot. Diehard cyclists, like Lawrence Dye, make tracks both ways, even the uphill trudge.

In 2005, the seventy-three-year-old Dye became a legend on the Virginia Creeper Trail after registering 100,000 miles of round-trips, relentlessly cycling in sunshine or snow. Once a schoolteacher like William M. Buchanan, Dye loved Green Cove just as much as Link. And he became predictable like a train. Dye once rode the trail for sixty-six miles a day, on a round-trip, five

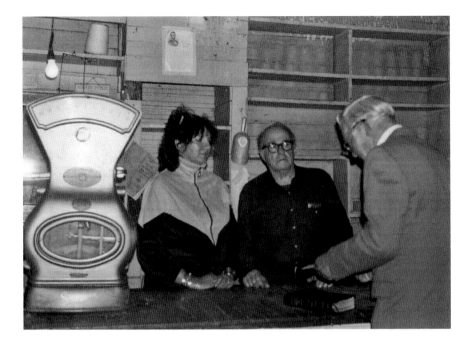

Above: Railroad photographer O. Winston Link, center, returned to Green Cove Depot in 1984 to marry his second wife, Conchita. *Courtesy Jim and Annette Goode.*

Right: Train tracks on what is now the Virginia Creeper Trail run along the dirt path of U.S. 58 in this 1949 scene at Damascus. The road sign, at left, warns, "Route 58 not recommended for through traffic." *Courtesy Virginia Department of Transportation.*

days a week. For years, too, Dye made daily stops at the Green Cove Depot, stopping to refuel himself with peanut butter and apple butter sandwiches. Then, bowing his head like Old Maud, he would pedal back down that rail-to-trail road to Damascus.

GREEN COVE: VIRGINIA CREEPER TRAIL

From Whitetop to Damascus, U.S. 58 rolls through the scenic Mount Rogers National Recreation Area—on the Mount Rogers Scenic Byway—like a roller coaster, twisting and turning but nearly always keeping the Virginia Creeper Trail in sight. To reach the Whitetop Station from the Whitetop Post Office at VA-600, follow U.S. 58 for 1.0 mile to a left turn at VA-754 and go 2.0 miles to the station, on the left, at VA-726. Then return to U.S. 58, turn left and go west for 2.5 miles. Turn left on VA-600 and go 0.4 miles to Green Cove Depot. Then return again to U.S. 58, turn left and go west for 5.2 miles to the Virginia Creeper Trail's Creek Junction Area, on the left, with handicapped-accessible fishing piers on Whitetop Laurel Creek.

Beyond Creek Junction, go another 6.0 miles west on U.S. 58—passing Beartree Recreation Area (with a campground, fishing lake and swimming beach) and the roadside waterfalls of the Straight Branch—to reach the Virginia Creeper Trail's Straight Branch parking lot, on the left.

The Straight Branch area affords access to Whitetop Laurel Creek. Turn right at the parking area and walk west for almost 1.0 mile to find Whitetop Laurel Falls, a 10.0-foot-high cascade that tumbles about twenty yards below the trail's Trestle No. 21. You can also easily reach the "Creeper Pool" from this parking lot. Simply turn left and walk east for 0.25 miles. Cross Trestle No. 22. Then turn right on an informal path leading to this natural swimming hole, bordered by large rocks and a sandy beach.

From Straight Branch, U.S. 58 runs west for 4.6 miles to the Damascus Town Park, where the Virginia Creeper Trail intersects the Appalachian Trail. West of the park, the Virginia Creeper Trail continues for about 16.0 miles to Abingdon, with other access points located near the South Fork of the Holston River bridge on VA-710 in Alvarado, along VA-677 in Watauga and along Green Spring Road in Abingdon.

45

HOLY GROUND FOR HIKERS

Damascus

From all over the world, people make tracks through Damascus—not by bus but by boot. These Appalachian Trail hikers start south at Springer Mountain, Georgia, and they will have walked hundreds of miles before reaching Damascus, where the world's longest continually marked footpath turns from moss to mortar, marching up Laurel Avenue on a brick sidewalk bordering U.S. 58.

There are no age limits. Some hikers are college kids calling themselves names like "Gypsy," and they'll tackle the 2,180-mile-long trail while looking for themselves, or maybe their next college major. Some are restless retirees, like the sixty-five-year-old mechanic who strapped on an outdated backpack and dubbed himself "65 and Alive."

Southern thru-hikers call this the "Ap-palatch-un Trail," while Northerners say "Appa-lay-shun." By many accounts, "Appalachian" is derived from the Appalachee Indian tribe discovered by the Spanish in the 1500s.

The Appalachian Trail grew from the dreams of Benton MacKaye, a forester who, in the 1920s, envisioned a footpath tracing the ridge crests of the Appalachian Mountains from Georgia to Maine.

Damascus adopted its biblical name in 1886, when Courtland, Virginia, was still called "Jerusalem." Confederate brigadier general John D. Imboden named Damascus, and he figured he would get rich from all the iron inside nearby Iron Mountain. Imboden formed the Damascus Enterprise Company with several partners, including brothers A.D. and R.J. Reynolds of Patrick County. But as it turned out, Iron Mountain was not so aptly

The Damascus Depot stood for much of the twentieth century along what is now the path of the Appalachian Trail at the Damascus Town Park. *Courtesy Virginia Tech.*

A sign notes the Place, a hostel for Appalachian Trail hikers in Damascus, just off U.S. 58. *Author photo.*

named, because the iron deposits were not enough to start a steel industry. Still, Imboden liked Damascus, and he spent his final years in town selling bottled spring water in the 1890s.

Inspired by the ancient Asian capital of Syria, the town's biblical name still fits. Damascus is holy ground for hikers, especially during Appalachian Trail Days in May, when thousands gather for what looks like a backwoods Mardi Gras. A tent city blossoms on the banks of Laurel Creek, and dozens crowd into the Place, a hostel that took its name from an unknown hiker who carved "This is the place" on some wood and left the sign at the hostel's back door.

Trail Days can grow crazy, especially during the Saturday afternoon Hiker Parade. This casual march down Laurel Avenue features a hodgepodge of colorful costumes, just like Mardi Gras. The long-popular water balloons have been outlawed, due to safety concerns. Yet hikers playfully still shoot squirt guns. Annually, it even seems all that flying water could be considered a baptism in the thru-hiking lifestyle: walk a week with no bath, never shave and sleep in trail shelters from Georgia to Maine.

DAMASCUS: APPALACHIAN TRAIL

The Appalachian Trail intersects U.S. 58 and runs down the sidewalks of Laurel Avenue to Damascus Town Park at the corner of West Laurel Avenue (U.S. 58) and South Beaverdam Avenue. The park includes a gazebo, a playground and a railroad caboose, where Forest Service officials distribute brochures on the Appalachian Trail and Mount Rogers National Recreation Area. The Place, 203 East Bank Avenue, stands behind the Damascus United Methodist Church, about a block off U.S. 58.

46

MARTHA GIRLS

Abingdon

B ill Clinton and Jimmy Carter checked in. So did Elizabeth Taylor. But the name that has won more fame than any other at the lavish Martha Washington Inn in Abingdon, Virginia, is not on the guest register. It is "Beth," the name of the college girl who haunts the four-star hotel on full-moon nights with her mysterious violin music.

Over several years, hotel guests and employees have reported feeling touched by spirits. And some have claimed to see the floating figure of a girl, often called "Beth," wearing what longtime hotel employee Pete Sheffey dubbed "an apron-type dress and high-buckle shoes."

Beth may have company. One story is told of a mysterious Civil War soldier hobbling down a hallway with a bloody leg or missing limb. Dates of this account have varied, but the ghostly soldier was reportedly seen by a policeman and left bloody marks on a floor before disappearing outside.

Yet another story of a stain dates to the Civil War. Legend says Union soldiers gunned down a young Confederate, and his blood stained the floor at the feet of his college-girl sweetheart. All attempts to remove the bloodstains were unsuccessful; the stains just kept reappearing. The marked floor, outside what is now the Governor's Suite, was eventually covered with carpet.

Conversely, some employees have worked at the Martha Washington Inn for years without even the most remote haunting encounter.

Blame the beginning, perhaps, on the "Martha Girls," the students of the Martha Washington College. For about seventy-five years, from the Civil War until the Great Depression, this school occupied the hotel

An eerie postcard of the early 1900s depicts the Martha Washington College—now the plush, elegant and allegedly haunted Martha Washington Inn of Abingdon. *Courtesy George Stone.*

buildings. The all-girl college students followed rigid rules that, likely, sparked great imaginations.

Boys from nearby Emory & Henry College could write notes to the Martha Girls, but the girls could reply only with the permission of the college president. The girls were not allowed to drink cherry Cokes, nor could they wave at train conductors.

"Dancing, privately or publically, while under College chaperonage, is not permitted," the student bylaws say. "There shall be no boisterous, disorderly or unladylike conduct within the buildings or on the campus at any time."

The Martha Girls could not keep their lights on past 10:30 p.m., nor could they turn them on again before 6:00 a.m. They were not allowed to tip the college's servants "for regular service rendered." And if they smoked, they got expelled.

Before it was a college, the central portion of the hotel was the family home of the wealthy General Francis Preston, who grew up at the Smithfield Plantation of Blacksburg, Virginia, and made a fortune selling salt that was extracted in nearby Saltville. As a twenty-seven-year-old attorney, Preston took a fourteen-year-old girl, Sarah Campbell, to be his bride in 1793. She came from good stock; her uncle was Patrick Henry, and her father was the late General William Campbell, who led the Overmountain Men to an American victory over the British at the Battle of King's Mountain in 1780.

Martha Washington College opened in 1860 inside the circa-1832 Preston mansion. Four years later, the first class graduated. That same year, Union troops marched through Abingdon and burned buildings during the Civil War.

"The Martha Girls" pose for a 1920s-era photograph at the old swimming pool on the Martha Washington College campus in Abingdon. *Courtesy Virginia Tech.*

About this time comes the story of Beth, a student nurse when the college became a wartime hospital. Beth cared for a wounded Union spy, but the man's condition only got worse. In his last breaths, he called out, "Play something, Beth. I'm going." And, with trembling fingers, she played her violin.

Today, some say, she is still playing that same melody as a musical ghost on the hotel's third floor.

Sheffey, for one, heard mysterious music in the hotel. But a guest who made a similar claim listened to a comic surprise—hotel employees discovered that this guest had actually been lodged next door to a concert violinist scheduled to play later that evening at Emory & Henry College.

ABINGDON: MARTHA WASHINGTON INN

From the Damascus Town Park, follow U.S. 58 west for 10.5 miles, crossing two forks of the Holston River (a watercourse named for Stephen Holstein, who took a canoe down its path in 1749). Reaching Abingdon, U.S. 58 overlaps I-81. Follow south for 2.0 miles to Exit 17. Turn right on Cummings Street, go 1.0 mile and turn right on U.S. 11 to reach the Martha Washington Inn, 150 West Main Street. The hotel sits at the center of Abingdon, a small town known for its art galleries and museums. Incorporated in 1778, Abingdon most likely takes its name from early settlers wanting to honor Martha Washington's ancestral home, England's Abingdon Parish.

47

BEANS FOR BARTER

Abingdon

Robert Porterfield provided miracles on Main Street. He turned Ernest Borgnine into more than a truck driver. He made Gregory Peck funny. He fostered the arts community of Abingdon, and he started the town's Virginia Highlands Festival. Porterfield also never stopped smiling when he told his Barter Theatre audiences, "If you like us, talk about us. If you don't, just keep your mouth shut."

Born in 1905 at Austinville, Virginia, Porterfield grew up in Saltville, a few miles northwest of Abingdon. Porterfield dreamed, at age ten, that he would become an actor. By the late 1920s, he was doing just that in New York. Then out of work during the Great Depression, he chose a change of scenery.

He came home to Virginia but stopped in Abingdon, tagging along with a ragtag bunch, hitchhiking into town. These twenty-two out-of-work actors were wild and hairy, especially unkempt for 1933, and certainly not a hand-in-glove fit with the white-gloved ladies of the genteel town. Why, some of the women in Porterfield's bunch even smoked!

But the clean-cut Porterfield could charm anyone, and he built a bridge in this small-town society by hauling his actors into an Abingdon church and showing how well they could sing "Rock of Ages."

Next, Porterfield got down to business. He announced that his transplanted troupe would be staging shows in Abingdon, and to get in, you could pay thirty-five cents or trade some victuals.

Call that crazy, but not here. Bartering had been a rule in Abingdon since the frontier times of the 1700s. And Porterfield's new Barter Theatre found farmers gladly forking over veggies to see a musical or comedy.

Barter's opening night on June 10, 1933, was hog wild. Somebody traded a pig to get in the door, and it was tied up outside, squealing like a barker.

Another time, a ticket taker squealed as a man tried to slip her a dead rattlesnake. That man promised, "Rattlers is good vittles."

Then came the guy with the cow. He milked it on Main Street but presented only enough milk to pay his own way. The ticket-taker asked the man about his wife's admission, to which the man replied, "Let 'er milk 'er own ticket."

And it went on like that, night after night. Turtles got loose in the lobby. A pig got loose on the street. One man handed over a calf but wouldn't give up its rope. The calf got loose in the theater, and show time was delayed for five minutes.

About 90 percent of theater patrons traded their way into shows with garden bounties during the Great Depression. Some earmarked ears of corn for admission. Some planted an extra row of beans for barter.

A local sheriff also helped the theater's 1930s production of *Mountain Ivy* when he staged a raid on nearby Whitetop Mountain and provided a moonshine still for the set. Still, there was a problem with the law—namely, the town jail. It was located in the basement of Barter Theatre's circa 1830s building on Main Street. Actors shared this brick landmark in the 1930s. Yet the inmates in the basement jail were at times so noisy that it was hard to hear the actors on the Barter Theatre stage.

But the crowds kept coming, and the theater's reputation grew, like the actors' waistlines and the Barter Theater's roster of stars: Elizabeth Wilson, Patricia Neal, Ned Beatty, Barry Corbin and Jerry Hardin.

In 1940, young Gregory Peck nabbed his first professional acting job at Barter Theatre. Yet Peck acted so serious that Porterfield made him practice loosening up. Peck was assigned to visit Porterfield's office each day and tell a funny anecdote. That exercise eventually relaxed Peck's nervous tension. The actor went on to star in acclaimed movies, playing attorney Atticus Finch in *To Kill a Mockingbird* and General Douglas MacArthur in *MacArthur*.

During World War II, the real-life MacArthur took center stage in the Pacific Theater while the Barter Theatre stage went dark. After the war, cash became common to pay for admission. The Barter Theatre reopened in 1946 and, that same year, won the State Theatre of Virginia title. Two years later, a 1948 show called *Papa Is All* featured a young Ernest Borgnine,

Robert Porterfield guided the Barter Theatre in Abingdon from its inception in 1933 until his death in 1971. Some say his ghostly spirit remains. *Courtesy George Stone.*

who first worked at the theater as a stagehand and truck driver. Porterfield discovered that Borgnine could act. Later, Borgnine starred in movies like *The Wild Bunch* and TV's *McHale's Navy.*

The personable Porterfield remained busy. During the 1950s, he renovated the three-story Adam Hickman House, standing a few blocks north of the Barter Theatre. Porterfield used one part of the 1857 structure to house actors; another portion became a restaurant dubbed "Chez Robert." Still, many did not understand that "Chez Robert" made a reference to French. So what should have been pronounced "Shay Ro-bear" was often—and mistakenly—called "Cheese Robert."

The Hickman house was nicknamed the "Cave Cottage" for the opening of a cave behind the house. This landmark boasts a sharp roofline with an icicle-shaped bargeboard. Porterfield leased the aging structure in 1971 to an artisans group, which opened the long-running Cave House Craft Shop. But this move, at 279 East Main Street, would be one of Porterfield's last acts.

Porterfield died in 1971. Still, the show went on at the Barter Theatre. Some say, too, that "Mr. P" never really left the Barter building. Actors claim the jovial founder has reappeared in Abingdon as a friendly ghost, often seen wearing a white dinner jacket or gray sweater, like he still beckons at the Barter, overseeing all.

But who knows what Porterfield would have thought of *Liquid Moon*, the most talked about stage show of 2003. This play, starring Elizabeth McKnight and Michael Poisson, won sensational headlines for its full-frontal nudity inside what was once a church—now a playhouse on Main Street called Barter Stage II.

Critics praised the thought-provoking dialogue of *Liquid Moon*. Clergy complained about the controversial content. Audiences showed up with curiosity. And the theater's artistic director, Richard Rose, simply stood on the stage and repeated Porterfield's immortal opening line: "If you like us, talk about us. If you don't, just keep your mouth shut."

ABINGDON: BARTER THEATRE

Barter Theatre, 133 West Main Street, stands across from the Martha Washington Inn (along what was once U.S. 58). Barter Stage II stands immediately north of the inn at Main Street's intersection with South Church Street. From here, retrace Main Street to Cummings Street. Turn left and go one mile to U.S. 58 (I-81) at exit 17.

48

AT THE MOONLITE

Abingdon

William Booker found himself in the spotlight of the Moonlite Theatre after trying to sneak through the gate without paying. Owner Walter Mays caught the twelve-year-old crouching in the backseat of a car but cut him a deal. Mays told Booker to pick up trash around the drive-in movie theater for four weeks.

That was 1970. By 1992, Mays was retired, and Booker owned the drive-in—he had fallen in love with all the nostalgia attached to the landmark Moonlite Theatre. It was a place where teenagers would pull up the hill to the make-out row. And the Moonlite sign lit up a show of neon stars, while opposite, flicks flickered on the sixty-seven-foot-tall screen.

Built by T.D. Fields, the Moonlite opened on June 9, 1949, showing *Down to Earth*, starring Rita Hayworth and Larry Parks. In the late 1950s, the Moonlite was one of more than four thousand drive-ins in the United States. By 2007, when the Moonlite was added to the state landmarks historic register, little more than four hundred remained in operation, less than a dozen in Virginia.

Mays once charged cable television with the demise of drive-ins. But rising real estate values could be the ticket. In growing suburbs, the acreage needed for a drive-in theater might be more profitable if the land were simply spliced and reedited as a scene for condominiums.

Then came the dawn of the digital age, a time when drive-in theaters like the Moonlite had to find $70,000—or more—to flip a switch on a more modern way of showing movies. The Moonlite did not make that move—at

The Moonlite Theatre opened in 1949 and was named a state historic landmark in 2007. *Author photo.*

least not initially. And many summer nights passed, in the dark, while the marquee read, "CLOSED FOR REPAIRS." Ultimately, in 2015, Booker put the Moonlite on the market—for $1.75 million.

In music, the Moonlite has been memorialized, with Rafe Van Hoy singing "At the Moonlite." A bluegrass band, the Blinky Moon Boys, named an entire album for the theater. Booker and the Moonlite staff, meanwhile, have affectionately memorialized Mays, saying the late theater owner could be moonlighting at the Moonlite—in spirit.

ABINGDON: MOONLITE THEATRE

From I-81 exit 17, go south on I-81 (U.S. 58) for 4.0 miles to I-81 Exit 13. Turn right at the ramp and go 0.1 miles on Spring Creek Road to the Lee Highway intersection. Turn left on U.S. 11/19 (the old route of U.S. 58) and go 0.5 miles south to the Moonlite Theatre, on the right. From here, retrace the route to I-81 exit 13.

49

FAKE LAKE

Bristol

Topographic maps say all this is supposed to be underwater: the ducks and the geese that splash into the shallow ponds, and the fox sedge sprouting in the swampy sanctuary. These are the Sugar Hollow wetlands, burrowed along Beaver Creek. Contour maps paint all of this blue, calling it "Beaver Creek Lake," immediately upstream from Beaver Creek Dam.

Those maps are wrong. Beaver Creek Lake is a fake. It's actually only a retention basin, a fort against flooding, guarded by an eighty-five-foot-high dam that looks like the natural hills of Bristol.

The dam forms the grassy centerpiece of Bristol's four-hundred-acre Sugar Hollow Park. In 1965, the Tennessee Valley Authority built the dam on land once belonging to the family of Margaret Brown Preston, the youngest sister of General Francis Preston, the original owner of what is now Abingdon's Martha Washington Inn. Margaret Preston married a cousin, Colonel John Preston, and lived part of the nineteenth century at Preston's Grove, a brick house standing on the northern edge of Sugar Hollow Park.

Low-lying land above the dam grows soggy in spring. Sometimes, when it rains, it looks like it has gone coastal. More than once, park personnel have fished picnic tables out of trees and lost lawn mowers in mud.

But they really had to work after 2002, when Bristol city leaders failed to meet a deadline to install a gas-extraction system at an old landfill a few miles from the park. Virginia's environmental regulators called foul on the failure but provided a choice for punishment: pay a fine, or create a project in the city to enhance the local environment.

Footbridges cross the wetlands of Sugar Hollow Park in Bristol at a site labeled on some maps as "Beaver Creek Lake." *Author photo.*

As it turned out, workers at Sugar Hollow Park would rake muck for months, building a bog, producing ponds and firming up a footbridge to stretch seven hundred feet above mud-crusted flats. This project made up for the mess at the landfill and created the Sugar Hollow wetlands, a swamp where the waters of Beaver Creek never fail to flow. The creek slips out of the fake lake and dives into the dam, rushing downstream to downtown Bristol.

BRISTOL: SUGAR HOLLOW PARK

From I-81 exit 13, go south on I-81 (U.S. 58) for 6.0 miles to I-81 exit 7. Turn right at the end of the ramp and follow Old Airport Road for 0.1 miles. Turn right on U.S. 11/19 (Lee Highway) and go north for 0.5 miles to Sugar Hollow Park, on the left. Continue on the entrance road for 0.2 miles to Preston's Grove (not open for visitors) on the right and the Beaver Creek Dam on the left. Follow the park road for another 0.5 miles to the Sugar Hollow wetlands parking area, on the left. The four-hundred-acre park includes trails, a campground, a picnic area and playgrounds. Beyond the wetlands, a fee-entry area leads to creek-side picnic shelters and a 0.5-mile-trail reaching the four-foot-high Beaver Creek Cascades. From here, retrace the route to I-81 exit 7.

50

BORDER BASH

Bristol

Virginia's southern border may look straight, but it's not. Slight variations make it dip to the south near Danville and then move slightly north before reaching Tennessee. Next, the border jogs up two miles and forms a crook in the line for another fifteen miles.

This big dent has become the Offset community of Tennessee's Sullivan and Johnson Counties. And no one knows for sure how that crook got there. But there's a legend that says a conniving woman gave surveyors some favors to alter the boundary. Another says surveyors were too drunk to draw a straight line. A third says iron ore deposits interfered with compass readings. Possibly, too, there was confusion in having four or more lines drawn over several years to separate the territories of Virginia and Tennessee.

Thomas Jefferson's father, Peter Jefferson, halted a survey crew marking about one hundred miles of the Virginia–North Carolina border in 1749. At a place Jefferson called "Steep Rock," the dividing line stopped on the border of present-day Tennessee.

Surveyor Dr. Thomas Walker tried to pick up where Jefferson left off. But Walker noted that Steep Rock in 1779 "could not be found, owing, we suppose to so much of the timber thereabout being since dead!"

Walker picked a new spot and headed west. So did Richard Henderson. But Henderson's line, surveyed for what was then North Carolina, did not match what Walker had completed for Virginia. Even so, both lines remained. And what lay between became a no-man's land, especially at the

The Offset lies just south of U.S. 58, immediately east of Bristol along the Virginia-Tennessee border. *Author map.*

Offset, where some settlers denied being citizens of any state to avoid taxes, the law and military service.

West of the Offset, along the state line, the city of Bristol was born with the arrival of the railroad in 1856. It was actually two cities—a Bristol in Virginia, another in Tennessee—with the state line running down a shared Main Street.

In 1881, at a time when Virginia's Bristol was then called "Goodson," leaders from Bristol, Tennessee, passed a resolution officially marking the state boundary at the center of Main Street. But not much later, hostility brewed on the border, largely over where companies could establish waterlines and exactly where the state line lay.

These disputes reached a boiling point during 1889 in what became known as Bristol's "Water Works War." An armed militia from Tennessee faced another from Virginia. Each stood on opposite sides of a water ditch in the middle of Main Street. Virginia officials had just arrested Sam King of Tennessee for trying to install a waterline in Virginia. Now Goodson town officials wanted to lay another waterline, and Tennessee officials planned to arrest them for trespassing into Tennessee.

At the brink of a showdown, Officer James Cox of Goodson caught his foot on a water pipe and fell into the muddy ditch. Sullivan County sheriff R.S. Cartwright also plopped into the mud. Then Cartwright laughed, seemingly at the absurdity of it all, and that laughter broke the day's tension.

The state line runs along State Street in Bristol, with Virginia on one side and Tennessee on the other. *Courtesy Tim Buchanan.*

The border bash was aborted. Still, the state line dispute remained, so Virginia and Tennessee took the matter to the Supreme Court to finally find out where they should be separated.

Much testimony was taken in the case, including a statement from an elderly woman who said she did not want the state line moved because that would put her home in Virginia, and she had always heard that the climate was milder in Tennessee.

The Supreme Court ultimately ruled on a compromise, saying a survey in 1802 had already properly marked the state line. Still, parts of that boundary were hard to find, so yet another survey had to be completed.

Bristol's Main Street became "State Street" in 1901 to match where the state line was officially placed—in the middle of the road. A few years later, a stunning show of unity arched above both Bristols: the landmark Bristol Sign, standing more than fifty feet tall and connecting the cities at State Street like a mammoth metallic handshake.

BRISTOL: STATE STREET

From I-81 exit 7, follow I-81 (U.S. 58) south for 6.0 miles to I-81 exit 1B. Then follow 2.5 miles into Bristol on Gate City Highway, which turns into West State Street, then State Street. The historic section of State Street lies east of the U.S. 11E (Commonwealth Avenue/Volunteer Parkway) intersection, reaching the Bristol Sign standing over the state line, at the railroad tracks. Erected in 1910 and moved to its present site in 1915, the sign is listed on historic landmark registers.

51

HANK'S LAST RIDE

Bristol

Nobody knows where Hank Williams died. And that apparently included Charles Carr, the chauffeur on Hank's last ride, as 1952 faded into 1953. Still, the mystery of Hank's final journey from Knoxville, Tennessee, to what should have been Canton, Ohio, has prompted people to pen songs, write books and even board a bus for hundreds of miles.

The trip began at Knoxville's Andrew Johnson Hotel on December 31, 1952. The eighteen-year-old Carr got the job of driving the country singer's Cadillac through wintry weather as Hank lay in the backseat, doped up from a doctor's medication. Hank had a New Year's Day show in Canton, and if he missed it, he paid a fine. So Carr sped the car north along U.S. 11W until he was stopped for speeding near Rutledge, Tennessee.

After that, Carr stopped for food—somewhere. And, somehow, Hank fans have come to think that he stopped at the Burger Bar in Bristol, Virginia. Carr asked Hank if he wanted something to eat or drink, and Hank said his final word—"No."

But that event couldn't have happened at the Burger Bar. At the time of Hank's last ride, the Burger Bar building housed the Bristol Cleaners & Furriers.

The site was called "Snack King Restaurant" in 1957. It had become the Burger Bar by 1967. Hank's Cadillac would have, at least, passed by this building while going north on U.S. 11/19 and crossing over U.S. 58. That does seem fitting. Hank's honky-tonk music had been inspired by the style of Jimmie Rodgers, a singer who made his first record in 1927 in Bristol, Tennessee, just a couple blocks east of the Burger Bar.

The Burger Bar has been a downtown landmark of Bristol since at least the 1950s. *Author photo.*

For Bristol, the biggest Hank hoopla happened in 1998, when thirty people stopped on a tour bus followed by a five-car caravan, all thinking this retro restaurant was where Hank had said his final word. Flying a banner that proclaimed "Hank Williams' Final Journey," these Hank fans inspected the Burger Bar while on a jaunt to Oak Hill, West Virginia, the town where the singer was pronounced dead on New Year's Day 1953.

Carr was not on that 1998 expedition. The Alabama businessman, who died in 2013, had then never retraced the path of Hank's last ride. But in 1999, Carr questioned where Hank said "no" and where he picked up a relief driver, the late Donald Surface.

"It probably was Bluefield," Carr said. "For forty years, I said it was Bristol, and that's where I thought it was."

The stop turned out to be the Dough Boy of Bluefield, West Virginia, about one hundred miles north of the Burger Bar. A waitress, Hazel Wells Schultz, remembered that Hank's Cadillac stopped that night and newspapers, just the day after Hank's death, had carried reports that Carr had stopped in Bluefield.

"We only gassed up one time," Carr said. "Wherever the restaurant was, I got a burger, and the cabstand was there. And that's where we gassed up. Wherever that was is where I got Donald Surface."

But the ride didn't last long. Going just a few miles north of Bluefield, Carr noticed that "one of the covers" had slipped off Hank, that the singer had his hand on his heart and that his hand was stiff. Hank's last ride had ended. He was dead at age twenty-nine.

BRISTOL: BURGER BAR AND THE BIRTHPLACE OF COUNTRY MUSIC

The Burger Bar, 8 Piedmont Avenue, stands immediately north of Bristol's State Street, about 0.2 miles west of the Bristol Sign. The city's Birthplace of Country Music mural, depicting Jimmie Rodgers, is painted on the side of the old Lark Amusements Building in the 800 block of State Street, one block west of the Burger Bar. Also pictured on the mural is the Carter Family, a group that also made its first recordings in Bristol in 1927.

The story of the 1927 "Bristol Sessions" is told extensively at Bristol's Birthplace of Country Music Museum, 520 Birthplace of Country Music Way, near Cumberland Square Park in Virginia. The Mountain Music Museum, 626 State Street, also showcases artifacts of local musicians on the Tennessee side of town. Music historians consider the "Bristol Sessions" particularly important because these field recordings by talent scout Ralph Peer of the Victor Talking Machine Company resulted in the near-simultaneous discoveries of Jimmie Rodgers and the Carter Family—among country music's first long-lasting stars. These "Birthplace of Country Music" sessions took place on the Tennessee side of State Street at the site of a man-size monument, about a block west of the Bristol Sign.

From the downtown district, retrace State Street/Gate City Highway for 2.3 miles to U.S. 58 at I-81 exit 1A.

52

JOHNNY AND JUNE

Hiltons

Johnny Cash showed up two days too early to note June Carter's birthday. He was also one month too late; June had died on May 15, 2003. The "Man in Black," still, sat onstage at the Carter Fold, and he said he found peace in coming to his late wife's "old home place here on the banks of Clinch Mountain, where we spent so much time and had so much love for each other."

As early as 1962, Johnny and June walked together along the dirt roads at Poor Valley where June grew up. They played with June's young cousins, and they ate country suppers. "I was impressed," Johnny recalled. "I just fell in love with Poor Valley and Scott County."

Frequently, the singers returned to this close-knit community. They also played homecoming concerts at the Carter Fold, a venue built by June's cousins Joe and Janette Carter to honor the Carter Family, the musical trio of the siblings' parents, A.P. and Sara Carter, and June's mother, Maybelle Carter. Discovered in nearby Bristol, Tennessee, in 1927, the Carter Family became a million-selling success by the time June was born in the Maces Spring section of Poor Valley on June 23, 1929.

June was a tomboy, constantly climbing the trees of Clinch Mountain. While still a child, she joined the Carter Family, dancing and singing on such standards as "Keep on the Sunny Side" and "Will the Circle Be Unbroken?" June later sang with her sisters, Helen and Anita, and "Mother" Maybelle. She became friends with Hank Williams, and she was a godmother to Hank Williams Jr. She also became a self-effacing ham, telling audiences lines like,

Johnny Cash and June Carter stayed for up to three weeks at a time in this Virginia house at Maces Spring, just below Clinch Mountain, near Hiltons. *Author photo.*

"I've got my hair parted in the middle. Daddy says I used to do that to balance my brain."

By the 1960s, June sang with Johnny Cash, a rock-and-roll pioneer and country music superstar. June steered Johnny off drugs. Then she married him in 1968. The couple lived in Hendersonville, Tennessee, but they also had the A-frame home of June's parents, Maybelle and Ezra "Eck" Carter, in Poor Valley. Johnny and June bought the house in 1981 on what Johnny called "the banks of Clinch Mountain."

The Cashes stayed in Virginia for up to three weeks at a time. Often, June scouted local flea markets and antique sales with her favorite cousin, Fern Carter Salyer. These cousins carted home so much loot that Johnny had to buy June a truck. Johnny, meanwhile, explored Clinch Mountain in a Jeep with June's cousin Joe Carter. But sometimes these men got into comical calamities, like once unknowingly running over a tree and noisily dragging it back down a mountain road.

Still, Johnny never met Joe's father, A.P. Carter, a songwriter and the leader of the Carter Family. A.P. died in 1960. Some years later, Johnny became the Carter Family's new musical patriarch. He re-inspired audiences with shows, records and television appearances, and he often took Mother Maybelle and

Johnny Cash, left, and his son, John Carter Cash, appeared on stage together in 2000 at the Carter Fold. *Author photo.*

the Carter Sisters on the road with him. Johnny also escorted a frail Maybelle to the Carter Fold stage for her final concert with Sara Carter in 1977.

Johnny consistently broke a house rule. He played an electric guitar at the Carter Fold while other musicians had to abide by Janette Carter's acoustic-only policy. But she did not mind. Janette would often say Johnny "was electrified before I knew him." Johnny also played many shows by surprise, mentioned mainly by rumors. "I don't advertise that he's going to be here too much," Janette Carter once said. "It's foolish to advertise when you ain't got no place to sit people."

The Carter Fold ran out of chairs in 2000 when Johnny played a concert for more than one thousand people. By then, his health had deteriorated from various ailments. But he still showed he could "Get Rhythm" and sing "Jackson" with June. That night, too, June said the couple was "hoping to retire" in Virginia. The crowd roared.

For the next two years, Johnny and June traveled together to Poor Valley for June's birthday parties. They also promised to help restore the fallen-down cabin where June's father and uncles were born. But June died just as that old cabin was being dismantled.

Without June, Johnny looked weathered. Once towering among the pines of Clinch Mountain, he now sat in a wheelchair. His hands twitched, and he sounded choked up at the Carter Fold when he made that spiritual pilgrimage to mark June's birthday, two days too early, on June 21, 2003.

Left: The late June Carter performs at the Carter Fold in 2000. The photo behind her, at upper left, depicts her aunt Sara Carter, an original member of the Carter Family. *Author photo.*

Below: June Carter's father, Eck, and uncle A.P. Carter, the leader of the Carter Family, were born in this cabin, a landmark restored in 2003. *Author photo.*

"The pain is so severe that there's no describing it," Johnny told his audience. "There's no way to tell exactly what the pain is. It's the big one. It's the biggest. When you lose your mate, the one you've been with all those years, I guarantee it's the big one. It hurts so bad. It hurts. It really hurts."

Johnny sang "Ring of Fire," a song June had written with Merle Kilgore. His crackling voice wavered. That singing, still, seemed to help his troubled soul. Staying in Virginia a few more days, he stopped again at the Carter Fold, singing a few more songs on July 5, his last concert anywhere.

Little more than three months later, just as that old Carter cabin was being restored, Johnny joined June at the family circle—"in the sky, Lord, in the sky."

HILTONS: CARTER FOLD

From I-81 exit 1A, head west on U.S. 58, passing small waterfalls along the Ketron Branch of Cove Creek, on the left, after 8.0 miles. Continue another 10.0 miles and cross the North Fork of the Holston River on one of U.S. 58's quietest portions. Beyond the Holston River bridge, continue another half mile and turn right on VA-709 at Hiltons (a village named for a local Hilton family). Go 0.1 miles, turn right on VA-614 (A.P. Carter Highway), and go three miles to the Carter Fold, A.P. Carter Museum and A.P. Carter

Travel tip: Two small hamlets, called Fido and Bruno, lie along U.S. 58 between the Scott County border and Hiltons. Fido, on the east, is believed to have taken its name from a dog, as did Bruno, the location of McMurray Grocery along Roberts Creek at VA-859.

Birthplace Cabin, all on the left, at Maces Spring. Continue for 0.7 miles to the privately owned former home of June Carter and Johnny Cash, also on the left; a marker in a roadside flowerbed honors Mother Maybelle Carter. Go 0.8 miles beyond the house to the Mount Vernon United Methodist Church, where A.P. Carter, Sara Carter, Joe Carter and Janette Carter are buried. A.P. Carter's gravestone, marked by a gold "Keep on the Sunny Side" record, stands about six rows from the back of the cemetery behind the church. Joe Carter's gravestone, nearby, is shaped like a guitar. From here, retrace the route to U.S. 58 at Hiltons.

53

THE TOWN THAT WOULD NOT DROWN

Clinchport

C linch River rolls through Virginia with no reservoirs, only briefly interrupted by small milldams, from its headwaters near Tazewell to the Tennessee state line. The water flows free and healthy for more than forty-five different kinds of mussels, creating one of the most diverse freshwater mussel habitats in the world. Still, that free-flow has also made riverside towns like Clinchport prone to problems.

In 1977, with no dam to hold back floodwaters, the Clinch River inundated the tiny town of Clinchport. The river also wreaked havoc upstream at St. Paul along U.S. 58A, an alternate route of U.S. 58 that splits from the main U.S. 58 route in Abingdon and stretches west for more than eighty miles through Castlewood, Coeburn, Norton, Big Stone Gap, Pennington Gap and Jonesville, where it meets U.S. 58 again.

Floodwaters continued to rise for days after the river in Scott County surged out its banks in Clinchport on April 4. In time, water rose as high as attics. Helicopters rescued stranded residents. And some mobile homes, meanwhile, washed through the submerged corporate limits of Clinchport.

When the waters receded, Clinchport was not rebuilt. Yet it also became the town that would not drown. Businesses dried up in Clinchport, and many of its residents scattered to nearby Thomas Village, a community that sprang up along U.S. 58 near Duffield. Still, Clinchport remained incorporated—with a population of fewer than one hundred people.

It would also make more news. More than a dozen years after the flood of '77, the townsfolk elected the country's youngest mayor, eighteen-year-

U.S. 58 crosses the Clinch River near Clinchport at Speers Ferry, a place named for Joshua Speer Sr., who established a ferry at this site in 1833. *Author photo.*

old Michael Mullins. In addition to his youth, Mullins also became known for posing at a town limits sign wearing a Motley Crue T-shirt in a widely circulated newspaper photograph.

Mullins's status even won him a guest spot on NBC's *Late Night with David Letterman* in 1990. "Actually, I decided to run three days before the election," Mullins told the talk-show host. "The night before the election, I went out onto town—me and one of my friends—and we went door to door and told everyone I was running."

Eighty-five people lived in Clinchport at the time. Just twenty-four voted the year Mullins won—with thirteen write-in votes.

CLINCHPORT: CLINCH RIVER

From VA-709 at Hiltons, turn right on U.S. 58 and continue west for 5.3 miles to U.S. 58's junction with U.S. 23 near Big Moccasin Gap, a natural passage through Clinch Mountain marked by a wayside park. Big Moccasin Gap was named in the 1700s by pioneers who found the prints of moccasins worn by Indians. From the gap at Weber City (a town named by service station owner Frank Parker Sr. for a 1930s skit on the *Amos 'n Andy* radio show), continue west on U.S. 58, passing Gate City (a town named for being a gateway in the mountains). Cross the Clinch River bridge at 11.5 miles. Continue another 1.5 miles west and turn right on VA-65. Go 1.0 mile to the Clinchport canoe and fishing access, on the right.

54

TALE OF THE TORNADO

Rye Cove

It might have sounded like a train, but it couldn't have been. There was no railroad in Rye Cove. The nearest track passed near Clinchport, about eight miles south along the Clinch River. This great noise was a howling wind. With it, the sky grew dark like night. "Then it got real light," remembered Lucille Cowden Necessary. "And the lumber started hitting us."

This was a tornado, the worst tornado tragedy in Virginia history. On May 2, 1929, the whirlwind ransacked Rye Cove in the shape of a dirty black cloud, whipping across rocky fields and arriving at the valley's Rye Cove Consolidated School just after recess.

Inside the school, ten-year-old Lucille watched a window fly toward her desk. She ducked. Then she blacked out as the two-story wooden schoolhouse was lifted into the cyclone. The schoolhouse spun and shattered, spitting students, teachers, books and desks back down to the ground.

"It struck the building," said the school's principal, Floyd Noblin. "The next thing I remembered, I was standing knee deep in a pond seventy-five feet from where the building stood before it was demolished."

Lucille awoke in the twister's trap of splintered glass and boards—all that was left of the school. Nails had pierced her knees. She had a broken foot and a severed finger—and she was one of the lucky ones. Other kids screamed as flames shot out of the wreckage from an overturned stove. Some were burned by acid in the school's science lab.

Maybe this is the end of the world, Lucille thought. Just days before, she had been sitting in church in Rye Cove when the preacher gave a sermon

Mountains enclose the scenic valley of Rye Cove in Scott County, the site of a tornado tragedy in 1929 that destroyed a school and the nearby Duncan Mill. *Author photo.*

saying that End Times were near and that some would be taken up and some left behind.

Wave Franklin, Lucille's thirteen-year-old aunt, was literally left behind—and presumed dead. Yet just in the nick of time, Lucille's mother saw one of Wave's hands move, and she was carried back home.

The tornado had hit around 1:00 p.m., but two hours passed before outside help arrived in isolated Rye Cove. Next, it was a challenge to evacuate the wounded on Rye Cove's muddy, rutted road to Clinchport, where trains could rush to hospitals in Bristol, Virginia, and Kingsport, Tennessee.

"Everything was a sea of mud," Lucille said. "The wagons took the bodies and the badly injured from where the school was to where the train tracks run."

That night, Lucille went to sleep trying to block out the clamor of hammers. Coffins were being made for those who were killed—a total of twelve students and one teacher, twenty-four-year-old Ava Carter.

The American Red Cross constructed a log cabin for a relief center. Musician A.P. Carter of the Carter Family also helped recovery efforts

The old Red Cross Cabin that was used to treat wounded students and school staff in 1929 was restored as part of a park at Rye Cove School. *Author photo.*

and penned a song, "The Cyclone of Rye Cove," which spun a tale of the tornado. But the following year would be a lost time, with no school for the 155 students of Rye Cove.

Haunted by memories of their real-life nightmare, children in the valley developed a habit of holding down their heads, afraid to look at the sky. Others would later swear that screams can be heard in Rye Cove each year on May 2, the anniversary of the tornado, like mysterious voices crying in the wind.

SCOTT COUNTY: RYE COVE

From the Clinch River access at Clinchport, follow VA-65 (Clinch River Highway) northeast for 3.5 miles. Turn left on VA-649 (Rye Cove Memorial Road) and follow for 2.7 miles to the site of Rye Cove School, on the right. The former school's belfry, perched on bricks in the schoolyard, serves as a memorial, listing names of tornado victims. The old Red Cross cabin, renovated in 2004, stands beside Rye Cove's present school at a small park. From here, retrace VA-649 to VA-65 and follow 4.5 miles southwest to U.S. 58.

55

STUPENDOUS SCALE

Natural Tunnel State Park

Nothing's haunting the Natural Tunnel except its old name: Natural Bridge. That's what the rocky landmark was dubbed for a good part of the nineteenth century.

It is not—to repeat, *not*—the same place as the Natural Bridge of Rockbridge County, Virginia. Only not everybody knows that. People often call wanting to check into the hotel or look for the wax museum, only to find that neither exists at Natural Tunnel State Park.

Once, too, the daughter of a 102-year-old woman from Georgia called the park office, saying her mother wanted to see the rock formation just one more time before she died. Park officials made every effort to oblige, even to the point of operating the chairlift to the tunnel during the off-season. But then the family cancelled just two days before the planned visit and said they had made a mistake. They were actually thinking about revisiting Natural Bridge.

Longtime Natural Tunnel State Park manager Craig Seaver blamed such mix-ups on "more of a marketing problem than anything else."

But factor in history. Decades before the first train passed through the Natural Tunnel in 1890, Matthew Carey called the formation "Natural Bridge" on an 1814 map. For the next few decades, the dark passage through Purchase Ridge retained at least some reference as a "Natural Bridge," once a generic term for any arch-type rock formation.

The Natural Bridge gives its name to Rockbridge County. It stands like a doorway, with one side leading to the Shenandoah Valley and the

A platform
provides a close-up
view of the Natural
Tunnel's swirling,
round entrance
and, occasionally,
a passing train.
Author photo.

other opening to Virginia's Southern Blue Ridge Highlands. Thomas
Jefferson owned the Natural Bridge and called it "the most sublime of
nature's works."

The Natural Tunnel sits in the woods of Scott County. It has not been
owned by anybody particularly famous, but it does form a general gateway
between Virginia's coal-mining region and the slant-sided farms of the
Clinch Valley.

In many early descriptions, Natural Tunnel was mentioned with
seemingly obligatory comparisons to Natural Bridge. Lewis Preston
Summers's 1903 *History of Southwest Virginia* contains a passage by writer
Charles B. Coale, who notes that the landmark is "not so perfect as that
of Rockbridge county, but is much grander in proportion and is laid out
upon much more stupendous scale."

Make that quite stupendous, even if the 850-foot-long Natural Tunnel
can't claim half the fame as the 90-foot-long Natural Bridge. It is, indeed,

Trains routinely run through Natural Tunnel. This postcard shows an early 1900s view of a steam train outside what's been called the "Eighth Wonder of the World." *Courtesy George Stone.*

grander in proportion. The curved limestone walls outside Natural Tunnel stand about 400 feet, compared to Natural Bridge's rise of 215 feet.

Scott County: Natural Tunnel State Park

From VA-65 at Clinchport, continue west on U.S. 58 for 1.2 miles. Turn right on VA-871 and follow for 1.0 mile to Natural Tunnel State Park, on the right. The 850-acre park features a playground, picnic areas, a visitor center, a swimming pool and a campground. A chairlift and trails lead to Natural Tunnel. Other attractions include the replica of a blockhouse, made to resemble the kind of eighteenth-century forts that once stood along the Wilderness Road in Southwest Virginia.

56

COLD WAR

Jonesville

For months, the Civil War interrupted the peace of Powell Valley. Once, Federal troops stomped through the quiet town of Jonesville and torched the Lee County Courthouse. Another time, in a unique case of friendly fire, the Confederates of the Sixty-fourth Virginia Infantry left some embers unattended and accidentally burned some cabins while occupying the Jonesville Methodist Campground.

Fortunately, no flames touched the campground's wooden shed. That landmark has been used for annual prayer meetings since the 1820s. Still, that shed was without a prayer in 1863 and 1864 as the war lingered. Church leaders opted to meet elsewhere, fearing a surprise attack by the Union army.

Such action arrived in bitter cold at the end of 1863. Union major Charles H. Beeres tried to occupy tiny Jonesville with about four hundred men in the Sixteenth Illinois Cavalry. Beeres's forces made a stand at the Dickinson-Milbourn House, a Federal-style brick home built on a knoll in the 1840s for prosperous landowner Benjamin Dickinson.

The news of Beeres's arrival made it to Lieutenant Colonel Auburn L. Pridemore, the Confederate commander of the Sixty-fourth Virginia Cavalry. Pridemore moved a force of 230 men into Jonesville from the east. Brigadier General William E. "Grumble" Jones marched north to Jonesville with more Confederate troops from Tennessee. The ensuing clash between North and South became the Battle of Jonesville on January 3, 1864.

Talk about a cold war; it was snowing and temperatures dipped below zero. At least one of Jones's men froze to death even before making it to Jonesville. Other

Confederates suffered frostbite after splashing through the cold Clinch River and climbing icy mountain roads.

Guns and cannons, by contrast, blazed hot. Clearly, the Union forces were trapped. Pridemore had blocked routes to the east and north. Jones had cut off roads to the south and west. And Beeres surrendered, giving up three pieces of light artillery, hundreds of men and more than twenty six-mule teams.

The frigid fight left dead and wounded on both sides. But, for a while, there would be peace in Powell Valley again.

Dickinson-Milbourn House stands near the center of Jonesville, a town that is known as the birthplace of Dr. Andrew Taylor Still, the father of osteopathic medicine. *Author photo.*

JONESVILLE: DICKINSON-MILBOURN HOUSE

From the junction of U.S. 58 and VA-871 near Natural Tunnel, follow U.S. 58 west for 3.5 miles to Duffield (named for a local Duff family). Turn left on U.S. 58 and continue west, reaching an overlook at the crest of Powell Mountain in 4.5 miles. Down the mountain, in 2.0 miles, reach Stickleyville (named for early settler Vastine Stoekli) and then pass through Dot (which is hardly bigger than a dot on a map) at the U.S. 421 intersection.

At 13.0 miles west of Stickleyville (or 23.0 miles west of the Natural Tunnel exit), reach the Lee County Courthouse on U.S. 58 at Jonesville and turn left. A cemetery with the graves of Civil War soldiers stands 0.2 miles west of the courthouse. At 0.4 miles west of the cemetery, the privately owned Dickinson-Milbourn House stands on the right, across from Jonesville Middle School. Continue on U.S. 58 for 1.0 mile west of the school. The Jonesville Methodist Campground stands near the VA-652 intersection at a historic marker, on the right. Both the house and the campground are listed on historic landmark registers.

PIONEER GRAVES

Lee County

Joseph Martin charged into Virginia's unknown wilderness, gambling that he could safely settle the isolated Powell Valley. The young man started with a challenge from Dr. Thomas Walker to claim twenty-one thousand acres of land. In 1750, Walker had surveyed Powell Valley with Ambrose Powell, a hunter who carved his name on a tree and later inspired subsequent travelers to name Powell Mountain, Powell River and the Powell Valley for him in what is now Lee County, Virginia.

Martin won his own name on a creek. Leaving Albemarle County near Charlottesville, Virginia, he raced hundreds of miles in 1769 and got lost in the woods. But he still beat a competing expedition by more than two weeks. That March, he set up a fort. He planted corn. He explored. But just as the corn crop ripened, Indians attacked. Martin fled and didn't return to Powell Valley for six years. He then built another fort along the same creek, and he attracted fellow pioneers, who shopped and slept at "Martin's Station." But along came another raid, and Martin was gone again after June 1776.

Such were the perils of Powell Valley. For pioneers like Martin, it was tempting to try to tame this territory. But conflicts with Native Americans seemed to always make the area impossible to settle.

Famed frontiersman Daniel Boone personally discovered the dangers. Boone came through the Powell Valley in 1773—a time when Martin wasn't around—while wandering west with family and friends.

On the morning of October 10, somewhere in the woods, Indians ambushed Boone's sixteen-year-old son James Boone and seventeen-year-old Henry

Russell at the boys' small campsite. Both boys were shot through the hips and stabbed with knives. Both had their fingernails and toenails ripped out. Finally and fatally, both boys were tomahawked. The Indians killed three more campers, another was kidnapped and two managed to escape.

A petty thief found the boys' bloody remains after he ran off from Daniel Boone's main camp nearby. The thief ran back and alerted Boone's group. They immediately prepared for an attack, stacking trees and quickly

The Pioneer Graves marker at Lee County pays tribute to Daniel Boone's son James and others who were massacred in 1773. *Author photo.*

making a fort. But the Indians did not return. Boone's family buried James and Henry together in an unmarked grave and then retreated east to the Clinch Valley.

Historians agree that the murders of 1773 slowed Daniel Boone's push to the west. But historians disagree over where the murders happened, on either the east or west side of the county, and where the boys were subsequently buried. Some say it was along Wallen's Creek near Stickleyville, the site of a state historical marker. Others contend it was in the west at Caylor, where, in 1951, a privately funded stone monument was erected with a description of the murders, titled "Pioneer Graves."

What is known, without an argument, is that Indians are buried in graves all over Lee County. Many lie in raised mounds, popping out of Powell Valley like perfectly rounded hills. One such grave site, called the Ely Mound, remained unexplored until 1877, when a legendary excavation for the Peabody Museum of American Archaeology and Ethnology helped theorize that Indians had built the mound between 1200 and 1650.

Local resident Charles B. Johnson discovered the skeletons of two Indian children below the top of the nineteen-foot-high Ely Mound. Then Professor

The Ely Mound is an Indian burial site rising just ahead of a white barn near Rose Hill in western Lee County. *Author photo.*

The Martin's Station replica at Wilderness Road State Park stands a few miles west of the actual Martin's Station constructed in 1775 at Rose Hill. *Author photo.*

Lucius H. Cheney climbed into a six-foot-long shaft in the Ely Mound and made an announcement that excited a crowd of onlookers.

He said there was an entire skeleton that could be saved, but it would have to come out delicately, piece by piece. Several spectators slipped to the side of the excavation to get a better look. But they rushed so fast and with such force that a section of the grassy mound collapsed. The excavators, Cheney and Johnson, were suddenly trapped inside the tomb.

It took about twenty minutes to pull out Cheney. The earth had fallen on his neck and the back of his head, killing him. Johnson was bruised but alive, and he finished excavating the Ely Mound a week later with Carr.

The Ely Mound owes its name to the family of Robert Ely, a prominent farmer who built a twelve-room mansion called Elydale in the 1870s. In the 1990s, Ely's mansion became part of the Wilderness Road State Park, the site of a life-size replica of Martin's Station. The park's fort represents what Joseph Martin constructed in 1775 when he returned to Powell Valley: a stockade with a half dozen cabins.

For the record, Martin didn't give up on Powell Valley after 1776. The pioneer established a new Martin's Station in 1783, this time a few miles west of the original site. Five prosperous years later, he sold off his land claims and retired at the foot of Virginia's mountains. His grave lies there at Martinsville, a city named for him, just as his name remains in Powell Valley at Martin Creek.

EWING: WILDERNESS ROAD STATE PARK

From Jonesville Methodist Campground at VA-652, follow U.S. 58 west for 12.7 miles. Turn left at U.S. 58 Business at Rose Hill (named for a hill blooming with roses) and go 0.2 miles to a historic marker, on the right, noting the original site of Martin's Station, near Martin Creek. Continue west for 3.0 miles through Rose Hill to another historic marker, noting the site of the Ely Mound, located across U.S. 58 (to the north), near a barn.

Continue west for 2.1 miles to Ewing (a place named for early settler Samuel Ewing). Turn right on VA-724 and go 0.1 miles. Turn left on U.S. 58 and head west for 4.3 miles to Caylor (a name that should actually be "Taylor," for local landowners). Turn left on VA-684 and go 0.1 miles to the Pioneer Graves monument, on the right. Return to U.S. 58 and go 1.0 mile to reach Wilderness Road State Park, on the right, at VA-690. The two-hundred-acre park includes trails, a visitor center and a picnic area.

Wheeler Depot once stood along the Louisville and Nashville Railroad on what has since become the Wilderness Road Trail. *Courtesy Carl Cheek.*

Beyond the state park, continue west on U.S. 58 for 6.7 miles. Go across Station Creek (site of the third Martin's Station) to reach the western terminus of the Wilderness Road Trail near the campground entrance of Cumberland Gap National Historical Park.

Covered with crushed gravel, Wilderness Road Trail parallels U.S. 58 for more than eight miles on the westernmost stretch of Virginia's Beaches to Bluegrass Trail. This path links Wilderness Road State Park with Cumberland Gap National Historical Park by largely following the former corridor of the Louisville and Nashville Railroad, running through Caylor, Wheeler and Gibson Station, on what was also once the path of pioneers like Daniel Boone.

BLUEGRASS

Cumberland Gap

D aniel Boone dreamed of the bluegrass of Kentucky—the untilled green, the wild turkey, the deer, the bear, the elk. It all waited to the west, beyond the ocean of the Appalachian Mountains.

But getting there seemed such a struggle. In 1767, the frontiersman stomped through the rocky Breaks Canyon on the Big Sandy River. But that area was too rough. Two years later, Boone made a trip to Kentucky through Cumberland Gap, a natural notch on a path used by animals and Indians. Hunter Gabriel Arthur became the first white man to walk through the Cumberland Gap in 1674 after being captured by Shawnees. But this cut in Cumberland Mountain remained a dormant doorway until 1750.

That year, Dr. Thomas Walker led a crew through the gap on a real estate expedition. The governor's council in Williamsburg granted Walker's group, the Loyal Company, a title to 800,000 acres west of the Appalachians in what became known as Kentucky. Walker returned with a journal bragging about coal deposits, buffalo and bountiful fields.

The gap was named for William Augustus, the Duke of Cumberland and the son of King George II of England. But there would be no rush through this "Gateway to the West," at least not just yet. In the 1760s, Kentucky became closed to further settlement and exploration due to the French and Indian War.

Then came Boone. The Pennsylvania native's first trip to Kentucky's bluegrass fields teased his imagination. He saw great herds of buffalo, and he returned often, even longing to settle in that mysterious, virgin land.

Boone's knowledge of the bluegrass and the narrow route getting there earned him a job in 1775. That year, the Transylvania Company made a deal with the Cherokee to buy millions of acres in Kentucky. Immediately, Boone and a group of thirty men marked the Wilderness Road, or "Boone's Trace," through dark forests to Kentucky.

This area soon evolved into Virginia's vast "County of Kentucky," stretching west to the Mississippi River. Thousands pulled wagons along Boone's Trace, especially after 1784, when writer John Filson described Kentucky as "the most extraordinary country that the sun enlightens with his celestial beams."

The bluegrass grew. In 1792, what was briefly the "County of Kentucky" became a commonwealth, just like Virginia. By then, Kentucky had been divided into three smaller counties, and the population of what became the Bluegrass State had reached more than 100,000, enough to qualify for statehood.

But Kentucky turned unkind for Boone. More than once, Shawnees captured the hunter, and for years, he fought in court to keep his land claims. By 1800, a disgusted Boone left Kentucky for good.

Cumberland Gap remained a gateway. It was called the "Gibraltar of America" during the Civil War and was considered a strategic passage to both the Confederacy and the Union. Soldiers built earthworks and stripped trees off Cumberland Mountain to make way for cannonballs. Still, little happened. The biggest battles, likely, were waged against boredom and starvation.

Then came Middlesboro. Settled along the gap's western border, this Kentucky city was first spelled "Middlesborough." That extra "ugh" came from Alexander Arthur, who named it for Middlesborough, England. Arthur acquired capital from English investors, and in 1889 he began to develop coal mining, iron ore and timber interests. Middlesborough grew from fifty to ten thousand people in fewer than eight months. And it all looked swell until a London bank went belly up in 1890. Then came a fire. Then the Panic of 1893 took finances on a continuing crash.

Middlesboro, as it was later more commonly spelled, had already experienced another crash millions of years earlier. A meteor dropped out of the sky and formed the three-mile-wide valley where the city grew. Possibly, that crash was similar to how a space rock slammed the Chesapeake Bay, slightly north of Cape Henry. At least, drawing a line between the two craters shows that meteors may have marked where Virginia should begin and end.

The Pinnacle Overlook in Virginia provides a bird's-eye view of the westernmost section of U.S. 58, ending just inside Tennessee, where the highway terminates at U.S. 25E. *Author photo.*

A pavilion marks the Tri-State Peak, where Virginia ends on a mountain, just above Tennessee, at the border of the Bluegrass State of Kentucky. *Author photo.*

In the west, Virginia ends on a mountain. Roughly five hundred miles away from the Atlantic Coast, even beyond the Cumberland Gap, the western tip of the Old Dominion overlooks the Bluegrass State. A wooden pavilion marks this spot, quietly hidden in the woods of the Cumberland Gap National Historical Park, a natural bookend on the trail from beach to bluegrass.

LEE COUNTY: CUMBERLAND GAP NATIONAL HISTORICAL PARK

The Pinnacle Overlook at Cumberland Gap National Historical Park stands in Virginia but can only be reached by driving through the Bluegrass State of Kentucky. *Author photo.*

From the campground entrance at Cumberland Gap National Historical Park, continue west on U.S. 58 to enter Tennessee in 1.2 miles. In another three hundred yards, turn right on North Cumberland Drive (the exit for Cumberland Gap, Tennessee) and go three hundred yards, passing back into Virginia, to reach the Daniel Boone Parking Area, on the right.

From the kiosk, the uphill trail through Cumberland Gap runs about 1.0 mile to the saddle of the gap. There, on the left, use the Tri-State Trail and go 0.6 miles—passing, briefly, into Kentucky—to reach the wooden pavilion at the Tri-State Peak, where concrete, stones and brass plates mark the boundary of Kentucky, Tennessee and Virginia.

To reach the national park visitor center from the Daniel Boone Parking Area, return to U.S. 58 and go 0.2 miles, veering right on U.S. 25E, and pass through the Cumberland Gap Tunnel. Exit immediately to the visitor center at Middlesboro. From the visitor center, continue left on the Pinnacle Road for 3.8 miles to the Pinnacle Overlook, a site actually located in Virginia but reached by car by going through Kentucky. During the 1930s, the Skyland Company promoted the view at the Pinnacle as the "Garden of Gazes."

BIBLIOGRAPHY

BOOKS

Beaudry, Mary C. *Colonizing the Virginia Frontier: Fort Christanna and Governor Spotswood's Indian Policy*. Boston: Boston University Archeological Studies Program, August 1981.

Bracey, Susan. *Life by the Roaring Roanoke: A History of Mecklenburg County, Virginia*. Mecklenburg County, VA: Mecklenburg County Bicentennial Commission, 1977.

Brown, Douglas Summers, ed. *Sketches of Greensville County, Virginia, 1650–1967*. Emporia, VA: Riparian Woman's Club, 1968.

Brubaker, John H., III. *The Last Capitol: Danville, Virginia and the Final Days of the Confederacy*. Danville, VA: Danville Museum of Fine Arts and History, 1979.

Bucklen, Mary Kegley, and Larrie L. Bucklen. *County Courthouses of Virginia Old and New*. Charleston, WV: Pictorial Histories Publishing Company, 1988.

Butt, Marshall W. *Portsmouth Under Four Flags: 1752–1970*. Portsmouth, VA: self-published, 1971.

Cohen, Stan. *Historic Springs of the Virginias: A Pictorial History*. Charleston, WV: Pictorial Histories Publishing Co., 1981.

Curtis, Claude D. *Three Quarters of a Century at Martha Washington College*. Bristol, TN: King Printing Co., 1928.

Dabney, Virginius. *Virginia: The New Dominion*. Garden City, NY: Doubleday & Co., Inc., 1971.

Dawidziak, Mark. *The Barter Theatre Story: Love Made Visible*. Boone, NC: Appalachian Consortium Press, 1982.

Drewry, William Sidney. *The Southampton Insurrection*. Murfreesboro, NC: Johnson Publishing Co., 1968.

Dunn, Joseph W., Jr., and Barbara S. Lyle. *Virginia Beach: Wish You Were Here*. Norfolk, VA: Donning Company/Publishers, 1983.

Edmunds, Pocahontas Wight. *Tales of the Virginia Coast*. N.p.: self-published, 1950.

Fields, Bettye-Lou, ed. *Grayson County: A History in Words and Pictures*. Independence, VA: Grayson County Historical Society, 1976.

Ginther, Herman. *Captain Staunton's River*. Richmond, VA: Dietz Press, Inc., 1968.

Goodwin, Doris Kearns. *No Ordinary Time: Franklin and Eleanor Roosevelt: The Home Front in World War II*. New York: Touchstone, 1994.

Gregory, G. Howard. *History of the Wreck of the Old 97*. Danville, VA: self-published, 1992.

Hagemann, James A. *The Heritage of Virginia*. Norfolk, VA: Donning Co. Publishers, 1986.

Hall, Louise Fortune. *A History of Damascus, 1793–1950*. Abingdon, VA: John Anderson Press, 1950.

Hall, Ronald W. *The Carroll County Courthouse Tragedy*. Hillsville, VA: Carroll County Historical Society, 1997.

Hanson, Raus McDill. *Virginia Place Names*. Verona, VA: McClure Press, 1969.

Hobbs, Kermit, and William A. Paquette. *Suffolk: A Pictorial History*. Norfolk, VA: Donning Company/Publishers, 1987.

Holloday, Mildred M. *History of Portsmouth*. File at Wilson History Room, Portsmouth Public Library, Portsmouth, VA.

Hume, Ivor Noel. *The Virginia Adventure: Roanoke to James Towne: An Archaeological and Historical Odyssey*. New York: Alfred A. Knopf, 1994.

Jordan, James M., IV, and Frederick S. Jordan. *Virginia Beach: A Pictorial History*. N.p: Thomas F. Hale, n.d.

Kyle, Louisa Venable. *The Witch of Pungo*. Virginia Beach, VA: Four O'Clock Farms Publishing Co., 1973.

Lee County Historical and Genealogical Society. *Bicentennial History of Lee County, Virginia, 1792–1992*. Waynesville, NC: Don Mills, Inc., 1992.

Lofaro, Michael A. *Daniel Boone: An American Life*. Lexington: University Press of Kentucky, 2003.

Loth, Calder, ed. *The Virginia Landmarks Register*. Charlottesville: University Press of Virginia, 1999.

Loving, Robert. *Double Destiny*. Bristol, TN: King Printing Co., 1955.

MacArthur, Douglas. *Reminiscences*. New York: McGraw-Hill Book Company, 1964.

Mansfield, Stephen S. *Princess Anne County and Virginia Beach: A Pictorial History*. Norfolk, VA: Donning Company, 1989.

Mapp, Alf J., and Ramona H. Mapp. *Portsmouth: A Pictorial History*. Norfolk, VA: Donning Company, 1989.

Mayer, Henry. *A Son of Thunder: Patrick Henry and the American Republic*. New York: Franklin Watts, 1986.

McDonald, Travis C., Jr. *Emporia: A Centennial Retrospective, 1887–1987*. Lawrenceville, VA: Brunswick Publishing Co., 1987.

McKnight, Brian D. *Contested Borderland: The Civil War in Appalachian Kentucky and Virginia*. Lexington: University Press of Kentucky, 2006.

Meade, Robert Douthat. *Patrick Henry: Patriot in the Making*. New York: J.B. Lippincott Co., 1957.

Nanney, Frank L., Jr. *South Hill, Virginia: A Chronicle of the First 100 Years*. South Hill, VA: self-published, 2001.

Neale, Gay. *Brunswick County, Virginia: 1720–1975*. Brunswick County, VA: Brunswick County Bicentennial Committee, 1975.

1908 Courthouse Foundation. *Bicentennial Heritage Grayson County Virginia, 1793*. Independence, VA: 1908 Courthouse Foundation, 1995.

Patrick County Historical Society. *History of Patrick County, Virginia*. Stuart, VA: Patrick County Historical Society, 1999.

Perret, Geoffrey. *Old Soldiers Never Die: The Life of Douglas MacArthur*. New York: Random House, Inc., 1996.

Pritchard, Emily A., and J. Rodney Lewis. *The Life and Times of the Boyd Tavern*. Boydton, VA: Boyd Tavern Foundation, 1998.

Reynolds, A.D. *Recollections of Major A. D. Reynolds, 1847–1925*. Winston-Salem, NC: Reynolds House, Inc., 1978.

Rice, Otis K. *Frontier Kentucky*. Lexington: University Press of Kentucky, 1975.

Salmon, John S. *A Guidebook to Virginia's Historical Markers, Virginia Department of Historic Resources*. Charlottesville: University Press of Virginia, 1994.

Schoenbaum, Thomas J. *The New River Controversy*. Winston-Salem, NC: John F. Blair, Publisher, 1979.

Simpson, Bland. *The Great Dismal Swamp: A Carolinian's Swamp Memoir*. Chapel Hill: University of North Carolina Press, 1990.

Stevens, William Oliver. *An Affair of Honor: The Biography of Commodore James Barron, U.S.N.* Chesapeake, VA: Norfolk County Historical Society, 1969.

St. John, Jeffrey, and Kathryn St. John. *Landmarks 1765–1990: A Brief History of Mecklenburg County, Virginia*. Boydton, VA: Mecklenburg County Board of Supervisors, 1990.

Sturgill, Roy L. *Nostalgic Narratives and Historic Events of Southwest Virginia*. Bristol, VA: self-published, 1991.

Tilley, Nannie M. *Reynolds Homestead, 1814–1970*. Richmond, VA: Robert Kline and Co., n.d.

Tucker, George Holbert. *Norfolk Highlights: 1584–1881*. Norfolk, VA: Norfolk Historical Society, 1972.

Tucker, George H. *Tidewater Landfalls*. Norfolk, VA: Landmark Communications, Inc., 1969.

Turner, Florence Kimberly. *Gateway to the New World: A History of Princess Anne County, Virginia, 1607–1824*. Easley, SC: Southern Historical Press, 1984.

Virginia Beach Public Library. *The Beach: A History of Virginia Beach, VA*. Rev. ed. Virginia Beach, VA: Virginia Beach Public Library, 1996.

Whichard, Rogers Dey. *The History of Lower Tidewater Virginia*. New York: Lewis Historical Publishing Company, Inc., 1959.

Writers Program of the Works Progress Administration. *Virginia: A Guide to the Old Dominion*. New York: Oxford University Press, 1940.

Yarsinke, Amy Waters. *Virginia Beach: A History of Virginia's Golden Shore*. Charleston, SC: Arcadia Publishing, 2002.

Zehmer, John G., ed. *Two Mecklenburg Towns: Architectural and Historical Surveys of Boydton and Clarksville*. Richmond, VA: Virginia Department of Historic Resources, 2003.

Newspapers and Magazines

Annas, Teresa. "The Hague." *Virginian-Pilot*, September 12, 2012.

Bonko, Larry. "WNOR Admonished by Federal Agency Over April Fools' Day Hoax." *Virginian-Pilot*, December 5, 1992.

Brown, Jamie. "International Paper Makes Commitment." *Tidewater (VA) News*, September 23, 1999.

Chaltas, David, and Richard Brown. "Battle of Jonesville (The Frozen Fight)." *Appalachian Quarterly*, March 2005.

Chase City (VA) News-Progress. "John H. Kerr Dam 50th Anniversary Edition," September 25, 2002.

Clancy, Paul. "First Taste of Luxury at the Beach." *Virginian-Pilot,* April 21, 2013.

Ernst, William. "William Barton Rogers: Antebellum Virginia Geologist." *Virginia Cavalcade,* Summer 1974.

Gilliam, Gerald T. "Crossing at Clarksville." *Southsider* 4, no. 2 (Spring 1985).

Griset, Rich. "Strange Brew: The Suspicious Death of Adolph Coors at the Cavalier Hotel." *Coastal Virginia Magazine,* January 2015.

Hairston, Douglas. "A Century of Charm." *Martinsville (VA) Bulletin,* May 25, 2003.

Harrison, M. Clifford. "Murder in the Courtroom: Sensational Newspaper Accounts Distorted the Hillsville Massacre." *Virginia Cavalcade,* Summer 1967.

Hunter, Elizabeth. "The Mabrys of Mabry Mill." *Blue Ridge Country,* July 2004.

King, Jan, and Liz Wissbaum. "Pony Roundup on Mount Rogers." *Bristol (VA) Herald Courier,* May 6, 1976.

Lindeman, Edith. "Porterfield Visits City to Complete Plans for Opening Abingdon's Barter Theatre." *Richmond Times-Dispatch,* April 17, 1946.

Lohmann, Bill. "Home Cookin': They've Gotten Themselves into a Fine Stew in Brunswick." *Richmond Times-Dispatch,* November 7, 2004.

Messina, Debbie. "WNOR Hoax Isn't Funny to Everyone." *Virginian-Pilot,* April 2, 1992.

Nelms, Willie. "A Divided City: Bristol's Border Disputes and the Water Works War of 1889." *Virginia Cavalcade,* Spring 1979.

Olson, Karen. "Where Mystery...Meets History: The Haunting of the Cave House." *Plow,* August 13, 1979.

Price, Charles Edwin. "Death in the Afternoon." *Blue Ridge Country,* May 1998.

Roberts, Dan. "Leader Saw Swamp's Potential." *Virginian-Pilot,* July 23, 2006.

Robertson, W. Glenn. "The Siege of Suffolk, 1863: Another Name for Futility?" *Virginia Cavalcade*, Spring 1978.

Schuster, Hendrika. "Roosevelts in Southwest Virginia." *Historical Society of Washington County, VA Bulletin* 2, no. 35 (1998).

Stone, Steve. "WNOR's Morning Team Is Suspended." *Virginian-Pilot*, April 4, 1992.

Sturgill, Mack. "First Lady Visits Whitetop." *Smyth County News & Messenger,* August 18, 1993.

Tarter, Brent. "'An Infant Borough Entirely Supported by Commerce': The Great Fire of 1776 and the Rebuilding of Norfolk." *Virginia Cavalcade,* Fall 1978.

Tennis, Joe. "Nearly Half-Century Later, Hank Williams' Final Journey Through Appalachian Mountains Still Poses Mystery, Conflicting Accounts." *Bristol (VA) Herald Courier*, December 26, 1999.

Troubetzkoy, Ulrich. "From Sophocles to Arthur Miller: The Barter Theatre of Virginia." *Virginia Cavalcade*, Summer 1960.

Tuck, Faye Royster. "Berry Hill." *Virginia Cavalcade*, Spring 1985.

Tucker, George H. "Butler Ruled With Iron Hand and Silver Pocket." *Norfolk Virginian-Pilot*, October 30, 1949.

Turner, Susan McNeil. "The Skipwiths of Prestwould Plantation." *Virginia Cavalcade*. Summer 1960.

Wagner, Lon. "Locals Liked the 'Chinese Corner' Label." *Virginian-Pilot*, July 22, 1999.

Walker, Wendy. "Coffins Float from Gravesites." *Tidewater (VA) News*, September 26, 1999.

Watkins, Raymond W. "The Hicksford Raid." *The Greensville County Historical Society* 1, no. 1 (April 1978).

BIBLIOGRAPHY

Wilson, Goodridge. "When a Roosevelt Found Health in Virginia Hills." *Richmond Times-Dispatch*, February 24, 1935.

Wilson, Patrick. "Wayside Village Shoppes." *Virginian-Pilot*, March 15, 2010.

INTERNET REFERENCE SITES

www.bartertheatre.com
www.berryhillinn.com
www.birthplaceofcountrymusic.org
www.blueridgemusiccenter.org
www.carterfamilyfold.org
www.cavalierhotel.com
www.chrysler.org
www.clarksvilleva.org
www.commodoretheatre.com
www.danvillemuseum.org
www.ingalax.net
www.jebstuart.org
www.macarthurmemorial.org
www.marthawashingtoninn.com
www.nauticus.org
www.oldcoastguardstation.com
www.oldhalifax.com
www.patcovahistory.org
www.portsva.com
www.rextheatergalax.com
www.reynoldshomestead.vt.edu
www.riddicksfolly.org
www.sbhcmuseum.org
www.southhillchamber.com
www.thecrookedroad.org
www.tourbrunswick.org
www.visitdanville.com
www.visitmartinsville.com
www.visitvirginiabeach.com

INDEX

Index

N

Natural Tunnel State Park 113, 181, 183

New River Trail State Park 126

O

Occoneechee State Park 77

P

Prestwould 78, 79

R

Reynolds Homestead 103
Riddick's Folly 53, 54

S

Sugar Hollow Park 163, 164

V

Village View 63, 64
Virginia Creeper Trail 16, 148, 150

W

Wilderness Road State Park 189, 190

ABOUT THE AUTHOR

Joe Tennis has spent nearly his entire life "Along Virginia's Route 58," watching the sunrise at the beach of the Atlantic Ocean and the sunset over the Bluegrass State of Kentucky at the Cumberland Gap. He was born a mile off U.S. 58 at Virginia Beach and grew up along the Elizabeth River near Norfolk. He later moved to Southwest Virginia between Bristol and Abingdon, also along U.S. 58.

A graduate of both Radford University and Tidewater Community College, the author has contributed articles and photos to *Blue Ridge Country*, *Bristol Herald Courier*, *Roanoke Times*, *Kingsport Times-News*, the *Virginian-Pilot* and *Coastal Virginia Magazine*. He has also written for *Virginia Living* and *Lake Country*.

The author's other books include *Virginia Rail Trails: Crossing the Commonwealth*; *Haunts of Virginia's Blue Ridge Highlands*; *Washington County, Virginia (Then & Now)*; and *Sullivan County, Tennessee (Images of America)*.

Photo by John Patrick Tennis.

Visit us at
www.historypress.net
....

This title is also available as an e-book